CLOGS

and

SHAWLS

Whitaker family group circa 1913. Parents Ralph Robinson Whitaker and
Mary Jane Jones Whitaker *in the center*. Daughters *clockwise from the far left*:
Doris, Frances, Barbara, Hannah, Ivy, Violet, Mona, Nellie.

CLOGS

and

SHAWLS

*Mormons, Moorlands, and
the Search for Zion*

A<small>NN</small> C<small>HAMBERLIN</small>

THE UNIVERSITY OF UTAH PRESS
SALT LAKE CITY

The Defiance House Man colophon is a registered trademark of The University of Utah Press. It is based on a four-foot-tall Ancient Puebloan pictograph (late PIII) near Glen Canyon, Utah.

Library of Congress Cataloging-in-Publication Data

Names: Chamberlin, Ann, author.

Title: Clogs and shawls : Mormons, moorlands, and the search for Zion / Ann Chamberlin.

Description: Salt Lake City : University of Utah Press, [2019]

Identifiers: LCCN 2019026437 (print) | LCCN 2019026438 (ebook) | ISBN 9781607817369 (paperback) | ISBN 9781607817376 (ebook)

Subjects: LCSH: Jones, Mary Jane, 1870-1946. | Chamberlin, Ann--Family. | Mormon converts--England--Biography. | LCGFT: Biographies.

Classification: LCC BX8695.J66 C43 2019 (print) | LCC BX8695.J66 (ebook) | DDC 289.3092/2 [B]--dc23

LC record available at https://lccn.loc.gov/2019026437

LC ebook record available at https://lccn.loc.gov/2019026438

Errata and further information on this and other titles available online at UofU-press.com

Every effort has been made to trace the copyright holders and obtain permission to reproduce the images in this book. Please contact the University of Utah Press with any enquiries or any information relating regarding the rights to the images herein.

Printed and bound in the United States of America.

CONTENTS

Part Three

ACKNOWLEDGMENTS

FIRST AND FOREMOST, I must thank my grandmother and her sisters for sharing their stories with me and, I believe, their storytelling skills that have been the mainstay of my life. I hope I have served them well.

My uncle, now deceased, Ralph Noel Maud, gave me the intellectual push and the tapes.

My mother stood always at the ready to correct dialect, details, and perceptions, as well as her usual stringent demands for good grammar and spelling.

My brother and sisters, cousins, and second cousins were a lifelong corrective on our joint experience of being the descendants of these remarkable women. These people number over a hundred.

My husband and sons take the ripples out further.

My niece Katherine Quigley, who promises to be another librarian, shared her trip to the Yorkshire of her great-grandmother and great-great-grandparents. She also visited the clog manufacturer when I could not and sent iPhone pictures.

This project has been blessed to have two spearheading editors over its long gestation. John Alley first embraced it while he was still at Utah State Press. He held on as that enterprise folded, and carried me and my pages to the U of U, right over my head where I toil at the Marriott Library. The patience of my downstairs colleagues, especially Leonard Chiarelli, is much appreciated.

When John entered his well-deserved—if heartbreaking for the rest of us—retirement, I had the pleasure of making the acquaintance of his replacement, Thomas Krause, who has seen the work through the final shoals of faculty advisement to completion. Ashly Bennett, patient copyeditor, Hannah New in marketing, and the rest of the press staff have all been very supportive.

I would like to thank those faculty members whose comments honed the work, as well as peer reviewers Martha Bradley-Evans and Kerry William Bate, supportive with suggestions and improvements I have done my best to match.

The women of the Wasatch Mountain Fiction Writers have beta-read my novels for twenty-five years. Although they prefer the sort of heroines whose character you can mold instead of reporting the given, I did read multiple chapters of this work to them and appreciate their interest and sustaining hand.

I also received helpful criticism from my new group, Paris Creative Writers. Ellen Bryson, in particular, is such a sharp, precise writer. She often dropped her own work to cut mine mercilessly but necessarily—and shared the view of Valletta Harbor in Malta with me.

Finally, that great, firm-minded Mormon woman Lavina Fielding Anderson served as a sympathetic sounding board for decades.

After all this help with something I can barely claim as mine, my stubbornness may have won out and still be responsible for shortcomings. I can only plead that the stubbornness is genetic. I will, no doubt, as my grandmother used to say, "Snort 'erself to death." I beg all these folks' forbearance, and the reader's, too.

INTRODUCTION

I N MAY OF 1983, I carried a portable cassette recorder over the shaky plywood bridge that had been thrown across Salt Lake City's flooded State Street. I was on my way, at my uncle Ralph Noel Maud's insistence, between bus connections to interview my great-aunts who lived in Rose Park. That year I interviewed my grandmother and all six of my mother's aunts who had made it to Utah. I attended every one of their parties, which were frequent and much loved—except by those of us of more recent generations trying to negotiate a Zion very different from the one those women imagined when they were girls in England.

Not one of the sisters ever fell away from the faith their mother taught them, and each endured to the end. How Great-grandma managed is one of the mysteries of this tale the rest of us struggle to unravel. Even God, the scriptures tell us, lost a third of the host of heaven.

Their adopted home in Utah found them as foreign as they found it; it did not readily embrace them. And so the Whitaker sisters—my great-aunts and my grandmother—clung to each other. Although at great sacrifice they had left the safety of home and family for something greater, and although social events had been among the deepest parts of their religious upbringing, they never found close friends outside the family group in Salt Lake City.

My grandmother and her seven sisters grew up in Bradford, Yorkshire, England, in Dickensian conditions, most of the girls having to leave school at twelve to begin work in the woolen mills. World

War I claimed many of the young men they might have married, but in the end they all fulfilled their parents' dream to emigrate to Zion. Mormon prophets for generations have sent out missionaries, fishing for converts. Converts, once attracted, were told to gather to Zion, in the shadow of the everlasting hills. Here was a more perfect society, people who were all fellow believers. Unlike immigrants to the U.S. from other ethnic groups who knew they would have language and cultural barriers to overcome, the women of my family thought they would at last be coming home.

In England, they had been poor, desperately poor. Their father, Ralph Robinson Whitaker, had been blinded at aged three and tuned pianos for a living. There'd been so many of them, and never the protecting brother. They'd had little education. And yet, for me as a child, listening to the roll of their stories around me, England in the past always seemed the promised land. I was Mormon? Every imperfect person around me was Mormon. Being English, belonging to that family—that was how I was truly blessed. Until I was not, until I was a teenager, and saw that I was out of the loop and ashamed of my poor, alien roots.

The mother of these girls—Mary Jane Jones, born in Swansea, Wales, in 1870—was the one to convert, having first met missionaries from Utah in Russell Square in London. Hers, along with that of the blind man she married, is the primeval story.

She gave birth to eight daughters between 1897 and 1910:

DORIS MAY—lively and fun-loving

ETHEL BARBARA—the nurse who married late, hardworking and no-nonsense

IVY—sickly and ill-fated, but always the best cook

MY GRANDMOTHER FRANCES LYDA—the best seamstress, ambitious, boyish until she became boy crazy

HANNAH MAUD—quiet and thoughtful

NELLIE THERESA—intellectually handicapped, the one who never immigrated

OLIVE MONA—had polio as a child and so was allowed to continue schooling into college

VIOLET—artistic and, as the baby, indulged

With such a mother, they would have strong personalities. Although they were inseparable, no one who knew them would confuse one for the other. There were those of her sisters my grandmother invited to help her cook Yorkshire pudding for the newspaper; there were those she didn't.

The recording portion of the project continued until early 1984 when I announced that I was pregnant with my first son. It was about time, I was told, and Auntie Doris and Auntie Ivy gave me quilted and crocheted baby blankets and a little crocheted doll for the expected addition to the family.

This memoir is divided into three parts. The first is a novelized version of the lives of these girls' parents, my great-grandparents. This seemed the most vivid way to tell their stories, which always rang so immediate to me from my aunties' retelling.

Part 2 covers the girls' lives at home growing up, the lost day-to-day mechanics that are at once so harsh but so nostalgic. I divided the topics into various subject sections. It was hard to make this either chronological or in a close point of view since something that happened to one girl was often reported by the others in interesting and telling fashion. But each girl did have her forte, and so gets a chapter to elucidate her character and strengths. I include the treasure of a diary written by a friend of the girls detailing a trip they took to the seaside.

Part 3 brings the seven women by various paths to productive adulthood and finally, reunion in Zion. The Whitaker girls produced enough descendants to fill a park with over a hundred souls at the Whitaker Family Reunion, none of whom bears the Whitaker name, of course. The sisters I interviewed—now all departed—are due most of my gratitude for sharing their stories so generously and for their part in teaching me how to be a woman. Thanks, however, are also due to the rest of the people in that park, whose lives and memories may differ. Now that I am nearly the age my great-aunts were when

I interviewed them, and have struggled with my own life paralleling theirs in many ways, I assure them, one and all, that I have the best of intentions and undying respect.

The title I chose comes from the tough clothes factory girls wore: wooden clogs and woolen shawls. And that is where most of this family went to work at twelve, leaving school forever. The icon is so prevalent that it forms the name of a subgenre of British popular romantic fiction: novels where the spunky heroine overcomes poverty, exploitative working conditions, and the lecherous overlooker.

> It's hard when folks can't find no work
> Where they was bred and born

says the first line of a traditional song from Yorkshire that goes on to describe the world I try to re-create here. The same is true of any immigrant, whether it be the flight from the eastern European shtetl to New York's Lower East Side, the African American flight from sharecropping in the rural South to the slums of the North, or those fleeing the clear-cut jungles of Latin America on the border today. So while my effort is individual and personal, I hope it may also echo in universal poignancy.

The poignancy, I feel, gains impact when I weave in descriptions of the times and places where I recorded these memories as contrast. For example, a motorcycle roars to life in the suburban driveway next door. Auntie Ivy doesn't hear it; she lost her hearing and the flexibility of her hands to the grueling, repetitive toil. Yet she sings the song for the tape recorder with such love, such nostalgia:

> Pretty clogs, pretty shawls,
> She looks fine and she's mine, all mine.
> Other girls, other girls
> May be fairy-like an' all
> But I'd rather be busy
> Wi' my little Lizzie,
> The girl in the clogs and shawls.

The stories from that time when one quiet but firm-minded woman made a promised land for her family in the poverty and two wars of Northern England may seem quaint and distant from the present. When quiet, shy Auntie Ivy endured her harassment at the hands of the mill manager on a job she had to keep. When Auntie Mona fought polio and the devil. But the courage, individuality, and joy these women found in this as in all their other challenges may bring the same to mine and to other lives. That is my hope and my purpose in writing these pages.

The time between my great-grandfather's accident and today has gone so fast.

Family Tree

Enoch Whitaker m. *Hannah Robinson*   *Henry Merton Jones*   m. *Jane Williams*

Ralph Robinson Whitaker   *Mary Jane Jones*
Feb. 6, 1871–Nov. 26, 1944   Feb. 23, 1870–June 25, 1946

↝ *Married May 4, 1897* ↜

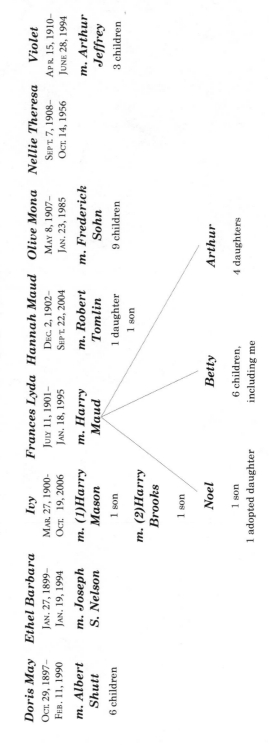

Doris May	*Ethel Barbara*	*Ivy*	*Frances Lyda*	*Hannah Maud*	*Olive Mona*	*Nellie Theresa*	*Violet*
Oct. 29, 1897–Feb. 11, 1990	Jan. 27, 1899–Jan. 19, 1994	Mar. 27, 1900–Oct. 19, 2006	July 11, 1901–Jan. 18, 1995	Dec. 2, 1902–Sept. 22, 2004	May 8, 1907–Jan. 23, 1985	Sept. 7, 1908–Oct. 14, 1956	Apr. 15, 1910–June 28, 1994
m. Albert Shutt	*m. Joseph S. Nelson*	*m. (1)Harry Mason*	*m. Harry Maud*	*m. Robert Tomlin*	*m. Frederick Sohn*		*m. Arthur Jeffrey*
6 children	6 children	1 son		1 daughter 1 son	9 children		3 children
		m. (2)Harry Brooks					
		1 son					

Noel   *Betty*   *Arthur*

1 son   6 children,   4 daughters
1 adopted daughter   including me

Doris May

Ethel Barbara

Ivy

Frances Lyda

Hannah Maud

Olive Mona

Nellie Theresa

Violet

PART ONE

DEDICATION

WITHIN TEN MINUTES OF MEETING ANYONE, my mother's mother would make this announcement: "I left school at twelve. I went to work in t' mill." Yes, that was pride in her voice when she said it.

My muttered "Please, Grandmas" were of no avail. I could only grit my teeth and vow, "I will never be like my grandmother."

Of all this life had deprived her, it had given her one thing. She had a voice "what would carry across t' weaveroom." The crack of sliding shuttles, the slam of beater sleighs, the rattle of heddles, the ratchets clicking on the beams, forty, sixty all at once, had left her husband and three of her sisters deaf in old age. On Grandma's part, however, this fourteen-hour-a-day assault on young ears had only strengthened her vocal chords; her aging relatives' infirmity held no dread for her. She could still give them orders.

The Saturday before Mother's Day that first year I counted myself among the feted—although I didn't show yet—Grandma and I went to take advantage of the sale at a local children's store. As we rummaged through tables of tiny bathing suits and sundresses, Grandma gave me a string of orders—advice—in that voice of hers.

Fortunately, if she had learned to make her voice carry, I'd learned to ignore it. No two women could be more different than Grandma and I, no two—I swore—would make more different mothers. It was hard to believe only one generation separated us; but I could not fret over trying to meet her expectations. Besides, I'd heard all her stories of birth and childhood a thousand times, since I was the baby and her daughter the new mother she was lecturing.

"Nowt 'ere," Grandma declares, tossing a pair of padded-knee overalls with the side seam unraveling back into the sale bin. "Tha can' make better thaself."

For once, I agree with her. She taught me.

We go next door to the fabric store and start on the remnant table. Okay, so we do have this in common: Neither of us will give a penny unless it goes for a bargain.

In her case, she had farthings to work with. And pins. Did you know that parts of a farthing could be counted out in pins, regular old straight pins? You could buy a paper of pins—not just at a fabric store, at the local off-license shop—for a farthing and pay your debts with four or five of them. Miser the rest.

"Mind them for'ners."

"Grandma," I plead.

Her voice hasn't dropped a decibel as a bevy of Southeast Asian women—grandmothers, aunties, mothers, sisters—comes to work beside us. Half a dozen dark-eyed children hover in attendance, some slung on backs in strips of cloth.

I smooth the front of my overlarge shirt. A practical carryall, that sling, if only one could figure out how to do it. This is how to be cosmopolitan while avoiding the expense of modern contraptions with patented names and no actual proof that they work. My sidelong glances at the women's wonderful, mousy smallness and soft, polite chatter fail to figure how the strip of cloth might be made to carry the big, wiggly American baby I expect to have.

By accident, my hand meets that of one of the two Iranian women also at work among the banded lengths of novelty cotton prints and wide-wale corduroy—

"Nowt to match t' nap," Grandma declares.

Are the Iranians mothers? No baby slings to tell for sure. Still their chadors and their very presence in this store tell me they are serious about wifely duties.

"For'ners ought to learn English like everybody else," Grandma announces in the same weaveroom voice. She who drops aitches and acquires them with abandon, whose copulas agree with their subjects so infrequently that disagreement becomes the rule instead. She who carries her native land with her wherever she goes, who can't see how very foreign she is, even after forty years. She should talk.

As of course she does. There is no stopping her.

So who really is foreign here? Those two blond women in designer jeans each with a single, pampered toddler in the latest stroller? Who avoid the bargains as if they are tainted?

No. I suddenly notice something even more serious.

There's a man in the store. An unaccompanied man. A redhead—or as Grandma would say, "ginger 'aired." This might not have been so very strange if something about him hadn't reminded me of my uncle Noel.

But my uncle Noel lives in Canada. Where he periodically "stands" for office on the Green Party ticket. He never wins more than 7 percent of the vote; too radical even for them. He only wants "to give folks an alternative."

I look again. The man has found something of interest behind the turning button display.

"When's that baby coming? October, tha sayst? Tha'lt want a nice woolly. I always loved to weave t' 'erringbone." Grandma fingers two yards of grey-and-black wool fondly.

In my opinion, no "woolly" is nice. No child of mine is going to wear scratchy wool in a world of central heating. Not to mention the trials of washing off baby spit.

The stray man covers half his face with a pattern book as I try to look over the Iranians' black-shrouded heads.

No fabric remnant here long enough to attempt a baby sling.

I look again. The male figure slips behind a mannequin just as I turn.

I buy the light blue twill.

"That'll do thee fer a pair o' pants." Grandma approves.

Thank heaven. She so rarely does.

We receive our purchases and carefully count change from the cashier—and there he is, full on.

"Give you ladies a lift?"

"Eee, our Noel!" and "What are you doing here?" Grandma and I cry together.

"Happy Mother's Day, Mother." He catches us both in a big, burly hug.

He's driven all the way down from Vancouver to surprise her and, when someone at home tells him where we'd gone, he is able to surprise her that much more. It's beside the point that Salt Lake just happens to be on the way to a conference on Jungian dream interpretation in Albuquerque from which he'll fly to the Caribbean. He plans to gather information for an article on the People's Republic of Grenada.

"But how did you find us?" I have to know.

"Well, I knew you wouldn't be in the ready-made shop, not with the remnant sale next door. The pair of you."

"You always were one for grand entrances," I tell him.

"And you know you really want a woolly," he teases right back.

"What? Oh—yeah."

"That voice of hers"—the ginger eyebrows move in his mother's direction.

Uncle Noel's grand entrances began, as my grandmother has only just finished telling me, the day he was born: "Christmas Eve, it were. So we called 'im Noel. Ralph first, for me dad, of course, then Noel." Every one of the girls has a first son Ralph, so there has to be some distinction.

He ripped her so she almost bled to death. While she waited to be sewn up, she prayed: "I care for nowt, so long as 'e's 'ealthy. And so long as 'e don't 'ave ginger 'air."

My uncle is the only person I have ever known who has what can be described, without a doubt, in either English or American, as "ginger 'air."

Grandma and Uncle Noel start in on each other before we reached the car.

"For t' first three months, we didn't know if 'e'd stay wi' us," Grandma trumpets. More motherhood training, I suppose.

"Believe me," my uncle says in his cool, studied Oxford tones, "I tried to go."

"'E were so sick and colicky. Wouldn't take 'is food. Should've 'ad soya or summat, but there weren't nowt like that them days. 'E weighed no more at three month 'an when 'e were born."

"Well, you know, she was always trying to kill me. She once sat me on a red-hot potty seat, hot enough to fry an egg on, never mind my backside."

"Aye, well, I were tryin' to warm it by t' fire for thee."

"'Aye, well,' it's a wonder you ever got me to sit on it again, after that."

∽

"There were always uncles at Christmas," Dylan Thomas wrote of his own childhood in Wales. My uncle—whom only the family is allowed to call Noel—is a *Britannica*-level authority on the great Welsh poet. And on being an uncle at Christmas.

Not a few of his grand entrances, including his birth, coincided with that holiday. I remember the year Uncle Noel came for Christmas with a stuffed toy buffalo for my brother and University of Buffalo sweatshirts in graded sizes for all five of us girls. I was young enough to covet the buffalo and to wonder about an institution of higher learning for bison only. More than my uncle that Christmas, I would have liked to have seen a graduate of his literature classes. Not only would that rare buffalo speak English, he would speak it eloquently with Oxford regimen and an acid wit besides. My uncle could only teach at that university, I decided, because, with his tawny, shaggy hair, stolid mass, weak eyes, and aloof, chewing-the-cud superiority, he looked enough like a buffalo to pass.

People who don't really belong make grand entrances: ice in hot water, crack! A strobe of light in a cozy world lit only by fire.

There was the time—another Christmas—when Uncle Noel had told everyone he wasn't coming. Grandma sat on her cheap plastic-and-chrome telephone seat taking the news. "Suit thaself." The weaveroom voice tightened with something between disappointment and annoyance.

Then, in the middle of our traditional lamb dinner, in he walks carrying the two large poinsettias he picked up at Albertsons down the street by way of gift buying: "an apparition with three red heads."

∽

This same Christmas, after having read only the blurb and opening page of my first published novel, Uncle Noel declares I can't write.

"Pathetic" is his exact word.

No, I refuse to cry. While I try to catch my breath from this body blow, however, he has time to fall into professorial mode.

"Take J. D. Salinger—"

"I hate J. D. Salinger." Two can play at this game. "He should be locked up."

"Well, then, Hemingway—"

"I hate Hemingway. All male grunts. He should have been shot with his own bull rifle."

"Who do you like?" As if there's no one left.

"Whom." Caught him. But then I have to confess. "Mary Renault."

"You'll never become great following in her dainty dancing shoes."

He's obviously never heard of her. "Dainty" is not a word I'd associate with Mary Renault. Her greatest crime, in his eyes, seems to be her gender. Of which there was always some doubt.

"When I write," I try to explain, "I like to think of myself tatting lace, delicate, intricate—"

"Oh, God! Look around you, girl! Do you see any lace? No. It's a vicious, hard world, like sandpaper and gravel, not flippin' lace. To be great, you have to tell it like it is. Write what you know."

"I need some distance to what I write, else I get too bitter. Besides, it's not my ambition to have my stuff dragged about through sterile English classes 'til kingdom come."

"That's libelous."

I smile. "Yes. It was meant to be."

"Who's the boss here?"

"Boss?" I hear my voice rise like Grandma's. I tone it down. "You're coming to my house for dinner tonight, remember?"

He concedes his dependency.

Real women, Grandma taught me, cook Christmas dinner. That includes Yorkshire pudding.

"And that stodge is what killed my father," my uncle grumbles, passing on the pud', passing on the gravy, passing on the mint pasty and custard.

ᴧ

Then there is the Old Year's Night (New Year's Eve), ghostly fog drifting over the Salt Lake streets all the way up to Tenth Avenue. When my brother lets Noel in that evening, my uncle makes another grand entrance. He gives my grandmother such a start, all in his muffler and tweed cap as he is.

"Dad?" I hear her say. Very quiet. Like a different person.

She quickly recovers and gives her more familiar shriek of laughter. "Eee, I thought tha'rt me dad there. Fer a minute."

Uncle Noel is more sulky than ever at that meal.

He looks around the family wheel, spoked by my grandmother and six of her sisters, all still alive in their eighties, rimmed by their innumerable descendants.

He cringes at the ongoing shouts of laughter, still toned "fer t' weaveroom."

When he can make his voice heard, that voice academics around the world stint to hang on, he demands, out of the blue: "I want to know how they did it."

"'Oo did what, Noel?"

"'Ow yer parents—" He goes back to fish up his dropped aitch. "How your parents did it. Raised all you eight on no money whatsoever. Did they preach to you out of holy scripture every night? Hellfire and brimstone? Tell me how they did it."

The sisters look at each other as if the question makes no sense. Then Grandma, who is used to this battle, raises her voice-from-the-weaveroom.

"Love."

She says it like an American advertisement. "A message from the Church of Jesus Christ of Latter-day Saints."

Now, nothing in this world embarrasses my grandmother. This, however, comes as close as I've ever seen. Someone at the ward must have been preaching vocalization of love. Please, we're English. English first, Mormons second. We don't speak about such things. They seem forced, phony.

Grandma's unnatural flush says she instantly regrets the word.

Uncle Noel rolls his eyes. "I was there. I didn't see love. All I saw was pathetic. A pathetic old woman, a pathetic blind old man."

"'E weren't pathetic. 'E were a wonderful person. I wish tha'd known 'im."

"And Auntie Nellie, good God. Fat, sloppy, simpleminded, pathetic Nellie."

Which causes the bigger fuss? That he has said such things about "our Nellie" (*My* Nellie. I always felt the burden of her, too)? Or that he has taken the name of the Lord in vain?

Within the bomb crater he's created, he continues. "Granddad—I was named after him, right? You thought I was he when I first came in. And I was told to emulate him. But I was only confused. What is there to emulate in a pathetic blind old piano tuner with eight daughters? Eight daughters. Not one son. Not one apostate, either. Not one black sheep in all the family. Until me. I have no role model, you see. No role model but that grinding poverty. That poverty. It was glorified. That gaggle of giggling girls. That ignorance."

He's said it. Red to the roots of his hair, he can't stop now. Because everyone is still dumb with shock, because for once he—the world-famous scholar—has made an impression. He doesn't stop.

"Because 'we' had such a sturdy foundation in Truth, things could only get better. God, the myth of Progress! But 'we' were already better than any of our teachers and classmates, see, because whatever they said, 'we' knew the Truth. All of this right there in Bradford. West Riding. Yorkshire—God, I couldn't get out of there fast enough."

"Tha'lt come back," Grandma says. "Back to t' fold. They's never an atheist in t' trenches."

"We'll just see about that. I hate people who go around organizing your life for you."

"Tha doesna, though."

"Oh, I do." He takes a fortifying breath for the next pronouncement. "I killed you, Mother."

If anyone was preparing a joke to get over this scene, this has them silent again. Silent and completely baffled.

Everyone looks at Grandma, as if they might have missed a funeral or something.

"Tha didna." She recovers on a shriek of scandalized disbelief.

"Like you tried to do to me on the potty seat. Only I did it first. In therapy, I did it first."

My uncle throws down his Christmas paper serviette—his nap-kin—napkin bought last January at discount—and gets to his feet.

"Tha'lt come back," his mother calls after him.

He slams the door and goes for a long walk in the dark, foggy Salt Lake streets.

Quickly restored to normal, irritant removed, the sisters launch into another tale about their childhood that has nothing to do with the unpleasantness we've all just witnessed. More than just the accent links the scene, all unconsciously, to the Monty Python skit of four Yorkshiremen sitting around, dressed in posh dinner jack-ets, drinking Château de Chasselas. Not the alcohol, of course, but memories of "them days" when "we'd 'a' been glad to 'ave the price o' a cold cup o' tea." (Only no tea, either, in my family's case.)

The television skit memories escalate to "t' three month" we lived "in a paper bag in a septic tank," ate an "'andful of gravel" for break-fast before going to work "twenty hour a day at t' mill for tuppence a month."

"We were 'appier, and we'd nothing. . . . 'Appier because we'd nothing."

"There were t' time me dad shaved off his beard, what he'd worn since they was courtin'—" Auntie Ivy begins.

Like the childrearing stories, I've heard it all before. "An' she didn't know 'oo 'e were."

They finish each other's sentences. It's always clear who "'e" is; there "were" only one in their world, and it wasn't my Harvard- and Oxford-educated uncle. They shriek with laughter. It's like tatting, round and round, leftover scraps of yarn on a wooden bobbin—they don't make those anymore—with five nails hammered in the head. Bright, clashing colors, red with orange, purple with lime green.

The tables and TV trays, black with pink flowers, the epitome of American life, have been pushed aside. Parlor games now, spin the bottle. A coal fire in the grate casts its light over a scene that might have played out three-quarters of a century ago.

The sisters are in their eighties. They are using an empty bottle that once held what my grandmother insists on calling "wine"—good Mormon that she is, it is only ever grape juice. Like she calls my baby sister Helen "Ellen" and calls both my husband Curt and Alice's husband Keith a combination of the two names, "Keirth." You can hear her voice across the weaveroom, but nothing goes the other way. Nobody can tell her a thing.

The bottle points to Auntie Barbara. Auntie Barbara, in her day, made extra Christmas money going from congregation to congregation (not Mormon; Mormon's don't pay) supplying the soprano for Handel's "I Know That My Redeemer Liveth." Now she's deaf as Beethoven. The rules of the game oblige her to sing "Ilkla Moor Bat 'At," the "unofficial national anthem of Yorkshire." The verses are about a man who goes to see his sweetheart without a hat and whom we all end up eating—either absurdly or with incredible existentialism—in a roast duck. Everybody joins in to help pull Barbara's age-shrill, sharp notes down to tune.

In the overheated room, I feel a cool presence at my elbow. It's Uncle Noel, damp on his tweed jacket from the out-of-doors. I smell the fog in the wool, like the house they grew up in must have smelled most of the time.

Grandma was right. Noel came back. Or rather, having so vehemently declared he hates people who go around organizing your life for you, he is now ready to give out assignments of his own. English 101.

"There's a story here," he tells me.

"Where?" I ask, careful to whisper. Not attending to spin the bottle is a sin right up there with denying the Holy Spirit.

"Here. The Family. The Sisters." I can hear the capital letters. "Parties like this."

"Ilkla Moor Bat 'At" concludes in full harmony—full harmony including Auntie Barbara a note and three-quarters above the sopranos—myself in there with the rest.

"And you're the one to write it."

"Me? Why don't you write it? You're the hotshot writer. You're the one with a good inch of cards in the library catalogue under your name. I'm 'pathetic,' remember?"

"Only because you try to write about what you don't know."

"You're the one who was born in Bradford, who knew the Parents, who spent Christmases in the House. I only visited once as a baby, and all I can remember is the old ginger tomcat that ate cheese, sitting in a window with lace curtains. He seemed the only patch of light in otherwise very gloomy surroundings."

Are spinning "wine" bottles attracted to agitated voices? This one is.

Or—bending down in the heat of competition like a teenager, only one with temple garments bunched around sagging thighs (she'd die if she knew)—Grandma can control the spin. I am called to order, required to "give an impression of Pablo Casals." At first I disgrace myself in this group "what always 'ad music in t' home" by not knowing who the greatest cellist of their generation was. I recover by impersonating the one cellist I know: my grandmother. Waves of emotional bowing. No care for the straddled legs. The laughter is, as my husband, musician from another generation, says, "Epic, like a room full of Albert Ayler free-form jazz solos."

I return to my place to find my uncle watching passively, his arms folded across his chest, where the bottle cannot possibly point at him. Again I have the impression that, to him, nothing has changed in fifty years, twice as long as I've been alive. We are in Zion, in Salt Lake, in a middle-class home. The future that kept all eight Whitaker sisters going with its bright promise, it's here. And yet, we are really still in the old, dark semidetached poor man's house at 4 Moulson Street in Bradford. A place that doesn't exist anymore and maybe never did.

"Yes, you're the one," my uncle says.

"Why?"

"Because."

"Because why?" Jeez, my voice is American, vowels ranging on for syllables. Surely he can hear the difference.

"Because you're here." He means more than just physical space. "I've run away," he says. "Escaped. And you have not."

In other words, I am pathetic. I am a woman, a wife, a mother, a romantic: all the things my uncle Noel has run from all his life. Killed, just like the therapist taught him.

"I'm out of college," I tell him. "I don't write to assignment anymore, thank you."

But Uncle Noel persisted. Throughout the seventies and eighties, he sent me old maps and blank tapes. He taught me how to make a grand entrance—to disrupt things with a whirring black box, juggling a microphone and making the trouble to find a plug behind "t' settee." He even accompanied me and asked the questions—brazen questions—manners always kept from my tongue.

Still, I was not really convinced I could do it, or that it was my own work rather than his I was pursuing. And still, there were "uncles at Christmas."

"Now that you have the recordings," he told me, "throw them away. It is not the facts that are important, for you see, the stories contradict at every turn. It's not the facts. It's the Myth."

It's the Myth. I wanted to raise my kids without myths.

Contrary to Uncle Noel's pronouncement, I had escaped. Two women could not be less alike than my grandmother and I are.

Or so I thought.

Then comes the day I am out in the garden with my own curly "ginger 'aired," blue-eyed, freckle-nosed son. We came from a land of back-to-back houses. A "bit o' dirt" is important to us, to grow "a few tomahtoes" in.

My son, who "tore me 'orribly when 'e were born," can't talk yet. He can't even walk, but sits in his little light blue twill overalls, made from a remnant, and picks up a stone.

"Dat?" he demands.

"A rock," I tell him. No, I will not let the visceral fear I get when I see a stone in someone's hand spoil the moment. He can't say it, but he rocks his body to and fro. "That's right," I tell him, so proud of my son, already making puns.

"Rock. Just like that."

He throws the rock. It doesn't go a foot, drops lightly on his own bare toes. I stifle a shriek.

I take a deep breath. No harm done. He's not crying. Spoiling the day might do more harm. I will not become my grandmother. Who told the tale her father told her to my mother who told it to me, out "amongst t' tomahtoes." I won't—

Another breath. "Oh, no, lamb." I stoop to kiss the little toes. "We never, ever throw rocks. Your great-granddad—No. Great-great-granddad. When 'e were no' but four year old—"

And here I am. Telling the tale, slipping into the same dialect. But is it Grandma's tale? Uncle Noel's? My son's? The baby can't even talk yet.

No, as in all families, even with family stories, all stories belong to the teller.

THE SHADOW

BRADFORD, WEST YORKSHIRE, that cancer of the Industrial Revolution, had grown to ingest completely what once had been the little farming hamlet of Thornton. Men and children here never saw the light of day. The knocker-up man came at half-past three in the morning, tapping his rattle at every upstairs window. The factory doors closed at six. Be late and you missed your ha'penny bonus. Those condemned to this life would not leave the clatter and dust of looms and spinning machines until after dark.

Hannah Robinson Whitaker's uncle had been big for a lad his age. The family lied and got him hired on at eight instead of the legal nine. But he was still just a child, in spite of his size, and fourteen hours a day was too much. One grey afternoon he fell asleep on the job, lulled by the horrible, monotonous racket of machinery.

Lulled to tumble into the crushing, tearing, insatiable jaws of the monster.

"They brought 'is body 'ome in a sack," Hannah'd been told. "Left 'im on t' step for 'is poor mother to find. ''Ere's your son,' they said. That were all."

Hannah's father and the rest of the lad's brothers were incensed at the murder of their baby. They organized strikes and protests, electioneering, "'stompin" they called it." They even resorted to waylaying wool shipments "on t' moors b' night"—and helped get the legal age raised to twelve.

Had all her forbearers' gumption left Hannah Robinson behind? For her, as for most girls grown into womanhood, marriage meant the only escape from the factory. Yet marriage brought constraints and dangers all its own in the shadowy kitchens and backyards of greater working-class Bradford.

Nothing grew there, no shrub, no blade of grass between the flagstones. There wasn't enough sun or space in four square feet of yard, or no yard at all in the back-to-backs.

Hannah had no place to hang her laundry but across the lane itself. Mr. Whitaker's three shirts, one for every two days of the week, had to overlap at the shoulders just to squeeze in. Before they dried, sticky coal soot would rain down in streaks. From the ground up came the grubby handprints of children playing at hide-and-go-seek. Or the muck of coal or rag-and-bone men if they didn't bother to yell: "'Eyup, missus, tha weshin'!" so you could run out and hoist up the middle of your line with a broom end to let them trundle their carts past. Did her dark, narrow life hold no more hope, ambition, or imagination than to marry her own first cousin and thus eke out the time allotted her in the second half of the nineteenth century?

No. One single bright spot lightened this life of Hannah Whitaker née Robinson. The photograph, she hoped, would capture it, so bright and clear, as if spliced in from a future full of promise. Leaning fondly against her knee, they had posed together: her only child, a little lad of not quite five years old. The doctor said she could never have another, she was too weak, but she would gladly die for just this one.

She called him Ralph and, oh, how she loved him! She fair got the colly-wobbles when she let him out of her sight. It was such a pleasure to see him and to hear him singing and prattling after her skirts from one end of the house to the other. He was four—almost five. Halfway to the eight when her father's brother had died mangled in the machinery. This uncle whom she'd never met but whose "body in a sack" had haunted every doorstep she'd ever crossed. Her life might be as narrow and dark as her grandmother's had been, but somehow, she would see her son did not suffer a similar fate. How, she couldn't tell, since her life seemed such a mirror image of those that had gone before. But somehow, she would do it.

One day in particular—November 13, 1875—it seemed harder than ever to let him go. She caressed his little limbs—so strong and lively—as she helped him into his little suit.

She'd made the jacket new for the photograph sitting just two days before. Yes, she'd used the fabric of an old jacket of Mr. Whitaker's that couldn't be turned one more time, but the grey wool left for such a small garment was sturdy enough.

Her son's sweet little belly rippled with laughter as she buttoned up the front. She pulled up the stockings to the pudgy knees and then—in a display that would have shocked any of her neighbors—kissed the knees on their dimples. She fitted the little woolen cap on his strawberry-blond hair that tended to curl, smoothing it with her fingers as if it were food and they, very greedy.

Best of all were his eyes. Even though they lived in such dark lanes, freckles sprinkled the pert nose that divided those bright, lively blue eyes. Those eyes missed little and got so much enjoyment out of everything they saw. The shadow she appeared to herself in them was better than her clear reflection in a mirror.

But she had to let him go. Though it was cold, it had turned clear and as sunny as the perpetually grey skies ever got. A bairn should play out on such a day. She wanted him to grow straight, not bow-legged like so many nippers in the lane. She did not fear for him playing with the other, older children, for he was such a cheery lad. He made friends with everyone, even the bullies.

And she had the washing to do. As she hoisted the heavy kettles of boiling water, she could not have him underfoot. She must take advantage of the few hours of sunlight as well as her boy. So she kissed him once again and sent him out across the flagstone step and into the lane. It occurred to her briefly as she swung the door—this was Friday, Friday the Thirteenth. But this was also 1875 and people didn't believe superstitions anymore. Besides, the laughter of little Ralph as he called out to his friends was soothing music to her ears. She shut the door and went to scrape the cake of lye soap. Its harsh smell scoured the inside of her nostrils. The small, precious packet of bluing to the kettle of Mr. Whitaker's three shirts—

"Mrs. Whitaker! Mrs. Whitaker! Oh, come quick!" It was one of the older neighbor girls. She ran in, clattering her clogs, without knocking. "Eee, Mrs. Whitaker! It's your Ralph. 'E's 'urt. 'E's 'urt bad!"

Hannah didn't even stop to dry her hands as she flew out the door and down the unpaved lane to the circle of children and now other mothers who had come out to see and to help. They parted to let her through with the sort of horror and fascination that grief always brings, even to those who know it well.

She thought he was dead. He lay, one leg in a puddle left from last night's rain. He lay so still and white, with blood all over his face and down his new little suit.

"It were a catapult," someone said, and told the name of the boy whose careless slingshot had thrown the stone.

Hannah hardly heard. She couldn't hear any name but the "Ralph! Oh, me darling Ralph" coming in sobs from her own throat.

She threw herself into the mud beside him and gathered him to her. The little chest rose and fell in shallow breaths. But the skin was white, too white against the splash of blood, too much blood.

"I've sent our Will for t' coal cart," Mrs. Next-but-One said. "'E were at bottom o' t' lane, past t' butcher's, not five minutes past."

Hannah tried to get to her feet with her son in her arms. She found her knees too weak. Another woman caught him up, carried him and held him while they waited. Two more women had to hold Hannah. Every minute she would find strength to lean over to the little body.

"Yer mam's 'ere, me lamb."

Once or twice she heard a whimpered "Mam, Mammy" and she had to go back to the supports.

They helped her into the cart—the open cart of the coal man— then handed her boy up to her. The coal man crowding her on the bench wore naught over trousers stiff with dirt but a leather waistcoat. She tried to protect Ralph from the jogs of one great elbow. Coal dust formed blackheads in the man's every exposed pore.

Oh, the cart went slowly! She begged the driver to go faster, but then it would jar Ralph's pitiful little moans into shrieks. She was afraid of losing either her seat or her son or both, so she would have to plead to go slower.

"Eee, make up tha mind, missus." The coal man glowered. "I've another 'alf ton to deliver afore it comes dark."

Thornton Road rolled at the bottom of steep hills running east to west, carved by the streams it followed: Mill Race, Middle Brook, finally Bradford Beck itself. The water grew dirtier and dirtier as the waste from fullers and dye works passed from one to the next. At this time of year, all day the sun barely rose over the humble terrace houses ridging the mountainsides. Where there were no houses, mining for the coal to feed the mills had eaten away the soil, leaving bare stone bones. The westering light cast deep, chilling shadows before the cart as they passed pubs, off-license shops, and seamy greengrocers. And everywhere, the mills' red sandstone chimneys stood stern sentry, as unflinching at Hannah's pain as the Queen's own guards, shakos plumed with black feather smoke: Leventhorpe Mills—where Mr. Whitaker toiled, ignorant of the grief awaiting him, unable to share her own. Brown Royd Works—well named—Lidget Green—all green utterly spun to cotton bobbins—and finally, on a southern rise, Lister's, the glowering grandfather of them all.

Oh, the nag was ready for the knacker. It was a miserable horse, a dirty coal man, and a springless cart over all five miles from their little hamlet to Bradford Infirmary.

The bite of alcohol in the great, echoing halls of the infirmary barely covered more putrid smells beneath. Poor mothers with sick children crowded on benches all up one side and down the other, all of them wanting to go first. The other mothers had other children clinging, fussing about their skirts with running noses besides the sick ones in their arms. Shrieks boomed in the halls and in Hannah's head until she grew dizzy.

But couldn't they see? Ralph was all she had.

"The doctor will have his tea first," announced the young assistant, his face pinched with distaste into a pair of wire spectacles. As if all the misery before him were her fault.

"'Is tea!"

Her Ralph was dying. All she had. The assistant's glare invited her to go elsewhere if she didn't like it.

At last the doctor came in, crumbs from his currant cake still on his waistcoat, picking at that left between his teeth. "It's the eye," he announced, coldly dabbing away the dried blood.

As if she didn't know. As if she hadn't looked down over these past endless hours and seen for herself—

"It'll have to come out."

No! Not his eye! Not his beautiful blue eye! But there was nothing for it. It had burst. It would have to come out or go septic. The assistant offered a glass of wine.

"No. He's too young!" she cried. "He's too young to drink wine." What she meant to say was that he was too young to lose an eye.

"Suit yourself." The doctor shrugged and got his knife.

She held her son on her knee. They cut his eye away without anesthesia while he struggled against the assistant's grasp, trying to hide his face on her shoulder.

≈

"Mammy?"

"I'm here, lamb."

For two days and nights without sleeping, she'd sat by her son lying in the master bedroom with a coal fire constant in the grate. She answered his every whimper with these words. In the kitchen below, her husband's shirts sat in cold bluing. What Mr. Whitaker did for his dinner, she had no idea. She herself ate nothing.

But here, now, was her son. The fever had passed, the bandages came away clean. His voice—his bright voice sounded much as she remembered it.

"Mammy? Mam."

"Darling, right—"

Her heart turned to ice.

"But Mammy, I canna see thee."

The left eye was whole. Infection, however, had spread beneath the freckled nose. Opposite the empty right socket, the left eye had turned cloudy.

Before the picture was back from the photographer's—the picture with the bright little boy at the shadowy woman's knee—he was blind.

～

My great-grandfather always said he had two birthdays—the day he was born and the day he went blind. They say sometimes he could see light—his father took him nine miles to Leeds to "see" the first electric light.

"It were like you can see with your eyelids closed."

He could see the color of a new dress, sometimes, if, pawing over you, he held the skirt right up to his left eye.

"'Tis blue."

"No, Granddad. Guess again."

"Green?"

Giggling with the tickles. "Russet red with narrow yellow stripes."

All he ever really remembered seeing was a green field, a startling rarity in the narrow lanes where he lived. His mother was only a shadow.

～

That is the primal origin myth of Paradise Lost, the source of the visceral clench in my gut when I see a stone in my son's chubby little hand, even when I simply look at his bright blue eyes and red hair and know they can all vanish in an instant. Generations have probably been made unsuited for Little League by this tale of horror: "On 'er shoulder wi'out anesthetic."

And the teetotalling Mormon virtue before they were Mormons: not even any alcohol.

Uncle Noel brings reprieve with the facts and figures he has uncovered.

～

At twelve years old Ralph Robinson Whitaker won a scholarship to York School for the Blind, founded in 1835 to the memory of philanthropist William Wilberforce, a Yorkshireman. Buildings original to the Abbey of St. Mary, after Dissolution the manor of the Tudor and Stuart kings, housed the institution, complete with fourteenth-century arches and ivy-covered stone walls.

The application form asks, among other questions: "Can he wash and dress himself? Free from fits and disease? Who will receive him when he leaves?"

If accepted, boys were told to bring:

Two jackets

Two waistcoats

Two trousers

Two hats or caps

Four shirts

Four pair stockings

Two pair shoes or boots

Two pair socks

Two handkerchiefs

Two strong aprons

One great cloak or coat

Hairbrush

Large- and small-toothed comb in a small bag

Girls brought:

Four shifts

Two flannel petticoats

Two pair of stays

Two skirts

Two frocks, one dark

Four slips

Four pair of stockings

Two pair of shoes or boots

Two nightgowns

Two nightcaps

Two pocket handkerchiefs

Two black hats

One cloak

Combs and hairbrush in a bag

All items were to be marked with the student's name and contained in a box or basket not larger than eighteen by twelve by twelve inches.

Ralph's mother sat in the shadows embroidering each letter of her son's name while the tears fell.

Time for rising:

6 a.m. in summer

7 a.m. in winter

Time for retiring:

Younger 8 p.m.

Older 9 p.m.

Breakfast 8 a.m.

Dinner 1 p.m.

Supper 6:30 p.m.

Recreation 12:30 to 1 p.m.; 5:30 to 6:30 p.m. Saturday afternoon

Religious instruction 8:30 a.m. Scripture reading and prayer by superintendent. Learning psalms. Church at St. Olives or Catholic unless parents provide otherwise. Read scriptures memorized for the week.

Industry 9 a.m. to 12:30 p.m.; 2 p.m. to 5:30 p.m. except when receiving general education

Pupils with ear for music to learn psalm singing

Mr. A. Buckle, BA, superintendent, reports in 1887:

Forty-six boys

Twenty-six girls

Eleven girls learning to bottom chairs

Fifteen boys basketwork [R. R. Whitaker listed among them]

Fourteen boys brush makers

"General education" included geography through the means of raised globes, and literature: all of Milton's *Paradise Lost*, memorized. Here Ralph learned to read and write Braille, passing notes to friends which some of the sighted staff couldn't read. He learned to mend clogs and more basketmaking. Tapping a white cane from house to house, peddling baskets and brooms, was the only trade most people could imagine for a blind man.

Music, however, was his first love. He learned to sing the psalms.

He came home to Thornton that first Christmas, negotiating train and tram all by himself. When he gathered his mother into his arms, he felt that he had grown as tall as she, the bosom that had been at a level for him to rest his head now meeting his. More disconcerting was the armful of brittle bones she'd become, the familiar "best dress" bunching where it never had before.

"Mam? Mam? Art tha not well?"

He sensed her plucking out her handkerchief and dabbing at her eyes, as if he couldn't smell her tears warm on his wind-blasted cheeks. "Of course, me lamb. I canna be ill when tha'rt 'ere."

But when he helped to clear Christmas dinner, he felt no goose gravy on her plate, no discarded bones.

He called her on it.

"I'm content with the dried bread and milk they give thee in t' school. If it's good enough for my poor lamb, it's good enough for me."

Ralph sought reinforcements. "Dad?"

His father said nothing but humphed in the corner, defended by his pipe smoke.

Ralph could have shown her the week's menu. Yes, breakfast and supper were usually naught but bread and milk, but dinners for the week were in fact listed as:

Sunday: Rice milk pudding, beef and potato pie

Monday: Bread and currant pudding, soup or fish

Tuesday: Suet pudding and meat

Wednesday: Rice milk pudding, beef and potato pie

Thursday: Batter pudding, roast beef

Friday: Bread and currant pudding, soup or fish

Saturday: Suet pudding, roast beef

Dessert on Sunday was coffee and currant cake, Monday through Saturday, more bread and milk. Ralph recognized the "beef" in those pies as being kidneys and the potatoes, mostly turnips, but he didn't need to tell his mother that.

Instead he thought he'd make her laugh by recounting the first pre-dawn he'd crept down through the school halls and stairwells, hand on the wall, until he felt the cavernous space of the kitchen all around him. He found the hearth by its banked heat. He raked out the coals neatly as she had taught him, told the heart of the fire by a hand over the spot and carefully laid the paper he'd saved from a Braille exercise in its heart. Then the kindling—

"Tha should 'a' 'eard t' cook shriek when she saw a blind boy playing with t' fire in 'er 'earth. But then she saw I had a nice fire going for 'er, all neat and tidy in the grate. I've wakened early and done it for her every morning since, and she's rewarded me. No more *Oliver Twist*, 'Please, sir,' fer tha lad, no Mam. We can all tell our own plates by t' different chips in t' rim, and Cook always sees to it right quiet like that I've a little summat extra on me plate—that one w' t' three deep snips in a row all on one side."

His mother laughed, and it did his heart good to hear it, except when he caught the bit of strangled tightness, even in laughter. Only later he realized his tale might have made her more jealous than anything, that another woman was seeing for him instead of her.

He tried again to tell his mother to stop worrying about him. He sang for her in the sitting room after the washing up. He wished he could accompany himself on the piano. The school had a piano, and although only the choirmaster was meant to play it, Ralph had found his way to the room often enough on his own that he could pick out any song they'd had them learn. Once he had even pried open the case lid and made an attempt to sharpen that B, so flat it always set his teeth on edge. He only succeeded in making it worse before he got caught. But at least he made it so bad that they'd got a tuner in for the whole instrument, and Ralph had been able to ask the man questions.

The psalm he chose for his mother was the twenty-third, his own chest thrilling at the sweet boy's treble it sent soaring:

"Yea, though I walk through the valley of the shadow of death—"

"Pathetic," Ralph heard his father mutter under his breath, as if he thought his son was deaf as well as blind and stupid besides. The school for the blind, he knew, would accept no student who had ever busked, playing or singing on a street corner for alms.

Ralph stood straighter and let the quaver fill his tones, willing his mother to hear him: "I will fear no evil: For thou art with me—"

Even when he would return to York directly after Boxing Day.

Ralph liked school and many of the boys he met there were life-long friends. Clearly, it was better for him in York than to be chasing around the lanes as he had done for seven years because they couldn't have him in regular school.

But on his thirteenth birthday—his first one, the one in February, not November—Ralph took train and tram home again from York to bury his shadowy mother.

In Exile with the
Children of Israel

T"'TIS THE NEW GIRL YOU ARE?"

"Yes, mum."

"Saints be praised." The woman filling the door with hips and bosom wiped her hands on a red-striped cloth. "I'm Mrs. Dougherty, the cook."

Under her white cap, Mrs. Dougherty's red hair was turning grey, but her green eyes sparkled. Her broad, pleasant Irish face made the young woman sigh with relief; she had left worse at her previous job. And though the cook must rarely step a foot outside, fading freckles still covered every broad inch of that face and the hammy forearms revealed by her shoved-up sleeves.

"How do you do, mum?" The young woman bobbed a curtsey.

"Hang up your coat and hat in the scullery there."

"Yes, mum."

"Now—put on this apron and let's have a look at ye."

The apron was a woven red with white checks that made it look pink. Strange, instead of plain starched linen. The young woman struggled to pin the bib on her bodice with her cold fingers. Then the little white cap to her hair—it had been such a long walk from her parents' home in Romford at the eastern edge of sprawling London here to the edge of Spitalfields (made holy during the Middle Ages by St. Mary's 'Spital, or Hospital, for lepers, nearby). Perhaps she should forgo the extra shilling a month and live under the roof like most girls in service. The house was so grand, with green shutters and an intricate portico—though of course she had come in the back. With her cold fingers, she was glad to be in the kitchen—and such a kitchen!

"Tsk." Mrs. Dougherty's brow furrowed. "We'll have to get Mrs. Plunkett to make you a proper uniform. The mistress likes everyone to have two plain dark cotton dresses for mornings, black merino for afternoons, and evenings with white collars and cuffs."

"I can sew, mum." Not with these fingers, but in a bit.

"Can ye, i' faith?"

"Yes, mum. If—if you'll show me what you want and provide the fabric."

"Well, sure, that'll be just fine. Lord knows, 'tis at her wits' end Mrs. Plunkett is, what with the ladies' dresses to make for the wedding and all."

"I'll be happy to, mum."

"In your spare time, of course."

What spare time? the girl asked herself. She nodded anyway.

"Fine. But—for the moment, you'll have to do. And to start, you can go and answer that door. Sure and it'll be the milkman. I asked him to call back with an extra pint of cream. I'm to make a trifle for Master Davey today. Here, you'll want this jug for the milkman to ladle it into from his can." Even as the girl trotted to the door carrying the blue-rimmed jug, Mrs. Dougherty continued: "And I can't tell you how good it will be to have an extra pair of hands around here."

Another pair of ears went without saying. The solid Mrs. Dougherty must have found gossiping to herself a sore trial for the past two weeks since her last scullery maid received notice.

It was the milkman.

"Are they—are they a very large family, mum?" the new girl asked warily, raising her voice a little as she pushed the door to with her hip.

"Oh, no, not so very large. Not so large as when I started here, what? Fifteen year ago now? Just a son at home—unmarried, mind—and not much entertaining."

The milk jug began to sweat the moment the girl carried it into the warm kitchen. She moved to set it down on the nearest counter—

when Mrs. Dougherty gave a sharp cry as if she'd been stabbed. The jug slipped in the girl's cold hand, but the cook moved even faster, like lightning for one so stout. Instead of merely landing hard on the counter, the jug crashed to the floor. Buttery cream splashed everywhere, including halfway up the girl's skirt—and Mrs. Dougherty's.

The young woman wanted to cry. On her first day. No, in her first ten minutes. But it wasn't her fault. Mrs. Dougherty had screamed—then actually shoved her. The order of events was completely confusing, but that's how it had been. The young woman knew better than to point this out, although she wanted to, in self-justification. She stammered. "Oh, mum. I'm so sorry."

Instead of worrying about the spill, Mrs. Dougherty scrutinized the counter instead. "All right, lass," she finally declared. "Not a drop on the board. No real harm done."

She could say that, with the jug smashed and a mess on the floor?

"Next time, dairy deliveries—over there." Mrs. Dougherty pointed to the other counter, across the wide table, on the other side of the room. She went on in a torrent more compelling than the cream slowly curling across the floor between them. "One drop on the fleishig side and we'd have to plane the whole counter down. And flush the lot with scalding water until it floods the entire kitchen. Probably call in the rabbi as well. The master would be very angry not to have a bit of meat for twenty-four hours. He does like his lamb chop. Fleishig on this side, milchig that side. Fleishig red plates, milchig blue. Fleishig silverware has the fleur-de-lys on them, milchig more plain. The soap comes in all the way from Mr. Rokeach in Poland, fleishig red made with beef tallow, milchig blue, only vegetable oil. You will see the bars have 'kosher' imprinted on them—only in Hebrew, of course, so's you can't read it. No washing red plates with the blue soap, hear? Same with the dishtowels, fleishig red, milchig blue. Do you understand?"

The girl was beginning to see—something. Now that Mrs. Dougherty pointed it out to her, that was what had been so very strange about the kitchen when she'd first stepped in. The room was much larger than any kitchen she'd ever seen, but she'd expected that, merely seeing the portico surrounding the house's front door.

Two sets of dishes? She'd expected that as well. The rich might have forty sets of dishes if it suited them.

But what the cook said was true. The right-hand side gave off a bluish glow, this left one, where she'd almost set the cream, red. Like baby boys and girls. Not a chance of turning one into the other, was there? As to what it meant here, however—

"No, mum. I don't understand. Is that some wild Irish you're talking?"

"Irish? Lands, no. Don't they tell you? They're Jewish. The family's Jews. We cook kosher here, for Jews."

"Jews?"

"You know what Jews are, I hope?"

"From—from the Bible."

"But you never actually saw such a creature in all your born days?"

"No—no, mum." Unless you counted the pictures in the Bible— well worn now—she had won at boarding school for excelling in biblical knowledge. Somehow, she didn't think that would count. She saw no signs of blue dishes or red dishes in those pictures of a world of wells and sandals and palm trees and very handsome, holy people. It was a world she wanted to enter, however, particularly on cold winter nights. Something like heaven must be.

Mrs. Dougherty gave a great sigh, as if rather than a new scullery maid, the weight of the world had just been thrust upon her shoulders.

"I'm—I'm willing to learn, mum," the young woman attempted.

Mrs. Dougherty nodded doubtfully. "Well, go on, then. Don't stand there staring. Now that you've splashed cream on your red apron, it will have to be washed. Put on another—red. We're still working on his lordship's chop. Mop and pail in the scullery. Get this all up, and we'll see what we'll see."

There was only one color mop—dirty grey—although the milky water had to be tossed out into the alley instead of down either sink.

"I'd be happy to run for more cream." The young woman made the offer as soon as she was certain her voice would not crack with tears. The last of the greasy slickness was coming up off the flagstones. "For Master Davey's trifle. I passed one on my way here this morning—"

"Goyim." Mrs. Dougherty used another new word, shaking her head until her white cap bounced. "I'll have to send one of the lads to Aldgate, the closest dairy we can trust to be kosher. I can't spare you that long. You've too much to learn."

"Yes, mum."

"Here, when you've finished that, I'll set you to peeling potatoes. Can't do too much harm with potatoes, I suppose."

Her arms wrapped around a bowl of scrubbed potatoes, however, the girl stared at the kitchen and didn't know which way to turn.

"Here, what do they call you?" Mrs. Dougherty asked. "Mercy above, if I haven't forgotten to ask."

"Mary Jane Jones, mum."

"Well, Mary Jane Jones. You can sit at the table to do them." The cook patted the broad, scrubbed surface. "Table in the center, pareve, neither meat nor milk. You can do potatoes there."

Mary Jane sat. Some tension went out of her, not just off her feet— already weary—but because she didn't have to worry, for a bit, which way to jump.

"Mary Jane Jones!" Mrs. Dougherty repeated, clattering a pan on the stove top. "With a name like that, I would have expected a Welsh girl."

"But I am Welsh, mum." Mary Jane struggled to catch her breath. At least, with the exercise, she wasn't as cold as she'd been. "I was born in Swansea."

"Swansea! Well, sure as sin, you don't talk like it."

"We've lived in London since I was six."

"You don't talk like a Cockney, either. You talk like a regular lady. The master will like that. Young Master Davey, too."

"Thank you, mum." Mary Jane dug at a potato eye, got a nod of approval from the cook. She thought she should do more to get on the woman's good side, to prove she wasn't a complete simpleton in the kitchen. She would say something of her own. "What will you serve with the potatoes today, mum?" Delicious smells had begun to fill the kitchen under Mrs. Dougherty's loving hands over the stove.

"The master will have them with his chop—gravy."

"My mother makes a lovely gravy, with cream and butter—"

Even as she said it, Mary Jane realized she was wrong.

"Cream and butter in gravy? Not in this house, Miss," growled Mrs. Dougherty.

Fully chastised, Mary Jane jabbed at the potatoes, wondering if she cut herself, would she have to transfer over to the red side of the kitchen.

Mrs. Dougherty's need for extra hands and someone to talk to did not let the awkwardness last long. Soon she was saying: "Aye, those eyes! That hair! You're almost as dark as the master. Aye, I can see the Welsh in you, now that you mention it. I suppose you come from a big family. All those Welshies have more kids than they can count, never mind feed. Much like my own Irish, I warrant."

"My mother has had a lot of children, mum, but only three of us lived. I have a brother, Edgar, and a little sister, Nellie, who is two."

"And you are?"

"Just turned nineteen, mum. I've been in service since I was twelve."

"How old's your brother?"

"Thirteen, mum."

"Thirteen. Well, that's two of you earning your keep now, sure. 'Tis a blessing to your parents such a great lad like that must be."

"I'm afraid, mum, he is quite a burden. He and I got the measles together as children. I recovered, but he was left blind."

"Lackaday, I am sorry," Mrs. Dougherty exclaimed and crossed herself—in that kosher kitchen. She was, however, the sort of woman whom others' griefs only spurred to more talk. "What sort of work is your father in, then?"

"He used to be in the coast guard, that's why we live in Romford, near the docks. He's lately taken employment with the railroad. He would miss the sea, if it weren't for the runs he makes when the trains join with the ferries." Mary Jane cut a peel deliberately, then asked: "I am surprised, mum, to see you here in a Jewish kitchen. Irish, aren't you?"

"As the day is long and the Holy Father Catholic."

"How did you come to be here?" And to grow so possessive of these rules I can't begin to fathom? She bit her tongue over that last question.

"I first came here during the famine, after my husband and our babby died, God bless them. The first post I could find was with the Rothschilds. The baron's house itself. So much food there, I'd do anything to get my share of it, learn anything they wanted me to. And didn't I just?" Mrs. Dougherty patted her ample belly fondly before pushing on.

"After that, on their recommendation, I came here, to my own kitchen. The mistress took a more active part when I first came, showed me just how she liked it. She's poorly and mostly in her bed these days, however. The chicken soup at the back of the fire is for her, poor soul. She can't eat much more, I fear. But I've been here fifteen years, thank the Blessed Virgin." She crossed herself again.

Mary Jane stifled the thought that the red dishes and the blue dishes might crack at such sentiment spoken in their presence. She didn't want to sound as if she were ready to give notice after only one day, but she had to know: "Aren't there Jewish girls you can hire? Girls who would understand this better than I?"

"Sometimes," Mrs. Dougherty confessed. "They know kashrut, but they come from the pogroms in Russia and don't speak a word of English."

"Pogroms?" Mary Jane asked, and Mrs. Dougherty told.

About Odessa and Warsaw after the death of the tsar in 1881. About the bodies of women and children stacked like cord wood. About dirt-floor shacks torn down over the heads of their occupants in the rain. About hollow-eyed survivors, starving. About a piece of a beloved teapot found in the mud. Although sometimes Mary Jane wondered if some of the vivid details the cook relished had not happened to her, in Ireland, and not so far to the east.

That all was another eye-opener. Biblical. Mary Jane thought of her Bible, the picture of the children of Israel in Egypt, the slave masters lashing their whips. It took on new meaning.

These details lingered over most of the morning, Mrs. Dougherty moved on to her original problem. "Once they start learning a word or two, bless me if the Jewish girls don't up and get married and start a two-sided kitchen of their own. I can't keep them long."

"Is that what happened to the girl in my post before?"

To Mary Jane's surprise, Mrs. Dougherty pursed her lips at this as if she'd just tasted her broth and found it bitter. Worse. Unclean.

"Mum? What happened to her?"

"Never you mind. Just see it doesn't happen to you. You're sleeping at home, that's good. Mind yourself with—with the family." The cook's gaze rose to the floors above. "That's all."

The previous girl must have offended the Jewish sensibilities in some very deep way. This was a matter of religion. Mary Jane was baffled—but intrigued all at once. How she was supposed to avoid such a pitfall when she couldn't even learn what it was?

"You don't have a young man, Miss Mary Jane?"

She didn't. Mrs. Dougherty's expression made it hard to tell whether this was a good thing or not. At nineteen, Mary Jane was beginning to wonder if she ever would. Service was not the best place in the world to be discovered. Isaac's servant finding Rebecca at the well. That was one of her favorite Bible pictures. She wanted love to be just that way—

"No, mum."

"Too bad. If you did, that just might make up for cream on the floor and the lad having to run clear to East London." The cook's resentment didn't even last to the end of the sentence. "He sails to the continent, then? Your dad?"

"Yes, mum." Mary Jane sighed, missing her dearest parent. "It means he's gone a lot."

"Calais? France? Mr. Wilson the butler is always on the look for the finest wines—only they must be kosher, too."

"Holland, actually. One run a week."

"Can't think of anything we'd want from Holland."

"My father brings home the loveliest ham—"

"Ham? Saints above, no."

"What? Does the master not like ham?"

"It's forbidden. Have you never read your Bible?"

Now, this comment hurt Mary Jane deeply, for she had always imagined herself to be religious. She had won her Bible at school for a composition she wrote on Christian charity. Her essay had been read before everyone in chapel. She'd worn the Bible out with reading. She read so much she often dreamed about it, the pictures, sometimes stranger things. Once she related to her father how these words had come to her in the night: "And I saw another angel flying in the midst of heaven, having the everlasting gospel to preach unto them that dwell upon the earth." The words of Revelation.

Her father had scolded her for not being serious enough.

∿

Mary Jane still opened her Bible whenever she got the chance. There was no part, she thought, that she had not read several times.

Over the next weeks and months, however, she discovered they hadn't taught her quite a bit in chapel. The Old Testament, which outside Genesis had seemed just a listing of "begats" before, took on new life as she saw it lived in this patriarchal household. She began to read the scriptures even more avidly than before and to the exclusion of the New Testament.

At first, Mary Jane made many mistakes in the kitchen and could not see what she had done wrong. "Unclean, unclean," Mrs. Dougherty would cry.

Cutting apples, Mary Jane sliced a worm. "Unclean, unclean!" Out she had to go into the yard with the horses and all to stick her knife ten times into ten different patches of dirt. Mary Jane found the dirt twice as "unclean" as the poor worm.

She carefully helped herself to a bit of butter for a slice of pareve bread with the butter knife—only to find she was in her pink apron instead of the blue. "Unclean, unclean!" Mary Jane quickly found it was better to eat only when the rest of the servants did, under Mrs. Dougherty's watchful eye.

But things of religion were always interesting to Mary Jane, and this order of the kitchen more than any she had come across. She learned quickly. She got Sundays off—which meant she worked on the Jews' Sabbath. She got a working view of what the seventh day meant when everyone in the household wished each other "Shabbat shalom," when the smell of warm challah filled the kitchen, its rich, eggy taste in the mouth even as the fire was banked and the cold meats prepared for dinner on Saturday.

Within a month, she was salting joints of meat from the shochet with the large-grained kosher salt on the very drain board where she'd almost set the cream. The sight of all the dishes stacked up in their proper cupboards after washing up—fleishig on the left, milchig on the right—let her set off for home singing a hymn. It was a clean, whole feeling; something, she thought, like the feeling her mother must have experienced upon baptism.

Service in the house with the large portico—like the sharply contrasted meat and milk dishes—meant more food to take home to her family. Eggs Mary Jane cracked carefully into a bowl before adding them to anything. If there were blood spots, there was a special little jar by the door for her to take them home in.

And when Passover—which she learned to call Pesach—brought the most thorough cleaning she had ever known, she got a ride home in the carriage. The ride wasn't so much because she was exhausted but to help her with the basket full of half loaves Mrs. Dougherty hadn't had time to put in the last bread pudding, vinegar, beer, crackers, biscuits . . . that helped her family have a happy Easter— but Mary Jane couldn't avoid the feeling that such gifts were tainted, tossed to her like to a dog because she wasn't clean—wasn't holy enough.

Come Sukkoth (she'd missed all about the booths in the Bible before), the master and his son built a tabernacle out back in the dirty alley. They carried the mistress down from her bed and settled her there. Mary Jane and the footmen served them outdoors as it began to spit rain. "Won't do the mistress's poor rheumatics a biteen o' good," Mrs. Dougherty prophesied.

One of the youngest footmen, a lad about Mary Jane's age, was let go at Sukkoth. He could not keep from laughing at the master as he returned from the synagogue: The master wore a top hat and frock coat, his blue-striped "bath towel"—prayer shawl. He carried a sort of lemon in one hand and a dried palm branch brought all the way from the Holy Land in the other.

Mary Jane was sorry about that. She had liked the young man. He'd even asked her to step out with him "once this dog-and-pony show of a holiday is over and we can all have a bit of a rest."

She never saw him again and thought it was just as well. If she married him, she would have to have her own kitchen, like her mother's no doubt, just curtained off from the tiny sitting room, with cracked basins and careless food. Besides, she thought the master—while, yes, odd for modern London—looked like a druid twined in mistletoe, a prophet from some ancient wisdom.

And then it was Passover again. She'd been in the house with the great portico over a year. Opening up the cupboards stacked with the two new sets of dishes—fleishig with a floral rim, milchig with the green pattern all over—was like greeting old friends. Reading Exodus to see what would happen next no longer seemed to matter. She was living those ancient words now. And for the occasion, she would stay over in the servants' quarters on the third floor to spare her the late walk home. She was bidden to set a place at the holiday table for the prophet Elijah himself. "And I saw another angel flying in the midst of heaven."

"Why is this night different from all other nights?" the little grandson intoned, looking like a precious jewel in his new suit of green velvet.

The ancient ceremony touched Mary Jane so she could hardly serve the platters of roast lamb and tender vegetables she knew were perfectly holy. Tears flooded her eyes. Just such a meal must the children of Israel have eaten, standing in their cloaks, ready to be delivered from Egypt. "And if a stranger shall sojourn among you, and will keep the Passover unto the Lord . . . so shall he do." The very words of the holy text were being fulfilled in her. "If any man of you or of your posterity . . . forbeareth to keep the Passover, even the same soul shall be cut off" made her think an awful thought: Somewhere all the Christian churches she knew must have gone astray.

Mrs. Dougherty had not slept since taking a brief nap the previous afternoon. The tension of production over and proclaimed a success, she succumbed to a splitting headache. She declared she could not wait up to see the master and his son retired for the night. Mary Jane, who felt so full of life she wondered if she'd ever sleep again, gladly volunteered to finish the washing up and take care of that duty for the older woman. It had already been arranged, as at other Jewish holidays, that Mary Jane did not have to walk home afterwards. She could catch a little sleep in Mrs. Dougherty's room, on the quarter of the bed the cook left her.

"'Tis like this every holiday" were Mrs. Dougherty's parting words, uttered with a heavy sigh. "Hopping on like Irishmen, the pair of them. At each other's throats 'til four o'clock in the morning."

And, shaking her aching head, she turned to climb the four flights up to the little room Mary Jane would eventually share with her.

Mary Jane knew young Master Davey usually avoided taking dinner with the rest of the family. He was a member of a gentleman's club and either ate there, or called for cold sandwiches to be brought to his room. But how anyone could be unmoved and rebellious after attending the ancient, glorious rite of that evening was incomprehensible to her. Of what went on in the parlor, however, she could hear nothing down at the pareve table where she was soon nodding, still in her pink apron. She dreamed of a world like the pictures in her Bible—

"Up, lass, up."

The sound of the cranking of a well handle in Canaan turned into the ringing of the kitchen bell. There was Wilson, the butler, shaking awake Rebecca about to meet her destiny with a water jug on her head. The angular old man's whiskers had grown out like a grey mist on his chin through the long night. He'd been busy running a steady stream of wine—"but absolutely no whiskey on account of the holiday"—in to the gentlemen.

"A pot of coffee and a tray of hors d'oeuvres are wanted in the library right away," he told her.

"What—what time is it?" Mary Jane rubbed the sleep from her eyes and hastily replaced the cap that had slipped from her head.

"Gone two, lass."

Her hair probably looked a fright. She tried to replace a few of the pins.

"Hurry, lass."

Very well. It didn't matter how she looked, did it? Stir the fire, set the kettle on. Roast the beans, grind them, boil the thick, brown liquid. Gone two, gone two. That was already going into breakfast, a milchig meal. Change the apron. Cream could go with the sugar and lemon on the tray. Matzo for the crackers, cheese kosher for Pesach, a little brick of gefilte fish, all on the special green china.

The tray looked very nice, if she said so herself.

Tray in hand, she learned that Mrs. Dougherty's warnings about the master and his son were true. The "discussion" held hardly more civility than she was used to in the working-men's pubs down where she lived.

The loud, angry voices kept her standing in the hall, hesitant with fear, as long as she dared.

Their shouting was so loud that her first, shy knock was ignored. Her second one, louder, ended the yelling abruptly.

A cough, a struggle for sobriety, "Come!"

She could still feel the echoes, like unsettled dust motes, swirling about her as she entered the room: the menorah on the mantel, the molding so difficult to keep clean of fire soot.

The old man sat in his brocaded wing-backed chair smoking a pipe. His last few puffs, taken in a great fury, clouded the air about him. In his holiday black silk and soft cloth hat, once again he looked nothing so much as like an ancient prophet: Moses come down from the mountain with the smoke of divine presence still drifting about him. If his own bearded face were somewhat obscured, it was for the protection of more lowly mortals. He was the very image of the etching facing the Exodus title page in Mary Jane's own Bible.

Agitation had forced the young man, Master David, out of his chair. He stood behind it now, grasping the back with both long, white hands to keep from pacing. Or from deeds of even greater violence.

He was not the "Davey" of Mrs. Dougherty's endearment, but a man approaching thirty, devilishly handsome with thick, curly dark hair and a well-tended moustache. He looked the very image of his biblical namesake—"withal of a beautiful countenance, and goodly to look at."

He was also very aware of the fact. His smoking jacket was ox-blood red, and the little black cap he had worn during the seder lay crumpled now on the table beside him, letting his hair curl unhindered.

Mary Jane had to nudge the cap carefully aside to set down her burden.

Still the tension in the room would not settle. The young man had words biting the tip of his tongue. He could not shake them free because she had entered. She would bob her curtsey, she would scurry away—

Master David could no longer keep something from exploding. They were not the words he had been about to say, but the same scalding sarcasm was there.

"Very well," he said. "Very well. Let's turn the question to Mary Jane here."

Dead silence followed. Although she didn't dare look up, she felt both pairs of dark eyes burning on her.

"I'm sorry, sir," she managed to stammer at last. "I'm sure I don't know what you're talking about."

"Of course you do. Everyone's an authority on religion."

"Religion, sir?" The essay she'd written in school was a long, long time ago.

"Leave the girl alone," the old man said.

Master David ignored him. He smiled, but she didn't find the expression pleasant. Handsome. But not pleasant. "Why don't you tell us, for starters, what religion you were raised as. Nonconformist, I assume, being a Mary Jane Jones."

"No, sir. Actually, my father is Church of England. My mother's a Baptist. I sometimes go to church with her, but I've never been baptized myself."

"All right for starters."

"Davey, leave the girl—"

The younger man brushed his father aside with a sweeping gesture. "So what did your parents tell you when you were a child?" he persisted. He stepped close enough that she could smell the quantity of alcohol on his breath. "What did they tell you? About religion and truth and all of that?"

"Not much, sir. I mean, they hadn't time, sir. I mean, they're only working-class people, sir, no education. I mean, I don't suppose my mother's ever dreamed there're as many books in the world as there are in this library, sir."

"Well, surely they must have told you something. A two-denominational family? Was there no battle for souls in that household?"

"No, sir. Not that I remember. Mother did say she felt—she felt very clean, very holy after her baptism, sir."

Master David gave a shout of wild entertainment. Even the old man smiled, and a twinkle replaced the burned-out look his eyes had held earlier.

"Anything else?" Master David asked.

"May I pour you a cup, sir?" Mary Jane asked the master.

He gave a nod, but seemed more intent on her answer. Emboldened, she said, "Once, sir, I did ask my mother which church was right, hers or Father's."

"And what did she say?" Master David prodded.

Mary Jane pulled herself up with dignity, like her mother. "'Mary,' she said, 'when you grow up, you're to find that out for yourself.'"

"There, you see?" The young man pounded on the back of his chair in triumph. "Wisdom from the English working class. That's what Christianity, a fractured Christianity, does for you. It frees you. It lets you leave superstition behind, and even uneducated women can tell their daughters, 'you're to find that out for yourself.'"

The old man took a long, slow draw on his pipe. Then he spoke: "So tell me, my dear, with such careful parents, how is it for you now that you have grown up? Have you found a true church?" The German accent came out in longer speeches, and late at night.

"No, sir."

"Still looking, eh?" he replied with a wink. "Still lost, adrift upon the merciless waves of life?"

"Yes, sir."

"But that's just it!" the young man interrupted. "Life is in the search, not in 'the Truth.'"

"The prophet Moses—" the old man began.

His son interrupted him again. "Moses kept wandering all his life, never settled down. That's what made Truth for him. What we see here is not Moses's life, but Moses's life in the five hundredth generation, in old, dusty books on old, dusty shelves—"

During this speech, Mary Jane tried to pick up the cup and saucer to hand it to the older gentleman. She found herself so infected by the passion in the room that she did not trust her hand to keep steady. Before she knew what she was doing, she had interrupted the young man. Or rather, purposely ignored him, in order to speak to the father alone.

"But tonight, sir," she said, and now her hand was steady, "I saw how beautiful what you and your people have is. It is beautiful, sir, the whole thing. It is—I can't find the words—"

The old man set down his pipe and accepted the cup, smiling and nodding gently at her. "Yes. I saw your eyes, my dear. Swimming, shiny. I remember my mother's eyes, too, just so—dark and bright and teary—at a seder table."

"Oh, God!" the young man exploded. "Now you'll try to make a Jew out of her as well."

He circled around the chair in disgust and helped himself to a wedge of gefilte fish. Halfway to his mouth, he stopped and, gesturing with it, made it wobble ominously.

"By God, will you look at that." Even drunk, his voice remained crisp with Cambridge in contrast to his father's smokey accent. "Not a year with us and she's as rigid as the rest of them."

Mary Jane did not think to correct the young master. It was more than a year. She put the table between them so she could pour for him instead.

Master David continued to eye the fish askance, as if it might eat him instead of the other way around. "Only pareve snacks lest, God forbid, we mix milk and meat in our stomachs and die, God forbid, because that is tantamount to 'seething a kid in its mother's milk,' God forbid. Have you ever heard of such a wild superstition? Compared to that, black cats and walking under ladders is serious business and the height of science."

"Now, don't be so smug in your all-mighty science, Davey," the old gentleman said. "They don't know everything yet. But I'll tell you one thing they do know they didn't know when Moses went up on the mount, and that's the fact that eating pork can give you trichinosis."

Mary Jane did not know what trichinosis meant. Anything that ended in "osis," however, she knew was vile and dangerous. All the pork she'd eaten—none of it under this roof—rose up from her stomach and sat sour in her throat.

"What is trichinosis, sir?" she asked.

"Come." The old man set down his coffee and got to his feet. "I'll show you."

"Jesus Christ! Not this again," the young man swore, flinging himself into his chair and feeding upon gefilte fish, which clung to his moustache in little grey blobs.

The old gentleman led Mary Jane to a bookcase from which he drew a heavy tome. She saw that, unlike most of the books in the room, it was not religious nor was it written in a foreign language. It was a manual of medicine.

The old man turned right to the page, or rather, the book fell open automatically there. Then he began to read in a somber tone, yet one full of emotion and drama, not unlike that in which he had read the Haggadah that same evening.

"Trichinosis. An infestation in animals and man of the parasitic roundworm *Trichinella spiralis*. In man, infestation most commonly occurs from the ingestion of contaminated swine's flesh. Almost invisible to the naked eye, *Trichinella* larvae are in an encysted state when eaten. Gastric juices break down the cysts, allowing the immature worms to escape and grow to maturity in the host's digestive tract. Within the intestine, they mate, and the female burrows into the intestinal lining to give birth to numerous live young. At this point, symptoms of abdominal pain and nausea appear, often accompanied by prostration, high fever, and urticaria. The young worms now enter the blood stream by which path they find their way throughout the body, lodging particularly in the large muscles of the host."

A pain stabbed at Mary Jane's belly. A flash of fever scalded her. Just the late hour, and how little sleep she'd had.

Then, with delirious clarity, a picture from her childhood appeared before her eyes. It was not from the Bible this time. It swam in place of the medical book's etching: magnified muscle infested with spiraling roundworms that had been painted a livid liver color.

Mary Jane had gone with her mother to the seashore to watch her father's boat come into Swansea. Near the end of the dock, a crowd was gathered. She and her mother had gone to see what the matter might be. A dredging operation had brought up the body of a drowned man whose pallid flesh squirmed with shrimp. Mary Jane's mother had hurried her away at once, but it was too late. The image stuck and gave her nightmares to this day. She grew light-headed whenever she thought of those little crawly things feeding on her own insides. It came over her again as the master continued to read.

"It is estimated that as much as half the population of modern Britain is infected with *Trichinella spiralis* in milder cases that are often misdiagnosed as typhoid fever and other diseases of similar symptoms."

Mary Jane clung to the edge of the table. Every muscle ached.

"Strong purgatives may help clean out the system in the early stages of infection, but once the larvae are in the bloodstream, there is no known cure. The physician may only do his best to shore up the victim's strength and ease the muscle pains caused by the still-living though encysted larvae that will be with him for life."

Mary Jane's eyes rolled to the top of her head. Strength swept from her limbs like a gale—

The next thing she heard was a great patriarchal voice intoning: "Science will prove everything that Moses taught."

"For God's sake, Father, do you have to read that bloody thing to everyone who comes through the door? You'll be standing on the step reading it to the postman next news."

Mary Jane tried to stir, but before she was able to open her eyes, a pair of strong arms lifted her.

The great medical tome closed with a snap. "There, my boy. That is the wisdom of the English masses when confronted by Truth. Knocks them right off their feet."

"We are not all hair-splitting clinicians in this house, Miss Mary Jane."

Master Davey's whisper came very close to her ear. She felt herself settled on the overstuffed love seat beside the fire, the buttons at her throat opened.

"Beware the strange handmaiden that is in your house," she thought she heard the old man say.

Then, she thought she also heard the young man whisper: "I will have you dress up in your finest, and I will take you dining at the Ritz. We'll have pork chops in orange cream sauce and candied ham and French grilled hare. We'll have escargot in garlic butter and plate after plate heaped with scampi flambé and melt-in-your-mouth shrimp cocktail and oysters on the half shell—"

Did he really say such things to her? She couldn't be sure, because the litany made her black out once more.

～

"You watch out for the young master," Mrs. Dougherty warned when Mary Jane tried to give an account of the event the next day.

Mary Jane laughed nervously. She'd been expecting to get the sack and felt she deserved at least this hearty tease for such foolish behavior as fainting in the masters' presence.

Mrs. Dougherty raised a plump finger of warning at the laugh. "Heed me, lass. 'Tis no joking matter. My last girl got the sack from under me because of him."

Mary Jane had almost forgotten about the girl she'd succeeded. She remembered now.

"Aye," Mrs. Dougherty answered her stare. "In trouble, as right as you could please, no more nor less. The man says, 'Do as I tell you or you'll have no job.' Well, I'm here to tell you, you do as he tells you and you'll have no job and a growing belly to boot."

"Surely Master David has no use for a poor girl like me," Mary Jane exclaimed, dumbfounded.

"No use in the marrying way, you may be sure. That's just what Sary said, mind you. But I'll tell you one thing, 'tis twice as pretty as her you are, she all buck teeth and freckles with a nose like an onion. No, you've twice the looks she had, so you be twice as careful, lass."

Mary Jane, who'd had no boy take a fancy to her since the footman who got the sack, refused to believe Mrs. Dougherty's gossip. The scientific evidence against pork drove her to renewed scripture study that consumed her every waking thought. She quite forgot the cook's warning. She was busy avoiding the leftovers of her family's Easter ham, contenting herself with mashed potatoes and turnips instead.

Mrs. Dougherty's warning, however, was forcefully brought to her mind again on the first Saturday after Passover. As a reward for her holiday exertions, she'd earned the half day off. She had just turned onto Bethnal Green Road, skirting the worst streets of Whitechapel, when there was Master David. He made a dapper show in a high silk hat, short morning frock coat and boutonniere, ivory-topped cane, white gloves and tailor-cut trousers in bold red-and-white shepherd's check. Fleishig, Mary Jane's mind parsed.

He tipped his hat and bade her good afternoon. Mary Jane blushed to the very soles of her feet, either for her own sake or for his for making such a spectacle of himself. And on the Sabbath. He had no doubt walked too far, shouldn't be carrying that cane—

After bobbing a curtsey and murmuring "Shabbat shalom, sir," she tried to hurry past.

"I'll accompany you a way, if I might," he said, turning to fall in beside her.

"I'm only going to my parents' house," she told him. "I have the afternoon off."

"What excellent fortune. I intend to avoid Spitalfields until sundown myself. A man needs a warm meal at least once a day."

Mary Jane couldn't decide which unnerved her more, that he might learn where she lived. Or that he was not keeping the Sabbath. Then he took her arm.

"I beg you, sir." The gentle tug she gave failed to dislodge her sleeve.

"You women!" Master David exclaimed as they walked, he holding them to a slower pace than she wanted. "How good you are at wrapping us poor males around your little fingers! The impression you made upon my father by fainting dead away like that! He hasn't stopped talking of it since. 'What an intelligent girl we have in that

Mary Jane, Mama,' he says. 'What a Jewess she would make. Just like my old mother, God rest her. I shall definitely leave that girl something in my will.' And all the while he's sending me looks as if he means to cut me off without a penny. If only I could faint dead away like that and get him to speak of me with such favor! Really, Mary Jane, you must give me instruction."

"I did not faint on purpose," Mary Jane protested. "I am very ashamed that I intruded upon you two gentlemen so. I never meant to ingratiate myself to the master over his own son." She even began to explain about the drowned man and the shrimp in Swansea, but she heard herself sounding silly and childish.

Master David began to chuckle. "Ah, idyllic scenes from a Welsh childhood."

Although he waited for one, Mary Jane made no reply to that but another deep blush.

He began again, taking another topic. "You may have wondered why a young man of my qualities and fortune should not have found a wife yet."

"Indeed, I do not wonder at all. It is not my place." She felt herself grow redder still.

"Well, the simple fact of the matter is that Father will only allow me to marry a Jewess—he will cut me off if I don't do so. And I—I will only have a Christian."

Mary Jane was shocked into silence. A greater shock was coming.

"I've been baptized, you know. Quite against Father's wishes, of course. His old heart would kill him if he knew, but it's a simple fact. What was it your wise mother said? 'When you grow up, you're to find out for yourself.' Well, what I've found out is this: One can't get ahead being Jewish, refusing to dine with Christian friends, taking all sorts of odd holidays. One can get ahead in modern Britain if one is a Jew—look at Disraeli, for example—but one has to play cricket, as they say. I mean to get ahead, yes, and MP is not too high for my ambitions. But I can't do it with a pudgy old Jewish wife who knows nothing but challah and smoked salmon. I need a wife who is witty and charming and whom I can take to dine anywhere in the kingdom. Do you know what I mean?"

Again Mary Jane was dumbfounded.

"Well, of course I mean you, Miss Mary Jane. You're pretty and a Christian, but Father likes you and, in the privacy of our home, you would know how to keep us kosher. There couldn't be a better compromise."

All temptations Mary Jane thought herself prepared for, but not for this: a proposal of marriage.

He's not serious, she told herself. The social distance between us—impossible. This is only dangerous, dangerous flattery.

Yet it was the flattery best calculated to sway her. He knew how attracted she was to his family's way of life. To be invited to join it as more than just an observer, "the stranger which is in thy gates"! So great was the temptation, that she didn't trust herself to open her mouth for a reply.

"Forgive me," Master David said. "I have been too forward. It's a tendency that comes with the positions, master and maid. I am sorry. Let us walk and talk and forget I ever blurted out the foolish dreams I have hidden in my heart. Here." He caught her arm, tighter. "Just look at the fine fresh sausages in this butcher shop. Come, let me buy you one. I'm sure after Passover in my father's house, there is nothing that would taste better to you. With a fresh roll and a good bit of mustard."

There. Mary Jane planted her feet firmly against the horror of the idea. A moment before she might have been unable to resist the arm on hers, but now she saw the sides of pork hanging in the butcher's window, a tray of pig's ears and trotters. Her eyes worked like microscopes, and she was certain she could see little cysts of *Trichinella* larvae imbedded between the muscle fibers just like the etching in the medical book.

She could also see that she could never respect a man who had so little respect for his own father, whoever that man might be. She pulled, more firmly, in the direction of her own home.

"Very well," Master Davey said. "Wait here. I'll be back in a minute."

The instant he let go of her arm and vanished into the shop, Mary Jane ran. She couldn't go straight home, in case he be on her heels. She wove the nearby streets.

At last, she reached the wall of her house. There, waiting for her, was the young master. No. He knew her house—

He was leaning against the door, his top hat at a rakish angle, a sausage in one hand and a roll spread with mustard in the other. If Mrs. Dougherty only knew how he profaned her kitchen!

"I wondered where you'd got to." He grinned. "Mile End is a dangerous place. It's terribly easy to get lost. Well, here, come and eat your sausage. I already ate mine, I'm afraid, because I thought it might get cold. Besides, I couldn't run and carry it at the same time."

"Sir, I thank you," Mary Jane stammered. "But I daren't—" She looked up, pleading to the mass of masonry in front of her. Wasn't there one of the neighbors in an upper window who might see her plight? Or, if not there, then heaven?

Master David pushed himself away from the door and let her pass with a little smile and a bow. Before she could reach the handle, however, he grabbed her arm and turned her to face him.

He leaned against the door again, but now she was between them, pressed so hard she couldn't move.

She could feel the pork grease on his fingers as he caught her chin around the ribbons of her bonnet. She smelled the meat rancid on his breath as he pressed his lips and prickly moustache against her right cheek. The kiss, like a nightmare, seemed to last forever.

Finally, Mary Jane managed to find the doorknob behind her and open the door.

"I shall see you soon in my father's house, my love." Master David laughed.

Mary Jane tumbled into the dark corridor and slammed the door behind her. She scrubbed at the grease on her cheek and could not make it go away. She couldn't face her mother, little Nellie. Poor blind Edgar fingering his way around the room. They needed her wage. And her father—who was away on another run. Even as she stood panting in the dark letting the tears fall, she knew she had not reached any kind of safety. She had to be back on Monday—in *his* house.

"Dear God, sweet Jesus."

She wept aloud. Pride goeth before a fall, and she realized now that her prided knowledge of religion wasn't the equal of this.

"What am I to do? I didn't ask to be beautiful. Oh, if only girls were given the defense of ugliness while they are young. Dear Lord, if You should see fit to make me ugly, so ugly that no man would ever look at me again, I would be the most grateful girl on earth."

O MY FATHER

~

"MORE THINGS ARE WROUGHT BY PRAYER than this world dreams of." All my great-aunts quoted Tennyson, with varying degrees of success, in connection with their mother, Mary Jane Jones. And all were agreed on this point: "She were a right good prayer."

~

A crusty scab began to eat away her cheek right where the pork grease from that first brutish kiss had smeared.

And she was grateful.

"Lupus," the doctors declared. They told her what they told every other victim of this tuberculosis of the skin—that she must have caught it using some filthy public towel. And that there was no cure for it.

Mary Jane wanted to sing for joy.

All the people who saw this beautiful girl ravaged in the face sadly shook their heads and wondered at a God who must take joy in laying such curses on the undeserving. Her mother wept, and declared there was no use for it: Her daughter would be a spinster all her life.

Mary Jane alone knew that the disease had come in answer to a prayer. Time and time again it did, in fact, make her the most grateful girl on earth. She lost her position in the Jewish household because of it; the old master was very particular about things that might be unclean.

Never to have to face young Master David again—How good God was to her!

In spite of her "osis," the old master gave her the highest recommendation and put in a good word with Mr. Moses. This got her a job sewing the high-end ready-mades for Marsdens, formerly Moses and Sons. Within a year, she went from there to Peter Robinson's, a very posh establishment, sewing gentlemen's opera capes to order.

The back room where she worked was not so posh. Full of steam from the irons, the air thick with drifting threads, pins crunching underfoot, the constant whir of the treadle machines. Nevertheless, she made more than she'd been making in the scullery, just to start. Raises came quickly and sometimes there were tips. She had no need to go in public where her face might offend; the girls she worked with soon got used to her and were kind. She did her best with the capes even when she imagined an unsuspecting Master David wearing her handiwork as he took his next innocent maid to the opera. Christian charity, she had learned, was sometimes safer given from a distance.

The only thing wrong with Peter Robinson's was that it was right in London, more than five miles from Romford and too far to permit Mary Jane to continue to live with her family as she would have liked. She would have to find another place to stay, but where?

"She were walking down t' street," the youngest daughter, Violet, told me, "and she were praying she'd find someone to 'elp 'er, some place to stay. She opened her eyes and saw a girl. She went up to 'er, and the girl said, 'Come back and stay with us.'"

So Mary Jane came to stay at the clean, quiet boarding house. The power of her prayer had worked again.

Though she never ate pork or shrimp the rest of her life, Mary Jane left her study of Judaism when she left service in the house near Spitalfields. Still, she continued a lively interest in religions. Because she was convinced she would never find a husband, disfigured as she was, she thought of becoming a nun. Though the doctrines of neither the Catholic Church nor the Church of England satisfied her, the notion of a life devoted to religion did.

Then her little sister Nellie died of the fever at the age of seven.

"Sure, 'tis a terrible grief." Noreen, one of the Irish girls she boarded with, sympathized.

"Aye, never to see the dear creature again," said Bridget, the other.

"Never see her again?" Mary Jane pulled the handkerchief from the sleeve of her black dress to wipe at renewed tears. "But she's in heaven. If only I am good enough, I'll join her—"

"In heaven?" Noreen shook her head dolefully. "Never a bit of it."

"The poor mite had not been baptized, had she?" Bridget agreed. "She'll not be among the blessed."

"Not even purgatory. Limbo."

"'Tis a great sorrow for you, indeed, indeed."

Mary Jane supposed the girls were well-meaning enough, but little Nellie in such a hell—she wouldn't believe it.

Then Bridget got married and moved out. An older woman with straw-colored hair moved into the room next door, a Miss Peacock. She colored her pasty complexion with quantities of rouge and lipstick in a most unnatural fashion. She was also fond of bizarre colors: purples, pinks, and lime greens. She wore them all at once in feathers and furs until she looked like some exotic bird. Or a circus clown. At first Mary Jane tried to befriend her, for an older spinster seemed a very sad—and a close-to-home— thing for her.

"I hope you'll join us in the dining room tonight," Miss Peacock told Mary Jane when they met in the hall one Saturday morning.

"Thank you. Will we have some music?"

"Oh, no. Not at all." Miss Peacock dropped her voice and filled it with echoes. "A séance." She grinned. There was lipstick on her teeth. "I have a spirit that could make your face as good as new."

"No, no!" Mary Jane cried, and hurried away. "I will not be indebted to the devil for anything."

"Or call up the spirit of your little sister—" the woman called after her.

All that day, Mary Jane worked with a cold, cavernous feeling inside.

Ever after that, whenever the dining room was dark and the doors closed for a séance, Mary Jane would keep the lamp burning in her own room. She would stay there, reading the Bible and praying all night while the ominous moans and groans went on below. And she would not eat a meal in the room until everyday life had returned the feeling of the place to normal.

Another, nicer woman moved in down the hall, and she was an officer in the Salvation Army. Mary Jane went with her to several meetings and soon "donned the bonnet."

⟿

Shiny black silk with black lace gathered under the brim, the aunties still showed off the famous Army bonnet in the House for a little girl to play dress up when my mother was that age.

⟿

Mary Jane sang with the brass band on street corners and visited "the sick and the sinful" in the gin dens of Whitechapel, so close to where she'd lived and worked in Romford and Spitalfields.

⟿

"She didn't know that it was the true church," my Auntie Mona said, "but she thought they were doing good. They were the most practical religionists."

⟿

And then her father died.

The tragedy struck the winter just before Mary Jane's twenty-sixth birthday. Her father was crossing the Channel when a storm came up. Although the ferry made it safely to shore, Henry Merton Jones had become drenched and chilled. He caught pneumonia, rambling in Welsh in his delirium in Belgium where no one could understand him. Far from the comfort of home and family, he died. Not bothering to bring his body home, they buried him at sea.

The night before they brought her word, Mary Jane dreamed of her father, the flesh of his face eaten by shrimp like the drowned man she'd seen as a child. Come the morning, the God for whom she'd so enjoyed searching seemed to have died as well.

Why were the strong and necessary always taken? she asked a cold grey heaven. As poor, blind Edgar stumbled into her arms, she asked again, Why were the sick and the weak, those least able to bear it, left to stand the buffets of life alone?

Did no one hear her prayers after all?

Her dear sister Nellie, such a bright, pretty girl, would have been able to work by now—had she lived—and been a comfort to them all. But now there was only a sick, old widow, a blind boy who couldn't tie his own shoes in the morning, and herself, a girl so ravaged in the face that normal people cringed to look at her.

～

"There weren't no pensions them days" is Auntie Barbara's moral.

～

Henry Merton Jones's boss took pity on the situation. He offered Mrs. Jones a little shop he owned in Lincoln. She could keep the shop, staying in the rooms above it, selling threads and packets of pins, and so make some sort of living for herself and the boy. Though Lincoln was very far from London, a place among strangers, Mrs. Jones decided she had no choice but to take it. She could no longer afford the rent on the house in Romford.

For some time, Mary Jane had been thinking of leaving sewing to devote herself to something the Salvation Army had taught her to love: nursing. Now she had the added incentive of wanting to be near her mother. She applied to many hospitals in the North, but was accepted only in Bradford.

"But 'tis in a different shire from Lincoln all together."

Noreen was no doubt right. Still, to a Londoner, anything "north" seemed like it must be in the neighborhood. It was closer than London, in any case.

Mary Jane gave notice at the boarding house, then at Peter Robinson's, and prepared to make the move. It was the end of February 1896.

∾

A light snow was falling in London as Mary Jane made her way home from work after the sorrow and tears that had met her announcement around the sewing machines. She could not cry these days without thinking of her father—every sorrow was caused by lack of him. Nightmares of his face eaten by shrimp still haunted her. The burden seemed to crush her into the slosh of new-fallen snow on the pavement. She couldn't see her way, she was so blind with grief. Her feet had to follow the well-worn route automatically: down Montague Place, past the British Museum and into Russell Square.

∾

Buckingham Palace, the Tower of London, the Globe, the British Museum. Of all the sites in London for the tourist to visit, a pilgrimage to Russell Square is always in order for my family. The hucksters are gone from this upscale neighborhood near the university. All is quiet under the ancient chestnut trees beside the fountain.

∾

"O Father," she wept silently. "O my Father."

> O my Father, Thou that dwellest
> In the high and glorious place.
> When shall I regain Thy presence
> And again behold Thy face?

Mary Jane stopped short, hardly able to believe her ears. At first she thought they were her own words. Now she realized they came from outside of her, and came as a song sung in the most angelic tenor she had ever heard.

> For a wise and glorious purpose
> Thou hast placed me here on earth,
> And withheld the recollection
> Of my former friends and birth.

So it was not her father, but the Father of us all to whom the song was addressed in such a personal, longing way. The singer was standing there under the bare, dripping branches of the square. The power of his voice had attracted quite a little crowd. Mary Jane's first thought was that it must be an Army band—without the band. But who needed drums and horns when they had a voice like that?

And the song. She drew closer to hear.

> Yet ofttimes a secret something
> Whispered, "You're a stranger here,"
> And I felt that I had wandered
> From a more exalted sphere.

> I had learned to call Thee "Father,"
> Through Thy Spirit from on high;
> But until the key of knowledge
> Was restored, I knew not why.
> In the heavens are parents single?
> No; the thought makes reason stare!
> Truth is reason, truth eternal
> Tells me I've a Mother there.

That certainly wasn't Army doctrine. But it was as wonderful as it was strange and unusual. Mary Jane had worked her way forward so she could see the singer now, a man in his forties with a full beard and neat but well-worn clothes. He closed his eyes with the effort of his song and seemed to be viewing the very heavenly glories of which he sang.

When I leave this frail existence,
When I lay this mortal by,
Father, Mother, may I meet you
In your royal courts on high?

Then, at length, when I've completed
All you sent me forth to do,
With your mutual approbation
Let me come and dwell with you.

Some in the crowd applauded; Mary Jane was too awestruck to do so. Some chuckled, some jeered as a companion to the singer began to scurry among them handing out pamphlets. Mary Jane took one gratefully; it might be the words to the song. She wondered if she could get the Army to include it in their repertoire. She squinted at the paper, but it was too dark to read. All she could tell was that, unfortunately, there was no music on it.

"Excuse me, sir."

Her high curiosity gave her the courage to touch the pamphleteer's arm when he passed again. She bowed her head as she saw the usual look of horror cross his face; the lupus registered with him. He quickly hid his reaction, however, and smiled. "Yes, Miss? Did you have a question?"

Mary Jane did the man the service of covering her right cheek with the pamphlet. She did it from shyness as well, for the sound of his voice made her feel even more brazen and confused. It was a foreign accent, from America.

"I just wondered," she stammered, "who wrote that beautiful song."

"Well, I'll tell you," the man said. "Her name was Eliza Snow."

Snow fell over the brim of Mary Jane's bonnet, between her and the man. "A woman?"

"Yes. And not just any woman. She was the wife of the late prophet of the true church of God."

"'Ey, you leave that good English girl alone, y'ear!" shouted a heckler in the crowd, and Mary Jane was too embarrassed to stay any longer.

Clutching the pamphlet to her, slipping in the dirty slush, she ran all the way back to the boarding house. The idea of prophets crammed her head—prophets who lived and died so that real people saw and knew them. Prophets who had wives who wrote inspired songs, and who weren't just etchings in the old Bible. "Come meet with the spirits tonight," urged Miss Peacock, meeting her in the hall. Lipstick smeared the lace of the older woman's collar, the fur trim on her wrap had worn down to the crumbling leather. "You'll be able to speak to your father."

Mary Jane pushed by, not wanting to warm up by the fire or have her supper first. When she reached her room, she quickly lit the lamp and read the tract all the way through with such greed that her gaze leapt from line to line. Meaning struggled to keep up.

"Men and women . . . sons and daughters of God, and Jesus their elder brother . . . Joseph Smith . . . the instrument . . . of restoration . . . divine authority under the hands of heavenly messengers . . . Infants . . . need no baptism . . . doctrine of celestial marriage . . . man and woman united . . . in an everlasting covenant . . . Prophet, Seer, and Revelator . . . The Gospel and Church and Authority of Jesus Christ restored to earth for the last days and . . . for evermore."

She was about to read it from the beginning again when her gaze was suddenly caught and frozen by the subscription as if it had been her tongue and she had licked a frozen railing.

"The Latter-day Saints (Mormons) meet for public worship at—"

She never got to the address. Mormons!

"It's true, I tell you," she remembered Hester at work saying as she pressed a seam. "I read it only last night. They take the poor girls in a passage that runs all the way under the sea from Liverpool to Utah where it ends up inside their temple. There they keep the girls—oh, hundreds of 'em—prisoner on bread and water until they can force them to marry some old codger, to be his fortieth or fiftieth wife." The steam rose all around Hester's chestnut curls like a whiff of brimstone.

Alone in her room, Mary Jane's insides withered with a groan. "My only love sprung from my only hate." How well the words of Shakespeare suited her despair! She could not, would not, plunge herself headlong into tragedy as Juliet had done. She swept the tract up and stuffed it down the chimney of her lamp until it caught. Then she tossed it into her empty grate.

As if a waft of the old spiritualist's perfume had just blown in under the door, she felt a dark, empty feeling come over her. She kept the light burning against it as she undressed, as she crawled, shivering violently, into bed. Still she did not dare turn down the lamp. She knew she couldn't fight sleep long, but when it came, its dreams would be awful. To the image of her father's shrimp-eaten corpse would come Hester in the steam: "They be devils. Young girls just like us be their prime prey, for don't they need myriads of wives for their lecherous old polygamists?"

Could even her God-given lupus spare Mary Jane from such a fate? She must pray now with all her might.

"O my Father," she prayed, then remembered that those were the words of the song. Such a heavenly song! How in the world could devils sing such divine words, and so beautifully? Still, they were devils. Had she reached up there in Russell Square and tipped off one of their hats, all London would have seen the horns for themselves. Like a beautiful siren that tenor had been, luring young women, like sailors, like her father, to their deaths.

"O my Father—" No, not those words again! Other words! There must be other words to address heaven. "My father—dear father—"

Even as she spoke (she was certain she was not yet asleep) a warm glow grew out of the lamp and filled the room. And in this glow walked the figure of her own father. He was not shrimp eaten and ghostly, but glowing and alive, dressed in white garments and smiling at her.

"Father," she exclaimed. "I thought you were dead."

Now the Myth diverges. Some say he opened his mouth and spoke in his singsong Welsh lilt, while others say he only looked down on his daughter, still imprisoned on earth, with such longing that she knew his message intuitively. Of the message, however, there is no doubt.

∿

"Mary, my child," he said, or seemed to say. "You have found the true church in these Latter-day Saints. I too, have found it, here on the other side. I beg of you, please, to work for me the saving ordinances only possible in the holy temples of these they call Mormons. Have my baptism done by the proper authority. Have my marriage to your sweet mother sealed for all eternity. And see, too, that all you dear children are sealed to us as well. Our little Nellie is here with me, besides all the other little souls your mother bore who died so young. They are beautiful, happy children. How I wish you could see them! But in time. In time we shall all be a happy family, for all the eternities, together. It rests on you. You must be true and accomplish the work."

The vision faded, but there was hardly time for Mary Jane to catch her breath before it came again, the same glorious picture of her father with the same remarkable message. After the dream had faded a second time, she thought it was appearing yet once more. Then she realized it was only watery dawn creeping in her little dormer window. She would have to hurry or she would be late for work.

First, Mary Jane had to jump out of bed and run to the grate to see if she could salvage anything of the tract that, overnight, had grown so precious to her. There it was, crumbling to cinders at her touch. Not a sentence of doctrine remained intact. As if preserved by a holy hand, however, was the address where the Mormons "meet for public worship," the day, Sunday, and the time.

It was two days to Sunday, and Mary Jane did all she could to make the time pass quickly. Both nights she took the same route home through Russell Square, but never did she hear the beautiful song again. Still, the tune was imbedded in her soul, and even a good number of the words returned to make her needle fly in the workroom.

Two days was a long time, a very long time, to maintain an other-worldly feeling over the many deep hollows of everyday life. Had she had someone with whom to share her burden, things might have gone better. But she didn't dare confide even in her friends from the Salvation Army. Without asking, she heard plenty from Hester at work.

"That's what I read last night." The iron hissed and the steam rose.

"But 'ow does the writer know all this?" another girl asked, wielding the big, heavy shears. "No one 'as ever been in them temples."

"They know because one girl 'ad the good fortune to escape. She dared to leap out of the 'igh window of the cell where they kept 'er. (Oh, they'd kept 'er months and months, and she was naught but skin and bones, but still she wouldn't marry. She'd pluck, she did.) She landed in the Great Salt Lake and managed to swim to safety. She was found half-dead by a CoE minister who was there, preaching amongst the 'eathen at the very risk of 'is life. 'Twas the minister 'imself told the story to the papers."

Come Sunday, Mary Jane's faith was wobbly indeed. She managed to say "No, thank you" to her Salvation Army friend, to get dressed, and to make it to the street given on the pamphlet in plenty of time. She even found the building, an old warehouse, and saw several men enter it. She saw no women, though, and so she didn't dare to cross the street to the right side. She walked up and down on the wrong side for nearly an hour, pretending to look in the windows of the shuttered shops, trying to evoke her father's voice again. All the while, she kept an eye on the old warehouse. It took on the aspect of, first, a terrible, crouching monster, then a dungeon, but then, often enough to make her stay on, a harmless old building offering shelter to a misunderstood people.

After about an hour, Mary Jane saw a young family approach: a husband, *one* wife, and three small children in clean but modest Sunday best. Picking up her courage with all her might, she ran across the street and allowed the man to hold the door for her as she entered.

Now she was inside. Her protection vanished. She found herself the ward (the captive, rather, for he all but pounced on her) of a large man with a very thick beard. After a moment or two of confused terror, she recognized him as the tenor from Russell Square. He did not flinch when he looked into her face. He was hatless, now, and she looked carefully. He had no horns. Still, she remained unconvinced about the tail. Why should he have such an avid interest in her? Why should he insist she take the seat next to him if he had no ulterior motives? Her throat constricted, her heart wildly raced. Her mind jumped alternately between fervent prayers and visions of the horrors waiting for her when she was snatched away. She heard little of the first portion of the service and was hardly able even to look around her.

The snatch didn't come. The other man, the American who'd handed out the pamphlets, rose to offer a sermon. In it, he gave an account of the first latter-day missionaries to come to Britain in 1837. Near daybreak on the day they were scheduled first to preach, an Elder Kimball said he was "struck with a great force by some invisible power."

Elder Kimball recalled, "My agony was so great, I could not endure it." Then, not the window, but the entire wall of their third-floor room opened up and, for "an hour and a half by Willard's watch," devils flew at them "in legions . . . within a few feet of us . . . like armies rushing to battle. They appeared to be men of full stature, possessing every form and feature of men in the flesh, who were angry and desperate; I shall never forget the vindictive malignity . . . on their countenances as they looked me in the eye."

These faithful men overcame the onslaught with prayer. Mary Jane felt she had suffered something of the same onslaught when she'd burned the tract in her own little room, and then in finding her way here. These men spoke with such authority and understanding of the invisible world she'd always sensed all around her. Against her own onslaught, she'd turned her own prayers. Her heart still raced, but about the devils now, not about these men who could subdue them.

The service seemed to be winding to a close. An awful black thought passed through her mind: she was so ugly even the Mormons didn't want her. She exorcised that demon as she realized with a burst of joy that the closing hymn was going to be "O My Father." Someone handed her a precious hymn book. Words and notes were actually printed there in black and white. She hardly needed that, however. The words were loosed from her as if her festering soul had been lanced, soon to regain health and wonderful strength.

Supported by solid basses, soaring with the sopranos, the song took on a new dimension now with all the parts chasing one another in echoes, encouraging one another to endure and improve upon every note. Even the monotones, as a subtle, artistic foil representing "this frail existence," had a place. Best of all was the wonderful tenor, ringing up from the barrel of a chest beside her. More than once she had to stop her own singing, overcome by the emotion of it all.

Mary Jane's head was clear for the final prayer. She "amened" with the rest. She welcomed the opportunity her host gave her to stop and talk with him as others departed in their little clusters. He told her something about the rites carried out in the temples for those who had already died—rites of which her vision father, not the tract or any other worldly thing, had already made her aware. It was supernatural how she knew, and neither coincidence nor devil's play.

Then the bearded man's talk turned to his home in Salt Lake City—Zion he called it. His tones were those Salvation Army officers used of a Zion in heaven, beyond the reach of mortal man. He showed her photographs of his wife (one, single wife) and their six young children. He rehearsed their names to her and their little personalities.

"I do not begrudge the Lord my time away from them," he said, "for He has given me all I have and will see we are all together in the world to come. But I shall certainly be glad when these three years are over, and I can return to them and to my dear Emily."

It was true. She saw it in his face. He didn't want another wife. He loved too well the one he had already. Mary Jane was safe, she was welcome, and she was almost certain she had found—

Again, there is some conflict of testimony among the sisters here. Some of them insist that their mother was baptized while in London and that, because of the haste in which the ordinance was performed, the records were lost. It had to be done again later. The rest of the sisters cannot allow that church organization could be so careless. For them, that day some five years later was the first and only time their mother stepped into those sacred waters—carrying my grandmother as yet unborn so that fourth daughter claimed extra virtue: she was baptized twice.

Whatever the case, it is clear that for the moment, the needs of a poor, dissipated family—a blind boy, a poor old widow, and a penniless girl of twenty-six—had to take precedence over a family resting in eternity. Before another Sunday came, Mary Jane found herself far away from London and from Russell Square. She was alone and lonely in the strange, cold North of England.

MEETING

FROM THE LITTLE WINDOW at the end of the student nurses' dormitory, Mary Jane could count thirty stacks belching black smoke into the pre-dawn sky. But these couldn't cause the unearthly sound that had awakened her. Every morning since she'd been in Bradford, she had heard it, promptly at half past five. The first time, she'd been too paralyzed with fear to get up to investigate. The previous five mornings, as now, she had climbed out of bed. Wrapping herself in a blanket, she went to the window. The past five days, as now, the streets were too dark to see anything at all.

The unnerving sound started very quietly, like a gentle rain. It crescendoed at a steady, scurrying pace until it grew to the roar of rushing water. Some heavenly child, Mary Jane thought, must spill his marble pouch down into the cobbled streets of Bradford every morning at this hour. Though she'd thought of that pretty image, it did not help her endure the daily event any better.

She was exhausted, physically, mentally, and emotionally. Young nurses on probation were always given the hardest, most degrading jobs: bedpans, soiled dressings, scrubbing the floors. She craved every moment of rest she could snatch, especially now, near the end of a sixty-hour work week. The rising bell sounded at six, but that one half hour she lost every morning was telling on her. The others, all native Bradford girls, managed to sleep right through the strange sound.

Of course, the other girls whispered and giggled 'way into the night, in the dialect she often couldn't understand. They were all younger than she, most had known each other before coming to St. Luke's, and all clearly had family, beaux, and other outside interests to chatter about.

"Never mind them," Matron had counseled Mary Jane privately. "All them silly girls—they'll never make nurses. Mark my words, the lot of 'em'll be gone afore t' year end. Married or back to t' mill where they belong. But tha'lt stay. I been 'ere fifteen year. I knows a nurse when I sees one. 'Tis a life of dedication, if you choose it."

Mary Jane's hand wandered up to her mottled cheek. She doubted Matron's kind words. The loneliness she felt in the midst of all those younger, happier girls was about to drive her away after only a week.

Lonely! She scolded herself as the first tear fell to the windowsill. How could she be lonely? Floor upon floor of the sick and injured lay in the hospital below her feet, craving her presence. She had never been so ungrateful as to be lonely when she was tending the sick in the Salvation Army. People are lonely and miserable, she always maintained, because either they haven't found God or they haven't found their fellow men. A single week of paid nursing, however, had taught Mary Jane a very important lesson: a great chasm stands between charity and efficiency. At St. Luke's Hospital, it was efficiency that counted. What Mary Jane had liked about "visiting the sick and sinful" in the Army was reading to them, talking to them, praying with them, anything to get to know them as the divine individuals they were. There was no time for such things in hospital. As she raced about with bedpans that filled faster than they could be emptied, she thought bitterly that Matron was more concerned with what came out of the patients than what stayed inside. What stayed inside and truly made them.

One man in the fourth ward, not so very old, was dying of tuberculosis. A trip to the fresh air of the Lake Country might have done wonders for him but, alas, he was too poor, and a life in the mills and this air thick with soot and cinder blacks had only aggravated his condition. Nonetheless, his spirits were high. Mary Jane's spirits lifted just to see his wasted but brave face. Once she had stopped by his bed and listened to a song he sang—or spoke, rather, rasping, coughing up blood—in the broad dialect she could hardly make out. A touching resignation quavered in the mournful ballad as he sang:

I've walked at night through t' Sheffield lanes,
Well, 'twere same as bein' in 'ell.
Where furnaces thrust out tongues of flame
An' they roared like t' wind on t' fell.
An' I've sumped up coal in Barnesley pit
Wi' muck up to me knee.
From Sheffield, Barnesley, Rother'am,

Good Lord, deliver me.
I've seen fog creep across Leeds Brig
As thick as Bastille soup.
An' I've lived where folks was stowed away
Like rabbits in a coop.
An' I've seen snow float down Bradford Beck
As black as ebony.
From 'Ull and 'Alifax and 'ell,
Good Lord, deliver me.

If Mary Jane had yet to see black snow in Bradford, it was only a matter of time. She did remember the conductor on the train calling "Sheffield, Barnsley, Rother'am" and "'Ull and 'Alifax," in just that order and cadence, "'ell" just around the next bend. She knew the dying man in the fourth ward was rehearsing the litany of a Yorkshireman in verse and melody. He, she thought, would be able to tell her, from very close experience, what the clatter in the streets every morning was.

He could teach me how to live, or at least how to die with some scrap of dignity in this town, she told herself. This town that seems no more than one great belching machine—so even caring for the sick is mechanized in these hospital halls.

But Matron had come by before she could ask, Matron, glaring, and announcing a dozen disasters in the next wards that needed immediate, efficient attention.

"I know no one in Bradford who isn't either silly or sick," Mary Jane admitted.

Then she bent her head down on the windowsill and gave in wholly to tears.

A good ten minutes' cry was enough to clear Mary Jane's head and her heart. She was, after all, a courageous and generally optimistic young woman. Displays of emotion, even in private, were uncommon to her. She trusted in God too much to make complaint when He handed her trials, nor to be too exuberant in her joy, either, when she was blessed.

The thought of God recalled to her mind that her complaint of knowing no one in Bradford outside the hospital was not exactly true. She left the window and hurried to the peg where she hung her coat. Yes, it was still there. She pulled a scrap of paper from the pocket, even though it was still too dark to read.

Two weeks before coming to Bradford, she had spent in Lincoln, seeing her mother and younger brother settled in their little shop and new life. While there, she had tried to discover if there were any Mormons in town, for the memory of Russell Square remained warm inside her.

"Yes," she had received the reply. The advert was pointed out to her in the back pages of the *Lincolnshire Echo* her mother sold in the shop:

TIME IS RUNNING OUT
Current events clearly indicate that it is God's purpose to overthrow the present order

Zechariah Chapter 5

It gave a local time and place. Mary Jane read the scripture: "Then I turned, and lifted up mine eyes, and . . . behold a flying roll." It sounded like a new revelation, like the Mormons.

The people she found gathered, makeshift, in the back room of a school, were not Latter-day Saints, however, but a group called the New and Latter House of Israel. They were good people, she discovered, even though they were not what she was looking for. They didn't drink. They preached of restored prophets, of a temple to be built above the Medway River in Kent. The men did not cut their hair, like Samson of old. These ideas of restoration, of progress in spirituality, all this spoke to her. Mary Jane returned to them the following Sunday. Their sorrow that she was to leave them so soon was genuine.

"But there are members of our group in Bradford who also haven't the means to gather to Kent," one woman assured her. "Enoch Whitaker, his wife and family. I know them well, and they are very faithful. I will give you their address and write ahead to let them know you are coming."

Mary Jane thanked her hostess, secretly doubting she would look up the family. But here in the dormitory of St. Luke's Hospital, she realized she had overestimated the satisfaction which nursing would bring to her life. And she had underestimated how desperate loneliness could be.

The bell to rise rang down the dormitory. Groans and struggles with sleep rose from the other beds. Mary Jane quickly slipped the address back in her coat pocket so she could be first in the washroom and impress Matron with her efficiency for one more day. Tonight, Saturday, when the other girls went to meet their young men, she, too, would leave hospital. She would go visit the Whitakers after all.

Never in her wildest dreams, of course, did she think that she, too, might meet a beau that night.

Mrs. Enoch Whitaker was as cold, sharp, and neat as a new paper of pins. So was her sitting room: bony furniture, the pleats of the drapes sharp, Queen Victoria glaring from a framed portrait on the wall.

There were two boys of ten and twelve who, Mary Jane learned, were not Mrs. Whitaker's sons, but her nephews. She had no children of her own and probably liked it better that way. When her sister-in-law had died and her drunkard brother had abandoned these boys as orphans, Mrs. Whitaker had capitulated to the suggestion of her husband's warmer heart. She had written that they would be willing to take one, preferably the elder, who would leave home sooner. The authorities had sent both, and though she dearly wanted to, she couldn't very well have sent one back after that. As it happened, both boys were very much like their aunt. They sat side by side in somber grey suits, sulky, spoiled, and sullen, staring at Mary Jane with a sort of mockery that made her constantly touch her ravaged cheek. She feared she might have spilled tea on her collar.

Mr. Enoch Whitaker seemed a more pleasant sort. He, at least, could produce a smile on demand. The present Mrs. Whitaker was his second wife. He seemed to apologize silently to Mary Jane, suggesting that it was none of his doing that this missus had first moved in, taking advantage of a poor widower and now, with her nephews, quite overwhelmed him. He had a pair of great, strong hands, which seemed, at the same time, to be agile and clever. He had, in fact, created the machinery for the waterworks of the town of Hull.

"There'nt nothing I like more 'an tinkering wi' summat 'at works," he said. "Fixin' it when it don't and taking me son to see the latest lightbulb, bicycle, camera, telephone, streetcar, 'ot air balloon, or ancient mummy exhibit at t' Natural 'Istory Museum."

Mrs. Whitaker gave a snort.

"I'd take me nephews, too—"

"Don't want to," the boys said in unison.

Now the great hands sat clumsy and restless, folding and unfolding, cramping to fit around a tea cup under the sharp, no-nonsense gaze of madam.

There had been a serious mistake. "We are not members of that deluded sect," Mrs. Whitaker informed Mary Jane. "Yes, Mr. Whitaker were attracted just after his first wife died."

"'New and Latter' sounded like t' billing for a zeppelin." Mr. Whitaker shrugged helplessly at his delusion. "Sure to be a step forward for all mankind."

"'E were lonely and confused," Mrs. Whitaker explained. She had soon set him straight. "We are now upstanding pillars of t' local Wesleyan chapel, naturally."

"Naturally," Mary Jane echoed.

Mr. Whitaker opened and shut his great empty hands.

"That long hair on gentlemen," Mrs. Whitaker complained. "Untidy! Un'ygenic!" Her voice was like a pair of barber's shears, and her gaze was clean on Mary Jane's cheek.

The woman, however, thought nothing of her own severe, black bun under her starched, lace cap.

Once the discomfort of this mistake had passed, Mary Jane found no other topic of conversation she could dredge up to fill the void. She finished her tea as quickly as she could with the two nephews' sharp eyes on her. Then she thanked the Whitakers for their hospitality.

They did not invite her to come again.

Just as Mary Jane was setting her feet under her so she could rise, a sudden noise at the front door made her lose her balance and fall back into the chair again. The same sound made Mrs. Whitaker grow white. She set down her teacup and clutched the rim of the tray as if it were about to be snatched from her. All Mary Jane could think of was that burglars were breaking into the house.

Soon, however, a merry tune whistled in harmony to the opening door. The tall, lean figure of the man who entered hung up his hat and coat on a peg that was obviously reserved for them. He tripped over the edge of a rug as he entered the room, but recovered himself as if it had been done on purpose—a clown's act to add a bit of life to the somber place.

"Mrs. Whitaker," he said, amusement covering any annoyance, "I do wish tha wouldna move t' furniture about wi'out telling me."

Mrs. Whitaker fumed silently, and the two nephews set their faces in grimaces of smug superiority. Mr. Whitaker chuckled nervously, but no one found any reply before the young man continued for himself.

"But now I see tha's' company, an 'andsome young lady. Won't tha introduce me?"

Mrs. Whitaker cleared her voice of a squeak. "Miss Jones, may I present me 'usband's son—by a previous marriage." She cleared her throat of another squeak to be certain the relationship was seen to be sufficiently distant, to disclaim all responsibility for it. "Ralph, this is Miss Jones."

"Miss Jones, delighted," Ralph said with a smart little bow. "Forgive me if I don't come and take tha 'nd, but there's no telling what me stepmother has rearranged between 'ere and there, and I don't dare to cross that no man's land."

"I will come to you, Mr. Whitaker," Mary Jane said, finding her feet with sudden ease.

"No, please don't bother," was the reply.

"No bother," Mary Jane said with a look at Mrs. Whitaker. "I was just leaving. It's on my way."

"Surely tha'rt not leaving so early?"

"I'm afraid I must. I feel I've overstayed my welcome already."

Then she continued, "How do you do?" for she found her hand quite by accident in the young man's. There was something curious about that hand, long and pale and terribly sensitive. It seemed to investigate by touch like the tendrils of a sea urchin. The sensation, however, was not unpleasant.

In fact, there was nothing unpleasant about the young man at all. His clothes were neat and even jaunty. His nose was rather large and rounded, but not ill formed. Beneath it, a scrubbing brush of red moustache met a red beard around gentle, laughing lips. His cheeks and forehead were high, and his hair, more brown than the red of his beard, though very long, was thick and curly upon his shoulders. It gave him the aspect of a saint, one of great compassion, not a stern judge.

If there was anything discomforting about him at all, it was his eyes. Up close, Mary Jane could see that his right one was missing: the lid hung lifeless over an empty socket. But she saw much worse daily in hospital. The right one was bright, angelic blue and had intensity for two. It fixed on her with a look that was only slightly too demanding, as if he were making an effort to see beyond the normal outward appearance and into her soul. The slightest flinch never passed through that gaze as he must have seen her ruined cheek.

"Tha'rt new in Bradford, Miss Jones."

"Yes. How could you tell?"

"Tha accent, of course. Clearly not a Yorkshire lass. London, p'r'aps?"

"Exactly."

"A man can tell a lot about a person from their speech, but few takes time to listen. London. And a lady."

"Well, you're wrong about the lady, I'm afraid. I'm only a poor working girl."

"Tha coat, Miss Jones." Mrs. Whitaker was urging them along.

"But tha must 'ave worked in some fine 'ouses." Ralph Whitaker seemed to know the best way to deal with his stepmother: ignore her completely. "Service, p'r'aps, when tha weret young and himpressionable."

"I have indeed been in service," Mary Jane admitted. She found she could do so with a smile, even remembering Master Davey.

"Good evening, Miss Jones," said Mrs. Whitaker.

Ralph went on ignoring his stepmother. "P'r'aps tha would' like some 'elp finding tha way back 'ome through these strange, narrow streets after dark."

"Well, I—"

"Please, Miss Jones," Ralph said. "Allow me to walk you 'ome."

He had now taken up his own hat and coat again, and a dapper cane which he tapped along. She could not refuse.

"T' 'ospital, is it?"

"Yes. But how did you know that?" Mary Jane shivered as she tied her bonnet under her chin as if the man beside her were indeed a prophet with second sight.

"Well, let's just say tha looks' like a nurse."

The young man so engrossed her that Mary Jane feared she did not take a very proper leave of the other Whitakers. And had she doubted for a moment she could hold up her end of the conversation with a strange man, her doubts soon ended.

Although he talked a lot about himself, Ralph Whitaker made it seem as if there were nothing she would rather hear. He made her feel honored, like a high-paying audience, in return.

He was, she learned, a musician. By day he tuned pianos and at night he entertained. During the summer holidays, he often went "busking" in the resort towns at the seaside to entertain the vacationers. He had been playing for a party of wealthy merchants and their families that evening, which was why he had not been home when she had called.

"What sort of music?" Mary Jane asked.

"Oh, I play t' piano, sing a song, tell a tale. I keep 'em entertained, tha may' be sure."

"I am sure," Mary Jane exclaimed. "What sorts of songs?"

"All sorts. Whatever is requested. If a chap 'ums a few bars, I can pick it up. I can play, I've been told, like tha can' talk."

"But nothing sad." Mary Jane had once heard a fellow who played a concertina in pubs declare that anything slower than a jig would lose the tapster his custom and the musician his job.

"Oh, I know me share o' slow ballads. If there be ladies present, they always like a romantic ballad or two to tear their eyes and blush their cheeks. Would' tha like to 'ear one?"

"Actually, I heard a very sad song the other day. Perhaps you know it. The chorus is 'From Hull and Halifax and—'"

Ralph Whitaker chimed in with a rich, full baritone and spared her having to say the word "hell." Then he continued with a full verse that seemed as if it would rouse all early sleepers in Bradford. The verse, however, was not one she had heard from her consumptive patient, but one that ended the song on a positive note.

> But now us children are all fled,
> To t' country we've come back.
> An' there's forty miles of 'eathery moor
> 'Twixt us an' t' coal pit slag.
> An' as I sit bi t' fire at night,
> Well, I laughs and shouts wi' glee:
> "From 'Ull and 'Alifax and 'ell,
> Good Lord, deliver me."

Perhaps it was only because Ralph set the tune at a livelier tempo— as if he could actually see springtime on the moors before him—and because he could sing without coughing up blood. Or perhaps it was because she learned that the name of the dalesman's beloved in the song was the same as her own: the first line was "When I were courting Mary Jane." Whatever the case, Mary Jane decided there just might be things in Yorkshire worth staying for.

"What is milady's next request?" Ralph asked after she expressed her delight at his first selection, clapping her gloved hands.

"Do you sing hymns at all?"

"Of course. And I'm a great favorite with the Irish Glee Club. I can do thee a 'Danny Boy' would draw tears from a stone. I've sung in York Minster, St. Luke's, St. Thomas's, besides Eastbrook 'All—just about any denomination that don't forbid music altogether as blasphemy—an opinion I don't 'old with meself. What would' tha like to 'ear?"

There was little chance, Mary Jane knew, but she asked anyway: "Have you heard a hymn called 'O My Father'?"

"Well, milady, tha'st stumped me there. But if tha'll' sing it in tha beautiful soprano, I'll improvise baritone underneath."

Mary Jane stammered, then lied that she could not remember it at all. She did not feel close enough to this man yet to divulge that part of her soul. They compromised with a very stirring rendition of "Hail, Smiling Morn"—"At whose bright presence / Darkness flies away"—with the long runs on "the gates of da-a-ay" like brooklets in the throat. They urged each other on to greater exuberance.

"Eee, aren't we good enough, though, to go on tour to t' seaside together?" Ralph asked when it was over. "Tha must have a bit of Irish in thee," he teased.

"Welsh," she smiled.

"Aye, that accounts for it then. Wi' dark hair and eyes?"

"Yes." Mary Jane felt herself blushing, but she wondered why the question hung in his voice. Couldn't he see for himself?

Ralph nodded. "I've 'eard tell 'at all t' Welsh babies what can't sing is put in little rafts when they's born and shipped over to Ireland. T' Irish think they can sing, but 'tis t' Welsh what really can."

"What a terrible story about the babies!" Mary Jane exclaimed, remembering her father lying at the bottom of the cold, black sea.

"Aye, indeed," Ralph agreed. "But I've 'eard an Irishman say t' same about t' Welsh, so 'tis bound to be a lie."

"Hail, Smiling Morn" had put them on the subject of religion, so Mary Jane cautiously asked Ralph's opinion. She'd had her hands slapped for inquiring too freely already once that night.

"The New and Latter 'Ouse of Israel, though tha wouldna know that sect," he told her.

"But I do," she said. "That was what brought me to your home." She watched the cane tapping ahead of them for a moment, then asked, "Mrs. Whitaker doesn't approve?"

Although he was polite enough to call her Mrs. Whitaker to her face, behind her back Ralph called his stepmother the name he'd first met her under—"Mary Birnley"—and the nephews were called, with equal irreverence, "the Birnley boys."

"Naturally she disapproves. But let it never be said that Ralph Whitaker would obey some fastidious old woman before God. An' she can't very well throw me out t' 'ouse. Even a Methodist wouldn't do that. I were there afore she were, after all."

"You believe, then, that the New and Latter House of Israel is the true church?" Mary Jane felt that if he answered "yes," she would forget all about the Mormons and confess herself ready to join at that moment.

Ralph smiled a gentle smile that suited his lips so well. "I believe 'tis what God wants me to do at this time. Why else dos' tha imagine I keep t' long 'air? I'm on me own, though. There's not another of t' faith left in Bradford. T' rest 'ave all got down to Kent to await t' second coming."

That was not quite the same as a definite "yes," but it encouraged Mary Jane to echo: "I feel I'm where God wants me to be, too, at this moment."

Ralph looked down at her with another smile that warmed her heart. They walked together in silence for a while, enjoying the air. It seemed very pure and, as in the song, "forty miles of 'earthery moor" from the smoke stacks and dragon's roar of the mills as well as the efficiency of the hospital.

They had been walking a very long time, Mary Jane realized. Surely they must be near the hospital by now. Perhaps just around this next corner. When it did not appear, she looked more closely at the buildings they passed. With a start, she realized that not one of them was familiar to her. She looked up at the man beside her. He was all but a stranger, she remembered—but he kept on walking carelessly—so carelessly, in fact, that he hadn't even bothered to step to the outside of the walk as she thought a gentleman ought to do.

Panic got the better of her. She asked, "Mr. Whitaker, where are we?"

"Why, don't you know, Miss Jones?"

"No."

Ralph stopped and that tapping cane with him. "Well, now what are we to do?"

"You mean, you don't know either? But you were to see me safely home—"

"Miss Jones, I am a blind man. I can no more see t' street in front of me than I can fly to t' moon."

"Blind—" Mary Jane strangled a gasp. She had had experience with the blind before—her younger brother Edgar and then several of her patients in the last week. But they were all helpless, pitiful people. Edgar would never dare go out alone. He tripped over furniture even when her mother was careful never to move it. Was it possible that Edgar just didn't want to try?

She remembered now how Ralph Whitaker had tripped over the rug when entering his own home, how he'd expressed annoyance with his stepmother. Still, not until she made a quick gesture with her hand near her companion's face did she know for certain that the one bright eye saw nothing. She gave another little cry of despair.

Ralph began to laugh. His voice was so rich and full that Mary Jane could not keep from joining him in a nervous chuckle or two before she grew angry. "Mr. Whitaker, how can you laugh when we are now so hopelessly lost?"

Ralph caught his breath. "Perhaps tha ar' lost, Miss Jones, but I assure thee, I am not. 'Ow can I be lost 'ere in Bradford? I spent seven years as a blind child 'ere wi' nowt better to do than to chase around t' streets alone and learn every nook and cranny because they couldn't keep me in regular school. Tha may' 'ave wondered why I was such a poor gentleman as to allow you to walk on t' outside."

"Well, yes, I did."

"The fact of the matter is, I keep me 'and on t' walls as we pass—Oh, Mary Birnley do complain at 'ow dirty me hands get. But I know every fence, building, and doorway by feel. 'Ere. This fence 'ere, for example. It's wrought iron."

"Yes," Mary Jane agreed cautiously.

"I'm afraid I can't tell thee what color it is, but I know they just painted it. A month or so ago I got me 'and full of wet paint, I can tell thee!"

"It's white," Mary Jane said, still dubious.

"White. Very well. I'll remember that, and t' next person I lead past 'ere, I'll fool even longer by commenting on t' new white paint. I must confess, I did get lost—once. I were walking wi' a blind friend of mine, and we was all wrapped up in our talk. Each of us 'ad expected t' other to keep tabs on where we was, but finally it dawned on us we should 'ave to ask someone.

"'You're beside t' town 'all,' replied t' man we asked.

"'Which side?' we says.

"'This side,' says 'e. 'E couldn't imagine just 'ow lost two blind men could be beside t' town 'all.

"So tha seest. Since then I'm always very careful to know exactly where I am, even with sighted folk."

Mary Jane chuckled weakly.

"Come, lass. 'As me joke upset thee?"

"A little," she confessed.

"Please. Forgive me, then. Can' tha blame me that I were enjoying tha company so much, I wanted it to last longer than just to St. Luke's?"

Mary Jane tried a stronger chuckle.

"A cruel joke, p'r'aps. But a blind man wi' a sense o' 'umor do get tired o' always laughing at 'imself—one week wet paint and Mary Birnley's displeasure. T' next, an upset orange cart. An' t' baby prams! Constantly running into prams. Look at this scar 'ere, above me brow. That's from an hunmarked workman's pit, couple year ago. Fell right in up to me neck."

"I wonder you go out of the house at all."

"Do you? Well, what would you have me do? Sit 'ome feeling sorry for meself?"

Mary Jane thought of Edgar. That's what her brother was doing, exactly what he'd always done, because their mother coddled him.

"Sit 'ome wi' Mary Birnley all day?" Ralph insisted.

Now Mary Jane laughed out loud. "No, I wouldn't wish that on—"

"On t' dog, yes, I know. Tell me, please, you don't begrudge me this little bit o' fun I've 'ad."

Mary Jane shook her head. Then, remembering he couldn't see, answered, "No."

"Don't fret, Miss Jones. I'll have thee back at 'ospital in no time. Look up over there beneath t' street lamp, and tha'lt see two street signs. The one running this way is St. Enoch's Road, t' other is Moore Avenue."

If the lamplighter had already seen to this part of town, his work had blown out through the frame from which one pane of glass was broken. Mary Jane had to go to the end of the walk to verify that they were, indeed, on the corner of St. Enoch's and Moore. She felt even more helpless than a blind man, to be so dependent on light.

"I can do better 'an that," Ralph declared. "This newly painted white fence 'ere belongs to a Dr. Brookfield. Exactly ten paces from where I'm standing, tha'lt find a metal plaque which reads:

NR. 7 St. ENOCH'S ROAD
DR. PHILIP R. BROOKFIELD, MD SURGEON
SPECIALIST IN INTESTINAL COMPLAINTS
NO SOLICITORS
SERVICEMEN PLEASE CALL AT THE BACK

"Go 'ead," Ralph urged. "See if I'm right. Only take big paces. They're my size, remember, not tha dainty ones."

Mary Jane paced it out, and it was exactly as he had said.

"I know because I missed the plaque t' first time I come 'ere. I could 'ave read the raised letters—like I can read Braille—but I missed it and went to t' front entry. Tha can't imagine what a fuss there was to 'ave me coming to tune t' piano at t' front door instead o' t' back! 'E thought I were a patient.

"'What's wrong w' thee, then?'

"'Nowt, sir. I'm fit as a fiddle. Except for me eyes, I'm fit as a fiddle. And thasel'?'

"'Well, I'm afraid I can't do anything for thee there.'

"'Then p'r'aps tha's' better let me help thee. Tell me where tha piano is, and I'll tune 'er.'

"I soon returned the joke. When I'd been shown to t' room where t' piano were, there was all these knickknacks and gewgaws on t' top of it, so I says, "Ere, I'm sorry, but tha'lt 'ave to take these off. I canna do it. I might break summat.'

"'Bessie,' t' doctor calls to 'is wife, 'Bessie, come down and take tha things off t' piano so this young man can tune it.'

"''Ave 'im come back later.'

"'Nonsense. 'Ere 'e is, come all this way—'

"'Philip, I'm not dressed yet." Er in a whisper.

"'Throw on tha dressing gown and come down anyway. 'E can't see thee. T' man is blind.'

"Finally, she were coaxed to come.

"'Really, Bessie,' the doctor scolds. 'You should be up this time of t' morning, Nancy's day off an' all.'

"'Why, I didn't realize it was late, cloudy day an' all. What time is it?'

"Quick as a wink, I opened me watch and said, 'Just gone eleven, missus.' Tha seest? I've taken t' glass out o' t' front of me watch so I can read t' 'ands."

Mary Jane marveled at the watch, and Ralph quickly concluded his story.

"Well, tha never 'eard such a shriek as come from Mrs. Brookfield then. She dashed from t' room and stood cowering behind 'er 'usband, crying, 'I thought tha said 'e couldna see! I thought tha said he couldna see!'"

Ralph's mimicry of a high-pitched women's voice was so perfect, Mary Jane laughed out loud. Then she scolded herself: "Oh, dear. They'll hear us inside."

"It'd be all right if they did," Ralph assured her. "The Butterfields an' me is now fast friends. They won't 'ave anyone else tune their piano or sing at their parties. They'd be 'urt if'n I was to go to t' back door now, but tha may' be sure them knickknacks is always gone from t' top o' t' piano afore I come. Nancy t' maid usually takes them down t' night before, and Mrs. Butterfield 'erself is always there, dressed and ready to greet me. When I've tuned t' instrument, she usually 'as tea and biscuits for me, and we sing a few songs. And Dr. Butterfield generally gives me an extra shilling or two as a tip. They're very, very nice people. If I don't drop in on them right this moment an' laugh with them about t' first time we met, I'm sure 'tis only 'cause I'd rather stay outside 'ere wi' thee."

"Very well, Mr. Whitaker. I do believe you know where we are. I also forgive you for the trick you played on me. What I do find hard to believe is that you're truly blind."

"Dost tha think, then, I just pretend to be? I just pretend so women like Mrs. Butterfield'll present themselves afore me in their dressing gowns all the time?"

It occurred to Mary Jane that she'd never had a young man broach such subjects with her. She didn't know if it was quite proper—but then, with Mr. Whitaker, "proper" seemed to melt away without a care. So, she simply, unapologetically laughed, as she longed to do. "What I mean is, I have a brother who's blind."

"'As' tha indeed?" Not a note of sympathy from this man.

"He does nothing all day but sit and mope."

"Well, now, that is a shame. I shall 'ave to meet 'im. In Lincoln, then?"

"Yes."

"Aye. I were certain there weren't a blind man or woman in Bradford I didn't know."

"I would love for you to meet my brother. And my mother."

"I figure, there's no use feeling sorry for meself. That never got no one nowhere, now, did it? An' if I can give a little joy and entertainment to others as well as meself, well, then, so much t' better."

Mary Jane agreed. "But I still don't understand. You certainly didn't seem blind when you first came into the house."

"Didn't I? When I tripped over Mary Birnley's rug, I didn't seem blind?"

"But you knew I was there."

"I knew someone were there. There were an extra coat on t' 'ook."

"But you said, 'a young woman.'"

"I felt t' fabric. Fine, light, not a man's coat. I smelled it, too. Tha must 'ave sprinkled it with lilac scent afore tha came. Very pretty. And nowt an older woman would wear."

"But then you said I looked like a nurse."

"Tha voice sounds like a nurse's: patient, soft, an angel of mercy. Aye, and there were summat on your coat 'at smelled like 'ospital, summat t' lilac didn't quite erase."

Ralph made another joke here, something about wishing that he "might get an in wi' t' 'ospital sin' they, wi' a piano on every ward, was good business." But Mary Jane, after promising to see what she could do, sensed that the levity, in this case at least, hid a painful sorrow from childhood. Something to do with hospitals, the smell of blood and alcohol, the knife as it cut his eye, the mother who had held him on her shoulder.

They began to walk slowly back to the hospital now, and the tone was soon lively again. Ralph told her other tales of things that happened to him as a blind man. He told how he and a friend liked to go out when the fog came off the River Aire and Bradford Beck so thick with coal smoke that sighted people couldn't see "t' 'and afore 'em." Even Bradford natives would get lost, fall in the canal or cry out helplessly in the dark. Ralph and his friend would go about answering those calls and leading people home. "For nice tips, tha may' be sure."

Then there was one April First before Ralph started to work on his own. He had worked for a firm that not only tuned pianos but sold and delivered them, too. On this particular day, they received an order for a delivery to number 14 Perseverance Road "in Leeds."

"There ban't no Perseverance Road in Leeds," Ralph told them. "There's one in Bradford, but not Leeds."

The boss wouldn't believe him. "'E can't even read t' street signs, much less a map or city directory."

The boss sent the movers out, and they searched all day. When they came back, dog-weary and unsuccessful that evening, the boss refused to give up. "You'll just have to start again in t' morning," he said.

Then another note came. It was in the same hand as the order and said: "April Fools!" It had just been a joke after all, and Ralph had been right.

"Mr. Whitaker, as a blind man, you must be used to using your ears more than others," Mary Jane suggested.

"Aye, I suppose I am."

"Then perhaps you can tell me. Every morning since I've come to Bradford, I've been wakened up very early—before light—by the most awful sound. It's like marbles spilling down the streets or something. I can't imagine what it could be."

"Aye, that. That's t' workers going to t' mills. They 'ave to be there by six."

"But why such a noise?"

"It's t' clogs. If you're poor in Yorkshire, you wear clogs. They're cheap and sturdy."

"I see." She knew what the women looked like by day, the heavy blocks of wood on their feet, stuffed with straw sometimes for warmth, the shawls, their only wrap, thrown over their heads and bundled across their chests.

"I learnt to make a good pair of clogs meself, in York School for t' Blind."

Mary Jane found herself thinking, Then with him, I shall never go barefoot. She had to stop that, her thoughts growing too forward, even if her tongue had not.

"Give it time," Ralph was telling her. "Tha'lt get used to it. Maybe even come to like it. A soothing sound when tha'rt 'alf awake, to remind thee all's well with t' world. Still, that's one reason I were always glad I were blind. I never 'ad to go and work in t' mill. Tha can' 'ear that sound an' stay abed.

"Now, 'ere tha be, safe and sound at 'ospital gate," Ralph announced.

She hadn't noticed, but so she was. Mary Jane was glad her escort couldn't see to be as embarrassed as she was by the couples—many of the nurse trainees she knew with their young men—billing and cooing in the shadows by the gate.

"Now, Miss Jones, dost not agree with me that the little trick I played on thee weren't so cruel? Not so cruel as 'twould 'a' been 'ad I brought thee straight back 'ere and not given us all this time to get to know one another?"

Mary Jane agreed and extended her hand in farewell. He couldn't see it, of course. She wanted to reach down and take his—dirty as it must be from the walls—of her own accord. Then, out of the corner of her eye, she saw the face of one of her fellow student nurses caught in the lamplight. This was one of the girls Matron had pointed out particularly, saying: "Mark my words, that's one won't last through t' training. She'll have 'erself married afore year's end."

"Mr. Whitaker." Mary Jane turned with a sigh to her new friend. "You were honest with me, and I appreciate it very much. Now I must be honest with you."

"You not be honest? I'll warrant, Miss Jones, tha couldna tell a lie if'n tha life depended on it."

"No, Mr. Whitaker. The fact of the matter is, I've been lying to you all evening. Well, not lying exactly, but at least letting you go on believing what simply is not true. I suppose I should have known you were blind from the first when you fixed your eye on me and did not flinch. The fact of the matter is, Mr. Whitaker, that I have—I have been afflicted by the grace of God with—with a rather severe case of lupus. The doctors assure me I cannot give it to anyone, but the fact remains"—and she laughed nervously—"I am quite a sight to behold. I would hate to have your friends talking behind your back and feeling pity for you. You are such a remarkable man that you should rather pity the rest of the world with their eyes and all. What I mean to say is, if this information should make you decide—I mean, I would understand if you never bothered to call—"

"Miss Jones, say no more. Tha's'—may I say it?—t' most beautiful voice in t' world. For a man like me, that is worth twenty of tha screeching, giggling misses. I don't care tuppence what a treat anyone tells me they look."

∼

Within six months, Mary Jane and Ralph were sitting in the Whitaker parlor once more. The Birnley boys had already been sent out, but were no doubt listening at the keyhole.

"We hope to marry," Ralph told his parents. "And we've come to ask your permission."

Mary Jane saw the glance that passed between Mr. Whitaker and Mary Birnley. They must have been expecting this. Her growing feelings and Ralph's could not have been more obvious, all the time they spent together. This couple she hoped to be her in-laws had had plenty of time to discuss the topic of a blind son's marriage, to steel themselves for it.

To decide to forbid it, so it seemed. Mr. Whitaker was the one who cleared his throat to reply, but Mary Jane was certain Mary Birnley had given him the words. "I'm sorry, Son. Tha stepmother and I feel a blind man 'as no business starting a family. 'E can't even take care o' 'imself. 'Ow can he be expected to care for a wife? And children? Nay, children can't be thought of."

"Some blind men, Father, p'r'aps." Mary Jane heard the tension in her fiancé's voice as he struggled to keep his temper in check. "Tha knowst me better than that. I take care of mesel', don't I? Pay me own way. Pay 'alf of this 'ouse, no less."

"Miss Jones." Mary Birnley tore at the handkerchief in her hands but must add her own words. "Tha canna realize the trouble tha'rt asking for. To 'ave a blind man stumbling 'round t' 'ouse day in, day out. Think of it. 'Tis enough to drive a woman batty."

"Mary Jane 'as a blind brother of 'er own." Ralph was trying to defend her. "She knows what she's undertaking."

Mary Jane had to add a few words of her own. "Then, Mrs. Whitaker, I wonder that you aren't very glad to have Ralph taken off your hands. I do have my mother's written permission from Lincoln."

Mary Birnley sniffed and pulled herself up stiffly. "I've to take on me brother's bairns, and that's quite enough. I won't approve a marriage for one that can't care for 'is own."

Mr. Whitaker cleared his throat again. "I'm sorry, Son. Your stepmother and I have decided. We cannot give permission to this match."

Mary Jane felt her heart sink to her bowels. Ralph was not so easily defeated. The red-haired anger flared up like a flue fire. "Then we will marry wi'out your permission."

"Son." Mr. Whitaker had anger of his own. "'Tis against the law in this civilized country, in case tha didna know. No one of any age can obtain a license wi'out t' express permission of both sets of parents. And we will stand firm. We will not give in."

Mary Birnley rose. "Miss Jones, tha'lt 'ave our son see thee 'ome. And then, if tha knowst what's good for thee, tha'lt never see 'im again. Find another young man, what 'as 'is sight."

They didn't go straight back to the hospital, of course. Ralph led them, his hand on the walls and fences, all 'round Bradford, talking, talking. What should they do?

"There's always Gretna Green." Mary Jane felt herself flush a little at the thought.

"I won't. I won't have it thought me wife and I 'ad to elope."

"Even if it was her idea? So what shall we do? Wait for the old woman to die?"

Ralph caught her around the waist and nearly crushed her against the back wall of a strange house. "I cannot wait that long."

"God forgive me for saying it, but she might not live so long."

Ralph laughed wickedly. "What a good idea!"

But no. In the end, the sin of murder was out.

What were they going to do? What were they to do?

IN THE FAMILY CLOSET

*I*WAS TALKING ABOUT Uncle Noel's grand entrances. I failed to mention perhaps the grandest of all. There was the year he brought home his wife, a Jewish woman half his age. Sigmund was her last name. Very Freudian.

Grandma disapproved of Liz Sigmund even more heartily than of Arthur's Chinese American girl. And Arthur had had to elope with her since interracial marriages were against the law in Utah in those days. They always called her "Lotus Blossom."

Six years later, after the divorce, I was the one who opened the door to find Uncle Noel on the porch with his son.

"Only 'e weren't 'is," Grandma told her sisters in what passed—for her—as a whisper. "She only said 'e were, to get 'im to marry 'er."

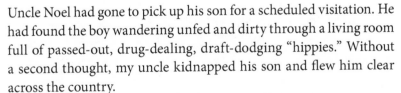

Uncle Noel had gone to pick up his son for a scheduled visitation. He had found the boy wandering unfed and dirty through a living room full of passed-out, drug-dealing, draft-dodging "hippies." Without a second thought, my uncle kidnapped his son and flew him clear across the country.

Four days later I also opened the door for my ex-aunt and her New York, Jewish, lawyer father and brother. I cheerily announced them

to all inside. I had no idea I was supposed to give the refugees time
to flee out the back in the case of such an event. I am held responsible, at any rate, for the fact that none of us have ever seen my curly-
haired little cousin since.

Uncle Noel will not marry again. A string of pretty graduate
students half his age hang about in the background when we visit.
"Helping with the research" is all the explanation we get, although
one of them did write Grandma a letter telling how it was all her
fault her son wouldn't marry.

I wonder. Was that an assignment, too? "In six pages, compare
and contrast your life with another's."

~

"'Ere." After one of Uncle Noel's more atheistic tirades, Auntie Barbara plunks a great leather-bound Bible down on his lap. This was
their parents' book. She inherited it of all the sisters because she is
the one who stuck it out to the bitter end.

"Auntie, I won't—" He tries to hand it back.

Auntie Barbara is used to dealing with recalcitrant patients. She
doesn't take "No" for an answer. "Read it. Pray about it," she says.
"Tha'lt learn."

"I won't, you know." He reads the "Mary Jane Jones" on the flyleaf. "So Welsh," he mumbles, as if wondering how a woman with
that name could so betray her heritage, then quickly closes the book
again.

> O may my heart's truth
> Still be sung
> On this high hill in a year's turning.

Uncle Noel takes on the Welsh accent of Dylan Thomas and
recites some of the master's words. Under their cover, he tries to
set the Bible down among the knickknacks of Auntie Barbara's end
table, in a house that's never known children.

"She didn't talk like a Welshwoman, not our mother," Auntie
Doris assures him.

"She didn't?" He's clearly stricken.

"No, of course not. She spoke like a 'true lady.' She learnt that in service, in London. That were what drew Father to 'er in t' first place."

Auntie Doris doesn't know this, but she's just snipped the last thread that kept him dangling to the family.

Auntie Barbara has caught him. She fishes the Bible up and hands it back. "Read. Pray."

"So how did this pathetic blind man and this pathetic old woman do it?" Uncle Noel asks again.

He gets the same old answers in the same old words. There's some more of this newfangled "Love" stuff, which makes everyone uncomfortable.

I'm not certain what this has to do with anything, but Auntie Barbara drifts from this into a tale about a woman she delivered once when she was a midwife. It's a rambling tale about riding her bicycle at night during the blackout of the Blitz in World War II. She hadn't been expecting to go to this house for a while; the woman was barely six months along.

"Nowadays they save all sorts. Them days, however, a six months' baby"—she shakes her grey curls—"Poor wee mite." The biggest drama, however, seems to be how she wasn't to use the lamp on her handlebars and how the constable stopped her for that.

Uncle Noel gets to his feet. On his way to the door he tries to set the Bible down on the hall table. Auntie Barbara is waiting for him there, too. "Take it with you. Keep it as long as you're in town. Just bring it back before you leave."

Uncle Noel returns from his walk in time to load up his car with as many of the nondriving aunties as will fit to shuttle them all home. I am astonished at the grin on his face. He looks like the cat that ate the canary. No one else seems to notice.

He sets the Bible down to help Auntie Violet into the coat she has retrieved, like everyone else, from the bed in the back bedroom. Auntie Barbara is there to force the holy book on him again. Uncle Noel drops the wool hastily onto Auntie Violet's slender, frail old shoulders and moves to snatch the Bible up before his missionary can get to it.

"Oh, no, Auntie. You said I could keep this. I'm keeping this."

Auntie Barbara smiles with satisfaction and casts a superior glance on all her sisters. "You see?" she seems to tell them. "A man like that 'as to be worked on with intelligence. Books. Books are the way to his soul." I can almost hear the tight Yorkshire "oo" in her eyes.

My house is the last one. I am alone with him in the front seat. Auntie Doris's Rose Park bungalow is hardly out of sight before he pulls over and parks the car. He shoves the Bible into my lap. "Read it," he says.

"You want me to pray, too?"

"Just the flyleaf."

I read the greying ink handwriting there, my great-grandmother's cramped hand. "Our Family Tree. Doris, Barbara, Ivy, Frances—" All the girls lined up like on the mantelpiece—"I know all this."

"Read it carefully. Pay attention to detail."

"Ralph Robinson Whitaker born February 6, 1871, married Mary Jane?"

"Keep going."

"Born February 23, 1870. She was older than he was."

"By almost a year."

"Okay. Mildly shocking."

"But that's not the important thing."

I keep going. "Married in Bradford, Yorkshire, on May 4, 1897."

"Keep going."

"First Child. F—female, of course—Doris May born October 30, 1897. Second—"

"Stop. There." There is triumph behind his black-rimmed glasses.

"What?"

"October 30, 1897."

"October 30, 1897. Auntie Doris was born the day before Halloween. So?"

"And Grandmother and Granddad were married?"

I catch my breath. "That's only five, six months."

"That's right. And what did Nurse Whitaker, the midwife who's delivered more of this family than any other, down to your own younger cousin Stephanie, just say about 'six month babies them days'?"

Uncle Noel and I stare at each other. I feel myself grow hot. He laughs out loud.

I try not to be shocked. But I am. Maybe because I know there's no getting around it. "They both were very religious," I protest. "Mary Jane seems to have joined the New and Latter House of Israel at the encouragement of her beloved then. Until the Mormons moved in—"

"The Myth presents them to us as religious."

"But why? They received special dispensation?"

"To get his parents' permission, of course, which was required then no matter how old you were." My uncle gets up to fifteen miles over the speed limit in his exuberance. "Every bit as tantalizing as 'why' must be the question 'where?' October, September, August—it must have been some time in February, the month when both of them celebrated birthdays. Anyone who has lived through a Yorkshire winter knows they cannot have trysted outside in the fields at the edge of town at that month. There were no backseats of cars then. What choice did that leave them? Between Mrs. Whitaker's eagle eye and Nurse Matron's?"

"She'd have lost her post at St. Luke's."

Just how true is our image of frigid Victorian England? Further close scrutiny of the family tree reveals that my grandfather's parents, on the other side, "had to" get married, too, the same generation, in East Yorkshire.

The car weaves as Uncle Noel starts laughing again. "Imagine." He struggles for breath. "Imagine a blind man and his lupus-faced lover scouring the grim streets of Victorian Bradford in—January? February at the latest. Looking for a place to make love. 'Tain't easy, even for the sighted. I've tried it myself. 'Tha's' bound to catch thee death o' cawld,' as the old song says." Uncle Noel is quoting the "unofficial county anthem," "Ilkla Moor Bat 'At." "The name of the woman he's courting on Ilkla Moor just happens to be Mary Jane, just like my grandmother's. And my grandfather must have lost more than his hat. 'Bound to catch tha death o' cawld.' That song meant something special to the old man, don't you think?"

He sees a print shop and swerves suddenly into the lot. After having xeroxed the important page—not in Isaiah or the Gospel of Mark—my uncle returns the book to Auntie Barbara and demands an explanation of all the gathered fruit of this sin. I am embarrassed, knowing how embarrassed they all are.

Did none of them really know? Did they never guess? Not even Auntie Mona, the family genealogist? They pretend they didn't.

"Well, they wouldn't let them get married, tha know'." This is the best even Auntie Barbara, the trained midwife, is willing to concede.

"We weren't there," says Auntie Doris, seeming extraordinarily hale for a six-month's baby born in 1897. "It weren't none of our business."

She's warning us. It's none of ours, either.

Two weeks later, they will all have forgotten what Uncle Noel tries to cram down their throats. He has to jab anyway. "Aye, there's great wisdom in that book after all."

At least he can leave, xerox sheet in his pocket, satisfied that his botch of a marriage has some time-honored precedent.

Mary Jane's mother must have had her qualms. She did have one blind son in the family already, after all. There does seem to have been some falling out between Mary Jane and her mother, for Mrs. Jones did not come to the wedding, nor to the births of her first grandchildren, nor does Mary Jane seem to have gone to Lincoln to visit. But Mrs. Jones was only a poor widow, living far away, and her daughter, after all, was twenty-seven years old and likely neither to get any younger, nor to marry anyone else with her face the way it was.

Mary Birnley Whitaker was the real wicked stepmother. She never set foot in her daughter-in-law's house until the day she died. Mary Jane was not a good enough housekeeper for her taste. "What does it matter, 'im being blind an' all?" And, all too soon, the children!

Enoch Whitaker did come to visit his son from time to time, and the children did go to visit their grandparents. Barbara remembers always having to show off her legs so they could make sure "t' rickets was going away." She'd had to go to the hospital as a two-year-old for her bent legs. The doctors had wanted to break them both and set them so they'd grow straight, but Ralph refused to let that happen. They had merely set the legs in plasters, and she remembers being "sat on t' table" in the cellar while her mother slaved to take the plasters off. The rolling, bowed gait came back to her in her eighties. As a girl at her grandparents' house, she was forever embarrassed because there was always a hole in her stocking, discovered during the inspection.

Barbara also remembers one day in particular, a bleak day in mid-November 1910, when she was nearly twelve. She and ten-year-old Ivy had gone to help their grandmother with some cleaning (instead of staying at home to help their own mother—"always help others first" might have been the motto she instilled in her daughters). Their grandfather was upstairs, sick in bed with some company.

When they'd finished their work, he sent for them to come up and join him. He had two little chairs set for them right at the head of his bed. "We 'adn't been sat down more'n a minute," Barbara said, "when 'e turned 'is 'ead 'round to see if we was alright. Then 'e just bent 'is 'ead and was gone in a second, without a sigh. I've always been 'appy that he were concerned and thinking of us to the very last thought."

Only Doris and Barbara went to the funeral. They got new black coats bought special for the occasion. "E, used to buy a lot o' black clothes, them days," Barbara comments.

Hannah remembers going to the hospital with her mother when "the old woman," Mary Birnley, lay dying.

"Mary Jane, can you ever forgive me?" the old woman asked.

"Mother answered in her quiet way, 'There is nothing to forgive.'

"I thought I stood on holy ground," Hannah adds. "If anyone looked like an angel, it were me Mother at that moment."

Ralph's perpetual optimism and good nature help a lot at that time. Mary Jane relies on him exclusively. When he comes home in those early days, she drops whatever she's doing to sit down and read to him for hours on end: religious works, the latest novel, the paper.

(They always took the paper. "'E 'ad to 'ave summat to start t' fire in t' morning.")

It is a warm evening in June or July. A too-early showing is making Mary Jane the talk of the lane. Being pregnant, she is irritable and prone to tears anyway. There my great-grandmother is, in her prudish nightgown and cap, weeping under the coverlet as if her heart would break. She is crushed by the guilt, by the rejection. Most of all, by guilt. The Lord our God is a just God, a God before whom the wicked "begin to say to the mountains, 'Fall on us'; and to the hills, 'Cover us.'" Though Ralph has not yet come to bed beside her, he needs no lamp to light his way. Around her all the house is dark and depressing, reflecting back her mood.

"Mary Jane? Mary, is that thee?" he calls up.

She refuses to answer, in a mood now where even her eternal damnation is all his fault. She tries to stifle her tears so he cannot hear and gloat at her sorrow. She manages fairly well until she thinks he's forgotten her again. Then the stifling only makes the sobs worse, gasping and coughing.

"Mrs. Whitaker, is that thee crying again?" He knows now. He only calls her "Mrs. Whitaker" when he wants to tease her by reminding her of the first Mrs. Whitaker, her sharp mother-in-law.

"All right, I'm coming up now. An' we'll just see what there is to cry about then." Ralph begins to stomp up the stairs like some giant in a child's fairy tale.

Suddenly, a fearful crack, a gasp of pain. Then all is dead silence on the stairs.

"Ralph?" Mary Jane catches her sobs to listen. No sound.

"Ralph, are you all right?"

Still no answer.

Clumsy in her haste, Mary Jane strikes a match, loses the flame. She strikes another and lights the lamp at her bedside.

"Oh, dear God! Oh, dear God!" she prays aloud. "More punishment for my sins. Ralph! Ralph! Are you all right?"

At the top of the stairs she trains her light, but doesn't dare follow it and look down for a moment or two. When she does, it is to see Ralph sitting on the bottom step, quietly balancing several pieces of broken crockery in his hands. He is very good at mending things, fitting together the shattered pieces by feel. Whether he can fit this together again—and make it watertight—is a different matter.

"I'm afraid, my dear," he says. He feels her presence behind him, the creak of the top stair. "I'm afraid I've gone and broken our best wedding present." Heaven knows there weren't many, the whole thing happening in such haste. "The chamber pot."

Now Mary Jane remembers. After washing the pot out in the morning, she had set it on the bottom stair so Ralph could bring it up later. Her arms had been full of clean laundry when she came. Either she had forgotten to tell him or he had forgotten he'd been told—it doesn't matter. He couldn't see it, and now the deed is done.

"Auntie Rachel's ceramic chamber pot with all the pretty roses on it?" she asks as if he could see it better than she. As if they had any other pot.

"Yes, my dear. I'm afraid 'tis so. I'll go out and buy us another just like it first thing in t' morning. I promise."

"But Ralph, we can't afford anything like that. Not with a baby coming and—"

"Tha'st the right o' it. We'll 'ave to content ourselves with a plain old metal one from now on, an' 'ave cold bottoms like everybody else."

Suddenly Mary Jane cannot think of the next line to this farce. Relief and, yes, joy so overwhelm her, flushing out all the sorrow and guilt. She cannot keep from laughing out loud. In a moment, Ralph has joined her, both in laughter and on the landing.

"Let's just hope—" Mary Jane gasps through her laughter as he takes her in his arms.

"Auntie Rachel never finds out?"

"Yes, that, too. But I was thinking—"

"Let's just hope tha'rt not sick in t' morning anymore. And that neither of us 'as to go in a 'urry tonight." Ralph finds breath enough to finish for her.

Mary Jane blows out the light. They can both find their way to the bedroom without it.

∾

Perhaps Mary Jane was just as glad the church lost the record of her first baptism in London. When, five years later, the missionaries found her again in Bradford, she could once more "have her garments washed white as snow." She kept her new slate mythologically clean after that.

And when, even later, Mary Jane found a doctor who, with "violet ray," was able to cure her lupus and leave only a slight scar on one cheek, people did talk behind Ralph's back. They wondered how he, a blind man, had managed to catch such a beauty.

Ralph Noel Maud:
the Harvard years

Ralph Robinson Whitaker,
photo taken two days before
the accident

Mary Jane Jones

Mary Jane's mother, Mary Williams Jones,
standing in the doorway of her little shop in Lincoln

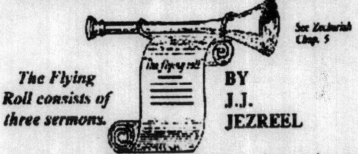

TIME IS RUNNING OUT

Current events clearly indicate that it is God's purpose to overthrow the present order, which has run nearly the allotted 6000 years, to be replaced by the glorious reign of the Lord Jesus.

This will bring unimaginable peace and happiness to mankind. Every Truthseeker should read.

See Zechariah Chap. 5

The Flying Roll consists of three sermons.

BY J.J. JEZREEL

It is a book which will appeal to those who are searching for a fuller life.

1st Book (208 pages) — £4
Make cheques, P.O.s payable to:
**New and Latter House of Israel,
18 Hawkstown Crescent,
Hailsham. Sussex BN27 1JB.**
The aim of the Flying Roll charity is to promulgate the 'Flying Roll'.

Nineteenth-century newspaper advert for the New and Latter House of Israel

St. Stephen's Church, West Bowling, where Ralph and Mary Jane as well as several of their daughters were married

130 Paley Road, Bradford, where Ralph tried to start a music shop. A different shop is having better success in this photo. This is the door on which the Mormon missionaries knocked in late 1900.

Ryan Street School

4 Moulson Street

Frances serves Violet (*left*) and Ivy (*right*) Yorkshire pudding, on the front page of the *Salt Lake Tribune* Lifestyle section, February 21, 1980.

Frances wearing the scandalous
cape she made to
visit Barbara in London

The sitting room in 4 Moulson Street

Our Nellie

Bowling Old Lane

Frances's husband Harry Maud with the loom he brought to the U.S. and eventually donated to a museum

The Sunday School on a ramble, with Frances (*far right*)

Frances and Ivy in the LDS orchestra (*first row, center*)

Ralph gives away his youngest daughter, Violet.

Doris with her first son, Calvin, in Canada

Hospital ward with Barbara in charge (*standing on the left*)

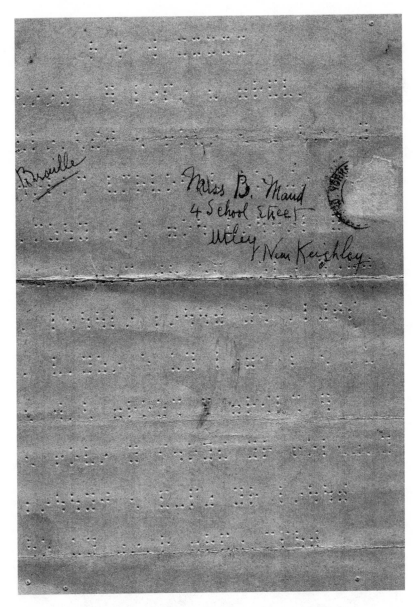

Braille letter from Ralph Whitaker to his granddaughter

Left, Mona sticks to history.

Below, Doris, Barbara, Ivy, Frances, Hannah, Mona, Violet circa 1984

PART TWO

INFANCY (OUR DORIS PLAYS DRESS UP)

"Is she still alive?"

Instead of his usual shouts of joy, for weeks now, ever since the baby was born, Ralph had come quietly home each day and asked the same question in a muffled whisper. All night, the rasping breath racked his sleep. She was their third child in three years, their third girl, little Ivy. She had been born with bronchitis, so sickly they did not expect her to live.

It was three tense, long months before the thin, infant wheezing began to fade, and along with it, the fears. Only then did he dare to follow the last tap of his cane on the doorstep with a loud "So where's me lasses, then?" And they would run into his arms as if he'd been gone for a year instead of just out on his tuning rounds.

Then he had a special little song for his Ivy:

> The verdant ivy clings around
> Yon moss be-mantled wall

The poetry of Henry Kendall set to music.

She was the only one, Mary Jane told him, who had fair curls and his same eyes, the blue eyes he had lost as a boy of not-quite-four.

But Ralph and Mary Jane made each of the girls welcome, each of them cherished in her own special way.

∾

We've crammed into Auntie Ivy's house today. There is no air conditioning, that thing nobody needed in England; the dry air is claustrophobic and breathless.

Auntie Doris and Auntie Ivy, as the first sisters to come to America, live in one of the worst parts of town, Rose Park. My aunties have been here over a hundred years between them. They've seen a lot of changes since they came looking for the promised better life.

Their homes are nearly identical, bungalows with a low pitch to the roofs and cheap siding. They are cookie-cuttered in the same old working-class development, although my aunties don't live close enough to belong to the same ward. Is a church true that doesn't let your widowed sister go to the same service as you? When the sisters and their mother once formed half of Bradford branch?

A black neighbor shovels Auntie Ivy's walk in winter, Hispanic brothers mow her lawn. None of them is Mormon. None has ever asked for a dime.

Neither auntie has ever been robbed. They are always home, except when they're at church, those dead hours known to the whole neighborhood when last year my mother's house in a better neighborhood was broken into.

The chain-linked yards are a decent size, but the houses are only two rooms square, and we're all trying to fit into one of them. Rap music throbs through the open windows from across the street. "There were al'a's music in t' 'ome."

We're at Auntie Ivy's because she's the best cook. Her English fare—a roast my mother bought her for the occasion and for her to pick leftovers from all week—and Yorkshire pudding do not help the stifle.

Interior decoration screams, "Cheap!" Cheap, faded plastic roses. A throw on the worn sofa Auntie Ivy crocheted herself—I got a similar one for my babies, and a crocheted doll—are cheap polyester, made-in-China yarn. The secondhand television is so old, it only gets three stations and won't support live caption. This is where she gets semiannual Conference; she doesn't bother with the sound. Photos of the temple and the head of Christ torn from

Ensign magazine. The visiting teacher message is ineptly xeroxed, the same platitude everybody else got. The message has nothing to do with my auntie.

The only spot where Auntie Ivy seems rich and honest—apart from her eighty-nine-year-old presence just come from the kitchen—is the old black-and-white photo in a solid frame of our Ivy at about eight. She is dressed as Little Red Riding Hood for a church play, eyes sunken in soulful dark rings. She'd probably just been ill.

I take the cheap plastic chair, giving more substantial seats to older behinds. This way, I face Little Red Riding Hood and can look up whenever I want.

There is poverty, and there is poverty that comes at you filtered through awakening China, the television, and the Xerox machine.

We sit in a sweltering circle and conjure up the dead.

Doris May was the firstborn. Mary Jane plied her needle for that little girl with something of Hester Prynne's guilt over her own Pearl of Great Price.

All the neighbors forgot the little girl was born three months too soon. "Doris May were t' best-dressed baby in Bradford."

"Them days," Doris describes, "babies' underthings was all made out of what were called flannel but what you'd call wool."

Grandma's notorious woolly.

"Babies and small children was always scratching in them hair shirts and pants." These underthings had to be "aired" in front of the fire "so there were no dampness left in them."

Following her own mother's practice, for each of her own children, my grandmother had six "nappies"—no more. Each night, she'd "bath t' baby in t' tub afore t' fire, then wash t' nappies in t' same water."

The baby suits and frocks her mother made, likewise of wool, might have been fashionable. But they must have also all been of very dark colors, for Doris remembers when she first came to America. The children playing in the park in their bright colors made her think they were "a field of little flowers."

Every day, rain, snow, or shine, a baby, like its underthings, was "aired." If the mother was busy, this involved no more than setting the baby, all bundled up in its pram, out in the yard. Or in the lane if there was no yard. Our Doris probably enjoyed the luxury of a walk with her mother more frequently that any of the others as time for Mary Jane became scarcer and scarcer. Whether around the block, down to the park, or just in the yard, a little English baby at the turn of the century was always covered with a silk veil "to keep t' weather off."

"Can you see a baby nowadays wearing such a thing?" Doris exclaims. "It'd pull it off as soon as it were born—so! They're born brighter these days, kids are."

"You think so?" I'm skeptical. I rather think that parents today are the victims of a whatever-youth-wants, youth-gets syndrome. But I don't tell Auntie Doris this. Mormons her age, I thought, weren't supposed to believe in evolution.

"Oh, yes, much brighter." So is that the secret?

Auntie Doris continues, "'E—"

Everyone knows who "'e" is by now, right? It's not Uncle Noel, who's only an annoying, passing glitch on the screen in a world where television doesn't even exist yet. Although forced to share a name and "ginger 'air," and even though Uncle Noel is still alive, his billing will never equal his grandfather's.

Surely that's part of the problem.

"'E'd come in to see us all every night, to make sure we was all in t' bed."

Often two or three to a bed.

"Running his hands over each one, so. Even in our sleep, we knew 'e were there.

"'E always knew me," Doris says, "by me skinny elbows." She laughs. "Funny, in't it? I were so skinny then"—when a little plumpness would have been fashionable—"and now"—at ninety, after six children of her own. So, which world is Zion? The place with no automobiles so poor folks' stodge gets walked off or the place where children make a field of flowers? Auntie Doris shakes her head at this fall from Eden—"I've grown so heavy."

Just as our Doris "were learning to toddle a bit," a second daughter was born in the Whitaker home. Our Doris was the only one of the girls to have a godmother, her great-aunt Ethel who'd never married and who'd been a lady's maid. Doris was sent to Auntie Ethel's when the new baby came. All she remembers about the visit was the commode. "It seemed to be a very serious business. Everybody were trying to train me in an 'urry!"

Ethel Barbara was the responsible one. Mary Jane used to leave the girls alone while she went out to church or to do works of charity. One day she came home, and Doris had all Mary Jane's hats and veils and gloves and dresses down to play dress up. Worse, she'd spilled scent over everything. After that, our Doris had to go with their mother on every errand.

"Our Barbara were left in charge" from the age of three. Even if Doris didn't go, Barbara, the second sister, was told: "Look after our Doris, will you?"

Pets added to the chaos of babies creeping underfoot. A blind man was allowed to keep a dog without a license, so the family always had one. For many years it was Tutti, a little Yorkshire terrier, shaggy white hair all in his eyes, obviously never meant as a seeing-eye dog. Our Frances put a rubberband around one little paw. No one noticed until the paw atrophied and fell off. We always got that story when we were young and putting a rubberband around anything we shouldn't. The lesson we got when we picked up a rock was just the beginning of our cautionary training. Tutti ran on three legs after that.

Mary Jane always had her cat, to keep out "t' vermin." Ralph tolerated this pet, but in general "'ated cats, sneaky devils." Mary Jane would often leave Ralph's supper out on the table for when he came home late from the pub. One night when he sat down to eat, he heard something at the other side of the plate. It was the cat, sneaking half of the food.

Ralph tolerated one cat, but kittens were another matter.

With every litter, each girl would claim one, name it, nurse it, dress it in baby clothes. When the girls were all out of the house, however, he would go to the nest with a sack.

She was hardly out of splints for her rickets, when our Barbara found him at this task.

"What art tha looking for, Dad?" she asked. "Let me help."

"I thought we 'ad five kittens this time. I only found four."

"'Ere's t' little tabby, hiding behind t' scuttle."

She held out the little blind, mewing thing, pulling away the bib our Doris had tied around its belly. Her father didn't immediately take it. She reached for his hand, so he could. He seemed guilty to be caught and about ready to give up on his project.

Barbara stood up as tall as she could. She was the responsible one.

He sensed her stance. He took the kitten and added it to the sack with the others.

"Willt tha come with me, lass?"

"Where, Dad?"

"Down to t' Bradford Beck."

He took her hand and they went, he carrying the squirming sack down to the river. At the grim beckside they stood, side by side. "Look with your good eyes and tell me when they've all gone under."

She did. After that, he always asked her when something difficult had to be done.

By the end of the year and the century, Mary Jane was pregnant again, with the girl who would become the sickly Ivy. That was when Mary Jane received the news that her mother had died. Our Doris was old enough to remember how long and bitterly their mother wept. Marriage, housework, and babies one after the other had kept Mary Jane so busy that she had put off reconciliation with her own mother. Now it was too late.

Jane Williams Jones had died of pneumonia above that cold, dark shop in the shadow of Lincoln Cathedral. If only she'd had someone at her side, applying poultices and pots of steam, it might not have killed her.

Leaving our Barbara with a neighbor and grieving heavily, Mary Jane took Doris on the train to see her mother buried in an unmarked pauper's grave near Lincoln Cathedral.

Mary Jane's troubles were far from over. She still had to worry about her brother, Edgar. Since their mother's death, Edgar had tried to run the shop on his own, but he couldn't keep accounts, blind as he was.

"My Ralph could show you," Mary Jane said. "You should just see—I mean listen to—how his fingers do pounds-shillings-pence on the abacus. He can do sums faster with that machine than others can do them on paper."

But even as she said it, the bell in the shop jangled.

Edgar went out to greet the customer. "Hello? Hello?"

From the back room, Mary Jane watched in horror as a pair of local hooligans helped themselves, one to fists full of penny candy from the jar on the counter, the other to coins from the till. They scampered away, guffawing, before she had time to rise in righteous indignation after them.

Edgar shuffled back, shrugging helplessly.

"Well, it's clear you can't stay here, Edgar," Mary Jane told him.

"What else am I to do? Just go to the poorhouse, I suppose. A good-for-nothing blind man like me."

It was true. Edgar couldn't even boil an egg on his own.

"You'll come home with Doris and me and just learn how my Ralph manages," Mary Jane said firmly, refusing to allow herself to be seduced into pity as she always had been before. "He doesn't feel sorry for himself, and he supports all of us besides. He's up first every morning, lights the fire so it's nice and warm before I come down. He makes up a big kettle of oatmeal, four-cups worth, all before I'm about. Then I read him the list of houses he must visit to tune their pianos. He memorizes the addresses, and off he goes, all on his own."

So Edgar did stay a few months in the Whitaker home.

"Our Doris had her photograph taken on our uncle's knee." There's some accusation of favoritism in the chorus of aunties.

Soon enough, Ralph had pulled in favors from all the friends he'd kept at York School for the Blind over the years. He got his brother-in-law in to learn a trade. Edgar made brooms and brushes of all sorts—stove brushes, boot and scrub brushes, brass or fiber brushes, hair brooms, carpet brooms—and sold them door to door.

Though he never had any children, Edgar did eventually marry a blind woman he met at the school, Auntie Bertha, whom all the children remembered with great fondness.

"When they'd come to visit, she let us brush out 'er long, thick chestnut 'air."

"And try to pin it up in fashionable rolls." Auntie Doris makes the gesture around her own white hair.

"All t' while, our dad and Uncle Edgar sat, one in t' settle, t' other in t' rocker, to either side of t' fire."

"And wouldn't they sing!"

"What would they sing?" I manage to squeeze my question in.

"'What Shall We Do with a Drunken Sailor?'"

"'Blow t' Man Down.'" I am glad to hear my grandmother is the only one who thinks the words are "Blow t' man up."

Sea shanties, favorites of Mary Jane and Uncle Edgar's seafaring father, lying at the bottom of the Channel.

Was it all our Ivy's illnesses as a child? Was it because their mother suffered such grief at the death of her own mother when she was carrying this third daughter? Each girl has her own theory for why Ivy, in her own words, "always were a bit morose."

"She's a reg'lar Calamity Jane, is our Ivy," says Doris.

Ivy's very first memory is of the dedication of the Victoria Monument in downtown Bradford, 4th of May, 1904 (Doris remembers the queen's death, three years earlier). The dour old woman stands twelve feet high in cold, grey iron, a little grim and neglected now.

The occasion of the dedication, however, was a festival to which people came from miles around. Rather than the joyful cheers, colorful banners, and flag waving others enjoyed, all Ivy can remember is herself, clinging to a wrought iron railing, screaming in fear at the "dancing legs" of the policemen's horses. Her mother, with "two or three other little babies to worry about," had no time to comfort her. Her life ever after never seemed quite free of nervousness, of woe.

My grandmother, Frances Lyda, "were always gayer," everyone agrees. And this is because of what happened when she was in the womb.

Ralph decided that, with this fourth child on the way, the family needed a new home. He also hoped he could fulfill the dream of owning a home of his own. He bought a two-story house on Paley Road with room on the ground floor in which to have his own music shop. Here he sold strings and rosin ("resin," we say in Yorkshire), sheet music, tuning forks, "'armonicas," violins, and pianos he bought secondhand and repaired. Barbara remembers "t' whole front room filled with pianos for sale." Little girls cut their teeth on stray ivory keys.

This plan seemed dubious to Mary Jane, even as they hired a man with a handcart to move their few belongings past Bowling Park with its famous Fossil Tree to Paley Lane. She knew, for all Ralph's skill with the abacus, if everything didn't go extremely well, they would not be able to make their payments.

Paley Road was a nice, quiet backstreet—fine for raising children in, but not the best place for a music shop. Mary Jane was also pregnant again, feeling queasy. To top it off, right in the middle of moving, all three of her girls got the measles at once.

"Our Ivy worse'n any of us," say Doris and Barbara together.

Besides the work nursing, Mary Jane agonized. It was the measles, she remembered only too well, that had blinded Edgar at about this age.

Ralph shared her concern. Every night, he would hold up fingers before each girl in turn and ask her if she saw the rabbit or the short-eared dog. He could hardly breathe until she gave the right answer. The room had to be kept dark, the drapes unpacked before anything else to block out the light.

The rest of the household remained packed up, the shop mostly still in its boxes.

At home at night, Ralph was working on one of the pianos. It was a cheap, blond-wood spinet. Its previous owner must have used it for dart practice. Glowing ashes from a pipe had been knocked on the lid and brandy spilled more than once on the keys. Ralph had never undertaken such a challenge. Could he do it? Not if our Ivy got into the broken strings and unpadded hammers strewn over the bench— if she lived through the measles. In the meantime, that instrument was all over the shop, too.

Mary Jane was upstairs with all three girls when a knock came on the door. She should have turned the shop sign around to say "closed" when Ralph stepped out to his appointment. They weren't really ready to open up. But they would need every sixpence for every lump of resin if they were to make the rent in one week's time. Leaving the children whining after her, she hurried downstairs.

Mary Jane caught her skirt on the edge of a box of sheet music as she reached for the door. Gilbert and Sullivan, concert party tunes, the purple-printed "Violets," and the ballad of how "Brave Grace Darling Nobly Saved the Crew" spilled like water through a weir.

"O my Father," Mary Jane prayed. She shouldn't open the door. She had to see to her children. And who would give the extravagant price of a full pound for any score fished from such disarray?

Two young men stood in the doorway. They removed their hats. "Good afternoon, ma'am." The accent—American. "My name is Elder Smith, and this is my companion—"

Mary Jane had grown too busy in the past few years to keep up her search for them, so the Mormons had found her instead.

Stepping over the sheet music, she pulled them in. She even asked them to bless her sick babies before they left that day.

Elder Joseph R. Smith gave Mary Jane her first Book of Mormon. He was the son of Joseph F. Smith, the prophet and president of the church, and also the uncle of Joseph S. Nelson, a young man who later came on his mission to Yorkshire, too.

Joseph S. Nelson—you will see—played a very important part in the family's life, unlike many of the missionaries "'oo forgot all about Bradford once their missions was over."

Now who interjected that? Today I scan the wrinkled faces. Not one shrinks in guilt. I see. They all might have said it.

"But my Mormon friends here would all tell me that his two years in the field are the best years of a young man's life," I protest. "He isn't likely to forget them."

"So they are. They prepare him for life." Auntie Barbara's memories are colored by my great-uncle Joe Nelson seated at her side.

"They prepare 'im for life in Zion," says Ivy. "Not in Bradford."

I understand that England is the plum of missions: easy converts, no second language to learn. Where general authorities' sons get sent—if they're not the brightest of the pack. Easy leap to the top.

"Never any letters back. Never come to visit again," sighs Auntie Hannah, "though they promised they would."

"Just keep our mother an' us doing all t' fellowshippin' and runnin' t' branch an' feedin' 'em," says Auntie Violet. Blowing her cover as one of "t' nice ones." "Whilst they get all t' credit. An' don't remember us names when we do cum 'ere."

"Not one of 'em'd think of marrying us." My grandmother never minces words, not when it's her favorite subject. With a flare of real jealousy, "'Cept Joe."

I'm never going to hear this again. Not with a tape recorder running—and I forgot it today. I try to take surreptitious notes, but am busy struggling with the realization that family was more religion to them than Elder Smith's Book of Mormon. And that my great-grandmother made her own religion, built on scraps from America and hope for a paradise that didn't exist—except for the sons of general authorities.

❧

On a cold January day in 1901, two months pregnant with my grandmother, Mary Jane Jones Whitaker was baptized by immersion in the Feversham Street Public Baths where one by one, on their eighth birthdays, all of her daughters would follow her.

My grandmother, Frances, has always prided herself on the extra sanctity of her two baptisms, one at eight, and the earlier one, before she was born. Her mother's recent conversion is also credited with the miracles surrounding my grandmother's birth: She was born without a pain. Her father hurried out to get the doctor. The doctor didn't come, so he ran to get another. All this time, Frances Lyda was born, the cord uncut, "lying at me mother's side, taking strength." It is to this time, nearly an hour, that my grandmother attributes her remarkable good health.

"Me first sickness," she declares, in her voice from the weaveroom, "will be me last."

"She were such a pretty baby, tha grandmother," Doris remembers, "with rosy cheeks and such a lot of dark, curly 'air. I wanted to 'old 'er, but they wouldn't let me."

They let our Barbara, though.

"Tell them why they named thee Frances, our Frances," all the aunties demand together.

"'Cause after three girls, 'e wanted a boy. I always were a bit boyish as well. I'd get a ball for Christmas or summat like that."

Perhaps she was a tomboy, but our Frances had more flair for style than anyone. Our Doris may have been "t' best-dressed baby in Bradford," but some of our Frances's hand-me-down clothes had stains on them that no amount of hot water could scald out. Mary Jane had no time to sew, often even to mend now, and what little money there was had to go ever farther. "Things was always held together with pins," Hannah remembers.

"When she weren't but three year old, our Frances got fed up wi' 'er pants."

This is her underwear we're talking about. Every sister can tell the story in the same words, even those who weren't even born yet.

"We 'ad a rag bag, kept for dusting and scrubbing, and where Dad'd get t' scraps 'e needed to make us rugs. One day, our Frances got an old shirt o' me dad's out t' bag and made 'erself a pair o' pants. One wi' better fashion. At three year old!"

"I never let nobody sew for me after that," Grandma declares.

Years later, when her doubts proved correct, when they'd lost the music shop and been forced to move from Paley Road, Mary Jane never regretted the time and difficulties it had taken to move there. It had finally brought her to the faith that was to sustain her and all her family the rest of their lives.

Ralph did not join the church with his wife. Later, when pestered by the missionaries, he would say he wouldn't lie to God. God knew that "as part of 'is job 'e 'ad to play t' piano in t' pub, and of course they'd buy a drink fer t' piano player." He couldn't earn a living this way, the best way he knew how, and be a good Mormon at the same time. He also liked to smoke his pipe a little too much to give it up. Mary Jane would always send him out for a walk when he began to tamp the tobacco in. He and God would both know when he was ready.

But one day, not too long after Mary Jane's baptism, another knock came at the Paley Road door. Our Ivy went to answer it and found a strange man there. She let him into the shop and went for her mother. When she came in, Mary Jane started laughing and cried, "Oh, Ralph! You've had your beard shaved off!" Our Ivy didn't know her father without his beard and his long, biblical hair. To this day, our Barbara still has the thick auburn plait that was cut off when he made this final break with the New and Latter House of Israel. I've handled it, like some sacred relic. It smells of mothballs.

At the end of 1902, Hannah Maud was born. Then, after a pause of five years, three more girls followed: Mona, Nellie, and Violet.

School (Our Ivy Is Lost)

I"Is she still alive?"

Once more, Ralph's hushed question was his greeting each evening upon his return. Our Ivy was sick. Again. This time, it was dropsy. Her whole little trunk from chin to belly swelled up twice its size.

"Insufficient strength of heart action," said the doctor at Bradford Infirmary, "allowing the serum of blood to wander outside the blood vessels." He would have nothing to do with the case. He sent her home in her mother's arms to die.

"Don't feed her, give her nothing to drink," their regular family doctor said. "Nothing but a few drops of this quinine twice a day. Maybe, on the off chance—" He actually sounded no more hopeful than his colleague at the infirmary.

Ralph found Mary Jane on her knees beside our Ivy's bed the next time he came to lay his hand on her shoulder and ask, "Is she still alive?"

Mary Jane got to her feet.

"Where art tha going, Mother?" He reached out a hand, found the little pain-wrenched face, heard the whimpered "Dad. Oh, me Dad."

"Sit with her a minute, will you? I am inspired to make her a bit of thin gruel."

"But I thought t' doctor said tha weren't—" Ralph protested as he sat in the bedside chair.

"Maybe she won't take it. But I thought—a voice told me I should try."

When there was sickness in the house in "them days," often a doctor would come right in without knocking, knowing no hand might be spared to answer doors. He walked in just as Mary Jane was dribbling another spoonful of porridge into the thin, white lips while Ralph helped hold up the little shoulders.

"Missus!" the man exclaimed in horror. "What are you doing? I told you not to feed that child anything."

Mary Jane stood firm. "I'll not stand by and see my child starve to death, not while she's willing to take something."

"I wash my hands of you, then." Out the doctor stormed.

The next time Ralph asked his question, Mary Jane had carried the little girl to the chamber pot

"She passed something," Mary Jane said. It looked like no more than the gruel having passed straight through her—only even more watery. Mary Jane got to her knees again.

"Slowly, slowly it all passed from me," Ivy relates.

That was the end of the dropsy, but that six months was not the only period Ivy would spend out of normal activity. At about sixteen, the noise and stress of the mill—including the overlooker "'oo were a mess"—gave her what a recent x-ray indicates must have been a bleeding ulcer. "Gastroenteritis" they called it then—she had terrible headaches and couldn't eat anything for weeks. Then her father said she could stay home from work for a year, "learn to play t' violin and help tha mother."

"Well, I helped me mother. I'd no time to play." Even after that healed, she suffered from "bilious attacks." "Well, there's no such thing as a bilious attack." It was gallstones, she's convinced now, after a modern operation removed a stone "so big, 'Arry [her husband] could've worn it on 'is watch chain."

Until one day, Ralph forgot to ask his question once more and called out instead, "Where are me lasses, then?" to have three squirming, joyful, healthy little bodies fill his waiting arms.

And thanksgiving was the prayer Mary Jane gave on her knees that night.

∾

Children went to school at age three.

"Our Barbara went at two," chimes the chorus.

They went as soon, my grandmother always says, "as they was clean in their 'abits." One by one, Ralph took his little girls on his shoulder and carried them down to Usher Street School, a cluster of brick buildings with tall, thin windows. Or, after the move, to Ryan Street School (for twenty years now a Muslim girls' school). Here, the Whitaker lasses stayed till they were five and could count and read.

Our Mona could already read a bit when she went, but she couldn't write her name, and a girl couldn't move on to reading until she could write her name. Mona thought it was foolish to sit around with the babies when she could be reading. So, when the teacher was out of the room, she climbed up on one of the little chairs, helped herself to the roll off the top shelf, copied her name, and so got to move on.

Doris remembers learning to count with bits of colored wool and seashells. "I liked that."

For the most part, their memories of school are not so pleasant. "Mind," Hannah says, "I do think American teachers are too lenient. But English teachers really were unreasonable." Students had to stand when the teacher came in and stand when they were called upon. Hannah hated being called upon. Caning, with a cane slit at the end so it nipped your palm, was a common practice.

Once our Hannah, during a singing class, was trying so hard to sing well that she forgot to smile. "Come out, you vinegar face!" the headmistress yelled at her, and made her go down to the lowest class for singing the rest of the year. Hannah tells it, self-conscious of the buck teeth that grew in after the event and now the stroke that keeps the right side of her face sagging and expressionless. Still, to me, it is hard to think of the word "vinegar" connected to the sweet, earnest features.

Barbara, though her punishment was a little more deserved, remembers the hot summer's day when she and Doris and some other children gathered the sticky, melted tar from between the cobbles to play with on their way to school. When they got to school, there arose the problem of what to do with it until time to go home.

One boy put his in his pocket, our Doris put hers in the school-yard corner. But our Barbara carried hers in with her. When she got in, since there was no under desk, she was obliged to sit on it. "Well, it got hot and t' tar melted," and soon the teacher discovered her predicament.

She was made to stand on the schoolmaster's desk with her back to the whole school. She walked home sideways, but once she reached the door, her troubles were far from over. She was sent to bed without any supper, and her mother labored all night to clean her clothes, the only uniform Barbara had to wear to school.

"That dreary incandescent lighting and living in fear of the teachers." Auntie Barbara shakes her head.

The teachers used to inspect faces, hands, and fingernails every day. "If tha face were' dirty, tha got a mop in tha face." Our Ivy usually managed to escape that punishment, but "I were always playing in t' dirt. I'd plant a pea between t' cracks in t' yard and reckon it'd grow. Me nails was always dirty." The punishment for dirty nails was to stay in after school.

One day when Ivy was kept after, the teacher forgot all about her. She went home and left her there. Ivy didn't dare leave. The teacher had told her to stay, and she always tried to do as she was told. It got cold and dark, and all the lights were out in the great old building.

At last, our Ivy got up the courage to try one of the doors. It was locked. All the doors were locked except for one, down behind the bakery. Our Ivy sneaked out of this one and crept home like a fugitive. When she got to school the next morning, the teacher said, "Oh, I've been all night worrying about you."

"But she never came to see where I was!" Ivy has the courage to exclaim now. Then, she was only glad her disobedience hadn't gotten her into more trouble.

Frances remembers one day when she was very little. It was raining terribly, with thunder and lightning, when they got out of school. All the other kids' mothers came to meet them with umbrellas and coats. She waited and waited, but her mother never came. She longed for her mother to come. "If she'd known 'ow I longed for 'er then, she would have come. But Mother 'ad two or three more little babies at 'ome" (that is a frequent chorus), and the Whitaker girls all had to walk home in the rain alone.

"Our Frances were left-handed." Sit next to her at a crowded family dinner and you'll soon learn this. Every time she reached for the pencil with her left hand to begin to learn to write, down came the cane, nipping her palm. She had to manage with her right. She only ever learned very poorly, and couldn't be inspired to spell.

When asked what they learned in school, Auntie Violet murmurs shyly, "To read a little and add two and two."

"Mental arithmetic," shouts my grandmother triumphantly. "I liked maths. I were always good at sums. Mental arithmetic, pounds-shillings-and-pence, I did like that." And hanging on to every one of them.

One day, when she was five and in the oldest class at Usher Street School, our Ivy skipped out of the building and among the other children milling in the yard in the late afternoon sunlight. Free for another day! Free from the terror of the teachers. Her little body was so cramped from the hours spent with hands tensely folded on the desk, staring with no comprehension straight in front of her. "You daren't peep. If t' teacher called on someone behind you, you daren't turn 'round to listen to t' answer."

Ivy, it seems, was too afraid, even to learn anything.

Maybe, if someone had given her more attention, she muses. "But we were eight at home and forty in a school class. No one could bother." Although faithful to the church her whole life, she never even managed to read the Book of Mormon. "Couldn't get past where they cut that man's head off and are told it's all right."

She got more from coming out of school than going in.

That particular day, coming out of school must have given her uncustomary exhilaration and confidence. One of the teachers of the babies' class noticed her as one of the oldest girls in the yard.

"'Ere, girl."

Our Ivy complied with a hung head and shaking like a leaf. Now what had she done?

The teacher told her, "Take this little boy 'ome."

It was one of the three-year-olds on his first day of school, only just "clean in 'is 'abits," hair shorn to keep rid of lice and squinty dark eyes.

Our Ivy didn't dare say no. She didn't even dare stop to find her younger sisters. She took the little fellow by the hand and led him from the yard, looking neither right nor left.

"Now," she asked him when she finally dared to open her mouth. "Where dos' tha live?"

"Down there," the little boy said. They walked down the street.

"Now where?"

"Up 'ere."

"Now where?"

It soon became clear that the little boy had no idea where he lived. Our Ivy walked him up one street and down the next for miles. None of the houses looked familiar to him. It began to grow dark. Ivy realized she could no longer find her own home, much less his.

If only she were as old as Doris or as capable as Barbara—then she would know what to do.

She walked through the lamplight blooming from the houses onto the sidewalk. To comfort herself, she remembered one day when she'd gone with their mother to take Doris and Barbara their dinner—fish and chips—to Usher Street School. Usually Mary Jane never stepped inside the school. "If you'd any trouble, you'd to sort it out yerself." This rare day, however, the teacher had been so impressed with the little family that she'd made them stand there in front of the class in a row, all five of them from Doris, five years old, to our Hannah, still in her mother's arms. In that lineup, Frances was still able to cling to her mother's skirts, and Barbara never minded standing in front of people at all. But even now, our Ivy shook to think about herself standing there, without a skirt to cling to. She got no comfort.

Barbara was so capable, the teachers told her, "Take care of Doris, will' tha?" as if she were the eldest. Or, "Take that child away from Doris, will you, Barbara?" their mother would say. "You're the only one who can 'ush our 'Annah."

Once our Barbara had even been invited into Doris's class to tell a story about an old man who lost a silver sixpence. Our Ivy loved to hear the tale at home by the fire.

"Once upon a time, Martin Crook lived in White Cottage with his widowed mother and grandmother—"

Martin Crook finds the purse and the crooked sixpence, drilled in three places, that the stone-hearted old squire lost. Accused of theft, he is able to prove his innocence by rigorous Christian virtue.

Barbara had done so well, they'd rewarded her "wi' a thrup'nny piece."

If she'd been asked to take the little boy home, our Barbara would know what to do.

In the cold, strange streets, however, our Ivy was beginning to realize that wanting to do good didn't always lead to divine intervention.

Still she and the little boy walked and walked. Our Ivy began to remember the walks, the very pleasant walks, with her father. If he had a tuning job out in the country, he would take one or the other of his daughters out of school and let her go with him so she could see the country instead of being hemmed in by brick walls all the time. Secretly, Ivy felt that none of her sisters enjoyed these walks as much as she. "I always loved growing things," she told me, tending to "t' tomahtoes" in her Rose Park garden. "Sometimes, at home, I'd plant a pea between t' flags. I wouldn't tell anyone else where I'd put it, but I loved to watch it come up and grow, secretly, by myself."

"Can you hear that cuckoo?" her father would ask as she walked with her hand safe in his big, strong one. "Can' tha hear that lark?" he'd say. "Can' tha see t' lark? It'll be rising. It rises as it sings, but stops when it reaches t' top of its flight. There. 'Ear? Can' tha see it?"

"Can' tha see that bank of primroses?" he'd say. He couldn't see their pale-yellow bloom in the warming spring earth for himself, but he knew where they were by their scent.

Whenever she would see ivy growing, Ivy made sure she mentioned it to her father. Then he would always sing her song:

And like the ivy on the wall
Will ne'er from thence depart.

That made her feel like the best-loved little girl in the whole world. Even when it was cold, she loved those walks, for then her father would let her put her hands in his big overcoat pockets where they kept warm as toast.

Something I don't think Ivy suspects to this day is that not all the girls went on walks to the country. All of them took turns going with him, but he suited each trip to the girl. The only thing that was the same was the feeling she got that she was the most important, best-loved person in the world.

"I never knew where we was going," Hannah, the fifth daughter, says. "'E knew, blind as 'e were, but I didn't. All I knew was that I were with him, and I were safe."

He knew where all the parks were with swing sets and slides. He would stop for lunch and let the favored girl of the day play for as long as she wished. Or he would take her to see the mechanical clock in Leeds. He knew when the hour would chime, and be sure they were there to watch the gilt figurines emerge, including a roaring lion and a host of beautiful, singing angels, all enacting the history of the town.

Mona, the sixth daughter, has the impression she was the only one who ever got to go with him. "I got to go 'cause I was bright," and her father liked her intelligent conversation.

Instead of the park or the country, which might have been too much for her lame leg, her father would take her to the Natural History Museum. Most of the exhibits he remembered from when his father had taken him, but Mona got to show off by reading the placards. Ralph had promised her an Egyptian mummy, but it was no longer in the place it had been when he was a boy. "They must have moved it because it got dusty" was the verdict they arrived at on the way home.

Frances remembers once when she was with him, they smelled a wonderful smell coming from a café. (The accent is on the first syllable in Yorkshire.) It was dinnertime and they were both hungry. They went in, but neither of them could eat what they were brought: "soup wi' carrots in an' lumps o' onions and vegetables an' stuff." ("Vegetables" is a definite and scornful four syllables.) Ralph never liked turnips since his days at the blind school when often there was nothing else. Our Frances would usually pass Ivy her vegetables when their mother had jumped out to the kitchen and their father couldn't see.

How Ivy wanted to share Frances's vegetables now, as she grew hungrier and hungrier in the darkening streets, and the little boy began to sob with his own stomach growling. There were no larks here, no primroses. The streets and faceless buildings seemed even more dingy in the twilight. She began to panic. Would she ever see the country again? She might never visit her little pea growing between the cracks to give it some water, or sleep again in the safe, warm bed with her sisters.

She might never sit for hours as she loved to do in the empty field near their home where there was a little hill. If only she could find that hill, and from it, her home.

On that hill, she could sit and watch the trains go by, speeding off to magical lands where there were no cities at all. They had no room to cultivate flowers in their yard, but in the field were "buttercups and 'arebells," and she loved them. When there were no flowers in bloom on the little hill, she liked to collect bits of broken glass in the field ("it's a wonder we're any of us still alive"), grind it up, brush it into little piles, "and reckon to sell it." ("We was very poor, you see.") "If I found a bit of blue stone, ooh, I were thrilled." Such little pleasures seemed lost forever. Would she ever see her dear parents again or sit, as she loved to do, with her ear against the piano as her father played?

"Is our Ivy still alive?" Her father was probably asking that right then, racked with grief, tapping through the streets he knew so well, calling her name.

Thinking such things, our Ivy began to cry. Her sorrow and fear fed the little boy's. Soon they could do nothing but sit side by side in the gutter, sobbing.

Presently, some friendly grown-up found them and brought them to town hall. Someone gave Ivy a teacake. The little boy soon had icing all over his face, but Ivy was too shy to eat hers. In an attempt to escape from all the big, official people in the hall, Ivy crept, crying, under the table.

There she found something even more terrifying—a dead duck. Someone had been caught poaching and this days-dead mass of feathers and dubious smell was the evidence. Still our Ivy didn't dare come out, so she sat, huddled up with the dead duck and crying.

At last her mother came to her rescue. Mary Jane took her daughter home to the house near the empty field of Bowling Park, to the pea plant in the flagstones and the great big bed she shared with her sisters.

~

Auntie Violet remembers going on a two-weeks holiday with her school class. The most memorable thing about that trip was how all the girls would try to get to the head of the line when they went down to meals because then they got to sit with the teachers. "There were quite a lot of glory wi' it." Shy little Violet, on the other hand, always tried to hang back to the end. She didn't want to eat with the teachers.

But one day the teacher called out, "'Round about turn!"

"I nearly died. There I were at t' top o' t' table wi' t' 'eadmistress! And I remember we 'ad some prunes, and I were too embarrassed to take t' stones out. I didn't swallow 'em, but I kept 'em in me mouth till I 'ad so many! That's how stupid I were."

"It's a shame," Auntie Barbara remarks, "that circumstances made it so I was happier working than in school."

At Home (Our Barbara Cleans and Our Hannah Listens)

"EVERY FRIDAY NIGHT—" begins our Barbara, the second daughter.

Today, my grandmother is throwing yet another party. The Fourth of July, that most American of holidays, and her most English of birthdays almost coincide, or close enough for Grandma to usurp the one with the other. Her Tenth Avenue house has a view of the whole Salt Lake Valley. After dark, we'll see every fireworks display from the university stadium to Sandy City Park. In the meantime are the "oohs" and "ahs," the "eees" and "'eyups" of verbal fireworks.

"Every Friday night—"

Auntie Barbara is surrounded by her sisters. Ergo, she is interrupted. Unlike Hannah and Violet, whose drops into silence before the deluge indicate shyness, Auntie Barbara's has a hint of superiority. Her sisters—my grandmother, in particular—are a silly lot and chatter on.

Auntie Hannah, I notice, is content to watch and listen.

I'll have to learn about those Friday nights when I have Auntie Barbara alone.

But first come the memories as I can pick them from the jostling party atmosphere. This gives a better idea of what it must have been like to grow up in that house anyway.

〜

After he'd lost the dream of a shop and a home of his own in Paley Road, Ralph rented a handcart, got a few friends to help him, and "flitted" to a new house; they couldn't pay for a horse-pulled van. They couldn't pay the overdue rent.

A number of houses came and went in the next few years: one was too expensive, one had too many stairs.

Finally, around 1905, they moved to a small house at the top of a steep hill at 4 Moulson Street. Large stones formed the street itself, smaller ones the pavements in front. If you stood looking at the family home, the Red Lion pub where Ralph did much of his entertaining was on the corner, behind and to your right. Around that corner was a sausage shop, a chemist's. Facing the home across the street was a long row of dark houses. In one of them, directly across, was the woman who made excellent pound cake.

Number 4 Moulson Street was built in the eighteenth century. Unlike the bleak houses it faced, it stood almost on its own. Instead of another house, to the left was a steep cobbled lane, "t' snicket," before the next line of terraced houses began. The home was attached "to t' big 'ouse" only on the right. At first "some rich people" lived there. Eventually, it turned into a Boys and Girls Club under the auspices of the Prince of Wales. Ralph thought, no matter how small, a house should be detached when ten people filled it.

Two stone steps, carefully scrubbed and delineated with yellow chalk, led to the door. The tiny vestibule, with hardly room to turn around, led straight to a flight of stairs climbing upwards. A dirty runner covered and softened the hollows worn in the old wood. The visitor was invited to hang her coat and hat to the right of the stair—if she could find room among the crowded pegs.

To the right, then, was another door set with glass in the upper half. Smaller, colored panes of alternating red, yellow, green, and blue framed a central pane of clear glass, only pebbled to translucency, a fascination to children's eyes. To keep drafts out, this door stayed closed, usually draped with a heavy curtain.

Stepping through door and curtain, closing them quickly behind her, a bundle of coal-fire warmth greeted the visitor.

Ralph set up a swing down the snicket at the side of the house. But since "it were nearly al'ays rainin' an' we needed summat recreation," he put another one in the long, narrow kitchen as well. Then the children could tip up the kitchen table on its hinge and swing to their heart's content. Frances used to touch the ceiling with the tip of her foot at both ends on this indoor swing. Needless to say, they made quite a racket. It was a good thing their house was detached.

One Sunday afternoon, Ralph came down very angry. The swinging had disturbed him from a nap to overcome his late night in the pub. Frances was the first one he managed to catch hold of. She knew he was going to hit her. She quickly said, "It wasn't me! It wasn't me!" in a voice squeaking unnaturally—a dead giveaway to us swatting evening mosquitoes in Utah, who know she is always the loudest.

"Well, why didn't you come and tell us then?" her father demanded.

Quick as a wink: "Because I love you."

"Typical Mother logic." We shake our heads at Uncle Noel's editorializing.

But it worked. Her father set her down and never laid a finger on her.

∼

Liberty Park has begun fireworks with a great burst of red, white, and blue. The Stars and Stripes? More like the Union Jack, with its crosses upon crosses. We sing "God Save the Queen" to "My Country 'Tis of Thee."

∼

Mary Jane, it seems, was not a very good housekeeper. She could cook, although in the process she tended to dirty every last spoon in the house. Clutter, heaps of things everywhere, dirt, dark and damp, impressed my mother. A challenge for a blind man.

I hate to confess, but I've inherited this gene.

"Friday night," begins the second daughter once again, straightening the afghan on the couch behind her and taking up another knitting project so time talking to the tape is not wasted. We are alone now, the end of July, so the subject is hers, and it will not be silly.

"Friday night, after ten hours' work in t' mill and after supper—whatever were to be found cheap in t' market—I'd be so tired I'd fall fast asleep in a chair for an hour. Then I would get up and tackle cleaning up t' kitchen. And if you know what it's like with ten people in a small 'ouse!"

I know. We started this conversation at Grandma's party. "Why did you do it?" I ask. "Were you assigned that particular chore?"

Auntie Barbara opens her eyes in surprise. She's never thought of it like that. "I were born with an instinct to clean up, you see. 'Tis a specialty of mine. Just 'ated to see things all cluttered 'round. And I didn't get much time to do it, only once a week on Friday, I just did it. Cleaned t' kitchen all up. I don't think they liked doing it very much. 'I don't care. I'm going to do it!'"

I also come to realize, sitting here in Joe's house that was his first wife's for so many years before Auntie Barbara even immigrated, that she was the one who stayed at 4 Moulson Street. She lived the longest there, and even now has no other home to really call her own.

"Our kitchen 'ad a bath in it—a luxury them days—wi' 'ot running water. 'E wanted it there even after a regular WC were added hupstairs. Father said, 'An 'ouse wi' nine women in it wants a bath.'

"T' bath were all boarded 'round wi' an 'inged lid—just a fine place to dump everything, mostly dirty pots. There'd be no Saturday baths till that were done. Me orderly mind tackled that first. There were t' great big baking bowl in which Mother, poor soul, 'ad baked two stone of dough. After that strain, she 'adn't strength left to do t' cleaning up, and the dough'd got hardened on. I usually filled it with water and did t' washing up of other pots first.

"Then t' problem were where to put them when washed. They 'ad to be packed and stacked carefully or they wouldn't fit. That's why they was al'ays left on t' bath top. It must 'ave been a joy for Mother to find the baking bowl clean when next she wanted it.

"When t' last spoon were finished, I'd tackle t' gas oven: a great big iron oven bought in 1902 wi' none of t' modern cleaning surfaces. Could never make it a beauty, but I knew it were clean. I used to scrub it and rub it and clean it off, all t' fat off and everything.

"Next, t' kitchen table 'ad to be scrubbed as clean as soap and elbow grease could make it.

"Now, fer t' floor. I would pick up all t' odd shoes and stockings and odd ends and put them where they belonged. Next, sweep up all t' debris [pronounced with the accent on the first syllable] and tip it into t' stove which kept the kitchen warm. Now, down on me knees. Flagstone floors: we scoured the edges wi' yellow stone which gave it a clean look. What rugs we 'ad were all prodded by Father of rags."

"Prodded?" For the record, I pretend I didn't learn this term at my grandmother's knee.

The floor of the entire main level, Auntie Barbara explains, was cold stone. To warm it, Ralph prodded rugs. The black scraps left from cutting down an old wool coat of Mary Jane's for Hannah, the trimmings from Frances's new red skirt, the houndstooth jacket Ralph had worn past another winter's use, all ended up in a great bag in the cellar. When the bag was full, Ralph would wash an old burlap coal sack, open it up at the seams, and set it on a frame.

Sometimes he would ask what color this scrap or that was, mostly he worked by feel. Having cut the woolen scraps into six-inch strips, he used a hook to prod the scraps into the burlap until the entire sack was covered in a geometric pattern. That became the new sitting-room rug. The older rug moved to the kitchen, then worked its way through the bedrooms for little toes dragging out of bed "to t' mill" on dark, cold winter mornings.

"Once, when Father and Mother were out when I were very young, I scrubbed t' kitchen floor, one of t' first times. They gave me a penny for that. But I were very disappointed. Not only did I get a penny, they all got a penny. Because I'd scrubbed t' floor.

"When I finished t' kitchen cleaning, it would be one or two a.m. Then I'd creep off to bed. For a time when I were working at t' other side o' town, I'd get up again at half past four to do a little piano practice before setting off for work at half past five to get to work by six."

Later, Auntie Barbara's efforts expanded to the whole house.

"There were two double beds in both big bedrooms and one three-quarter bed in t' small room, clothes for ten of us everywhere you could put them, shoes everywhere. I remember fixing a corner shelf wi' a curtain behind which I could 'ang me clothes. We did 'ave a clothes closet in t' front bedroom, but when t' WC were made upstairs, it were incorporated to make t' toilet wi' t' upper part of t' tall staircase. Getting under them beds for cleaning were a job! They never bothered with 'anging.

"Bedroom floors and steps were wood and 'ad to be scrubbed weekly. 'Ouse floors and cellar steps were flagstones and were washed and scoured. A red-letter day were when we got linoleum on t' living room floor and later in the bedrooms, too. Windows were sash windows, and I sat on t' sills to clean them. I will ever be grateful to my father for 'is effort to clean all our windows, before I started. I marveled to see 'ow well 'e did when 'e couldn't see 'em. 'E must 'ave 'ad a systematic way of covering them completely so as to make such a good job of it."

As an aside, she tells how the Catholics built a beautiful new church in Bradford, and Ralph got the contract to tune their pianos. The first time he went, the priest showed him around the edifice, of which he was duly proud. But Ralph, with his hands all over, discovered they'd put one pane of glass in the great main window "t' wrong way 'round." The smooth side should have been outside for ease of washing. The priest didn't much like hearing that; the window stayed as it was.

"I loved to clean the backyard. Even though 'e never used t' dog to guide 'im, 'e loved dogs, so we al'ays 'ad one and a big, strong kennel that someone 'ad given Dad. When Dad and t' dog were gone, t' kennel were a store for junk, and strangers were never sure there weren't a dog in there.

"The atmosphere were putrid throughout t' yard, from t' dog, and there were soot and dust around everything. I would sweep first and then swill wi' buckets of water carried from t' kitchen until we got an 'ose pipe. A tax were charged on t' length of 'ose, you see, so it were only a very short one.

"I loved to swill that old flagstone yard. I'd even put some strong soda in t' water to make it special. T' water ran out through the gate into t' side snicket. You'd to make sure that didn't get blocked up wi' debris. Finishing touches were putting some yellow ocher on t' edges of t' steps. It helped to see better in t' dark. I once tried to grow some plants in a box, but t' cat were so pleased to see a bit o' green, 'e made a toilet of it, and nothing grew then.

"At t' front, where t' door came level wi' t' street pavement, I washed t' steps and edged them wi' yellow as well. Some people used white stone to trim t' steps. Often Mother would come to t' door and forbid me to wash any more of t' city's pavement.

"T' first furniture I remember were a big, square table wi' stout legs, good, solid, strong stuff, as big around as that." She arcs her arms out to their fullest length, never dropping a stitch of knitting. "Some people protected those legs by putting stockings on them so you couldn't kick t' polish off. We didn't bother."

And I don't bother to tell my auntie I'd always heard that was because Victorians were excessively modest when confronted by bare legs, even when they were made of wood.

"We 'ad a rocking chair, four wooden chairs, and nearly al'ays two or three pianos. We bought a polished sideboard, drawers, and cupboards. We also 'ad a glass-doored bookcase. There were built-in cupboards and drawers in t' sitting room. Dad fixed high-walled cupboards in t' kitchen. There were three: one for pans, one for crockery, and one, with wire mesh in front to keep out vermin, for dry goods.

"There were a little fireplace in each bedroom that were so useful in times of sickness. Otherwise t' bedrooms were never 'eated. T' fireplace downstairs were an 'igh mantled, primitive one wi' a side boiler for 'eating water, the only source of continuous 'ot water for washing and bathing.

"On t' other side were an oven. When t' 'ot water system were installed, an iron tank were fixed behind t' fireplace and a big copper tank upstairs. Water must al'ays be in t' tank or it would burst.

"Later, another fireplace were installed wi' new arrangements. It 'ad some plated steel parts which made it look better about t' 'andle and trim. We now also 'ad a more elaborate fender and brass parts to polish and give glitter.

"There were a lower mantel shelf which could 'old a few ornaments—"

I notice she's not specific about the "ornaments," only more things to dust for her. Nothing about the ceramic shepherdess and her flute-playing companion, Victorian kitsch, that managed to make it to the States to become a bone of contention here. Cousin Raymond has them on his mantel in Bountiful today. And he's adopted!

Oblivious, Auntie Barbara continues. "—And a clock. Dad did love 'is clocks!

"Decorating 'ad to be done every year, in spring. If you'd papered the place, by next spring, the patterns would all look much t' same, uniform coal-dust grey. At first we lime washed t' walls. The ceiling were al'ays whitewashed wi' calcium. T' walls were often dark green or maroon. Then Mother learnt 'ow to paper, which made things prettier. Then, during t' war, paper got scarce, so we 'ad to go back to calcium coloring, stippled wi' a roller or even a rag to make a pattern.

"I remember once putting water paint over some oil paint. I were living alone, and I kept 'earing funny little noises all night. T' paint were just curling up and dropping down. It were all over t' floor next morning in little curls. I learnt!"

Beneath the stairway running up to the second floor—what English-English calls the first—was the flight going down to "t' 'orrible cellar." The cellar was tiny and dark, lit in later years by a single bare gas burner. The walls ran with damp. The washtub and mangle were here. The loaves of fresh bread in a big crockery bowl, covered with a lid or cloth, nineteen at a time; any food that needed to be cool in a day before refrigeration; all these things could be found—if any child dared to venture.

One inducement for the brave grandchild to go down at least one step was the gas meter. "Some people 'ad electricity. We still 'ad gas lighting," Auntie Barbara tells me, "but we now used mantels, which was a good improvement on t' incandescent light that were still in most bedrooms yet."

Gas entered the house through a meter which, rather than being read once a month had to be fed with pennies when the lights flickered and threatened to go out. "'Ere's a penny," my mother remembers her grandfather telling her. "Go stick it in t' meter."

"I lived in that house on and off for fifty year and saw such changes in comfort!" Auntie Barbara is rolling to a conclusion, exhausted as if she'd just done all she talked about. "I 'ad replaced t' pot-bellied stove wi' a slow combustion, enameled fire wi' oven and water 'eater, and a modern gas oven.

"After t' first ten years renting, me father negotiated to buy t' 'ouse for five 'undred pounds. T' city paid me one 'undred and fifty for it in a compulsory purchase in 1961. They tore it down to build t' council 'ouses what are there now."

The tape recorder has clicked off; I've run out of tape.

"But it 'ad been 'ome, and they couldn't take away t' memories." Auntie Barbara shoves the stitches down on her needles and pushes the points through her ball of yarn to lay her work carefully in the workbasket beside her easy chair.

~

"Your parents must have been very strict disciplinarians." Uncle Noel pushes as sloppy pieces of Grandma's birthday cake get passed out.

Auntie Hannah is so quiet, she would not get a piece if my mother didn't fend for her.

The only punishment any of them related is this of Barbara: She was once, when very young, "the receiver of stolen goods." I suspect it was Doris (although Barbara won't tattle on her by name in company) who stole a shilling from their mother's purse and told her younger sister which candies she was to buy at the shop: licorice whips, "'umbugs," and jelly babies. Barbara went to sleep that night with them in her hand. Her father discovered them on his nightly visit, while she still slept.

In the morning when she awoke, the loot had vanished.

"Then I got it real and strong."

She had to watch her younger sisters eat all the candy and "labored in fear for several hours" while her parents went out. They'd threatened her with the police.

"What a blessing this was to me!" she exclaims. "It cured me of theft for me life."

Ralph could tell each daughter by touch. "Oh, 'ello, Doris," he'd say, she of the skinny arms. About the rest of them, he often joked that if they fell and he went to pick them up, he might set them on their heads, they "was all such dumplings."

Every girl says over and over, "We all loved him." When alone, each one says, "I think he liked me best because—"

Violet remembers once when she was out strolling with her husband, Arthur casually mentioned, "There's me dad over there." She found his nonchalance hard to believe. Had it been her father, she would have shouted, "Eee, there's me dad!" and run to him immediately.

This same impulse got Barbara into trouble once. She was playing truant from school and happened to see her father. She was so glad to see him that she forgot she was playing truant, ran right up to him and threw her arms around him.

"And why a'n't tha in school?" She never played truant again.

They used to have a canary that would sing at the top of its voice whenever Ralph came home. When the girls heard their father, they'd all drop whatever they were doing and run to greet him. Sometimes he would throw his hat in the door first, as a joke. Then one would take up the hat, another would take his coat, a third would take whatever he was carrying. Then they would lead him to his chair—no one else sat in it when he was home, you may be sure—and they'd fight over who got to fetch his slippers.

He always had a joke to tell them when he came home, about something funny that had happened to him. There was the day he knocked over a pair of orange carts set in a new place in the street. He left the two merchants arguing loudly over which oranges were whose.

Then one girl would bring the paper and read to him. The *Telegraph and Argus* was only two leaves "them days," and they read it from beginning to end. If by chance they couldn't afford a paper for a while, one girl would be sent out to read the news on the placard in front of the stationer's store. Then she'd come back and report what it said.

One day my grandmother came running in. "The Almighty is coming! It says 'The Almighty is coming!'"

Mary Jane came from the kitchen and caught her breath. The Almighty was coming? This event she'd prayed for all her life, and the Mormons were the last to know? "For goodness' sake, Doris. Run out and see what it says."

Bulging the webbing on her Salt Lake lawn chair, Auntie Doris comments, "I always were a good speller."

And it goes without saying that our Frances "weren't." She always read what she wanted to read. Oh, the frustration I suffered as a child with the Christmas carol "Once Upon an 'Ousetop" and the nursery rhyme "Little Boy Blue Come Blow Up Your 'Orn."

The headline actually said: "The Admiralty is coming."

"Mother—pathetic" is the note Uncle Noel adds to the general Catherine wheel of laughter beneath the warm Utah summer sky.

After supper on long winter evenings, they would all draw up chairs around the coal fire. There would be "Mother in a rocking chair, nursing a baby." All the little girls would be in a circle, and Father would read to them from big Braille books he got from the library. He read "the classics," frequently Dickens, all by firelight, for he didn't need a lamp.

He would read till he could tell by the breathing that half of them had begun to nod. Then he'd wrap them up in blankets and carry them up to their cold, unheated rooms, tucking them safe in their beds.

～

Because she is so quiet, our Hannah is a good listener. She listens to sounds in the night.

The greatest difference between America and England, Auntie Hannah says—I get her alone on another day when she is not in danger of missing out on her cake—is the air and especially the sounds it carries. She used to lie awake at night and listen to the air.

I add details later, from the communal stew, but Hannah is the one who encourages me to listen in the rare, precious quiet time.

Our Hannah was, in some respects, a "baby." There were five years between her and our Mona, the next youngest. (Barbara says their mother had two miscarriages during these years, both little boys. Nobody else knows this.) Hannah would crawl into bed early, before the older girls, and then listen as Barbara rocked and sang the babies to sleep in the other room.

> Sleep, baby, sleep.
> The Lord's stars are the sheep.
> The little ones, the lambs, I guess.
> The gentle moon's the shepherdess.
> Sleep, baby, sleep.

> Sleep, baby, sleep. Away to tend thy sheep.
> Away, thou sheep dog, fierce and wild,
> And do not harm my sleeping child.
> Sleep, baby, sleep.

Sometimes Ivy or one of the others would lullaby the little ones, too. Ivy sings her favorite in her gentle, somber voice:

> Pride of the Prairie, Mary, my own,
> Jump up beside me, right to my home.
> My heart is lassoed, no more to roam,
> Pride of the Prairie, Mary.

There was even a lullaby especially for Nellie:

> Nellie Bly shuts 'er eye, when she goes to sleep.
> In the morning, when she wakes, 'er eye begins to peep.

I remember my grandmother using that one on us.

Our Hannah would listen and listen and usually fall asleep, too. But then, sometime after midnight, the pub owner at the Red Lion just down the street would call: "Time! Gentlemen, time!" She would hear the men wandering off to their homes, singing snatches of song in drunken notes. Most of the songs our Hannah recognized. They were songs her father had been entertaining the men with in the upper-class room, songs Hannah herself or one of the older girls had helped him learn by reading off sheet music he'd bought or borrowed.

I wonder what 'e's going to do next.
'E took me wife on 'is shoulder.
'E took 'er down the stairs and I followed in the rear.
I bet 'e didn't know that anyone were near.
'E took 'er in a van that 'e 'ad outside
And I stood there quite perplexed.
Ah, well, I never.
That were wonderfully clever.
But I wonder what 'e's going to do next.

Auntie Hannah remembers once listening to her father and a friend practicing "Excelsior!" in their sitting room below. She lay transfixed at the glory of it as each tried to outdo the other in the charge.

They had to keep the door downstairs locked or one of the drunks might wander in, thinking it was his house. But Father had a key. After bidding a loud, cheery "Good Night" to all his mates, he would quietly let himself in. Sometimes there would be a bit of supper left for him in the wooden food safe. Our Hannah could hear him pull up a chair to eat it in the kitchen all by himself. Our Hannah heard the row the night her father caught the cat lapping at the other side of his dish.

Most nights he ate, checked to see that the fire was well banked, and came up the stairs with no light and almost no sound. He would step into each room, set his hands briefly on each sleeping head.

Auntie Hannah remembers the other row, the row when he felt for one girl and found her missing. Our Frances had rocked herself so violently in her sleep that she rolled "clean out o' t' bed" and under, all without waking up. Their father soon found her, but not without rousing the household with his hue and cry.

Most nights weren't so eventful. Finding all his lasses safe, Ralph went to his own room where he took off shoes, suspenders, trousers, and soon joined their sleeping breath.

The soft breathing of her family asleep filled the air all about her: Doris and Mona in the big double bed with her, Frances in the single bed in the same room "'cause our Frances al'ays rocked and kept us all awake." In the little room at the top of the stairs were Barbara and

Ivy. That room was meant for the two eldest, but Barbara had kicked Doris out because she was so untidy. From the big bedroom came the heavy baritone of Father, Mother's gentle soprano, and the fairy breath of the two babies, Nellie and Violet.

Once that peace settled, all was silence, save the ticking of the clock and, once an hour, the chime. Their father loved clocks and they always had a lot of them he'd tinker with: a great big grandfather clock at the top of the stairs, a marble clock. He even rigged an alarm clock himself "wi' a sort o' batt'ry" for our Ivy when she started to work at Lister's mill across town and had to get up earlier than anyone else.

One clock in particular had a jarring chime. The girls got used to it and tended to ignore it, but Hannah always liked to pause and listen. Her father, holding her face in his great, searching hands, had told her how it had come to sound so jarring. When she was being born, her mother had sent him for the doctor. He'd been in such a rush, he ran into the pump organ he'd been mending at the time and knocked the clock off. It was just a broken wire. For the rest, it ran well. But though he had a good hand with mechanical things, he never fixed the chime because it reminded him of that little fifth daughter. Hannah listened, and was reminded that, although she was number five, she was still loved for herself alone.

Silence. The wail of the two-twenty train, bound for "'Uddersfield and 'Alifax," as the conductor announced, echoing the words of the old song.

Then silence again.

Once a week the night soil men would come with a cart and clean out the midden (the outhouse) in the back. The men had a contract with the city of Bradford and took the waste out to manure farms. They would make quite a noise as they urged the horse to back down the steep, slippery cobbles in the alleyway. If the noise woke up any of the girls, they would groan slightly before turning over to sleep again.

A visit from the night soil men meant a very unpleasant chore in the morning. The girls would have to fetch buckets of water and swill out the inside of the toilet and all down "t' snicket" shared with four other houses. The toilet had a wooden seat and a drop of ten or twelve feet to the ground below. For a child, it was a frightening business.

ᗝ

Their outhouse shared the midden itself with the people in the big house next door. Once as she cleaned, our Frances found a box of chocolates the big house had thrown away. There was a whole chocolate still inside.

"You never ate it," we cry in horror.

"Of course I et it." Grandma downs a large forkful of her birthday cake. "Then went on wi' t' swilling."

"Waste not, want not." Uncle Noel's comment.

The rocket's red glare.

The chore was not usually so exciting. It made a big, smelly lake "down at t' bottom o' t' snicket."

ᗝ

Around four in the morning, the knocker-up man came down the street, rattling wires and bones fixed on a long pole on the upper-story windows where he knew the millworkers slept. "All right!" the workers would call back, stumbling out of bed. "If it were summer an' t' windows was open," they'd hear Mrs. Who-Is-It across the street calling for her son John to get up.

They've forgotten what the last name was, but always remember "our John," for the missus had a fine pair of lungs. In an hour or so would come the great clatter of clogs on the cobbles, and another day had begun.

ᗝ

"I liked to watch when the lamplighter would come," Auntie Hannah confides quietly. Better than the knocker-up man.

In winter, the lamplighter came around four or five in the evening. It was wonderful to watch him with his lamp and his ladder.

The bubbles and imperfections of the window caught and fractured the light and turned it into a million lights, "like fairyland."

Like the kids dancing with sparklers out on the lawn, after dinner. Dinner of roast beef instead of hot dogs and hamburgers. Marshmallows are anathema to my mother: too sweet. And barbeque? What foreign language is barbeque?

FOOD

Of all the girls, Ivy is the best cook. During the forties, she worked as a cook for Mrs. Tracy of the Tracy-Collins Bank, Salt Lake City, in the Tracys' summer cabin. Often the language at these summer retreats was pretty loose, but "Ivy doesn't like swearing," Mrs. Tracy would warn the guests. She set a cup on the table into which anyone who swore had to pay a dime "for the cook."

Even today, Ivy gives a dinner party once a week for her sisters. She does it for sheer joy and all without recipes. As everyone knows, it's no fun to cook for one, and then she has leftovers all the rest of the week.

Being a grandniece, I can invite myself to these parties, be the youngest in the room by twenty-five years or more. I've got this ongoing project of tape recording going at the behest of my difficult uncle. I've read enough anthropology to understand that "food is identity." But can I endure the weight of guilt at having left my own family with pizza at home? Mythic tales of family meals like these only underline the guilt. My family's identity is pizza?

Does trying to capture this world mean I've lost my own?

Sometimes, it's enough to make me wish there were still a cup in the center of the table so I could swear. "Not another family party!"

"We've eaten many a piano," Ralph always used to say.

Whenever things became desperate, he managed to sell a piano he'd repaired.

Although work was plentiful in winter when people were cooped up in their sitting rooms with their untuned pianos, it always grew scarce with the good weather. Sometimes in summer the girls would be sent to gather currants and bilberries on Ilkley Moor, wandering among the stones of the circle called the Twelve Apostles (not just in Salt Lake) or the natural formation called the Cow and Calf. My sisters and I have done the same with my mother on Haworth Moor. I know they take "a lot of picking"—hours of bending and getting scratched will hardly cover the bottom of the bucket. Then the girls would trudge home as the late summer sun faded, holding the buckets between their knees on the train.

Much more than berry picking, the girls loved going into the woods to hunt mushrooms with their father. Mushrooms, he told them in a voice weaving mystery, grew on the sites of old battle-fields. One of the best sites was north along Canal Road. Whenever they would find such a site, they would bring home "sacks and sacks, stones and stones." Grandma doesn't like mushrooms raw, and she never tires of letting us know this every time they appear in a salad. But fried in butter with a few potatoes on the side—that made a meal! "We thought it were manna from 'eaven," my grandmother says. That particular "u" in "mushrooms" does not exist on this side of the Pond.

Once when they were courting, my grandparents wandered 'way off the beaten track, outside of Bierley. There they found a great field of mushrooms, which my grandmother told her father about as soon as she got home. The very next day, he took Violet out of school to help him collect them. "I wonder what our Frances and 'Arry was doing when they found these," he teased.

"Only this kind. Only this kind. That's right, only this kind," their father warned as they picked. Somehow he could tell them by touch.

Seventy years later, my grandmother recognized a handful of the safe kind of mushrooms growing in her yard on Tenth Avenue.

"Nonsense," we said. "Nothing that grows wild in England could possibly be growing in Salt Lake's desert."

But with utter confidence, she cut and cooked them and never suffered ill effects.

"Mushrooms picked by a blind man" has become a byword in our house for something so miraculous that it takes the faith of Lazarus to believe. Perhaps it is only sour grapes. I, armed with the best mushroom book money can buy, head out into the garden or the mountains after a rain, determined to gather ourselves some fresh mushrooms. I pour over the pictures, stare at the fungi before us, and then return empty-handed, defeated by my doubts and lack of faith.

"Mother didn't bother much about breakfast," the girls relate.

She would usually stay in bed until eight while their father saw to the fire and the porridge. They were Mormon; there was no tea. So other days there was a pot of cocoa, warm milk, or just plain warm water to wash down a slice of toast and jam (with lettuce, perhaps— ugh) or drippin' 'n' bread. Drippin', that's the "lovely" fat and juices left in the bottom of a roast pan, kept without refrigeration, spread thickly on toast. Not only did the Sunday roast make their own drippin', it was the cheapest thing to be had in the butcher's, 7d. for a full crock. It's greasier than whole slabs of butter and takes some getting used to.

"I think we lived on that," my grandmother says. "Drippin' 'n' toast an' a pot o' cocoa."

Supper, too, was rather haphazard. Barbara's memories of "sandwiches and fruit in summer, stew or fish in winter" are elaborate. Grandma remembers more drippin' 'n' bread.

When Mona was born, Mary Jane kept eight-year-old Barbara out of school for a month or so to help. She couldn't afford to hire the usual nurse. A truant officer came around, very angry. When Mary Jane explained the situation, how little money there was, how many mouths to feed, and how impossible to hire help, the man relented.

"And why don't you send your children to t' Methodist Hall for breakfast and dinner every day?" he suggested. Here free meals were given to the poor, and for many years that helped out, although perhaps my great-grandmother was disturbed it was the Methodists and not the Mormons doing the charity.

"They were always good meals," Mona remembers, who was old enough to go herself before the dole closed down. She remembers especially the rice pudding, so rich and creamy, that would come to the table steaming in big metal milk jugs. Barbara remembers the bread and jam for breakfast, but Frances only remembers that when she'd help serve the warm milk to the other kids, there often wasn't enough left for her.

But Mary Jane always made certain her family had a cooked meal at noon. When they walked in the door from school or work, it was ready for them. They only had to stick their knees under the table, eat, and be off again. That was good when they only had half an hour dinner break.

My vegetarian brother-in-law gives his general recipe for all of that infamous English cooking, as thick with scorn as Grandma's gravy: "Put orange carrots, green celery, peas and beans, white potatoes and turnips, creamy parsnips, and a hunk of dead animal all together in a roasting pan and cook in the oven until everything is one uniform brown." The Whitaker girls, however, praise their mother's cooking with one voice.

The week generally began with roast on Sunday, either beef or, especially, lamb. Mary Jane liked lamb a lot—perhaps for religious reasons, as the family always has lamb on Christmas Eve today. In her globe-trotting seventies and eighties, Grandma visited the Holy Land. In the old city of Jerusalem, the whole skinned lamb carcasses, eyes still intact and staring, hanging in front of the Arab shops, delighted her. She "'adn't seen such a good bit o' lamb since me youth."

In the drippings beneath the roast, huge slabs of Yorkshire pudding were baked. Grandma still thinks a bread panful of pudding will only do one person. That's a far cry from the muffin-tin size my mother makes, traditionally with liver on a dreary weeknight because, she reasons, "if they won't eat the liver, they'll eat the Yorkshire and at least I know they're getting eggs."

Ralph, being the Yorkshire man, had charge of this regional specialty. He would make it while the rest of the family was at Sunday School. This is his recipe:

A good tablespoon of flour for each person around the table—
then one for the pot. If there are more than five people, use three
eggs; two if fewer. Make it the consistency of thick cream by adding
about half a pint of water (or part water and part milk—judge by a
pub pint) and half a teaspoon salt. Beat well.

Place a little less than one tablespoon roast fat and juices in the
bottom of the tins. Put the tins in the oven to get right hot. Pour the
batter evenly into the hot tins and bake about half an hour or until
puffed high and golden brown.

The recipe Uncle Noel wrote down for me includes more precise
directions: the oven is 425 degrees, one cup of flour to two cups
of milk, the use of a bread pan six inches by three, "no bigger, no
smaller," and "NB taste it" after adding the salt. Who but Uncle Noel
would have a nota bene in a recipe?

Our Americanization of sprinkling the leftovers with powdered
sugar is anathema to him.

After Sunday, the week's meals went to a rhythm like the familiar "Monday, washday, Tuesday, iron—" It explains how they "made
do" with little more than that one roast for the entire week: "Roast
beef Sunday, cold meat Monday, shepherd's pie Tuesday, 'Ash
Wednesday"—this is the cue to repeat, "'Ash Wednesday!" to emphasize the joke and maybe even cross yourself in mimicry—"stew
Thursday, fish Friday, fish and chips Saturday."

Not so poetical, perhaps, but more exact is Barbara's adage to describe
what they ate: "whatever were to be 'ad cheap in t' market." Sometimes
Mary Jane would go to Newby's, "a real class shop" in town, and buy at
cut rate all the perishables they couldn't keep overnight. The butcher
around the corner was a good friend of Ralph. Every Saturday night,
after their father had finished up at the pub, he'd stop by the butcher's
shop and buy whatever was left at half price. Once he brought home
twelve pounds of sausages, which they steamed and ate for days.

The girls went with their mother to the wholesale market to buy
green—what we call blue—cheese, sugar, and sardines.

Sometimes they would buy fish heads and make a soup with that,
or a whole halibut which Mary Jane would put in the oven with some
butter—"That were lovely!"

Street vendors sold everything from meat to fruits and vegetables, calling out their wares:

"Grey peas, green peas, all hot. A penny a pot!" or

"Cockles and mussels, alive, alive-o!"

Venders carried trays of hot meat pies; others tended old rubbish bins on which they roasted chestnuts. Men selling kitchenware, scissors sharpeners, and tinkers joined the fishmongers and travelling butchers.

But doorstep service generally cost more, so if a meal could not be rounded out from the usual source of bargains, the Whitakers would go themselves to the shops. There were no big supermarkets—every imaginable food was segregated into its own little shop.

As for the scissors sharpener—a few good whisks of the blade on the back step avoided him. Many's the time I've come home from church on a Sunday to hear that same sound as my grandmother gets ready to carve our roast.

Mary Jane got heart as well as liver from the butcher. Both were more tender "than what they 'ave 'ere." Liver baked in the oven with onions and forced meatballs (dumplings) on the top made a nice meal.

Pork butchers were separate, and nearly always Germans who suffered prejudice during the war. There were tripe shops, too, "what sold tripe, chitt'lin's, pig's feet, cooked potted meat, and black puddings."

> 'Ere comes an old woman as stiff as a stump,
> Selling blood pudding a penny a lump.
> You must neither laugh nor smile,
> But say outright, "I will."

This game, still played at birthday parties and on Old Year's Night, is always full of shivering terror. It's enough to make one laugh out loud (and lose the game) with nervousness when Auntie Mona comes at you with her cane. Perhaps some of Mary Jane's horror of pork lingers on in that jingle as her daughters repeat it for, though she'd cook it for her family, she never did eat it herself to her dying day.

"Then there was t' fish an' chip shops. A penny'rth of cooked, battered fish and an 'alf a penny'rth of fried potatoes for an adult;

a child got an 'a'penny worth of fish and an 'a'penny worth of potatoes." (During the war, sometimes it was chips and fries, no fish, just
potatoes sliced and potatoes wedged.) "They was al'ays wrapped in
newspaper to keep them warm until you got home with them. And
that were a dinner, you see, them days.

"There was wet fish shops, too," Barbara continues. "Fish were
very fresh on a Tuesday and Friday. It'd come from t' seashore by the
night train packed in ice and were good. But not on Thursday night.
By then, it were already getting smelly."

Often the chickens bought at the poultry shop had to be plucked
and cleaned. This was a job Ralph did with help from Barbara—as
they drowned new kittens together, too. Rabbit was not unusual
fare. Once our Doris planned a rabbit dinner for a young man's visit.
When she "were out t' kitchen for a minute," the cat jumped up on
the table and began eating the carcass.

Throwing such good meat away was unheard of. Doris simply
washed it off, put the rabbit eaten-side down in the pan and cooked
it anyway.

Green grocery was separate; Ralph tuned a green grocer's pianos
and would collect his fee in kind.

Off-license grocer's shops did sell a little of everything "from yeast
to firelighters, beer to milk." They were called "off-license" because
they were licensed to sell beer to go off the premises. You took your
own jug to them for milk or—if you weren't Mormon—beer. Barbara
remembers "tripping along t' sidewalk, dancing a coin in t' empty
jug," singing a little song she made up:

An 'a' penny milk an' an 'a'penny back

to help remember what she was to buy and what change bring home.
That would be skim milk, probably. The Whitakers would buy milk
from the milkman who came to the door, too. He brought a big
five-gallon can and a pint dipper to measure it into your own jug.
The family bought milk frequently but never in large quantities.
There was no refrigeration, and it would sour quickly otherwise.

In the off-license shop, "we children was al'ays most interested in
t' 'spice' or the candy jars with 'ard pear drops, 'pinehapple' drops,

raspberry drops, and fishes, jelly babies, licorice allsorts, and mint 'umbugs."

Sometimes a girl would be sent to the corner shop with a little mug to buy that mug full of jam out of the big pot. An alternative to the ladylike voice story of their budding romance tells that when Ralph first tasted Mary Jane's homemade strawberry jam, that's when he fell in love with her. She always did try to make one batch a year. But it was quicker and easier to run down to the shop, especially when the missionaries dropped in unexpectedly. That would call for "pudding"—dessert—something the household usually did without. The easiest thing was a slab of parkin, rich with ginger and poured over with egg custard, or "jam roly-poly"—jelly roll. Jam pasty was also possible.

Any sort of pasty: mint pasty, currant pasty, pasty with raisins. Pasty is close to what we in the U.S. call a pie. It comes in so many variations, yet is so much the same that my younger sister invented the name "rice pasty" to describe Grandma's attempts at Chinese cooking. "Yorkshire salsa" is "tomahto" sauce without a trace of heat or garlic.

On Pancake Tuesday (more commonly known as Mardi Gras or Shrove Tuesday in America) there would be lots of pancakes yellow with eggs baked on a griddle over the open fire. Barbara remembers one such day when all the girls were sick with the mumps, and their pancakes were made with what they called "Egyptian eggs"—tiny Bantam eggs that were twenty-four for a shilling, very cheap.

Of course, there were bakers, and bread was a penny or tuppence a loaf, rising to 9d. only in the worst days of the war. But most of the Whitaker baking was done at home. Mary Jane used olive oil in her recipe and solved many a Relief Society crisis with a loaf of bread. At home, they ate great quantities of bread: sandwiches, toast, bread and jam, bread with gravy on it to finish a meal and, of course, drippin' 'n' bread. When they first moved into the house on Moulson Street, they had to rake the fire out of the oven and shove cinders under the loaves to bake. It took a lot of know-how to keep that oven at just the right temperature by adding fuel throughout the process.

Six or eight loaves of bread went into the oven at once and two whole stones of flour (twenty-eight pounds) would be kneaded together. Auntie Hannah remembers standing "on a little buffet," helping to knead in the great big yellow bread bowl. Usually, there were two such bakings a week, that bread was such a staple. When the loaves, all nineteen of them, had cooled, they were carried down to the cellar to be put in earthenware crocks with lids on.

All those trips up and down the cellar steps for everything that needed to be kept cool! My only disillusionment about "them days" was that Mary Jane used white flour instead of stone ground. It was cheaper because it kept better in the shop.

Food at home, when not taken to the cellar, was kept in a big wooden "safe" that Ralph built with a wire screen door to keep out insects and mice. There were mice, which was why Mary Jane always kept a cat. Cheese traps were set, too, our Barbara's task. Once she shocked everyone by catching a little mouse in her bare hands and showing it off to everyone. Ants posed a problem, as well, which were fought with boiling water poured on the hole. The safe, of course, did not keep things cool, but good management (and hungry mouths) kept most things from ever going bad before they were eaten.

I can see them all now in my mind's eye, "sat 'round t' table" as they must have been "them days": table leaves stretched between chairs to make benches to seat three or four, side tables to lengthen the main table so they could all eat together. Ivy and Frances sit side by side then as they do now. If Ivy ever ate a bit of fat (including drippin'), she'd throw up, but our Frances loves fat, and will help herself to any piece she sees (on Ivy's plate or yours) to mash into her potatoes and gravy. But our Frances cannot eat cooked carrots, turnips, parsnips, or lumps of onion. She'll toss a spire of root taken by mistake onto Ivy's plate with the well-primed fork clutched in her left hand.

So betwixt them both, you see, they kept the platters clean.

I can see it before me because I've been there, at Auntie Ivy's in Rose Park.

Then, as now, grace is often sung. There's a sudden hush in the chaos of voices. Uncle Arthur hums a pitch and we begin.

Oh, how I love the meals when everyone is here, from bass to moving tenor on through to the top-heavy sopranos!

Praise God from whom all blessings flow.
Praise Him, all creatures here below.
Praise Him above ye heavenly host.
Praise Father, Son, and Holy Ghost. A-men.

This isn't Mormon. This is so British.

I'm always glad we all have our heads bowed, for tears come at the beauty of it.

CLOTHING
(OUR FRANCES SEWS)

~

I WON'T LET MY CHILDREN OUT OF MY LAP at my grand-mother's when they are small. Pins litter the rug in every room. She's not seeing so well—"I'll never see t' stars again," she says—and what once passed as precious change for a farthing now often slips through her fingers. She's still sewing, though. From that first day at "four year old," (some insist three) "dissatisfied wi' 'er pants," my grandmother has sewn, twelve, eighteen hours a day.

When I was much younger, she would sew uniforms for all the pep clubs in town. If her sewing room was black and white, Highland High was having their fittings. Red and black was the West High Panthers, red and white what would be my own East High or maybe even the University of Utah.

She also made Miss Utah's wardrobe every year. Photos cut from the paper are not for the sake of this year's beauty, but for the smart pink suit with a Jackie Kennedy pillbox hat she's wearing, Grandma-made.

So what did I learn from this intersect of the world of the Myth and the world into which Grandma's following the Myth had dumped me? Me, who had to keep quiet for hours on end while Salt Lake's most popular teenagers trooped into the house in the Avenues. They trooped in and dismissed me with distaste. With one glance, they knew that fat, nearsighted little girl, bursting out of the seams of a dress patched together of last year's red-and-white remnants, with such a grandmother, would never belong to their club. They turned with relief to the three-sided mirror instead.

What did I learn from that being quiet besides that we don't write our foolish stories about giants and fairy princesses on the white bass and high notes of the piano because Grandma had failed to provide me with paper? She thought I'd be content with a crochet hook and some yarn unraveled from an old sweater. I liked how the yarn smelled—of my grandfather and his cigarettes—but it didn't make a story.

Don't put any hope in your clothes. Not in your looks at all. They will get you nowhere, only scornful glances. That's what I learned.

I did learn to sew. I even like it, although the machine is piled with manuscripts these days. This is not because of my grandmother, but because my mother hates it, having had to learn from her mother. These things have to skip a generation, at least when certain personalities are involved.

Once I asked Grandma, who "'as t' button 'oler," to provide a blouse I'd made for a friend with buttonholes, marking carefully where each should go and providing the fancy buttons. I was reduced to tears of frustration when she'd put them where she wanted them. The blouse was ruined.

I understand why my mother hates to sew, why she bought all our clothes from Deseret Industries instead (as I do now). But none of this helped me through high school.

A woman in France, so I'm told, can hold fashion and existential philosophy in her mind at the same time. In my experience, the ambitions are mutually exclusive, as exclusive as different buttonholes in that same expensive blouse material would be. The French have it easy. The French don't have pep clubbers tossing their curls, flashing their straightened teeth, changing into purchased matching skirt and sweater sets, shaking their pompoms, swishing a perfectly synchronized swish of my grandmother's perfect red-and-white pleats. A football field full of the West High Pantherettes gratified my grandmother more than her own granddaughter ever could. And Miss Utah—

That's what I learned, my grandmother's granddaughter in Salt Lake City.

～

My grandmother is such a good seamstress because clothes are so very important to her. Even today, her first comment upon arrival is about something new she's wearing: new pockets in her beloved fake leopard-skin coat, a new purple sateen lining—scraps from last week's bridesmaids' gowns—on an already loud-patterned polyester dress, new pink plastic beads, a huge red silk rose to add interest and color to the black dress she remade from one the neighbor threw out. Grandma will perform with the ward orchestra in this rose. Everyone else will be sober black so as not to detract from the music, but Grandma will have her rose.

Most of the lectures we had to endure from childhood until now are about how we should "make an effort to look nice," "boys 'ave to look at you first," and "men like their wives to take care with their dress, don't you, Kierth?" Never does it occur to her that we, like her own mother, might long for a man who considers our souls first, or that there might be something more important than fashion, such as comfort or practicality. Oh, the all-white wool summer suits we have endured! Oh, the gussets and loud bows emphasizing curious body parts.

Grandma often brings us fashion magazines—we never bothered with them ourselves—having just discovered a model that looks "just like our Franny, don't you think?"

"Well, maybe," Fran mutters under her breath. My sister inherited the fashion gene with modern improvements, no sewing and much more cash, as well as—to her eternal mortification—the name. "Maybe—on a bad day."

"Wouldn't you like me to make you a dress just like she has on?"

"No, thanks, Grandma."

"I could put a gusset in 'ere and some nice little tucks in the sleeve—" In the orange fabric she calls "red" and insists on matching such colors together in remnant lengths of nylon.

"No, thanks, Grandma." Sometimes one has to be quite firm.

You'll notice she never offers to make a dress for my dumpy body.

⤳

Barbara remembers "our Frances" at the sewing machine at ten. Grandma will only confess to beginning to sew at twelve "from necessity." Her mother had taken the four younger girls to a little country cottage for the summer "for our Nellie." They had begun to notice that there was something wrong with this daughter and hoped the fresh air might do her some good. Left alone in the city to keep her first half-time job at the factory, Frances found that her everyday dress no longer fit her across the shoulders and at the wrists. If a new pair of sleeves was not put in, it would never last until next Whitsunday. In fact, it wouldn't last another week.

"They must 'ave looked a sight," Frances remarks about this uninstructed attempt to perform one of sewing's most difficult operations: set-in sleeves. But at least they lasted until her mother came home and showed her how to do it properly.

"Your grandmother 'as a natural talent," every sister says. "But our 'Annah—she 'as persistence. 'Ow many tears she shed learning what came so naturally to our Frances." Through those tears, Hannah eventually learned the skills necessary to work in a sewing shop and, like all the aunties, to make their own clothes. But she never did it with the sheer joy of our Frances.

By the time our Mona was old enough to begin sewing projects of her own, Frances helped her instead of her mother. "Oooh, I 'ad to keep me mouth shut," Mona recalls. "Our Frances were so superior. It 'ad to be done just so."

I know what that's like.

Frances helped Mona make two new dresses when she started secondary school, at about twelve. They were "like milkmaids' dresses," of blue-and-white gingham check. Frances also made her a beautiful black velvet dress with bright orange silk lining for her first dance at the school.

Number 4 Moulson Street "were a 'ouse full o' petticoats" in spite of the fact that each girl got only one new dress a year. The new dresses

were made for Whitsunday, when they became best dress worn only on the Sabbath. Last year's dress then became the dress for weekdays. The dresses were usually dark colors and made of wool. White, starched pinafores were worn over them.

The girls knit their own black wool over-the-knee stockings using four needles from a very young age.

"It took so long to make a stocking." Doris hated the job.

Barbara, on the other hand, loved to knit and does so to this day. Mona remembers the first day her mother went and bought a ready-made pair of woolen stockings for her. In her haste, Mary Jane got navy blue instead of black. It was already Sunday before she realized her mistake. Then it was too late to take them back, and Mona got to wear her first pair of lovely navy-blue stockings.

They made their own underwear, too, with crochet on the bloomers and crocheted camisoles.

Much of this needlework was learned or at least perfected in school. Auntie Violet remembers being required to bring a stocking from home for a darning lesson. Looking in the drawer, she chose the one with the biggest hole, thinking, "Won't it be summat if I mend this!" She made such a mess of that big hole that the teacher made her stand on a chair in front of the class all day, holding up her shame.

Auntie Mona, on the other hand, remembers being allowed to ring the bell at school for a whole week for having the neatest knitting.

Mary Jane made all her daughters' clothes—when they didn't make their own. With a weary sigh, Violet remembers having to stand for hours "this way, and then this way" as the clothes were fitted.

"We was al'ays pinning summat," Grandma remembers. As a teenager, "our Doris were al'ays called back into t' house to pin up a neckline that were too low."

Shops would sometimes give a paper of pins as change when they didn't have a little copper farthing piece. Pins stuck in pinnies served as currency in childhood games. There were always pins in mouths while a seam was mended or straightened, pins on the floor.

Once our Hannah swallowed a pin—right down—when she was quite young. "Eee, I've swallowed a pin," Grandma remembers her saying in a small, weepy voice. They took her to have an x-ray—a device newly invented—and sure enough, there was a pin inside her. "It were a miracle" that, with "castor oil, castor oil, castor oil" it passed right through her and caused no harm.

The girls always tried to look their best and make do with what they could sew or mend themselves. Violet remembers being jealous of the little girl she sat next to in school. One day they had to share a book to read a history lesson. Rather than reading, Violet, "wi' a 'ole in me 'ead," spent her time looking at her companion and daydreaming: "If on'y I'd 'air like 'ers. If on'y I'd a dress like 'ers. If on'y I'd a ribbon like that—"

"Violet!" the teacher snapped. "Come out and tell us what you've read."

Violet stumbled to her feet and had to confess she had no idea what the lesson was about. She was sent back to try again.

"Monday, washday, Tuesday, iron—" Although each girl had only two dresses apiece, both made of wool so they were neither of them ever washed, laundry was still a massive, hard, and drab project. The dresses were sandwiched in between the underwear and petticoats inside and pinafores outside. "Everybody looked twice as fat as we really was 'cause of all them clothes we 'ad to 'ave to keep warm," Auntie Violet remarks. These innermost and outermost layers were what got washed.

Auntie Barbara, with her ever-great interest in the details of hard work, gives most of the following description.

By the fireplace in the kitchen was a "set pot"—a big pot made of iron with stone built all around it. It came with a "piggin," a half-gallon-sized enamel mug to ladle the hot or cold water in. Underneath the "set pot" was a little place where a fire could be started. The clothes were put in this pot and boiled: "It were t' one way of gettin' 'em clean; now you've got such a lot of good detergent 'at you don't need to do that."

After the clothes were boiled, they were lifted with the dolly stick into the dolly tub, which "were as big as a garbage can" and set on wheels. Across the top, the dolly tub had a bar through which the dolly stick was threaded once the clothes were in. The end of the dolly stick "were summat like a three-legged stool. An' then you worked it like this—oooh, talk about 'ard work! It took skill to work it backwards and forwards amongst t' clothes," doing manually what agitators do in machines today.

In the dolly cycle were usually added either "dolly blues" or "dolly yellows," sheets of paper one bought at the chemist's permeated with dye. Blue was put in with handkerchiefs and aprons to make them look a brilliant white. ("You'd al'ays to 'ave an 'andkerchief", what with no Kleenex and frequent colds.) Yellow gave curtains an old-lace tint, and curtains had to be washed quite often, what with the soot from the fires.

One day during the war when Mary Jane was sick in bed, Ralph decided he would do some washing himself. He got the boxes mixed up, however, and put dolly yellows in a load of handkerchiefs. How terribly dingy they came out that time! And when he went to the pub that evening to play, the men commented on his yellow-stained hands: "Ralph, 'as' tha a new job in t' munitions fact'ry? 'Ow shall we get on wi' t' war now, blind men making us weapons an' all?"

Finally the dolly tub was rolled over to the wringer where the clothes were fed through two great wooden rollers turned with a crank at the side. Frances remembers once when Hannah got her fingers caught in the wringer. "Everything 'appens to our 'Annah. Mother gave her a banana to make her feel better."

Although my grandmother doesn't much care for them now, bananas were an unheard of luxury then. She says, "I'd 'ave put me own fingers through t' wringer for a banana. But I never got nothing." She still washes everything with a wringer washer in the basement of the house of Tenth Avenue.

As time went on, Ralph made every effort to get each new washing machine that came out for his wife. They had everything from a great rolling iron machine and a "steamer" that cleaned the clothes with hot steam, to one of the first electric machines. I suspect he was as interested in them as toys as he was to help out with the washing for ten people.

Drying clothes in a humid climate like England was no easier or less tedious than washing them. Sometimes it took two or three days. Some, like Ralph's mother, set up lines right across the street in front of their back-to-back houses. If a cart needed to get by, the driver would shout out, "Coal man!" or "Dustman!" and the house-wife would have to run out and prop up the line with a pole or mop end so he and the horse could drive by.

The house at Moulson Street was fortunate, however, in having a backyard, and here the clothes were hung. Sometimes as many as eight lines threaded the space and filled the whole yard. Frances liked to hang clothes, but usually you'd no sooner get them hung out than "down 'd come t' rain" and you'd have to rush to bring them all inside again.

Inside, most people dried their clothes on clothes horses set up around the fire. Ralph, however, wouldn't have a clothes horse in the house 'cause he'd trip over it. He rigged up a system of racks that hung from the ceiling of the kitchen and could be raised or lowered with a pulley.

On cold, wet nights, Mary Jane would hang up all the clothes, then stoke the fire and go to bed. The house would fill with steam, even when she was careful to leave a window open.

One morning, when they woke up, the window she had left open was down. "Somebody's been 'ere," Ralph said. Later he found out who it was: the neighborhood bobby out on his beat that night had taken advantage of the open window to come in out of the miserable weather and warm himself by the fire.

"Policemen in England," Violet explains at the end of this story, "are not like they are 'ere." They'll come in and have tea with you and get to know most of the people on their beat, not just the trou-blemakers. Violet remembers once when her own children left their little cart in the front yard. That night, she and her husband heard someone moving by the side of the house. Alarmed, they got up to investigate. It was only the bobby, who tipped his hat and said, "Just moving t' cart 'round to t' back, missus. We've 'ad some stolen recently."

The friendly police demeanor that she grew up with got my mother thrown off jury duty once here in the States. The lawyer asked if she would believe the testimony of a policeman over that of an ordinary citizen. (The "ordinary citizen" was the young man sitting very uncomfortably in a borrowed suit, looking suspiciously like one of her Head Start fathers.) She replied, "Of course," and was immediately dismissed "for cause." "I thought the policeman, the judge, and I were a team," she complained. "I assumed we were all hoping to see justice done." She has obviously not watched enough television.

When she was in her teens, my grandmother liked to wait up until everyone else had gone to bed and then do her own washing by herself. She would hang it up and then wake early and take it down before anyone else got up. She says this is because she wanted to save her mother work. This seems to be only a secondary virtue. The main reason for her action was that she was as particular about how her clothes were washed as she was about how they were sewn.

One night when my grandmother had all her clothes hung, Hannah pushed the kitchen table under the rack. On the table was a lamp—one with a tall glass chimney that periodically had to be washed of soot. The flame shot up that chimney and caught all the clothes on fire. What a time they had tearing down the clothes and throwing them in buckets of water! Hannah certainly felt the brunt of my grandmother's wrath that night!

Finally there was ironing. Tongs were used to fill a box-iron with glowing charcoal. They also used the same old, black, heavy, flat irons (they really are "irons") that we use now for decorative paper weights. After setting it into the clear red fire, a girl grabbed the handle with a folded up towel and tested it by setting a wet finger on it to hear it bubble.

"I like that sound," I exclaim.

Uncle Noel surprises me when he mutters, "I 'ate it," dropping his aitch with the passion. He'd run from the room when he heard it as a boy, as if someone were dragging his fingernails across a chalkboard. No doubt something Freudian to do with his mother and her passion for clothes.

Uncle Arthur has more reason to "'ate" the sewing: when he was very small, Grandma's heavy-duty sewing machine swung down on its hinges and hit him on the head. A weakness remains in his left hand from this accident and kept him from ever fulfilling his dream of becoming a concert pianist. But he is not so outspoken as his older brother Noel.

Capes seem to have been what made a "bobby-dazzler" ("all fer t' boys 'n' all") in Grandma's youth. "I went to London to visit our Barbara in a cape," she says in a flirtatious tone that even now must make her poor mother quake in her grave.

"But I never did anything wrong," Grandma insists. "I wouldn't do anything wrong."

"But isn't fashion sex, Mother?" Uncle Noel interjects. A few moment's discussion of this philosophy is required.

Grandma, as usual, simply cannot abstract sufficiently to get any-where. She ends up justifying her point of view with "'ats."

"We all wore 'ats them days," she says. "'Ats wi' feathers, posies, cherries. Ivy 'ad such a lovely 'at wi' a big blue bow on to go to America. I made 'er a coat, too. A right smart coat what tapered at t' knee and fastened at t' side, mandarin style. You know, there were a young man took a fancy to 'er on t' boat. 'E would 'ave married 'er, too, if—"

"Fashion is sex." Uncle Noel thinks his point is won.

Everyone has his delusions.

◠

No doubt there's something Freudian about shoes as well.

Shoes for everyday were clogs. The girls' great-grandfather (father's mother's father) "were a clogger." Any pair of shoe uppers could be taken to him to be fitted with a pair of wooden soles. Ivy once had some made from a pair of real button boots.

"Oooh, I were jealous of 'er," Frances says.

Their great-grandfather also made Mona some real little red clogs for a doll—which the dog chewed up on Christmas Day.

On the bottom of the sole, clogs would be fitted with iron bands "like horseshoes" to keep the wood from splitting. This added to the clatter on the cobbles. Ralph, who had also learned to make clogs at the York Blind School, used to hammer little bits of leather in between these "taps" to make them wear longer and quieter.

"They were too 'eavy for me feet," my grandmother says. She used to kick "one against t' other" and always had sores on her ankles.

Why do I think a lot of this had to do with the fact that this was poor folks' footwear, fashion conscious as she still is? Their father gave her special dispensation, and she got to wear regular shoes every day.

Sunday required no less walking than any other day. Nonetheless, all the Whitakers contrived to have real shoes for the Lord's Day and the one-way hour's walk to Westgate Hall.

One Sunday Doris had a pair of brand-new shoes, but on the walk to church, she had to pull Hannah off into a side street. "Eee, our 'Annah, change shoes wi' me. These nip my feet so's I can't walk in 'em." How lucky Hannah felt that day! A pair of brand-new shoes for church! Usually by the time they got to her, the fifth one down, shoes were all worn out.

They used to have to buy boys' shoes for Barbara because she had hammer toes that hurt, sometimes even when the shoe had that extra breadth.

Ralph used to go to "bankrupt sales" and buy up all the shoes. He'd bring them home in a big sack, dump them out in the middle of the living room floor, shouting, "Right, then. Take what you can use!" There'd be a scramble for the best, trying to make them fit like Cinderella. Anything that fit at all or might possibly be grown into was kept. The rest Ralph took to the home of a blind friend who also had a large family.

Ralph used to mend all his family's shoes himself, hammering on the last shoe he owned. At Bradford's Blind Institute, there was some talk of teaching the young men to cobble, but the city aldermen said that would be impossible, given the handicap. One alderman, however, knew my great-grandfather. He brought a big carpet bag to 4 Moulson Street and asked him to fill it with shoes he'd mended. Then the alderman took the bag to the council's next meeting and dumped the contents, all the Whitakers' shoes, on the floor in front of them.

"There," he said. "A blind man's done this, an' 'e taught 'imself. Just think what they could do wi' summat instruction."

A cobbling class was added to the curriculum.

For wintertime skating on the frozen pond in Wibsey Park, our Frances had a pair of old button boots. Such things were out of fashion by then, but "I didn't care!" They served very well in place of real skates. And they were much more practical than the fine white pumps she once wore when she took the three babies to the park in a little wagon. It began to rain. By the time she reached the top of Bowling Old Lane, soaking wet and dragging at that wagon full of three wailing sisters, there was nothing left of those wonderful new pumps. "An' me mother warned me not to wear 'em!"

Our Violet used to like to clean her father's boots for him. For polish, they used "blacking what come in packets an' you'd to mix it up in an old saucer or tin," using water or spit or—in other houses—tea to make it the right consistency. Once her father gave our Violet a whole shilling for her efforts.

"Eee," my grandmother says. "She were the favorite."

"It were worn thin," Violet protests. "'E thought it were a ha'penny. An' I says, 'Eee, Dad, that's a shilling.'" Usually he could tell a shilling because they "'ave a ridge on t' edge."

~

Many years later, stuck inside an old pair of winter boots, Auntie Barbara brought a pair of my great-grandmother's shoes with her to America. They are solid brown leather and have thick two-inch heels—soles much mended by Ralph's neat, fancy broguing—and lace up with many tiny eyes. Somehow they ended up in our dress-up box and appeared in many a skit as granny and school marm's shoes over the years. At some point, I decided such a life was too indignant for them. The leather is tearing now and cracking in the Utah dryness. Once every two years or so I find an occasion special enough to bring them out and wear them myself.

I cannot gratify Grandma and be dainty, but her mother's feet and my big clumsy ones are just the same size.

Our Violet Is Born and Our Mona Sees the Elephant

THE MOST IMPORTANT RITUAL of Christmas dinner "them days were t' plum pudding." My great-grandfather Ralph used to sprinkle raisins all around it, dowse it with brandy, and light it on fire. (Remember—this is a blind man!)

Fire dancing across the surface of the pudding, all the little girls would try to snatch at the raisins and pop them in their mouths, flaming hot. Inside the pudding would be hidden various things: a thimble, which meant you were going to be an old maid, a ring, which meant the opposite, and a shiny silver sixpence or a thrup'nny bit, which portended wealth.

My own grandmother puts dimes, quarters, or half-dollars in hers. Once there was a silver dollar after one of her (always successful) jaunts to Las Vegas.

English plum pudding, "with a stake of holly through his heart" as Scrooge cursed all who go around with "Merry Christmas" on their lips, is an acquired taste. Think fruit cake batter boiled in a muslin bag for ever-so-many hours. They never had it more frequently than I did, but they certainly seem to relish it more.

At first, those in my generation thought it was the brandy that tasted so bad. We pleaded that only half of the pudding be fired. Now I realize that there aren't even any plums in the concoction—at least, not the way Grandma makes it—but only things like carrots and treacle. The nuts are usually hand-cracked, too. Where Grandma has the patience to pick out seams twenty times (not that they ever need it), she never bothers to pick out broken bits of shell.

Bah, humbug.

Christmas was always Ralph's busiest time. Everyone wanted their pianos tuned so they could sing carols and have entertainment during the holidays. He just couldn't do it all.

It was a busy time for the girls, too. Father Christmas wouldn't come, they were told, unless the house was spotless. So there "were a reg'lar thorough cleaning" from the attic to the cellar.

Baking had to be done as well. The Christmas cakes used to be made quite a while before Christmas and set in crocks to ripen. My own mother remembers how three cakes were always made in her house above and beyond the number required for Christmas itself. Two were for her brothers' birthdays, which were both within a week of Christmas. The third was for her birthday; it would be left to ripen clear until the end of April when her mother would decorate it with marzipan and the first spring violets. Mincemeat and Christmas plum pudding had to be made, too.

Our Barbara would always climb up and find the presents from Uncle Edgar her mother had hidden. On top of the "safe" in the kitchen or in the closet in her mother's room—it didn't matter where they were hidden, Barbara would find them.

The house was decorated with chains made of red, green, and white paper. This was a pleasant task for whichever child was sick in bed around Christmas—and "there al'ays were at least one." Candles, little elves, and black golliwogs ("like on t' marmalade jars"—rather grotesque blackamoors) went on the mantle.

The Christmas tree was artificial, used over and over each year. It was only a little one that sat in the middle of the table. But the girls all thought it was beautiful, "an' as big as could be," this new tradition made popular by Queen Victoria and her German consort. Real candles trimmed it: "You'd to watch it all t' time" so there were no accidents. Instead of the glass baubles we're used to, confections such as a sugar pig or a candy birdcage or a chocolate watch were the decorations.

"On Christmas Eve," Grandma relates, "Dad would come 'ome, tired but 'appy, with a big sack of oranges an' apples on his back." He would throw his hat in first, and the girls would run to meet him. That evening around the fire he would read the story of the First Christmas from his Braille Bible. And before they went up to bed, each girl would hang her stocking on the great fire guard. They were plain black stockings from everyday, stockings they had knit themselves, though carefully chosen to be without holes as a testimony to Father Christmas of their tidiness.

When they got to be about twelve years old, the girls would start to go out with the carolers, usually a group from the church. They wouldn't begin their rounds until midnight, and then they'd start off with "Christians Awake!" They'd sing outside the home of a person they knew, and then sing just walking down the street. The cold air seemed to be full of music, for all over the city, groups were out making merry, carols rising on their frosty breath.

"They'd generally finish up at our 'ouse," Auntie Doris remembers. "They'd come in, 'alf dead, and rest on t' floor or on t' stairs." On the long staircase leading up, "there'd be somebody on every stair. And we 'ad, before 'and, made a number of mince pies and things to offer them." Muscatel raisins and almonds in candy dishes stood "instead of chocolates."

Twenty-five years later, Doris returned to England during the war. Her father had just died and, instead of carols, "there was a bomb went off early Christmas morning and killed a family a few streets over. It were one of them buzz bombs, wi'out a pilot.

"'Ow different, I thought, from when I were 'ere before."

Early Christmas morning, Father would get up and go down to light the fire as he did every day. This special day, however, they would hear him talking up the chimney in a voice like Father Christmas. "On t' top shelf in t' kitchen, right at t' far back, our Ivy, Father Christmas 'as left thee some 'air ribbon."

"Eee, I thought, she's favored," says Auntie Hannah, the listener, who remembers this. "She's got some 'air ribbon."

Then, "Our 'Annah, for thee there's some nuts and candies behind t' piano."

Then their father would open up the piano and begin to play:

Christians, awake, salute this 'appy morn,
Whereon the Savior of this world was born!
Rise to adore the mystery of love
Which 'osts of angels chanted from above.
With them the joyful tidings first begun
Of God Incarnate and the Virgin's Son,
Of God Incarnate and the Virgin's Son.

Only then were all the little girls allowed to come trooping down.

They never got much in the way of gifts, never more than would fit in the stocking: an apple, an orange, a shiny new penny Father had gone to the bank special to get, a new handkerchief, a bit of hair ribbon. Doris always wanted a book with pictures, but Mother said they couldn't afford it.

Mary Jane used to buy little wooden dolls with painted features, dress them in scraps, and stick them in the stockings. "We longed for the big china dolls we saw in the stores," Auntie Doris says, "but they wasn't for us. We knew they wasn't for us, and so we were content."

My own grandfather did once actually get some coal—and nothing else. His family couldn't afford anything else that year; he was glad to have it to help heat the house. Even in Salt Lake, a sack of coal is the best gift you can get my grandmother; you go down to the rail yards to get it and keep it hidden out "in t' garage until after Christmas dinner."

"I do love a coal fire," she says, working her poker at it with her left hand and adding all the wrapping paper too torn to keep for next year as our gifts are revealed.

The girls remember a few prized gifts, but perhaps only for the items' short and tragic lives. Mona got that pair of little red clogs for a doll from her great-grandfather, but the dog chewed them to pieces. Doris got a set of real little wooden furniture, but the son of a friend of her father, come for a Christmas visit, sat on them and purposely broke them.

My grandmother was given a football. "I guess I were summat boyish," she says. "They did call me Frances, so they must 'ave wanted a boy, at least." She took it out on Christmas morning to play in the street. A boy kicked it and burst it. "That were me Christmas."

"That were me Christmas" is a chorus my own children say whenever something disappoints.

But there were more important things than gifts.

My mother remembers one Christmas dinner at her grandparents' during the war. There were her grandparents and our Nellie, Frances's five, Hannah's four, Violet's five—and one scrawny chicken among them. "That was the best Christmas."

The day after Christmas was Boxing Day in England. That day, all the men in service professions—the milkman, the night soil men, the coal man—would come around to the house for a tip. As an example of their mother's ladylike qualities ("She spoke real English, not Yorkshire") the girls cite the story of how a man came to the door and said broadly, "'Av cum fer t' larns."

"I'm sorry," Mary Jane replied. "We have no larns."

Ralph was on a stepladder behind her at the time, fixing a clock. He laughed so hard he nearly fell off. "I've come for the allowance" was the translation. The man had come for his tip; Ralph quickly gave him one.

The final rite of the holidays was a little party on Old Year's Night. (We say New Year's Eve here, as if to emphasize the brash newness of all things American, we who, as teenagers, had no patience with a "party" that consisted of no more than sitting around playing parlor games with a lot of old people.) The tree was untrimmed at this party and packed away for next year. Their father would hold a lottery with the prizes being the confections that had served as trimmings. Each girl got one or maybe two sweets, and that way they didn't feel so bad about Christmas coming to an end.

Over the years I've come—no, not to love plum pudding.

That's too much to ask. But I do cry out at the suggestion that it's too much work to steam one this year. Today, for me, the Christmas gorge is incomplete without a hefty spoonful, brandy and all. Drowned in plenty of egg custard, warm, slightly bitter spice, it's like an old fuzzy blanket in the belly. Grandma's woolly. I eat it for my sins, which life in Zion does not let one escape.

When my own mother was growing up, a great part of the ritual was still to go for Christmas Day dinner at Grandpa and Grandma Whitaker's home. Auntie Barbara would dress up as Father Christmas and dispense the gifts.

When they came to Utah, my own grandmother made a red suit with an unraveled white sweater for a curly beard, and first my grandfather and then my father had to take a stab at the charade. Of course, being American children, we called him Santa Claus—if we didn't spoil the fun altogether, as I did as early as five, pulling on his red pants' leg and saying, "Grandpa, Grandpa, look!"

Was it the change in name to Santa Claus or the change from the Whitaker line that lost us the spirit? I must admit the game, complete with phone calls to the North Pole and jingle bells outside the front door, was played with best success the year Auntie Barbara finally immigrated and reclaimed the part. I'd thought I had it all figured out—Grandpa went off to the sewing room and always managed to miss the old elf's arrival because, he said (ha, ha) he'd "'ad a nap." That year he stayed for the whole ritual and made a true believer out of me once again. That year we had a rather stern and unsympathetic Santa, one who wanted a clean house, lacking my grandfather's cigarette smell.

And that, as Grandma would say, were me Christmas.

～

Some of the aunties' tapes run longer, some are shorter.

Auntie Mona and Auntie Violet are the two youngest I interviewed. Mona's is the longest; she is the family genealogist. Violet's the shortest; everyone else seems to have said it all by the time she comes along, even about her own birth.

Grandma, who was eight years old, remembers coming home from school one day in the middle of April just after the move to Moulson Street. She found her mother standing up at the top of the stairs in her nightgown.

"Mother, what's t' matter?" she asked, for she had never seen her mother in her nightgown at four in the afternoon before.

"Run across the road to Mrs. Brooks. Tell Mrs. Brooks I want her."

Frances did as she was told, but she had no idea what her mother wanted the neighbor for. Frances had no idea, at eight going on nine, where babies come from and hadn't even noticed the difference in her mother's shape. "It were better them days," she adds philosophically. "Your thoughts were purer."

Ivy, a year older, was just as innocent. She had been sick that day, another splitting headache. Usually, she had to go to school anyway. But that Friday, wonder of wonders, her mother had let her stay home in bed.

When the doctor came and told her her mother was having a baby, Ivy thought the doctor must have brought it in his little black bag. Then, feeling better, she went out to play with the rest of the girls. "You wouldn't pay no mind."

Used to getting their own suppers, the girls were sent to bed early by Mrs. Brooks, who told them: "Your mother's sick, and you're to be quiet."

Being quiet was difficult. It was still so early; they weren't tired. The girls burrowed under the covers and talked and giggled. Usually, they got in trouble for this. ("It were always Doris," Ivy complains. "I never talked.") They didn't talk about their mother, who never made a sound in the next room, but only of the day and things at school. Then, suddenly, they heard a baby cry in the night. They stopped talking and wondered. Soon their father came in to tell them they had a new baby sister, and that they could go in and see her.

Even Doris, who was nearly thirteen, seems to have shared in the joyful naïveté. She describes how the oval fireplace in Mother's room was lit and surrounded by a big, six-foot screen. "Mother had a little rocking chair before the fire and a little table for the water. Here she'd bath t' baby on her knee." Sometimes she let Doris help "because I was the eldest. I thought it was so cozy and so pretty to see that little tiny mite being bathed."

Only Barbara, always so fiercely practical, has a different tale to tell. Doris, as the eldest, might have been allowed to help with the bathing, but it was Barbara, the most responsible one, whom Mrs. Brooks the neighbor sent to call the midwife.

Barbara found the woman in a house with black crepe weighing down the windows and door, laying out the season's first typhus victim in the bedroom—"something which was absolutely forbidden when I practiced midwifery.

"Our Violet were a breach baby," she continues. "That's an awful birth, buttocks first."

Our Barbara also had to brave the smoky, crowded Red Lion on a Friday night to make her way up to the first-class room to tell her father when mother and baby were delivered well.

"'Ere," her father turned from his next tune. "I almost forgot to ask. What is it?"

"A girl, of course."

Ralph said the whole family might help in choosing a name for that last little girl. Ivy remembers she suggested Rose. Another said Lily and another Daisy. By coincidence, they were all names of flowers. In the end, they called her Violet, a tiny, shrinking flower, because she was so very small and delicate.

The song sung in church the day our Violet was blessed was this:

Earth with her ten thousand flowers
Air with all its beams and showers,
Heaven's infinite expanse,
Sea's resplendent countenance,
All around and all above,
Bear this record, God is Love.

"You'll never raise that one," Grandfather Whitaker told his son Ralph, sadly shaking his head as he looked down at tiny baby Violet.

But the record in the family Bible now stood complete:

Ralph Robinson Whitaker m. 4 May, 1897 Mary Jane Jones

Doris May b. 30 Oct, 1897

Ethel Barbara b. 29 Jan, 1899

Ivy b. 27 Mar, 1900

Frances Lyda b. 11 July, 1901

Hannah Maud b. 2 Dec, 1902

Olive Mona b. 8 May, 1907

Nellie Theresa b. 7 Sept, 1908

Violet b. 15 Apr, 1910

～

Our Mona was all set to take her turn on her father's shoulder and go down the road to Ryan Street School when she caught a cold. Within a week, the cold had settled in her lungs. Five or six times a day, she would have coughing fits so bad she would vomit. The fits ended with the telltale whooping gasp for breath that tore at her mother's heart. Instead of going to school, she spent most of the summer coughing and then, slowly, recuperating from the dreaded whooping cough. Only Mary Jane's prayers managed to keep the disease from the rest of her girls.

Finally, come August, our Mona seemed stronger. On a warm and sunny day, to celebrate, Ralph decided to take his whole family—leaving Mary Jane home with only Nellie and little Violet—to the zoo newly opened between Halifax and Ellend. By the time they caught the crowded tram running between Halifax and Salterhebble every two and a half minutes, Mona was showing herself not as strong as they hoped. Our Barbara took her up pickaback, however, and the trek went on.

The zoo stood on thirteen acres of a farm left for civic purposes by a former mayor of the town. Its attractions included a "pleasure city" complete with concert hall and a tea room, its tiny square tables decked with linen. These were not for the Whitaker girls, but plenty of other things for them to see filled the rest of the grounds. A miniature railroad carried them through a mock African native village and ostrich farm. A lion and lioness stalked their cage, a Russian bear played dead in one far corner, a pair of wolves loped, a hyena laughed, and a white Arabian camel spat at anyone who got too close. Arctic foxes suffered in the heat. Rare breeds of ducks and geese from Australia and Japan preened and called; pygmy cattle and pelicans did what such creatures do in rusting cages.

Elsewhere, a family of acrobats built a human pyramid four men high and unfurled three Union Jacks at the top to the patriotic cheers of the crowd. The girls and their father went boating on the little lake, bringing scum up with their oars.

The older girls longed to make the visit last until after sundown when fairy lights were promised around the lake: the King's Cross band would play and there would be fireworks.

Meanwhile, for the younger ones, there were donkey rides and sand to dig in the children's corner.

For his part, Ralph had come to "see"—have described to him— the heroic deeds of the goggled and leather-helmeted flying men in Yorkshire's first airship. He could hear the fragile motor start up, the gasps of the crowd as Herbert Spencer and his assistant Frank Gooden took to the skies in the flimsy bamboo structure. Ralph timed it on his pocket watch as the machine climbed a thousand feet in three minutes. And he marveled only slightly after the fact as one of the brave men, high above the earth, walked out across the body of the frame to check on the engine—leaving the audience speechless and Ralph demanding "What? What?" of his excited girls.

"Aye, but i'n't 'uman progress wonderful," he said then. "What wonders all me lasses will live to see."

Barbara didn't see. She had had to take Mona away from the airshow when those around had complained of the little one's whining.

Barbara and Mona found, instead, the cage of chattering monkeys more accessible now that the crowds were at the airshow. "Look, our Mona. Look at the funny monkeys."

Barbara set her little sister down to rest her arms. Still, she couldn't interest Mona in the antics of the creatures swinging by their tails from dead branches, grooming one another and eating messy handfuls of what looked like porridge. Mona pulled away from the cage, pulled on Barbara's skirt as if afraid of the animals, whining, whining to go home.

That was when the elephant approached. The trainer, under a tweed slouch cap and banded waistcoat, had found no further audience for how he could make one huge, pachyderm foot after another lift in time to his penny whistle. Leading his great charge off by a length of chain, he went for a break behind the monkey cage, the one for a cig the other to drink a trunkful of water out of a low tub. Although this day in August was warm, still that native of Africa must have been miserable in the Yorkshire grey and cold. The elephant "had caught a cold." As our Mona pulled away from the monkeys, the elephant gave a loud, trumpeting sneeze, spraying her with water.

Now Mona ran. Barbara lost sight of her in the crowds. She had to find all the rest of the family and enlist their help before they finally found this littlest one, far at the other end of the park, sobbing and trembling. That ended the outing. All the way home, through the stations of "'Ull and 'Alifax" with 'ell seeming just around the corner, Mona shook in Barbara's arms.

Come morning, the little girl with dark hair and eyes was still trembling and feverish. Mary Jane took her to the Royal Hospital where Mona was quickly whisked away from her to quarantine.

Little Olive Mona had what until very recently had only struck infants and hence was still called infantile paralysis—polio.

"She won't live," the doctors said.

And then, once that crisis had passed, "She'll never walk."

Mary Jane got to her knees.

Mona's first memory of this world is of sitting under the great family's table, eating a lump of sugar she'd stolen from the bowl above. This childish wickedness, rather than the elephant, is what she blames for divine punishment. Her second memory, and everything after, is colored by her touch-and-go time in the Royal Hospital.

There, in an effort to lengthen her one leg to match the other, they cut the tendons clear across. It hurt and she cried.

The day nurse told her to be quiet and when she didn't, spanked her hard.

Mona liked the night nurse better. This woman in her nun-like veil drifted quietly through the ward, stopping to say a little prayer by each afflicted child's bed: one over Mona's friend who would always have to wear a special boot to make her legs match, one over the little boy who did not survive, one over Mona herself.

When at last they allowed Mary Jane in for a visit, she brought Mona a little packet of pink candies, each set on top with a Barcelona nut. Mona was still too sick to eat them.

Finally, they could bring their sixth daughter home. But there was no time to rejoice. Every day showing a scrap of sun, Mona had to be set out in the yard, all bundled in blankets. How her mother labored over her, after all the prayers that had brought her back to life and kept the dreaded disease of summer from infecting the rest of the house. Mary Jane gave Mona warm baths, packed her leg with warm cloths, rubbed it with warm olive oil until the smell clung to both of them. That was when this daughter dropped her first given name, Olive, and began to go by Mona instead.

Ralph, too, gave encouragement. "Come stand on tha leg, lass." Mona had to stand "for hours" on that one leg. "Just through one more chorus of 'Excelsior,'" he'd say.

Still, "she'll never be strong," he had to confess to his wife. "We can't send 'er to t' mill. To be knocked about?"

"She'll never marry, either," Mary Jane agreed.

"We shall 'ave to see that she comes by an education."

"It won't be cheap."

"No, it won't. But some way, some'ow, we shall 'ave to see our Mona to an education."

It would be a tall order for a child who started school late on account of her illness and who could never "trip" (American, "skip") like the others. Still, Mona could already read a bit when she did start, after all those months in bed with no entertainment.

And it was the elephant in Halifax zoo and the zoo itself that died first. By the end of the Great War, both were gone.

And Mary Jane in the kitchen sang the chorus:

All around and all above,
Have this message: God is love.

∼

Mary Jane was often asked, "Which girl do you like best?" The answer comes from every auntie now at once, as once it came so readily to their mother, "Whichever one is sick."

After a reverent pause to let the import sink in, someone has to complain, "Aye, and our Mona 'ad polio."

"Don't forget our Nellie."

"Or our Ivy. She were al'ays sick. 'Is she still alive?' 'e were always asking."

Grandma has to get in the last word. "Aye, an' I were never sick. She never loved me."

Laughter reigns once more.

OUR NELLIE

"WERE THERE EVER ANY ROWS AT HOME, at 4 Moulson Street?"
Uncle Noel, helping with my research although he won't claim it
as his own, asks the congregated aunties and assorted descendants
this question.

"A row—" I have to explain to my very American cousin, "not
what you do with a boat, pronounced differently—is an argument,
a fight."

Wiser grey heads purse their lips, confessing nothing.

The Tabernacle Choir–perfect "Love at Home" must be maintained before the heathen.

Auntie Hannah, the quiet innocent who heard everything, finally
admits she remembers one: "It were our Nellie. She'd lost 'er soother."

"Her what?" my cousin asks.

Not every branch of the family had babyhood peppered with foreign words: "tushy pegs" (not to be confused with the American rear
end), "gob" (not meaning a lump goo comes in), "pandies" (which I
can't find on the internet at all), "nappies" (nothing to do with sies-
tas or table serviettes, either), "swot", "Bovril," and "'eyup." Which
translate as teeth, face, hands (as in "wesh tha pandies"), diapers,
to study or one who studies an excessive amount, that nasty stuff
like bouillon cubes and—well, what is 'eyup? Something like oops or
hoopla, used for surprise or caution.

Auntie Hannah is laughing through her stroke-crooked mouth.
"'Er soother. It were under t' bed. She were cryin' 'er 'ead off."

"She'd lost 'er dumb-tit," the auntie closest to my cousin stifles the question so we can get on with the story.

"She lost what?" my cousin insists.

"'Er dummy."

"What?"

"Me father couldn't stand t' noise," Grandma says. Hannah has spilled the beans. There was a row, and Grandma is obliged to put the best spin she can on it. She knows how to be popular.

"She lost what?"

"Her pacifier," someone finally translates. That stuns the uninitiated into silence.

Finally the cousin bravely dares, "How old was she?"

Hard to say. Turns out our Nellie kept her pacifier till her death—at nearly age fifty.

"Well, that doesn't sound like a great conflict of personalities," Uncle Noel says, thwarted once more in his search for scandal. He was thinking Faulkner, Dostoevsky.

Our Nellie had fits. She'd fall down and bite her tongue. "You'd to shove a spoon in 'er mouth."

Our Nellie had a violent temper, too.

"She'd chatter to 'erself," remembers Auntie Ivy, "and called me 'Avy.' She'd say, 'Our Avy wants some fish and chips' when it were 'er 'at wanted 'em."

And, of all the talk of angels in the house, "our Nellie weret one 'at saw 'em." And an unpleasant cohort they were, too.

My theatrical mind re-creates the scene.

It's closing time at the Red Lion pub on the corner where their father sings and plays. "Come on, Charlie, lad," calls the publican, giving his counter a final swipe with his rag. "Drink 'er up. That's right. We'll see ye on Monday, lads. Good night to ye."

The noises disperse. Ralph taps his cane down the cobbles and quietly closes the front door to 4 Moulson Street as he does every night. The last sound is one final verse of "Ilkla Moor Bat 'At" fading off into the distance.

"Then we shall 'ave t' bury thee."

All is quiet darkness for two beats. Then a frightful scream and a crash shatter the night. Lights come on all up and down the street.

"Good Lord!" says the publican, his head having just hit the pillow in his bed above his establishment. "What were that?"

"Angels!" It's our Nellie—twelve, perhaps, fifteen—screaming in the front bedroom she shares with her parents.

"Nellie! Nellie, dear, what is it?" Barbara and their mother are both at the girl's side. She's standing, staring out the window to the street, yelling, in her nightgown.

In the other room, the other girls groan, pull the covers over their heads and hope the noise won't carry too far. They have to hold their heads up in the neighborhood come morning.

"Angels! Angels!"

"No," says Barbara firmly, "there are no angels."

"Mam, there's angels. Ban't there?"

"Yes, love," says Mary Jane.

Some days—and nights—my great-grandmother's faith must have wavered. Didn't Joseph Smith the prophet see angels? Isn't the angel Moroni on the pinnacle of the temple? Mary Jane had always thought that such visitations were blessed events. How can her careful presentation of God's Truth have become so distorted in Nellie's head? Why, of all her daughters, must this be the one who sees them?

Before her daughters, however, Mary Jane refuses to lose faith. "Guardian angels are with us always. But—"

"Angels!"

Our Nellie is pointing out the window, trembling. And it's not just fright. The window is broken, new-broken, cold, damp air pouring in.

Mary Jane has never heard that the prophet's heavenly visitors broke windows.

"Where? Show them to me," she asks. If only, only she could see them, too.

Our Nellie runs back to bed and pulls the covers over her head.

"There ban't no angels." Our Barbara has found the soother, but it's no use.

"Angels! Angels!"

"You see angels there, dear?" Mary Jane is determined not to destroy the simple faith of a child—terrible though that faith might be.

"Angels! Angels!"

"All right. There are angels there. But angels are good. Our guardians—"

"No! No! Bad!"

"I'm sure they're your guardian angels, lamb. Keeping watch while you sleep."

"Git! Git, you bleedin' angels."

Violet has come timidly to the door. "Mother? What is it? What's wrong with our Nellie?"

Barbara is busy changing the bed over and around the screaming girl. "It's nothing, lass. She's only wet t' bed."

Outside, the publican can't be grateful that someone on the street makes noise, more and later than his establishment. "'Ere! Why don't ye keep it quiet up there?" he calls.

"Angels! Angels!"

"Are they making fun of you, lamb?"

Our Nellie nods vigorously. Not content with setting the neighborhood bullies at her, heaven also sends its minions.

"Come on. Leave off. Let a body get some sleep," shouts Him-Next-but-One who's joined the publican in the street.

"Git! Go 'way!" Nellie throws a wet blanket.

There's pounding on the door, and Ralph goes downstairs to soothe with his cheery demeanor.

"This must be the only house in the world a publican has to yell at to keep quiet," mutters Barbara.

More glass gives up the frame at the blow from the blanket and tinkles into the street.

"'Ere. What tha tryin' to do?" storms the publican. "Kill me? I only said—"

"The only house that tries to kill its guardian angels," Barbara mutters again.

Nellie is poised to throw more things. Mary Jane struggles with her. Barbara tries the soother again.

"'Ere we go! 'Ere, our Nellie. 'Ere's your dummy."

Nellie seizes the pacifier and begins to suck. Things immediately calm.

The girls can still hear the publican's voice raised outside. "I'll call t' police, mind! Tha'r' a good man, Ralph, but that idiot of yours—"

Barbara can't bear to hear the low murmur of her father struggling to cover such behavior with his charm. She calls through the broken glass: "It's all right now. She's calmed down."

She finds Nellie a clean nightgown and thinks about the morning wash.

"Ought to have that one in t' asylum, that's what they ought." The publican delivers his parting shot. "She's not right. Not right at all."

He stumbles over something in the dark street. He picks it up and wants to throw it back, but he restrains himself.

Instead, he hands it to Ralph, grips his shoulder, and re-enters his establishment. Ralph's slow trudge comes up the stairs. He has a bit of cardboard to fix into the broken window.

"Won't get to t' glazier to beg a bit o' glass till Monday," he says.

"What's that?" Mary Jane takes the other thing from his hand. In the light from the quieting lane, she sees it's the glass paperweight, with the lump of coral in it.

~

"Mother wouldn't 'ave a paperweight in t' 'ouse after that," says Violet in the calm of Salt Lake, their sister twenty years dead.

Paperweights are missiles to be hurled at heavenly visitors.

~

"Run me, our 'Annah, run me." Four-year-old Nellie gave herself a good head start, her golden curls bouncing.

"Tha'rt not to run," our Hannah scolded her younger sister. "Tha'll' fall."

But our Nellie paid no mind. School was out for the day, and she was exuberant.

"Tha'll' fall!" Hannah warned again, louder. Guilt tinges her recollection all these years later. Even as she said it, it happened. The little girl tripped and fell full length across the rough cobblestones.

"There. Didn't I tell thee?" our Hannah said as she went to pick her sister up.

But she found herself unable to lift her. Our Nellie, though sobbing heartily, made no move of her own to help the struggle. Ivy, who was twelve, left her older friends further down the street and came to try to pick our Nellie up, too. She couldn't do it either.

At last a friendly man came along and carried her home. "From that day on she were sick and nearly died."

The doctor said she'd caught infection from Mary Jane's lupus and had it all through her body. Violet thinks it must have been appendicitis, because eight years later our Nellie actually did have appendicitis and was able to tell their mother what she had.

Hannah still wrings her gnarled old hands with guilt because she let our Nellie run.

Mona gloats to see the devil dealing just punishment to sinners. She reminds us all that their father's parents were first cousins: "The sins of the fathers visit the children to the third and fourth generation."

My grandmother, never at a loss for words, doesn't want to talk about it. Not a thing about Nellie.

Meningitis may be the most reasonable explanation. Or maybe autism?

There were no specialists to diagnosis, let alone to help treat. Only prayer.

Now it was our Nellie about whom their father asked, "Is she still 'ere?" every night when he came home. Our Nellie lay in a coma for two weeks after her fall.

"You're to pray for our Nellie to live," their father told the huddled family the evening that the elders came and prayed over her for a long time upstairs. All the little girls bent their heads and prayed that their sister would live and live and live.

The prayer was answered. Nellie lived. "But she weren't never right after that."

"Our defective sister," the girls call her.

"Our funny aunt," says Uncle Noel.

Nellie Theresa—the seventh girl, the one Mary Jane named for her own dear little sister who'd died so young, the only one, besides Ivy, who inherited their father's blue eyes and fair, naturally curly hair, "the prettiest girl"—was intellectually disabled.

I actually met Auntie Nellie before I was two. The ginger cat that liked cheese and the lace curtains in a window full of light and the narrow, dark stair are all I remember of Bradford from that time. No shadow of a "funny" aunt. She was dead by the time I was three; she is the only one of the eight I could not interview.

"Oooh, she were a big baby," Barbara says. "It wore me arms out carrying 'er around."

Barbara is also alone in dating the defectiveness to before our Nellie's fall as a four-year-old. Barbara recalls a certain strange hoarseness in her younger sister's voice and how she'd tremble when she'd come down the stairs in the morning, even as a toddler. And Nellie did always sleep in the parent's bedroom in a crib, even after Violet was born. "Our Nellie were sick."

"It were from birth," Barbara insists. "It were some injury she had in utero. My theory is that all people who have mentally defective children don't want to believe they are born like that. If our parents said all these things [the causes the other sisters have given], then it's because they didn't want to believe it either." Perhaps—the unthinkable—it was hereditary, and we are all potential mothers of—

Hannah remembers that she was so quiet their father feared she might be a little off, too. One evening he asked her to say her times tables and was so relieved to hear her recite them perfectly through to twelve that he gave her a whole penny. "That were like the bank to me."

They sent Nellie to regular school for a while. But they couldn't keep her there—she never did learn to read and write. Their father, always a believer in special schools because of what York School for the Blind had done for him, sent her across town on the tram to Macmillan School for children with "deficiencies."

"She were good. She 'elped take another girl on t' bus 'at were summat like 'er an' all," they praise, but "all they taught her at that school—"

And it doesn't matter who's been telling the story thus far. They chime in together now. "Were to swear!"

"She never learnt them words at 'ome."

My own mother's memories of her grandmother are surprisingly vague. All she remembers—the most important thing to be noticed about any woman, to my gardening mother—was a little window box in the kitchen where Mary Jane grew geraniums and maybe some herbs. My mother does remember Grandma Whitaker raising her voice to say one word only, "Nellie!" Nellie was always swearing, and even if she hadn't just sworn, Mary Jane could tell she was about to. The notion of an adult out of control unnerves my mother with her always-stiff upper lip.

Uncle Noel has more vivid memories.

～

Spending the year doing research in Wales and studying at Oxford years later, Uncle Noel comes to Bradford for Christmas. His grandparents are dead by now. Auntie Barbara, still working as a midwife, lives there taking care of Auntie Ethel, Doris's godmother for whom Barbara was named (nursing homes, of course, unthinkable), and Nellie.

"Three pathetic old women."

As his contribution to the festivities, Noel has bought some Spanish grapes from a man in Bradford rail station, and set them up in a vase on the sitting room table. He now sits by the fire with Auntie Ethel, showing her the literary magazine he is editing.

Barbara is out.

Our Nellie, large, untidy, and forty, has said nothing. She sits playing quietly with her "baby" on the top stair until Barbara returns from a late delivery.

Barbara sings the hymn that might be called her personal theme song:

Have I done any good in the world today?
Have I helped anyone in need?

Have I cheered up the sad,
Helped make someone feel glad?
If not, I have failed indeed.
Has anyone's burden been lighter today
Because I was willing to share?
Have the weak and the weary
Been helped on their way?
When they needed my help was I there?
[*Chorus*]
Then wake up, and do something more
Than dream of your mansions above!
Doing good is a pleasure,
A joy beyond measure,
A blessing of duty and love.

And her favorite lines, for when she can't remember the rest:

Only he who does something is worthy to live
The world has no use for the drone.

Chorus again, as she shoves the front door shut with one hip
and trundles in all her parcels: "Then wake up, and do something
more—"

Nellie hears her coming. With shrieks of joy, she clomps down the
stairs and into Barbara's arms, a confusion of hugs and groceries.
"Our Barb'a! Our Barb'a! Our Barb'a!"

"Hullo, our Nellie, dear. How has' tha been today?"

"Our Barb'a! Our Barb'a!"

"Aye, I love thee, too, dear. But look. Look who's here. We've a
visitor. Tha's' made it, Noel, dear lad."

"Hello, Auntie," Noel says. There's no kissing here, no hugging.
We're British.

Most of us.

Barbara takes off her coat and hat and hangs up Noel's things, too,
that he has left draped over a chair. This gives her a chance to say to
Ethel what Noel should not hear: "Hard delivery. But we made it. A
beautiful baby girl—" She stops, having noticed the grapes.

"Our Nellie, lass, did' tha do this?"

"Actually, Auntie—" Noel begins.

"Our Avy do," Nellie confesses.

"Please, our Nellie, tha musna play with Mother's fancy vase," says Barbara, carrying the groceries back into the kitchen. "Tha know' she wouldn't like it." As if their dead mother was bound to walk in at any minute.

"Mother don't like."

"There's a good lass."

Reentering the sitting room, Barbara dismantles the grape stand. "Now, Noel, lad, how good—"

Auntie Ethel speaks up for the first time from her seat by the fire, facing the "enemy"—the draft blowing through the front door and bending the flames up the chimney. "It's Ralph, Barbara."

"Eh?"

"He goes by Ralph these days. He's done all his writing under the name Ralph." Auntie Ethel might not have the strength to do much anymore, but she does read the magazines Noel sends to 4 Moulson Street—if she can get to them before our Barbara uses them to light the fire.

"That were me father's name. I were there the day they blessed him. Weren't we, Nell? They called him Ralph Noel. And weren't Dad pleased!"

"He was only Ralph number three."

"But 'e were t' first in England. T' first Dad took on 'is knee. Come, our Nellie. Don't you remember our Frances's little Noel? Oh, I do think you look more like 'im than any of 'em. That same 'air. Nell?"

Uncle Noel makes an attempt: "Hello, Auntie Nellie."

Our Nellie has been hanging back and scowling. At this advance, she grows violent. "Son of a bitch!"

Barbara smiles awkwardly. "Tha liked to take him on tha knee when 'e were a baby, didn't tha, our Nellie? Tha liked to nurse 'im. Such a skinny little thing 'e were, too, and all red. Just like Dad."

"Red son of a bitch."

Barbara takes on their mother's tone. "Nellie."

"Red and skinny son of a bitch."

Barbara raises a cautionary finger aloft. "Nellie. Jesus is listening to you."

Nellie waves aloft. "Hullo, our Jesus—"

"That's right."

"You damned son of a bitch."

"Please excuse her, Noel."

"It's all right, Auntie," says Noel, a glint in his eye.

Nellie is still looking heavenward. "Tha're a right booger, tha ar'."

Barbara continues her mortified apologies. "She's not quite right, tha know'."

"Indeed." Noel struggles to keep a straight face.

"Tha' scabby-'eaded get," says our Nellie.

"Mother and Dad did t' best they could by 'er," says Barbara.

"I'm sure," says Noel.

"Saved t' aftermath, they did," interjects our Nellie.

Barbara: "Even sent her to a special school, soon as they realized she weren't—"

Nellie: "Threw t' baby away."

"Went on t' bus all by 'erself clear across town, didna tha, our Nellie?

"God damned bleedin' bus."

"She'd go on t' bus with other bairns that were—were a bit like 'er. And she'd look after 'em. Tell 'em where to get on and off and all. Didna tha look' after t' other kids, our Nellie?"

"God damned bleedin' kids."

"They thought they was doing good by 'er, sending 'er to that school. But all that school—"

Barbara and Nellie in chorus: "—Ever taught 'er were to swear."

Our Nellie beams proudly. "'Ell, aye."

Barbara is at her wits' end. "Our Nellie, dear, why don't we—?"

"Tha'r' a right booger."

"'Jesus Wants Me for a Sunbeam,' our Nellie."

"Sunbeam?"

"Yes. Let's sing 'Jesus Wants Me for a Sunbeam.' Then tha can' help me get our tea. Ready?"

Barbara and Nellie sing, our Nellie with a huge explosion on the "beam":

Jesus wants me for a sunbeam
To shine for him each day.
In every way try to please him,
At home, at school, at play.
A sunbeam, a sunbeam.
Jesus wants me for a sunbeam.
A sunbeam, a sunbeam,
I'll be a sunbeam for him.

Once she is certain our Nellie is hooked, Barbara can leave the song. Speaking over the booming "beams," she busies herself about straightening things for tea. "We were a very musical family. Always 'ad music in t' home."

"Soothes the savage beast, eh, Auntie?" comments Noel.

Barbara: "Aye. 'Ere, Noel—"

Ethel, from her corner: "Ralph."

Barbara: "Lend us an 'and with these groceries, willt tha?"

"Certainly, Auntie."

Barbara cannot keep the vanity from her voice: "I've lugged them all the way up t' 'ill meself. Bring them in t' kitchen 'ere. That's right. I'll put them away and then make us some tea. Tha'd' like tha tea?"

"Fine, Auntie."

"I'll make us some."

Busy as she is, our Barbara cannot allow anyone else to sit still, either. Running to put the food away and start the tea, she keeps the others from falling into sloth by calling out her rhythm to them.

"Let's see. Noel, why don't tha take tha things up to t' smaller back bedroom? I've cleared Nellie out of there. She'll sleep with me in t' big room while you're 'ere. Won't tha, our Nellie, dear? A sunbeam, yes, that's right."

"Maybe I'll just stay up there till teatime. I have some books—" Exhausted, Noel is ready to make his retreat.

"Well, all right. Suit thaself, dear. But when tha can', be so good as to—there are a couple of boxes under the bed in there. They're full up of Mother's Christmas decorations. I should have 'ung them a week ago, but I just 'aven't 'ad time. Can' tha bring them down?"

"All right, Auntie."

Barbara on an errand into the sitting room, gives encouragement to Ethel in passing: "Auntie, dear, has' tha dropped tha mending again? 'Ere it is, right by tha chair. There we go. Tha'r' on the same sock tha was last night? Dear, dear. That's right. We need them socks mended."

Noel comes downstairs with a box.

Barbara: "Yes, Noel, dear. That's one of them. Wasn't there two?"

Noel: "Yes, there were, Auntie, but I couldn't carry—"

"Well, go up and fetch t' other one. There's a good lad."

When he comes panting down with the second box, Barbara and our Nellie have gone to bring the Christmas tree up from the cellar. Noel gratefully sits down across the fire from Auntie Ethel.

"Just imagine how it must have been with all eight of them here," says Auntie Ethel.

"This chaos to the third power? No wonder my mother's never had a lucid thought in her life."

"Noel, dear," Barbara calls from the kitchen, "did' tha see the card we got from tha mother?"

"No, Auntie."

She can tell he's sitting down from the other room.

"'Tis on t' mantel there. Why don't tha get it down and read it? She sent a lovely parcel, too, but I've put that away 'til Christmas Day."

Noel speaks in an undertone to Ethel as he shoves himself out of his chair: "Then how do you know it's lovely? White wool. Mark my words. It'll be white wool."

The old woman chuckles at their shared joke.

The mantel stymies Noel. "Which card is it, Auntie?"

"They're in order, dear," answers the unseen Barbara. "Starting with our Doris at t' left and working down all t' sisters to baby Violet. They're all there."

"And all purchased at discount," Noel observes.

"All except Mona," Ethel adds in an undertone.

"Our Mona's hasn't come yet." Barbara puts a good face on what she can't possibly have heard over the clatter in the kitchen. "But there's space for when it does."

"When it does come, it'll be Eastertime," says Auntie Ethel, still sotto voce. "And the parcel with it won't be a parcel at all, but the latest installment of 'The Whitaker Family Genealogy,' a ream thick."

"What does tha mother say, Noel?" calls Barbara. "I'm sorry, I haven't had time to read her letter yet."

Noel: "Hard to say. Her handwriting's impossible to read."

"Yes. Our Frances were left-handed."

"She still is left-handed."

"But at school they made them write with their right."

"I know, I know." Noel is still struggling with the writing.

"She'd get a good caning every time she went for the pen with her left."

"So, lo and behold, today nobody can read a word. Well, yes, it looks like here she says something about a fall fashion show she helped organize for the ZCMI." Noel has an unpleasant visceral reaction to the letters "ZCMI." He worked for the Zion's Mercantile Cooperative the very brief time he spent in Salt Lake.

"Our Frances always were a smart dresser," Barbara comments.

"I'm not sure 'smart' is the word." Janitorial staff at the ZCMI was not a happy experience for one with academic ambitions.

"When I were at midwifery school in London," Barbara wages on, "she come to visit me in a cape. A cape!"

"Scandalous," Noel agrees.

"Mother nearly wouldn't let 'er come. 'What kind of a girl will they think you are?'"

"What kind of girl was she, Auntie?"

"Oh, she were a good girl. We were all good girls."

"Of course. I've heard that before."

"I've heard she made her own pair of pants from one of your dad's old shirts." Auntie Ethel gives Noel a wink. She's feeding Barbara her lines.

"She were only three, too." Barbara bites. "Nobody showed her 'ow to do it. None of us 'ad time. She just did it on 'er own. Didn't like the underpants she had—well, they'd been through the three of us older ones already—didn't like them, so she made some new ones from an old shirt. Very smart, is our Frances."

"I've no doubt she'll go to her Maker, her graying hair crimped and in little yellow ribbons like a schoolgirl," says Noel.

"What else does she say?" Barbara asks.

"Well, here she says something about a new suit she's made for herself from some fancy castoffs at the store. 'Camel-colored brown with'—something—'lapels.' What do you make this word out to be, Auntie? Fish lapels? Fin?"

Auntie Ethel's eyes aren't what they used to be, but she works on intuition. "Fur maybe?"

"That's a long shot," says Noel. "But must be fur. 'Fur lapels.' Lord, she never does get off the wardrobe, does she? When she mentions Betty and Arthur, it's only to say what she's forced them to wear most recently. Dad she doesn't mention at all. He's a hopeless case.

"No. I was wrong. Here she does have something to say unconnected to clothes. About me. 'See if you can get our Noel to go to church with you while he's there. I fear he is coming under evil influence at Oxford and is falling away.' Well, enough of that." Noel replaces the card on the mantel.

Barbara enters the room with a tea tray. "And 'ere's our lovely tea."

Our Nellie follows, singing "tea-beam." She clumps into things; her large size fails to fit her childish movements.

"Terrific. I'm famished." Noel helps Auntie Ethel to the table and then prepares to dive into sandwiches of potted salmon and butter.

"Noel, as the only man present, will tha ask t' blessing?" Barbara's words are kind enough, but there's a glare in her eye.

Noel chokes.

"Our Nellie. That's enough singing, dear. Noel's going to ask the blessing."

"Our Avy wants to say the blessing."

"No, dear. Tha say' it all the time when Noel's not 'ere, but when 'e—"

"Let her say it, Auntie," Noel says, spying his way out.

"No." Barbara insists. "The man of the house should say it."

"Our Avy wants to say it!"

"I really think patriarchy is a concept somewhat beyond her ability to comprehend," says Noel.

"'Tisn't," insists Barbara, then recites: "It's our Heavenly Father's plan for 'is children, and all of 'is children can come to know its truth. Why tha, Noel, 'ave fallen away. A lad as bright as thee—fallen from the gospel which, besides being true, is so partial to men."

"I like to consider myself a pleasanter chap than your average patriarch."

"Our Avy wants to say it!"

"Ask the blessing, Noel," Barbara orders.

"Yes, ma'am."

"Our Avy wants!"

"Nellie, hush!"

Quickly, Noel gives the "Christmas Carol" grace:

"Er—for what we are about to receive may the Lord make us truly grateful."

"Amen." Barbara sighs.

"But he didn't say—" protests Nellie.

"It's all right, dear."

"Tha didna say' 'In the name of—'"

"That were a fine prayer, Noel."

Nellie's distress has reached a fever pitch. "Jesus Christ!"

"Patriarchy driven to new heights," declares Noel.

"'E didn't say 'Jesus Christ.'"

"'Tis all right, our Nellie."

"Our Avy says a better prayer than 'e does. Our Avy says a—"

Barbara uses their mother's voice again: "Nellie!" Then calmer: "Would' tha like a cup o' cocoa?"

Our Nellie's ready. She claps her hands. "Cocoa!"

"Yes, cocoa, dear."

Nellie takes the mug—her mug, very solid stoneware—and is happily quiet with cocoa and lots of little sandwiches and cakes.

"Tea, Noel?" Barbara asks.

"Thank you."

"It's all that cake, makes her so fat." Barbara shakes her head.

Noel sets down his cup with a dangerous clink. "Auntie, you are guilty of fraud."

There is an awkward pause before Noel deigns to explain himself: "For the last twenty minutes you've been promising us tea. This is not a pot of tea. It's a pot of cocoa. I call fraud."

Barbara pulls herself up self-righteously. "We don't drink tea in this 'ouse."

"Yes, I know. Book of Mormon, Word of Wisdom, all of that. I was raised in a house, satellite to this one, where a pot of cocoa signaled teatime. But really, it is shocking. In the interest of being 'honest, true, chaste' and all of that, you might at least decorate the tray with a token sprig of the weed. Either that, or have the decency to call it 'cocoa time' instead."

"I'll 'eat you up a pot of warm milk if you'd like."

"Our Avy wants 'ot milk."

"Tha's' thy cocoa," Barbara tells her.

"Our Avy wants 'ot milk, too."

"Sit down, Auntie," Noel says. "I'll drink your cocoa."

Grown suddenly stately, Auntie Ethel rises from her chair to her full height. "I think I shall—"

Noel: "However, you miss my point."

Ethel: "I think I shall go put on another pot of water."

Barbara: "Auntie Ethel?"

"I feel like a cuppa—a proper cuppa—myself." Auntie Ethel draws a tea tin from the sideboard drawer and heads for the kitchen.

"Well, I'll be!" says Noel. "A clandestine cache of Earl Grey."

"Babies are born at the strangest times," comments Auntie Ethel. "They often need midwives—at four o'clock in the afternoon. Perhaps not as often as four o'clock in the morning, but often enough. I shan't take a moment, Ralph."

"Tha know' 'tis not good for thee," Barbara shouts after her.

"No use telling that to a woman twice your age." Auntie Ethel shuffles out of the room.

"Or to a man, world-weary, at half it," adds Noel.

Barbara: "It says in the scripture, 'Hot drinks are not for the body or the belly.'"

Noel takes a sip. "Cocoa is a hot drink."

"Our living prophet has determined that cocoa—"

"Besides. It only says 'body or belly.' No word about 'soul.' It's a very poor religion that considers body and belly before soul."

Auntie Ethel pokes her head in from the kitchen. "Well put, lad, well put."

"A man's—an Englishman's—soul needs his tea."

"'Tis with a 'ealthy body first that t' soul—" spouts Nurse Whitaker.

"No. With some of us, the soul has priority." The tea kettle whistles, and Noel adds, "Now there is a sound! Doesn't it thrill the heart of every Englishman? Like brass bands and 'God Save the King.' Mormons make sorry Englishmen."

"Here you are, Ralph, my dear." Auntie Ethel offers him the cup.

"Thank you, Auntie."

Barbara, biting her tongue, begins to put up the Christmas decorations, cocoa cup in hand. "'Ere, Noel. Give us a 'and with this garland, willt tha?"

"Just a minute, Auntie." He is not good at hiding his annoyance. "I've only just got my tea."

"Some of us don't have time to just sit."

"Not even for tea—or cocoa? You are iconoclast."

Our Nellie tries the word out like a new swear word. "Iconoclast."

Barbara: "I've always been a good worker."

Nellie: "Iconoclast."

"'Twere a specialty of mine. Born with an instinct to clean up."

Ethel: "The house, the yard, other people's lives."

Barbara: "I got a recommend from Matron at midwifery school—I 'ave it still. 'Nurse Whitaker's capacity for work,' she says, 'is unfathomable.'"

Ethel and Noel together: "Indeed."

Our Nellie: "Iconoclast."

～

My grandmother, Frances, seems to have had the hardest time accepting "her" Nellie. "If I'd 'ad a child like that," she says, "I don't think I could 'ave lived. I'd 'ave run mad.

"I once took 'er on a day trip to Morecambe on t' train. It took us two 'ours. I thought I'd give 'er a treat. I never should 'ave done it. I were working at t' time, earning a bit o' money. I were probably eighteen or summat like that. I never should 'ave, 'cause, you see, I were good lookin' fer t' boys. An' I 'ad 'er wi' me an' oh, I 'ad a time wi' 'er on t' front wi' boys. You couldn't trust our Nellie wi' nobody. So I couldn't speak to nobody. I daren't speak to nobody."

"What would you 'ave done if you 'adn't been with Nellie," my uncle presses.

"Well, I should 'ave spoke to 'em! I never should 'ave gone alone, mind. I should 'ave gone wi' a group, wi' Mother and Father. But then I should 'ave gone off an' 'ad a bit o' fun."

Violet comes to our Nellie's defense with much more vigor.

As the two youngest, they were often lumped together. They were bathed together until they were quite old, and were even baptized together in 1918.

Violet relates how Alex Kirkwood, a large fellow "down t' street, were always teasing our poor Nellie." One day, tiny little Violet stood between her great, big sister and this great, big rowdy and shouted at the top of her shrill little voice: "You leave 'er alone."

Alex sauntered away, defeated by shame but not letting on. "Brainy! Brainy!" he shouted at Violet as he went.

"Proud to be brainy! Proud to be brainy!" Violet shouted back, shrill and fierce as a little bird protecting her nest.

Many years later, Violet remembers when she was sixteen and had a job in a stationer's shop. The bell on the door rang. She looked up from the novel she kept under the counter to read between customers, and "there were Alex Kirkwood." He bought a packet of cigarettes. As she handed him his change over the counter, he smiled at her and said flirtingly, "Brainless."

But he'd already disqualified himself with that packet of cigarettes, hadn't he?

Even as a young married woman, Violet would put her two babies in a wagon and come and take our Nellie for a walk. She remembers she once bought a bottle of green soda pop, something her mother would never let them have at home unless they were sick. "How our Nellie enjoyed that!"

"I've seen me dad crying over our Nellie," says Auntie Hannah. "But 'e never complained. 'E'd say, 'I never grumble about our Nellie. I prayed for all me girls to live. 'E's given me what I asked for, so what can I say?'"

～

As he left to catch the train back to Oxford, the last thing Uncle Noel remembers our Nellie doing is pulling the soother out of her mouth and calling him "Iconoclast."

AROUND EAST AND WEST
BOWLING

"DID YOU ALWAYS LIVE in this district of Bradford?" Uncle Noel makes a great show of turning the tape over, silently scolding me. It had reached the end. I've been too involved in the stories as they happen to remember the tape recorder and posterity. I hope we haven't missed too much.

"East Bowling?" Auntie Ivy and Auntie Violet ask together.

"Yes," says Auntie Barbara.

"Why?" demands Uncle Noel. The tape is rolling, and for once, the sisters stare at him and at each other blankly.

"Because—" What a foolish question, is the unified subtext.

The pause for thought lengthens.

"Because me father were married there," Grandma finally says, as if it were self-evident. As if only a fool would live any place other than this crumbling slum.

"An' 'is father always lived there afore 'im," chimes in Auntie Doris.

In 2007, Uncle Noel invites (orders) his siblings to accompany him on a barge trip down the Leeds-Liverpool Canal in memory of their other grandfather who kept the lock at Goole. Of course, Uncle Noel needs my uncle Arthur to steer the barge and my mother to man the galley.

I meet Uncle Arthur, a composer and choirmaster who has heard his work performed in Durham Cathedral, and my mother for a few days touring on our own agenda before these duties begin. Uncle Arthur found us a wonderful sixteenth-century working farmhouse bed and breakfast in Keighley. The proprietors are two spinster sisters with whom my mother had been at school. They inherited this bit of heaven from their father, who inherited it from his. It goes to the state upon the sisters' deaths.

Uncle Arthur also rents the car, which he is confident he can drive. He immediately breaks the mirror off, driving narrow streets on the wrong side.

It is Sunday so he takes us first to St. Stephen's, the church where their grandparents were married in that hasty wedding more than a hundred years ago.

Our entrance doubles the size of the congregation in what is now a mostly Muslim neighborhood. When my great-grandmother, four months pregnant, gave her vows, she must have had a view of saints and angels above the altar blessing her union. The view she had is impossible for us to gain: stage flats sporting American cartoon characters block the nave, "attractive for t' kiddies."

There are no kiddies.

Massive new sound equipment provides pop music for the service, anathema to my uncle who left the Mormon Church for the Anglican because the music was better. "A snooker table," the website now offers as a further lure.

Back at the farm, our hostesses direct us to a massive black stone jutting out of a cliff over the valley. Druids might well have made their sacrifices here. We take the stone's measure and agree that more religion molders here than in town.

We escape the depression of St. Stephen's as soon as we can by visiting Bolling Hall.

～

The Bolling Hall estate, which gave its name to two main districts of the city, East and West Bowling, is today across from Bowling Park and situated in a lovely, walled sanctuary of lime and sycamore trees.

It sourced the name of the thoroughfare that Moulson Street ran into, Bowling Old Lane.

The girls remember how popular playing at bowls was—still is—in Yorkshire. On a level, untrafficked street—if you can find one—or on the carefully tended lawns in the park, in infrequent fair weather or drizzle, weekends or any week day when the pensioners appear: teams of men in their grey tweeds patiently deliver their black and brown fist-sized "woods" towards the distant, smaller "jack."

Quirks of archaic etymology, of dialect, make Bolling of Bowling, and even Ol' of 'All. Confusing. My grandmother, who was born here, never distinguished between the two, just as she never distinguished my husband Curt from my sister's Keith. She cannot enlighten my study of the map.

Although now a museum open to the public, in my grandmother's day "t' squire" still lived in "Bolling 'All" with its long history.

After the Battle of Adwalton Moor in June 1643, parliamentary forces under the younger Sir Thomas Fairfax decided that Bradford could no longer be held. A town built for manufacture and trade, the antitheses of defense, it was not a medieval fortress set on a hill. The forces withdrew, leaving the citizens—who had fought bravely with nothing but scythes and staves—at the mercy of the Earl of Newcastle, head of the King's army in those Northern parts.

Now, the Earl of Newcastle was in a livid passion against Bradford. Miserably armed and defended as they were, its citizens had still managed to repulse him, with a little help from the weather—much the same now as it was then—throughout the winter. He had lost men, time, supplies, and honor in the fruitless endeavor. Now he had won at last, and every man, woman, and child in that Godforsaken town, he declared, must die on the morrow. He set his guard around so none could escape this terrible fate.

In the time of these Civil War events, Bolling Hall stood as the main house of substance in the district. The Earl of Newcastle naturally took it for his own quarters and, in order to appear fresh for the slaughter in the morning, retired to an upper bedroom.

On toward midnight, he was awakened by an apparition. A ghostly young woman, all in white, stood by the damask curtains at the foot of his bed moaning: "Pity poor Bradford! Pity poor Bradford!" (My grandmother's voice goes all squeaky as she tries to modify her "voice from t' weaveroom" to haunting tones.)

The war-hardened general got no more peace that night, and in the morning, he gave the whole town pardon.

Is this the tale that was taught in history lesson at Usher Street School? I do not know. That's the way the chronicles have it. Ivy says it was the ghost of Cromwell who visited the Earl of Newcastle. (Cromwell was alive and leading the Southern army at the time.) My grandmother insists that a malevolent ghost haunts Bolling Hall to this day. My mother says she saw a blood stain on the rug at the top of the stairs when she visited the estate-become-museum in her school days. My mother, who hasn't a dramatic bone in her body, she assumes foul play, too.

Grandma also says an underground passage runs from Bolling Hall to the parish church through which someone (she can't remember who) helped someone else (also no memory) during the Wars of the Roses. I've been able to find no verification of this tale at all: Bolling Hall wasn't built until the century after the House of York had its little bid for freedom.

Ah, the wonders of popular legend: what was to their ancestors a Godsend made the little girls run for all they were worth every time they could not avoid passing the great stone wall and dark park of Bolling Hall.

❧

My uncle, my mother, and I are the only visitors in Bolling Hall this afternoon. We observe the great hall with its many coats of arms and an upper bedroom that must be the site of Bradford's salvation, but no ghosts haunt the day. I like the well-equipped kitchen best, and linger by the baskets and the dry sink.

❧

Some local philanthropists ran a club for poor children called by the illusory name of the Cinderella Club. Violet remembers they once came around to her school and asked for all those children whose parents were out of work to raise their hands. It was summer, and she had heard her parents talking about how little piano tuning there was at that time of the year. So she raised her hand.

Her mother later scolded her—her father wasn't out of work at all. Violet got to go anyway, to the concert the club gave where they gave a pantomime of Cinderella. "The coach came on t' stage and all."

The Cinderella Club used to give parties in a hall which would be decorated all 'round with great big china dolls. "'Ow we longed for 'em." But when each child left, she was only handed "a little thing—nowt at all."

The club also ran a home near the seaside in Morecombe where children could go in the summer—forty girls at a time for two weeks. Once while my grandmother was there, Mary Jane sent Frances two-and-six spending money, but only addressed it "To my darling daughter" and signed it "Mother." It could have gone to anyone. Frances recognized her mother's handwriting and so got the money.

Frances also remembers going once when she was thirteen.

She was one of the oldest girls then, "Number Two, so that were t' next to t' biggest girl. Us big uns 'ad to go into t' farm to get milk an' all sorts o' things."

She stopped some bickering among the younger girls. "I says, 'What ye're all quarrellin' fer?' I says, 'Look, ye're 'ere in a lovely place, Morecombe. Ye're supposed to be enjoyin' yerself and ye're quarrellin'!' An' I were lecturin' 'em like this." She turned 'round and saw the man who ran the place standing in the doorway. He came and patted her on the back.

"But 'e didn't pat me no place else!" Grandma assures us. This man, "'e were a mess. 'Is wife were an invalid an' 'e used to take some o' these young girls into t' [h]uts in t' grounds at t' club. You know, tales goin' round. 'E knew not to take me," she finishes firmly, "'cause 'e'd a got kicked in t' be'ind or summat. We were morally clean! We were!"

Why does Uncle Noel chuckle and find this so hard to believe?

～

They used to call Bradford the "Dead City" because everything used to close up on a Sunday. The girls insist that that's why they were never as hard hit as Coventry or London during World War II, even though it was such a central place for manufacture, "an' haeroplane fact'ries an' all." One airplane factory where Violet's husband worked was built underground and camouflaged with plastic cows and sheep. But all remained safe "'cause we kept t' Sabbath day 'oly."

～

Whitsuntide, seven weeks after Easter, was Doris's favorite holiday. The weather was always settled then and everybody got off work. All the children of every chapel would go marching down the street two by two in their single new dress for the year. A band played at the head. "It made the air seem so gay because we didn't 'ave much excitement, you know."

Each child would carry a little mug. When they finished their march at Bowling Park, each child would get some milk in their mug and a hefty, sticky Bath bun with a few lumps of sugar in the icing.

At the park, games and races were held with prizes for the winners. In those days, adults didn't think it was naïve to play as heartily as children at London Bridge is falling down, in and out the window, nuts in May, and musical chairs.

"It shows a different trend," Doris says sadly, for she always thought "it were lovely to watch t' grown-ups enjoying themselves like that."

My grandmother and her sisters buck the trend. Their parties always include musical chairs with my uncle Arthur induced to play the piano.

Easter was celebrated with at least two days when nobody worked. Everybody went to the seaside or somewhere on holiday. When she came to America, Doris thought, "Eee, they don't give 'em enough 'olidays 'ere."

Bowling and Manningham, other districts of the town, each had their own holidays which were called "the tides": Bowlingtide and

Manninghamtide. Bowlingtide was in August. The mills closed for a week, and the fair came and set up in the empty lot at the back of the Whitaker house. From their attic window, the girls could look out and watch the fair: the bright lights at night, six or seven rides all going at once to their different calliope tunes.

And the colorful "gypsies" (travelers), the girls were warned, would try to steal them if they weren't careful.

I'm assured that a friend of a friend did lose a baby boy that way, when she set him out in the yard to sun. An image of this cautionary tale is hard formed in my mind, but I realize it is the large lawn of the house we lived in until I was ten on which I see the pram and the exotic woman wearing bangles and scarves.

We're back to the tides.

"Mother wouldn't let us go at night," my grandmother says.

"But you could go during the day, couldn't you?" I assume, from what I've heard the other girls relate.

"I don't know if she'd let us go or not. Maybe she would."

Is Grandma being coy? Trying to impress us with the deprivations of her childhood so we'll see how well she's done for us? I can't tell why she won't talk about these fairs, and it's no use pressing her. Uncle Noel's not here this day.

"If we did go"—she'll concede this much—"if we got a bit of brandysnap, we's lucky."

Barbara has more positive memories of the fairs (because she's not trying to impress anyone?). She speaks so fast we can hardly keep up with her, like a child just come, flushed and out of breath, from the fairgrounds.

"It were an exciting time. We could 'ear t' lions roaring in their cages. I were always afraid they would escape, and I've had a fear of lions ever since. The roundabouts had great, loud organs. Dozens of shows and games and fat ladies and dwarves and deformed people." The brandysnap is here, too, not just a sop, but greatly enjoyed along with "other sweet-toothed things."

Ivy liked the flying boat ride at the fair best, but she had to put it off till last because it always made her throw up. She enjoyed throwing up? Calamity Jane is a martyr.

～

Remember, remember, the fifth of November, gunpowder, treason, and plot.

"Guy Fawkes were a Yorkshireman." Such pride in the statement, as if the rebel is someone we'd do well to emulate. Bradford always celebrated his day in a grand fashion. All kinds of rubbish—old sofas and chairs, baby prams, old boots and tyres, paper and rags—were collected over the space of weeks into great piles on the street corners throughout the city. On Plot Night, the piles were set ablaze. The children got to stay up and watch. They'd hear firecrackers going off and maybe have a sparkler or two of their own. "The authorities won't let them do it anymore," Barbara comments. The rebellion is quenched at last after all these centuries—except when race riots flare now in the same streets.

Birthdays brought little celebration, usually just a special dinner. Auntie Ethel would always send a handkerchief or a piece of hair ribbon, but "that were about all." On her eighth birthday, however, Ivy got a blue ribbon in the mail from someone who hadn't signed his name. Her father had her trying to guess who might have sent it until she found out he'd done it himself. He'd gone into the stationer's shop down the street—which, like many a newspaper and magazine shop, also served as a post office—and had the woman there write out the address for him.

Even if there wasn't a holiday, plenty of things could still keep a young girl entertained. Any evening a girl wasn't too tired, she could go to Wibsey Park and row the boats in the lake there.

Vendors always walked the streets: the ice cream man; the coal man with his hundred-weight sack shouting, "Ony coils?"; chimney sweeps all dressed in black with their ladders and brushes; and the paperboys calling *Telegraph and Argus!* Barbara remembers the special editions when the Titanic sank on a Sunday, 1912, and when war was declared.

The rag-and-bone man would come around pushing his cart and shouting: "Any old rags? Any old rags?" The children would run and ask their mothers if they had any bones or rags to throw out because in exchange the man would give them a balloon, a goldfish in a bowl, or some other small toy. Sometimes the man would give away kitchen utensils—teacups, saucers, mixing bowls. That's how the Whitakers furnished their kitchen. The man would take their junk and sell it to the factories to remake into shoddy cloth. But finally the health authorities put an end to this colorful way of getting rid of rubbish, too.

The tingerlary man played a hurdy-gurdy with his little monkey, and beggars begged. Violet remembers seeing a man and a woman carrying a little baby walking down the street, singing and rattling a cup. "I think my parents always had a great fear of the poorhouse themselves," she comments as she recalls how her mother gave her a penny and said, "Go put that in his cup."

Doris remembers how a friend "'oo were real smart" set up a magic lantern show in his cellar. He used a candle to project the colored images on the wall "and we'd 'ooh!' and 'ah!'" Pictures of gardens and woods, little cats and rabbits, pretty children and Father Christmas all came to flickering life against the dank stone wall.

Children played hoops, skipping rope, rounders, or pizeball— which is something like baseball, only "ye 'it it wi' yer 'and"—run, sheep, run and statues—where someone twists you around and "ye've to fall as you go." "Then we used to turn us 'ead to t' wall and run a little bit and if ye catched anybody, they 'ad to go to t' wall"—like our red light, green light. They'd play in the street with the neighbor kids in the evening with no fear of traffic.

Ivy's favorite game was diablos (pronounced with a long "i"). It consisted of two sticks connected with a piece of string. A bobbin was spun, tossed up in the air, and then caught again on this string. But she could hardly ever afford to buy such a toy and had to borrow it from others at school.

Spinning tops were purchased toys, too. Two types of tops were carefully segregated as to sex. Boys wound theirs with a string while girls used a whip. I remember a set of heavy iron boys' tops from my grandparents' house when I was a girl. My grandfather would draw patterns in many colors on bits of cardboard and put them on the tops. He would spin them for us to see how the colors blended and changed.

The girls also had "checkers"—what we call jacks. (The game we in the U.S. call "checkers" is "draughts.") "Checkers" were made of stone and came in different shapes. My grandmother says her nails were always worn away from scooping them up off the paving.

In the yard of 4 Moulson Street, two stone retaining walls ran with a lower path in between. The girls used to play at jumping from one to the other. Once our Frances fell and cut her brow right over her eye. Her mother came, picked her up, and carried her into the house. That's the only time she can remember her mother carrying her. Any bleeding from the area of the eye was a serious thing in that home, for they all knew what it meant to be blinded. Catapults and even throwing stones by hand were both absolutely forbidden. My own mother will still stop any stone-flinging child in her Head Start class by saying most severely, "My grandfather—" Just as I did to my own boys.

At one point, the big house next door was turned into a Boys Club. The Prince of Wales himself—Edward (VIII) it would have been—dedicated it. Whenever royalty came to town, there was always a general holiday, and everyone went down to wave a flag. This time brought even more excitement—"it were right next door."

The wall between the houses "were twelve foot 'igh," but by standing on top of the dog kennel, the girls could just see over. Others watched from the attic window. "Mrs. At-t'-Bottom-o'-t'-Snicket—Mrs. Stubbs, they called 'er"—had come to watch, too. As she was climbing up, she stepped on her skirt, and it broke at the waist. "There she were, stood in 'er corsets on top of a dog kennel with the Prince of Wales next door!"

All the girls were laughing so hard some dignitary had to come to the wall and tell them to be quiet. The Prince of Wales thought they were laughing at him!

Violet finds some satisfaction in this flagrant disrespect. She never cared for royalty much. Once when she was in school, the Prince of Wales (I don't know which one it was this time) made another visit. All the children practiced for months to get a couple of songs ready to sing for him. On the day of the visit, and for several rehearsals beforehand, they had to march miles across town to practice in their places on the steps of the town hall.

When at last the prince arrived, however, he didn't stop to hear the songs at all, just hurried in, then hurried out again without a sidewards glance at the several hundred young subjects assembled in his honor.

Doris, however, is a "regular Royalist," and follows the royal family's doings devotedly. Isn't it curious that Doris was the first to leave England and Violet one of the last?

In her teens, Doris became a "regular opera buff." She used to go to the opera, by which she doesn't mean anything the likes of *Figaro*; more often operettas, pantomimes, and concert parties, often at the brand-new Alhambra, opened in 1914, on Morley Street. Since she had to be home by ten and the opera never ended "while ten," she always had to miss the last scene in order to run all the way home.

Dance performances, skits, and little plays marked the days at school and in church as well. Barbara remembers being an orphan boy and having to eat some food greedily in a production of *David Copperfield*. She also devised some machinery that actually worked with gears and a crank to portray the inside of a factory for another show.

Ivy hated the notoriety of actually appearing in the show, but she loved to make crowns for the fairies out of silver paper. Once she made the donkey's head for a production of *Midsummer Night's Dream*. Every bit of cardboard or colored paper was saved for such projects. In one road show for the church, Ivy did appear as Little Red Riding Hood; it makes a lovely picture. She got the mumps while they were on the road, however, and cried all the way home.

Our Mona didn't care for dancing and such things: With her lame leg, she couldn't "trip" like the others. But our Violet loved to dance. Once they danced with tambourines, once to "How are you today, sir? Very well, I thank you"—"like lancers." They did traditional dances "like your Virginia reel" to a piano played by a teacher and to their own singing. For one production of five dances, Violet was appearing in four of them and longed to be in the fifth, although most of the other girls were only in one or at most two. At the last moment, a girl in the fifth dance bowed out, and our Violet quickly volunteered to take her place. But she discovered it takes more than desire to perform a dance: she mixed the whole figure up in the middle of the performance by making wrong turns.

Their mother would sometimes help her hang a curtain across the yard on a clothes line, and our Violet would put on little shows at home. Neighborhood children would either appear in it or pay one of the multitude of pins they always had about them to come and watch. One little girl from across the street came so dirty that seven-year-old Violet gave her a good scrubbing and combed her hair herself before sending her home again.

Later, when motion pictures came in, the girls would sometimes stay in town after work, buy fish and chips for their dinner, and see a show. They liked Charlie Chaplin and Mary Pickford. My great-grandmother went to one picture show in her life: *Abraham Lincoln*. The U.S. president was one of her heroes, but she couldn't stand the atmosphere: everyone who wasn't smoking was eating oranges and dropping the peels on the theatre floor. She never went again.

My own mother takes after her; she's had no use for movies since that last one she saw—*The Music Man* when it first came out.

ᔕ

Uncle Arthur's actress daughter, the only Whitaker descendant to sometimes still make Bradford her home, meets us and gives us a tour of the new theatre in the center of town. She looks very like her Chinese American mother, except with our grandmother's wavy hair, my wavy hair. My cousin has directed plays in which the multicultural inhabitants of today's town get to tell their own stories.

Then we all go to see if we can tell where Moulson Street once ran. We fail.

My mother and Uncle Arthur find the house where they both were born. Long gazing at the upstairs window behind which the very bedroom lies makes the present lady of the house in bright shalwar kamis very uncomfortable. She keeps a keen dark eye on us as she goes out to fetch her laundry from the line.

We move on from a place where we don't belong, even though two of us were born there.

She might not approve of the cinema, but sometimes the girls' mother would take them to the Mechanics Institute Hall to hear lectures, travelogues, and later, informative slide shows.

Ivy, Frances, Hannah, and Violet would go once a week on their lunch break to the West Bowling District Baths. The pool itself was sixty feet by thirty feet; decorative stone dolphins swam along its walls. There were also four first-class and eight second-class slipper baths—great clawed tubs—vapor baths, showers, douches, and medicinal needle baths that shot the body all over with a very fine spray from many jets. All these were for women, but cost extra, not to mention the mysteries of what went on beyond the doorway marked "Men." Even in the pool, any man who thought to wear a topless suit got scolded by the lifeguard while women made their own, very concealing suits.

Mona went to the baths once a week, too, with her school class. The first day she fell into the deep end and nearly drowned. After that, she was more careful and passed the third- and second-class certificates. She never earned first class because her bad leg prevented her from getting up speed.

A branch library was in the same building as the swimming bath, at the juncture of Wakefield Road with Metcalfe Street. Mona particularly loved the library. She read every historical novel they had. Harrison Ainsworth was her favorite: *The Lancashire Witches, Windsor Castle, The Goldsmith's Wife, Old St. Paul's: A Tale of Plague and Fire, The Tower of London: A Historical Romance.* ("'E's not like Sir Walter Scott. 'E's one of the lesser lights.") She learnt much of her history that way.

We leave the tarmac for the old farmhouse's dirt road, exhausted from our touring and the dinner at the Chinese restaurant in Utley where Uncle Arthur made them turn off the music, he found it so objectionable. "A chippy tomorrow," he decrees.

My uncle suddenly stops the car and leans on the steering wheel. "Look." His hushed tone silences whatever my mother in the front and I in the back might have been about to say.

We look.

Across the green valley cross-hatched with mortarless stone walls, looking towards Aire Gap and Ilkley Moor, the first lights of the villages along the Aire River are just beginning to come on. It's not "forty miles of 'eathery moor," as the old song says, perhaps only half that, but as far as the eye can see. Cows in the next field chew their cud. Sheep look like the rest of the tumbled boulders.

"This," breathes Uncle Arthur, when anyone can say something. "Isn't this how all the world should be?"

A man who lives in the tall woods of Minnesota, a woman from the western desert, and one from the Rockies' alpine meadows just caught a glimpse of what their genes tell them is paradise, having looked all day, for years, in the wrong places.

When it grows too dark to see and rain begins to spatter, my uncle restarts the ignition and drives on. In the back seat, I wipe away my tears.

CLOGS AND SHAWLS

HER VOICE CRACKING WITH AGE and competing with the boom box outside on a hot Rose Park afternoon, Auntie Ivy sings:

Joe in London settled down
Left 'is little cotton town,
Left behind 'is sweetheart fair,
Workin' in the fact'ry there
'E would watch the passersby,
Then 'e'd say without a sigh,
"I'd rather 'ave me little factory lass
In 'er clogs and 'er shawls."

A scene from one of these popular British novels of the spunky heroine overcoming poverty, exploitative working conditions, and the lecherous overlooker.

~

When she "were twelve year old," our Doris, the eldest, decided she should leave school and get a job to help with the family finances.

"Are you sure it's what you want to do?" her father asked.

Her mother was expecting Violet at the time. That was ten people, trying to live on a blind man's earnings. As the eldest, Doris felt the responsibility too keenly.

Mary Jane had been in service. She knew what it was like; she remembered Master Davey. She didn't want any of her daughters to go through that; the lupus on her face tingled when she thought of it. The factory was the main alternative Bradford had to offer.

"An' she'd never been to t' mill," the girls say ominously. "She didn't know what that were like."

A year after Doris, Barbara went to work. Her father gave her much the same talk he'd given Doris, perhaps with even more emphasis, since Barbara had a better mind for school. "If you go, you'll have to stay. You'll never stop working all the rest of your life."

"An' I never 'ave," Barbara declares proudly, not regretting her decision. "I've always been a good worker."

Ivy remembers no choice in the matter. "When you were twelve, t' 'eadmaster would come. 'Off to work wi' thee.'"

Barbara remembers her mother went with her to apply for the job at Ripley's at the bottom of the hill. The month was January, bitter cold, and not quite her twelfth birthday. She had her birth certificate clutched in her hand. The authorities required that in an attempt to keep children under twelve from going to work, unlike in her great-uncle's day when he had gone and died in the gears at eight. Barbara remembers her mother had made her a new, warm wrap for the occasion. "'Oundstooth check with black frogs, very fashionable"—but very out of place for someone applying for a factory job.

"It were inevitable," she sighs. "I were soon wearing clogs and shawls like everybody else."

Clogs became fashionable in my teens. My friends spent fortunes to have the latest from Denmark to clatter (rather clumsily, I must say, with many a twisted ankle) down the high school halls. My mother couldn't believe I wanted a pair, too. To her, they'd always been a sign of dire poverty. Shawls and clogs, wooden clogs and great squares of dark woolen weave folded in half with a fringe to throw over your head or your shoulders, to bundle in against the cold. That was the "uniform" of the "little army" of factory workers in those bleak Northern towns.

And year after year, as regular as the clockwork their father mended, another Whitaker girl joined that "little army" until all the five eldest were working and none of them out of their teens. "That's why I'm on'y little," my under-five-foot grandma sighs. "I never got t' chance to grow. I were al'ays in t' mill."

At first it was only half-time. Still the schedule was rigorous. "Up at five thirty in t' morning. You 'ad to be there by six or t' pennyhoilman locked t' door and you'd lose your ha'penny bonus. Push back up t' hill 'ome at eight for 'alf an 'our's breakfast—a pot of cocoa and a slice of drippin' 'n' bread. Run back down t' 'ill, up all three flights of stairs at the factory to be back at your place again by eight thirty. 'Ome again at twelve thirty wi' 'alf an 'our to eat dinner, change your clothes, and be at school. It were dark when you got up and dark when you got 'ome at night."

They all recite it in these exact words, in a singsong like "The Rhyme of the Ancient Mariner." Ivy and other girls "'at were dumb like me" added to this another run up and down those steps to fetch great trays of tea mugs for the other workers on their break before they were free to run off to their own. "An' we didn't even drink tea!"

Every other week was the reverse for half-timers, with school in the morning and work till five thirty in the afternoon. But this only lasted a couple of years. At fourteen, if you were up on your schoolwork—as the Whitakers were—you left school and went full-time: ten hours a day and half a day on Saturday among the whir and thud of dangerous steam-driven machinery under poor gas lighting.

The first thing a girl learned was to pin her hair up or stick her plaits in her pinnie, to keep it away from the slapping belts overhead and the bobbins blurred with speed. Then she took on her first job, "sweeper-up." With a big push broom, she had to keep all the lint swept up under the machines. On Saturday she had one nasty job—the men's and women's latrines—and then she was free to go.

She did this until she learnt to be a "doffer," which meant she watched bobbins on the machine until they were full. Then she took them off and put on new ones—like doffing a hat.

How ironic that when the old mills were dismantled in the last twenty years or so, wooden bobbins like these should be salvaged. They were made into ballpoint pens for the tourists or simply left as they were to collect dust on coffee tables with a sort of perverse nostalgia. Like the knickknack shelves made from old New England barns and the stuffed Christmas ornaments made from old quilts with which they appear side by side in glossy catalogues: they make objects of idle conversation from what was once the fabric of a very rigorous life indeed.

As a girl "doffed," she watched the others and soon learnt to "mind sides" as a "spinner" or "piecener." Any description of these processes is very difficult for the uninitiated to follow, not because the words are too technical but because rather than verbalize the work, my great-aunts simply feel it in every arthritic bone.

The basic outline, however, seems to be that the thread would come spinning through "rovings"—"little things"—getting finer and finer in the air on its way to the bobbin—one bobbin of a whole bank of bobbins. If the thread on one of her bobbins broke, it was the spinner's job to stop the wildly whirling bobbin with her finger, quickly catch the loose end coming from the rovings, attach it, and get the bobbin going again. Auntie Ivy displays an index finger made permanently crooked by stopping bobbins.

The best job was twisting, to which a girl finally came after spinning for several years. Twisting meant she only had to mind two sides, or banks, of flying bobbins instead of four. It took more care, however, for here the thread was made even finer and finished, "ready to go to t' weavers."

I have visited the industrial museum in Lowell, Massachusetts, the curators all wearing ear plugs and handing them out to us, too. No such thing in Bradford. The steam-driven machinery made a great and constant noise. My grandmother complains that she couldn't chat to make the time go, a great deprivation indeed. She could only yell over the noise to the girl at the next bank of sides from time to time. "That's why I 'ave such a strong voice now," she says. "You can 'ear me voice anywhere." It's true. I've heard it, syllable for syllable, a block away and inside the house.

This phenomenal effect of machinery was not universal, however. It seems to have driven soft-spoken girls like Ivy and Hannah further into the ground—and in old age, made them deaf.

My grandmother remembers one day when all her ends were "beautiful." She sat down for a rest in the great big basket at her side where she set the full bobbins when she replaced them. "'Ead o' t' mill come by just then. 'Ey,' 'e says, and I jumped up. You 'adn't to sit down, even if all t' ends were fine."

Barbara says that Doris's beginning wage was two shillings and that she herself got "two and six" a week when she began a year later. Doris and Ivy, however, both claim that the starting wage for a half-timer was "four and six."

"That were about a dollar," Doris says.

"Fifty cents," says Ivy, always more pessimistic.

Until she was twenty-one, a child gave her whole pay to her parents. At twenty-one, when she also got "t' key to t' door," she'd give a pound and keep the rest. Of her first "four and six," Ivy remembers her mother returned thrupence spending money for the week. Ivy would buy candy with one penny and put the rest ("Two pennies! They'd die if you tried to do it today!") in the co-op bank. This wage, each of the girls was told by her mother in turn, was tiny, but important. It could buy the flour for the family for the week.

At the end of two years half-time work, Barbara was earning five shillings a week, which became "a precious gold ten-shilling piece" at fourteen and full-time.

One Saturday after they'd been paid, Ivy and Frances decided to treat themselves to a fish and chip dinner and a silent picture show. "That were a night!" they exclaim to one another and, giggling, remember the pears they bought to eat in the theatre. Frances found half a worm in hers. They giggled so much about the other half that they were sent out of the theatre. Only then did Frances discover a worst disaster: her pocket had been picked and all her wage was gone.

"I remember our Frances were sat at t' top o' t' stairs, crying 'cause she'd lost her wage. Tell us what our dad did then," Hannah encourages.

"'E come up and shoved two shillings in me 'and."

"That's the sort o' man our dad were."

I always loved the rollicking, thumb-your-nose-at-authority song no one in my family sang, but they must have known it.

Resuscitated in the rebellious, communal folk-rock of the sixties, its name is "The Doffing Mistress." I knew what doffing was.

> Oh, do you know her or do you not,
> This new doffing mistress that we have got?
> Oh, Elsie Thompson, it is her name
> And she helps her doffers at every frame.
> Fol de ri fol ra
> Fol de ri fol ray.

In spite the fact that they were serving machinery and not the whims of humans as Mary Jane had feared, the girls still had to deal with mortals.

~

"And mind that overlooker, Mr. Sims. 'E's a mess."

Our Barbara's laconic bit of advice on Ivy's first day of work had almost been forgotten in the stretch of two years since. Now that she'd left school and started full-time, Ivy was only just coming to understand what her older sister had meant.

The unpleasant man with the weak chin and bad teeth had the power of God over the factory floor. And in the last two weeks, he'd started hovering near Ivy's machines a good part of every day. Sometimes she could tell he was there, watching her, before she saw him. He smelled of cheap cigarettes. A hint of that smell, so completely different from the comfortable fragrance of her father's pipe, made the skin on her spine crawl. He had no business watching her. She knew her work, minding sides, stopping the bobbins with her finger—so—if something snapped. Getting it all going again. Yet Mr. Sims kept coming to her with helpful hints he had to bend very close to almost whisper in her ear. He would stand so close she couldn't move, here by her machines. And she'd been so happy when he switched her to these rovings near the window—unfortunately she saw now, a little too removed from the rest of the floor. Once or twice he had even trapped her against the spinning frame and scraped the stubble of his chin along her cheek. It made her sick to her stomach.

"Doesn't our overlooker have a wife?" Ivy even dared to step in and dry dishes for our Barbara in order to get this question answered.

"'Course 'e does." Barbara didn't like help when she was washing up. Nobody else did it right.

Ivy hung up the towel and left the kitchen, feeling sick again. X-rays many years later show she had had a bleeding ulcer.

At break the next day, she made certain she lingered near Doris and her friends. The older girls hadn't any patience for her, though, with their giggles and their secret beaux. Besides, what Ivy truly wanted every minute she could claim away from the clatter of machinery was not chatter—but peace and quiet.

"I can make things easier for thee, lass," Mr. Sims offered then. "Meet me in t' stairwell after work, and I'll see tha gets a Leicester side."

The Leicester fibers were best, strong and rarely breaking.

She couldn't find her tongue to say "no" that day. She simply grabbed her shawl before the final bell rang and clattered down and out before any others. Oh, those clogs did make a lot of noise!

That night, Ivy asked if she couldn't bring a Book of Mormon to read during break. Her mother looked at her as if she were coming down with yet another fever. Ivy herself felt as if she might be. She wished she were. She wished she never had to go to work again.

She got the Book of Mormon instead. Sitting in the deep sill of the high windows, she tried to read. "Brief Analysis of the . . ." What did "analysis" mean? Was that really a word God would use? "Testimony of Eight Witnesses . . ." Maybe she could skip that part. "I, Nephi, having been born of goodly parents . . ." Why did the word of God have to be so difficult? It was worse than being in school.

Ivy turned to look out of the window instead. A milky sun tried to push through the clouds. She had the view over Ripley mill yard to the place where once, before she was born, over fifty people had died. A massive millworks chimney, built on the hillside riddled with the abandoned tunnels of a mined-out coal pit, had collapsed. Just at break time, they said, when workers had gathered around the fire in the yard to keep warm. "You can still hear the wailing of their ghosts when the wind blows," older girls told her. Ivy was always careful to hurry past the spot. But the same Ripley family who had built that chimney still owned and took the profits of this mill. They hired this overlooker. Maybe one or two girls had been glad to die in that disaster, plagued by a "mess" of an overlooker of their own.

These windows faced northwest. When the wind blew, even if you couldn't hear ghosts, the panes ran with threads of rain so that even here she couldn't escape the sights of spinning worn into the back of her eyes. The web of a monstrous spider.

Today she could just see one tree, of all the vista, one tree beckoning with bare arms over Manchester Road.

Suddenly, her heart was racing. Cheap cigarettes filled her nose. Oh, why had she let her eyes wander from the safety of the scriptural page, no matter how boring? Now all she could do was to jump down from the sill, clutching the book protectively before her.

"What are you reading?" Mr. Sims asked.

When she didn't answer, he drew the book from her hands, letting them idle between book and her blouse a little too long.

"Mormon, eh? I sort of envy those fellows, you know. When one wife doesn't understand you, perhaps another, younger one would be more biddable."

Ivy snatched back the book and tried to move around him. He stepped to block her path. His grin lost even the pretense of friendliness, swallowed up in the slope of his chin. "I missed you last night in the stairwell. How about tonight?"

"Busy."

Ivy scuttled back to her sides before the bell even rang.

This gave Mr. Sims the chance to shove past her—very close. Hadn't he heard her one strangled word, that she was busy? He'd heard. He just didn't care. "If tha want special favors—tha must give special favors. Tonight—or else."

Ivy grabbed her shawl even earlier. If anyone saw her, she'd be docked in her pay.

The next morning, she learned what "or else" meant. By the time she got home for dinner, she couldn't eat. All she could do was sit in a chair and sob. She couldn't even explain to her mother or sisters what the matter was. She felt too dirty; she was too ashamed.

This was during the very first days of the war. The factories were making lots of khaki for soldiers' uniforms. "It were rotten stuff," made from rags collected by the rag-and-bone man and then recycled. It was called "shoddy" and broke constantly. Mr. Sims had taken her from her nice machines and put her—not on the Leicester wool, but minding four sides of shoddy. She simply couldn't keep all the bobbins going, though she ran all morning from one end to the other. Mr. Sims seemed to have nothing else to do than to hover over her, yelling at her for every broken thread, until she could hardly see the ends for the tears. She couldn't catch them, either, her hands were shaking too much. Her stomach felt like a knife stabbed in it. And this had all been before breakfast.

Our Frances threw Ivy's shawl at her. "Come on, then. Tha can' eat or not as tha like, but tha mustna be late for t' after dinner shift."

"I won't." Ivy heard herself say. "I won't go back to that mill."

They all stared at her, even their mother, jostling two babies. Nobody thought quiet Ivy had it in her.

"I won't," she said again.

And, having heard herself say it, she amazed herself by getting to her feet. She took up her shawl, but instead of walking left with her sisters, she turned right out the door instead. There were other mills, weren't there? If there's one thing Bradford had no shortage of, it was woolen mills. Their chimneys stood like prison bars, all around.

> And when the boss, he looks round the door,
> "Tie your ends up, doffers," he do roar.
> Tie our ends up we surely do
> For Elsie Thompson but not for you.

To Ivy's own surprise, within an hour she'd found another job. This was at Lister's, which was clear at the other side of Bradford, the biggest factory in town, so big that a whole range of hills was named for it. Lister's meant getting up at five, before anyone else did, before the knocker-up man, even. Her father contrived an alarm clock for her, but she only let it ring the first day. It made such a racket, she was scared to let it ring again, and was always up to stop it after that. Working at Lister's meant she couldn't run home for breakfast or dinner, either. And for a while, she hadn't any friends on the floor.

A friendly girl named Alice Maud worked in the office at this factory doing odd jobs. Her task was to make tea, coffee, or, for a little Mormon girl to buy for a penny, Bovril, to warm up those cold mornings. Ivy would skip a tram ride and walk the whole way, just to be able to have that cup of Bovril. Usually she took a cold sandwich for lunch. Sometimes, when she could afford it, she took a potato and bought "thru'pence o' meat" in a little tin which Alice would have cooked along with others in a big oven in the factory yard by noon. Alice soon befriended Ivy.

In spite of all these inconveniences, Lister's was still much better than Mr. Sims at Ripley's. One overlooker at Lister's was particularly kind. He found her making another attempt to read her Book of Mormon at break, before she had won many friends. Instead of talking polygamy, he asked her interested questions about her religion. Ivy's present-day missionary zeal makes her say, "I should've spoke to 'im." At the time, she was too scared to do anything but hang her head.

Another sidelight of Lister's: I have a sister named Alice.

She was named for this very Alice Maud who used to put the potatoes and meat in the mill yard oven and stir up the Bovril. And my name is for Alice's sister Annie who, they say, I resemble a little too closely when I lose my (very short) Maud temper and refuse to be "a good mixer." Like Aunt Annie, I'm "bound to snort thaself to death." Their brother Harry "were just learning to twist"—to be a warp twister—at the same mill, where he stayed until he had to go into the army. Although Ivy met him first, it was another of the Whitaker sisters Harry Maud eventually married: Frances, my grandmother.

Ivy doesn't tell this story when Uncle Noel is present. She couldn't tell her mother or sisters about Mr. Sims at the time. Ninety years later, she entrusts me when we are alone. I am so honored.

> We'll tie our ends and we'll leave our frames
> And wait for Elsie to return again.
> Fol de ri fol ra
> Fol de ri fol ray.

～

Twisting (different from warp twisting in the weaveroom, like my grandfather) was as far as a young woman could go in the spinning room. For an ambitious, hard-working girl like Barbara, the lack of challenge soon bored her. Weaving, a step up on the pay scale and a prided craft, was guarded by its practitioners. Ralph paid a woman quite a sum of money to teach it to that precocious sixteen-year-old of his. Barbara learned plain weave, then the complicated box pattern, then plush and velvet weaving. "An' when I'd learnt it all, it grew monotonous, too." Again, Barbara was looking for a change.

So the price of lessons wouldn't be lost, Barbara taught first Doris and then Ivy to weave. Doris didn't like weaving. The flying shuttle "were about to give me a nervous breakdown." She moved on to "burling and mending," which was quieter and, what was most important to Doris, "more fun." A bunch of girls, all her good friends, would chatter the whole day long and, incidentally, take the bolts of fabric from the weavers and "perfect" them: if there were threads missing, they'd sew them in by hand, or they'd pick out burrs.

Ivy liked weaving better. She remembers minding two looms, one with blue serge for navy uniforms and the other with heavy drapery material in lavish patterns and colors. The drapes, she was told, were going to rich men in India.

"Englishmen?" I ask.

"No. Them as 'as lots of wives," she answers. "Rajas and such."

The romance appealed to her, no thought given to the mechanics of empire that destroyed native economies with one hand and provided the armed forces to keep them crushed with the other. Ivy stayed at weaving until she, too, went overseas—to America.

At sixteen, Frances was earning thirty shillings a week when she decided to leave spinning and go with a friend to learn dressmaking. Entering the dressmakers' shop would mean a drop down to two shillings as a beginner. Doris had gone to sewing for a while earlier among her many job shifts. All the woman had had her do was pick up pins, for which she was paid nothing. The move was a big, perilous step for Frances.

"Dost tha think tha'll' better thaself?" the mill boss demanded, gruffly skeptical when she went to tell him she was quitting.

"Yes, I do," our Frances replied with spunk.

"I were a good worker," she explains, "an 'e were sorry to let me go."

A dressmaker didn't have to start work until eight, so Frances waited around almost an hour for her friend to come and meet her at the dressmakers' shop. When at last she walked into the place, she knew she'd made the right decision. Instead of the dingy factory, she walked into the workshop with the bright morning sun streaming in through high windows. All the women, chatting and laughing as they worked, were wearing gay white paper hats to keep the sun off. And by the end of the week, they'd put her on piece work and Frances was earning more than the thirty shillings she'd left behind in the mill.

In sewing, a girl started on simple skirts, then worked up through underclothing to dresses and finally tailoring. Soon Frances was making samples, for which she won prizes.

One girl at work wrote this poem for her on a birthday:

To Frances from Viola:
There's a grey little room built close by me
For hours on end it's as quiet as can be.
A nice person is there sewing, with deftness and haste
Dresses to please ladies of discriminating taste.
Out of this quiet rise peals of laughter,
Giggles and squeals to reach the rafter.
Whether sober or jovial, she's very sweet.
Happy Birthday, Frances, and thanks for the treat.

In a year or two, Frances took Hannah into the shop to teach her the craft, but it was never as easy for her as Frances made it seem. Hannah tells how, the first day she went, Frances told her to go iron a blue sash. Well, as any cramped family meal spent seated next to my grandmother will teach you, she's left-handed. At the shop, they'd fixed her up with a left-handed iron, a great big heavy thing that got gas fed to it with a long, awkward pipe. All the other irons were in use, so Hannah was obliged to use this monster. She could hardly lift it, let alone iron with it. By the time she had hoisted it off the board again, the sash had disappeared. It was stuck to the bottom of the iron, burnt to a crisp!

"Tha'll' 'ave to do better'n that. Tha'll' 'ave to do better'n that," Frances scolded in her busy fashion.

Hannah also tells how she cut a blob out of the center of a simple skirt pattern, ruining the length of fabric. I've shed tears myself, picking out seams under my grandmother's sharp eye. I have great sympathy for my poor, gentle auntie! "Our Frances never understood how hard it was," Mona, who watched this all as a younger sister, explains. "Aunt Frances has a natural talent, but Auntie Hannah has persistence, and she developed hers."

Both women stayed at sewing until they were expecting their first children. ("In them days you wouldn't think of working when you was showing! But they do now, don't they? They don't care.") Then they continued to do dressmaking and alterations in their homes and helped their families this way. "Dressmaking isn't well paid," Hannah says. "But you make it up in what you can do for your kids."

⮌

Violet, the youngest, did not go to the factory like the others. When she reached twelve years old, she answered an ad in the paper and got a job in the swankiest florist's shop in Bradford. She longed to be able to go in the back and have a hand in making the bouquets. She'd always been a bit of an artist. "I liked to mess about, waste me time."

Of course, she never got to do that. All she got to do was wait on customers, then go to the till and give them their change. No cash register or adding machine helped her. She had to do it all in her head and "twenties and twelves"—the British money system of pounds, shillings, and pence—was too much for her. She could do it all right when she was alone, but when a customer was watching, she got flustered and jumbled things up.

Usually, the shop had a boy to deliver boxes for them, but on her first day, the boy wasn't there. Violet herself had to take four big boxes of flowers on the tram to a wedding. She quite liked that. It made a change from the shop, and weddings always gave a big tip. But negotiating the tram was difficult, a twelve-year-old with all those boxes. The trams were the sort that could be driven from either end, but if you got on with packages, you had to leave them at the front before going to find your seat in the rear.

When her stop came, Violet had to jump off and rush around to the front, fighting crowds and always afraid the conductor would take off again before she'd reclaimed the packages.

At that first wedding, they ushered her in. "Eee, we're so glad tha'st come. Come in, come in." They were all in their "flower dresses," ready to enter the church. "Now, tha must show us 'ow to 'old these bouquets."

"Well, I'd never seen a bouquet before." Violet looked down, bewildered, then decided they shouldn't be held downwards so no one could see them. "'Old them well up," she said. "That's right. Well up."

She also had to pin the boutonnieres on the men's lapels. "That were too close to a man for me."

So she went to work in a sweet shop, then a stationer's, a hairdresser's. Finally, Violet went with Frances and Hannah to learn dressmaking where she eventually worked her way up to sample hand for the wedding dresses. She made all the dresses for her own wedding party.

When a girl left school at thirteen or fourteen, she was given a certificate that entitled her to attend night classes. If she kept up attendance and did well, the certificate would renew itself each year until she was twenty-one. All of the Whitaker girls continued to take a selection of the classes offered in millinery, dressmaking, cooking, embroidery, shorthand, bookkeeping, first aid, and home nursing. My grandmother did so well in dressmaking that she passed an exam, which entitled her to teach courses on the subject anywhere in England, although she never did. She used to win prizes, too, for attendance, which entitled her to select a book of her own to keep. She chose a Bible one year, the next a collection of romantic poetry by the American whose name my grandmother loves to say in a squeaky little voice: "Eelie Wheelie Weelcox" (Ella Wheeler Wilcox). Barbara took classes in home nursing and first aid, loved them both, and passed exams to teach in them.

When she describes all she did, work, school, hard playing in between, my grandmother leaves us speechless. "What about your sisters?" we ask her.

"Oh, they never did as much as me."

"Were they lazy?"

"I wouldn't say lazy. I'd say tired. I remember our 'Annah would come 'ome from work and sit—so—all evening." Grandma slouches in a chair with her head in her hands, mimicking being worn out.

Ivy remembers wrapping her shawl around Hannah on the way home at night and feeling her sister tremble beside her. She was too tired, almost, to carry those heavy old clogs up Bowling Old Lane to Moulson Street one more time.

CHURCH

"How did she do it?"

Once again, Uncle Noel is trying to solve the mystery. How did my great-grandmother manage to keep all eight girls faithful members of the Church of Jesus Christ of Latter-day Saints that had captured her own heart? Her husband, the bright parent who could "tell a tale and sing a song," the one they all loved, was no strong disciplinarian and wasn't always at her side at home.

At first, I don't get the point of the question. I take the answer as much for granted as the aunties do. "It were t' church teachings." Nothing can be more self-explanatory than that.

Now, in my fifties, I've seen the best of Mormon "families are forever" cracked by divorce. I've seen the sweetest mothers produce "ungrateful daughters," stalwart men beget renegade sons. All the church teachings in the world, delivered from the pulpit of the new "hanging gardens of Babylon" conference center, I've turned from myself with a stifled yawn.

"'Church teachings'?" Uncle Noel scoffs. "If it were as simple as that, anyone could manage a family of eight just as well.

"What is particularly suspicious," he goes on, "is just how little time the interviews actually dwell on religious matters."

He's right. "You'd think religious matters would permeate everything." They don't. In fact, the aunties turn from the subject, as if we'd brought up sex or something. With the possible exception of Auntie Mona, we are the ones who bring it up.

"Was there a preacher you particularly liked?"

"No."

"An inspiring Sunday School teacher?"

"Don't remember much about Sunday School. 'Cept it were fun fer t' kids."

"How was it then?"

"You should read t' books. Then you'd know."

"At what age did you read your books, Mother?"

"Well, I—I don't think—"

Later, Uncle Noel tells me the obvious: "She never read the books. No more than Auntie Ivy." Who got as far as God telling Nephi to kill Laban in the first pages of the Book of Mormon and gave up.

Now, Grandma insists, "It were bred in me."

"That's what I mean," Uncle Noel insists. "How was it, then?"

Rare spectacle: my grandmother, at a loss for words.

"Didn't your mother ever talk to you about her conversion?"

"No. Me mother were a very quiet person."

Says Mona: "Like Shakespeare's Cordelia, ''Er voice was ever soft and low, an excellent thing in a woman.'"

"Now, that didn't carry on," Uncle Noel, watching his own mother distracted to some bit of shrieking laughter.

When he can bring her back to the interview, he tries again. "Was your mother strict? Did she force you to go?"

Ever and again, the answer is "No. Never. I only remember my mother raising her voice once." For some of the girls, the answer is not at all.

At first, Mary Jane went to church alone, leaving little Doris, who can't have been over five years old, at home to look after the rest with their father nearby in case of disasters.

But we remember how Doris got into her mother's clothes, in particular getting scent on the old Salvation Army bonnet.

After that, the black bonnet disappeared and Mary Jane took Doris with her, leaving Barbara in charge instead. Doris remembers so well standing small at her mother's side as that beautiful Welsh soprano raised in "Sweet Is the Work, My God, My King," reading from a hymn book without notes. "There were a lot of men with long black frock coats. At the close of the meeting, someone came and said something pleasant to me. I felt Mother wanted to stay a little longer, but she were anxious to get 'ome to t' others."

When she was about eight, a girl was baptized and joined the weekly trek to church. What a flurry there was Sunday morning as the girls hurried to get dressed and then lined up, as many as five abreast, to walk nearly an hour, up hill and down, to "t' right o' Westgate Hall and up a backstreet to a side door, up some wooden steps into a sort of club room over a factory workshop" where the Saints would gather. They also rented space in Sackville Street for a time. For Conference, they would rent a large hall, and there would be quite a to-do to get ready for the numbers of people who would come "from all over t' district to 'ear an apostle of the Lord."

The girls would often take their lunch with them and stay at the meeting house all day. During evening service, Grandma remembers, she would sometimes fall asleep. But she tried not to. She would look up at the lights and "think of angels and things."

The Myth insists that all went to Sunday School without a second thought. But Violet, in spite of the fact that she is now a Relief Society president herself, has one memory. "I don't think anybody rebelled." She insists on that first, then continues, "Except our Frances. Once. I do remember that."

"What?" Frances can't believe it.

"Tha were' late for church."

"Were I?" Still incredulous.

Frances was sixteen or seventeen, and Violet, who was still too young to make the long trip across town, was always fascinated by the dressing-up process of her older sisters. She recalls, "Tha were' late for church and tha were' just stood in front o' t' mirror, preening thaself."

"I never were. I never put on lipstick or anything like that."

"Aye?" Violet dares her to continue.

Violet may be small, but she's no coward. "An' I've never seen me mother as cross. 'Cause tha were' just stood there and tha were' late. I don't know what she said to thee, but tha just shrugged tha shoulders. 'I won't go.'" Again, mincing. "'I won't go.'"

"Did she go?" Cousin Delia asks. We are all on the edge of our seats.

"She'd go," Hannah insists, though not without anxiety. It unnerves her to find a hole in the Myth.

Violet can't say. Much as she loved to watch and idealized her older sisters, she hated a row more and fled upstairs to escape it.

Frances, when her sisters aren't around, admits her mother did lecture her. She puts on an authoritative tone so the message will sink into us as well. "You can gain your whole—but lose—"

Now the authority fails. Grandma can't remember the scripture she meant to quote.

I cover the microphone and ask Uncle Noel in an undertone, "Did she even hear the words when she was a girl, or only the tone of her mother's voice?"

My uncle ignores me. "I know just what you mean, Mother," he says.

It wasn't until 1934—the girls were grown—that Heber J. Grant, president and prophet of the church, came to Bradford to dedicate a new chapel in Woodland Street. It was their first building not used for something else during the week. Here the Saints worshipped for many years. They loved that place and cleaned and redecorated it with care from time to time.

Unfortunately, the neighborhood began to deteriorate rather rapidly, faster than they were able to gather the funds to build a new chapel in a better location. Neighborhood rowdies kept breaking in and "pilfering." Of all the things they took, the saddest loss was the nearly life-sized plaque commemorating Mary Jane's many years as Relief Society president that once decorated one wall.

The wooden plaque, portraying a pioneer woman with a child on either side of her, was carved and inlaid by Arthur Jeffery, Violet's husband. He was a carpenter who, at a later date, when I was a teenager longing for castles in the air, turned his craftsmanship upon my bedroom—the first of my own—and truly made a palace of it. At the bottom of the plaque, Mary Jane had asked there to be carved what had come to be her motto: "More things are wrought by prayer than this world dreams of."

"'Tis true," the girls insist. "No one knew 'alf t' things she did. She were a lady, a very quiet person, and she never talked about 'erself."

The plaque lauds her twelve years of service in the Relief Society. Doris insists "it were fourteen or fifteen years" that her mother stood in this post of heavy charity giving, "mother of t' branch." My grandmother, with her usual exaggeration, a great believer in and perpetuator of the Myth, says it "were twenty year at least."

When she first received her call to be president, Mary Jane asked for and received her patriarchal blessing under the hands of Patriarch James H. Wallis. It says, in part: "Thou hast been called to labor among his handmaidens, even those who are mothers to the choice spirits that are waiting and longing to come on the earth and take their part in this great work. The Lord will inspire thee, dear sister, if thou will' seek him, and thou will' be mighty in counsel. His handmaidens shall come unto thee for guidance and for direction in the management of their homes and to discuss with thee the many problems that pertain unto the purpose of their creation. . . . I bless thee with health and strength, and seal it upon thee by the power I hold from the crown of thy head to the soles of thy feet. . . . I bless thee that thou may' feel the presence of the spirit of the Lord in thy home, and that love and peace and union may abound there; that thy children may respect thy counsel and follow thy Godly example and bless thy name for having taught them to live uprightly before the Lord."

My mother suggests Mary Jane was "like Mona," or maybe even like my saintly mother herself. Mary Jane was often sick, stayed in bed while Ralph tended to things like the fire and breakfast that most other men of his time wouldn't be caught dead laying their hands to. Mary Jane was a woman so caught up in doing good for others that her own family was neglected. The scrapings always hardened in the great yellow bread bowl, my mother says, because Mary Jane had run off to deliver fresh loaves to someone she thought needed them.

"She's al'ays at church," Ralph complained good-naturedly of his wife. "She'll die at church." Which all agree turned out to be prophetic.

When Mary Jane was first made Relief Society president, Sister Emma Rae Riggs McKay, wife of the European mission president and later of the church president, came to visit Bradford branch. Going over the books, she became angry because the women's society had quite a lot of money in the bank. "The Relief Society is here to give money away," Sister McKay said, "not to hoard it."

When Mary Jane told Ralph this, he said, "Oh, don't worry, Mother. You can soon alter that."

And she did.

When Mary Jane went to visit widows or shut-ins, she would often take one or two of the girls with her. The women would sit upstairs and talk while downstairs, the girls were set to work cleaning and scrubbing floors, whatever needed to be done.

Hannah remembers one time when an old woman, keeper of a little shop as their grandmother had been, had a floor so filthy with the condensed mixture of coal soot and oven grease that it was like sludge. It took Hannah hours to clean it all up, and when she had finished, the woman gave her two little sweets from her shop. "That were all!" But, Hannah says, now that she is old, she realizes how much those women must have appreciated the help.

Harvest Thanksgiving Sunday caused great excitement when gifts of fruits and vegetables decorated the chapel. After the meeting, they were taken to the sick and the poor.

In 1916, a slight young missionary from Salt Lake City came to Bradford to serve as district president. Although not yet twenty, his hair was already thinning. He nonetheless caused the usual flutter among the hopeful Whitaker girls. A missionary had to give his two years to the Lord before he considered marriage. And if they were clear sighted, like Barbara, the girls would understand that these Americans, still not burdened by the European war, would never stay in England, but would go home to marry sweethearts waiting there.

The name of this young man was Joseph Smith Nelson, of the best Mormon pedigree.

Ivy was suffering from a stomach ulcer at the time. So severe was her ailment, she sometimes had to keep to her bed. More than once, Ralph had to ask again, "Is she still alive?" when he came home. Elder Nelson gave her a blessing. Later that night, he wrote home to an aunt: "I've just been over to the Whitaker house: a blind man with eight daughters. The mother and daughters are all members." After that, Ivy's stomach healed.

Again, this was during the war, and all the Englishmen were gone. Only women, very old men, and young boys were left to man a patriarchal church organization. As his assistants, Elder Joseph Nelson had only two fifteen-year-old boys: Reggie Saunders and Harry Clark as district assistants. Mary Jane served as a district missionary with Sister Walker of faraway Halifax. Young girls were sent on preaching assignments to other town branches. A good friend, Hettie Gelder, was branch clerk (say "clark").

Frances, too, served a stint as clerk. "Can you believe me, wi' me 'andwriting?" Grandma exclaims, gesturing with a fork in her preferred left hand.

"Yes, can you believe me?" says Violet, nine years her junior. "I'd to substitute for 'er and read that 'andwriting."

Substitute when Grandma was? Well, she won't tell us where.

Barbara, at seventeen or eighteen, taught the adult Sunday School class "wi' old Brother Turner." She says it in such a deep and ponderous fashion—like the bassoon plays Grandpa in *Peter and the Wolf*— that we make no mistake of just what a doddering old man he must have been. And everyone participated in street meetings.

The family was always having the missionaries over for dinner.

Once the young men came early while Ivy was still in the kitchen taking a bath. Doris ran in and shut the bath top down on top of her.

"She'll tell you to this day I tried to drown 'er," Doris says with spunk.

"She did an' all," Ivy insists.

Hannah remembers what a privilege it was at eight or nine years old to finally be allowed to stay up to listen when the elders came. Father would always sing and play for them and discuss scripture late into the night. He always knew the Bible better than they did. And he was the one still unbaptized.

George F. Richards was another one of these missionaries.

He spoke fondly of the fifteen children he'd left at home in Utah, one of whom was LeGrand Richards, a longtime member of the quorum of twelve apostles. His "fifteen assets," Elder Richards called them.

"Assets!" Ralph exclaimed. "I thought they was liabilities!"

One evening, one of the missionaries gave a prayer in which he promised that one day every Whitaker girl would have the opportunity to come to Zion if she wanted. "Me father were dumbfounded" for a response to this, Hannah says, for "'e never thought any of us would ever 'ave t' money to go anywhere."

Ralph paid tithing, a full 10 percent of his income, long before he was baptized. He put off actually joining for years. Although he knew the church was true, some of the girls suggest, he never felt good enough. Sometimes Mary Jane would walk him to the pubs or clubs where he was to entertain, but she'd never go in.

"There's an evil influence there," Mona makes sure to quote her mother.

She says her father felt it, too, but it was his living. He despised one man in the branch who passed the sacrament. Ralph recognized the man's voice as one of the rowdiest in one public house he played at. Ralph hated hypocrisy and would not descend to it himself.

Mary Jane often read the church magazine, *Millennial Star*, out loud to Ralph. It made an impression on the girls. My grandmother remembers one night when they were coming home from a visit with Ralph's parents, they saw a new star in the sky.

"We thought the Millennium 'ad come at last," Grandma says.

"Must have been Venus," Uncle Noel says.

One rare day, Mary Jane was the guest of honor and had to speak at a secular Mother's Day program. This happened only because the lord mayor and his wife had to bow out at the last minute. Mary Jane was given flowers and had to sit on the stand with all the dignitaries. That embarrassed her.

This speech cannot have been particularly profound. And indeed, "If my mother is any example," Uncle Noel says, "we can see the sort of doctrine they imbibed. It came in the form of misquoted, misunderstood scripture and Articles of Faith, anything from Shakespeare to Dickens taken as holy writ, and rather wild faith-promoting coincidences."

"No wonder she is so cheery," agrees my skeptical husband.

It was neither the fervent Mona nor the practical, meticulous Barbara who converted her friends. "It were our Doris," Mona says, not without a hint of envy.

Happy, fun-loving Doris was so popular among the girls with whom she worked that she earned the jealousy not only of her sister but of a spiritualist who was also trying to win converts. The Mormon girls knew about spiritualists: "They were of the devil, and they 'ad it out for our family," Mona says, "ever since that one tried to convert Mother in the boarding 'ouse in London."

A pair of missionaries once asked the president of the mission if they could attend a spiritualist meeting. "All right, you can go," the president said. "But you must fast three days before you do." When they went, none of the medium's tricks would work. "The spirits will not come," she said in her hollow, eerie voice, "until you two young men leave."

They testified to this the next Sunday.

Despite such warning, Doris, never-say-die, was enticed to go to a meeting one evening not long after. All the way up the hill to the meeting place, she kept telling her friends: "You know, I don't believe in it. I really don't believe in it."

When they got to the sitting room with the lamps turned down low, the first thing that happened was that the medium stood up and, "in the very voice of Doris," repeated all that she had been saying as she came up the hill. Doris got up and fled and never was enticed again.

Doris wasn't even conscious that she was converting anyone.

To this day, she doesn't know how her two best friends, Annie Groom and Lily Briggs, came to ask for baptism. Lily's family were very strict Catholics. Her father said, "If you join that church, I'll go and burn it down." Nevertheless, she did join in a private baptism with Annie one night.

More than doctrine, it was the good times the girls remember and that seem to have impressed their friends. Connected with the church were concerts. They dressed up as fairies, Little Bo Peep, and Little Boy Blue, and gave shows. Later, they formed an orchestra and played together at rich people's garden parties ("'cept they was al'ays midges," Grandma says), competitions (which I doubt they often won), and dances.

Ivy and Hannah played violins, Frances the cello, and Barbara sang. Once, during a blackout in the war, our Frances fell coming home from a concert and broke the neck on her cello. Her father had to fix it.

Frances even managed to get my own nonmember, no-nonsense, poor-mixer grandfather to grow out a "ginger beard" and play the king in one church concert before they were married. None of us can believe that.

"Eee, an' t' rambles!" Every Saturday afternoon, rain or shine, and sometimes longer ones over holidays.

When Auntie Ivy pulls the bundle of yellowed papers out of the shoe box and hands it to me, I hold my breath. Inexpertly typed, blurry as the fourth or fifth carbon copy of a stack, it is as I've reproduced it below. Mormons were instructed, "in them days," to keep careful records and diaries. "The scripture of the future will be written from them, like the Book of Mormon from the time of Nephi, the Doctrine and Covenants from the time of Joseph Smith," was preached in so many words.

This diary is as close as Ivy knows to future scripture, a careful record of events that were faith affirming for her and which she hopes will be for future generations. I find it so illustrative of the relationships of young women before they got boxed into cell phones and parent-driven activities, as to their language and pastimes and self-confidence during the dark days of the First World War, so telling of their view of the physical layout of their world and details of language and food and prices, that I will not tamper with it.

THE TERRIBLE EIGHT—A WALKING TOUR TO BLACKPOOL WITH EIGHT GIRLS

This is an account of a walking & tramcar holiday in Aug 1917 from Bradford, Yorks. to Blackpool, Lancashire, Eng. with my sister Doris & myself Ivy Whitaker & friends, Alice Brooks (who wrote this diary), Sarah Pace, Eva Pace (Peg), Lily Briggs, Annie Groom, Moyra Holmes. Eight young ladies. Ivy was the youngest, 17 yrs. Sarah, the oldest, about 25 yrs. All were members of the Latter-day Saints' Church except Moyra. ["Well, poor Moyra."]

∾

Saturday Aug. 10th, 1917

Arrived at Town Hall Bradford at 5:25 AM. Took a tramcar to Queensbury at 5:30 AM (1 1/2d). Arrived at Queensbury 6:05 AM. Left there at 6:15 AM. Boarded a tramcar for Halifax (3d). Arrived there at 6:45 AM. Then caught a car to Hebden Bridge at 6:50 AM (6d). Arrived there at 7:40 AM. Set off walking through Sandbed to Todmorton. Arrived there at 8:55 AM, having walked 5 1/4 miles. Then took a tramcar at 9 AM to Portsmouth (4d) & had our breakfast which we had brought with us & eat it on the top of tramcar (double-decker). Arrived at Portsmouth at 9:30 AM. Then walked 6 miles to Burnley, Lancashire, passing through Walkmire & Holme. Rode on a flour wagon about 1 mile up hill. ["Someone gave us a lift."] Then had a tramcar ride (1d) into Central Burnley. Arrived at 11:50 AM & took a tramcar to Rose Grove (1 1/2d). Walked from Rose Grove to Grusold Twistle, 3 1/2 miles, then took tramcar to Acerington (1d). Arrived there at 1:20. Took tramcar from Preston Yew Road to Billing (2d). Arrived 1:40 PM. Then walked 7 1/2 miles to Farrington Park. Then by tram car to Preston (2d).

We walked almost 20 miles. It rained heavy part of the time. Then a thunderstorm overtook us so 4 of the girls took the train from Preston to Blackpool, costing 2s & 3d. Arrived at Tabbot St. Station at 5:40 PM. The rest who continued on foot arrived much later.

At 5:45 set out for lodges. Still pouring rain. Moyra Holmes was there to greet us. She was the rich girl who came on the train from Bfd. to Blackpool. She welcomed us & took us upstairs to change out of our wet clothes & then we came down to tea. Some very nice girls staying at the same house. After tea, 3 of us went to Winter Gardens [Europe's second-largest theatre and newly opened to the public during the Great War] & we put our things away in drawers & waited for the rest to arrive. Then we had family prayers & prepared for bed

& that is where the fun came in. When we were all undressed we just remembered we didn't know where to sleep for we knew 2 of us had to sleep in another room so we sat on the edge of the beds & laughed until our sides were sore & someone happened to see an emergency bell so we pressed it but there was no response. Annie kept her finger on it until she heard footsteps on the stairs. As we were all in bed but Annie & Lily, they bobbed down. Then in walked the Landlady, so Sarah told her there were 2 girls stranded in their nightgowns and of course she had to laugh especially when she saw us all peeping out of the bedclothes. She then came around & gave us all a gentle tap somewhere. (Whack, whack!) Then she told Annie & Lily, who were pretending to be shy, to go with her. She showed them to their room, so they went, dancing down the hall. Then I put out the light & tried to get some sleep. But all in vain. First one cracking jokes & then another. Some fun we had, but finally we went to sleep.

Next morning Doris woke up at 6 AM & went to the window to watch the bathers. She then commenced to wake us all up. Some task! All started to parade around the bedroom in nightgowns. Then Doris decided to dress herself so we all followed suit. There was some shouting and searching for clothes. Those ready first go down & order breakfast, then we all went down to partake of it, cracking jokes all the time with the other room girls. They were nice and friendly. The Landlady came in to help us to laugh—a nice, friendly, motherly old lady.

After breakfast, Doris, Annie, Lily & Ivy went to see Lily's mother at Bloomfield. Some house & some garden! All kinds of vegetables & flowers were growing & we watched them dig potatoes. Then we sat on deck chairs lounging until time to return to our digs. While we were there we saw real tiger skins & daggers & knives from Africa.

We set out for digs about 11:45 AM. Arrived at 12:15 for dinner. We had leg of lamb, new potatoes, peas, mint sauce & rice pudding. As usual, another lively time at table. After dinner Moyra played the piano to digest it. We then decided to get ready for a ride on the Ferris Wheel. Some sensation! Not much excitement, rather slow. When we reached the top, we could see almost all over Blackpool & nearly seasick. We then went on the North Pier (some jetty!). Mussels were growing up the ironworks. The band was playing live music. Then we left for tea, arriving back at 4:30.

After tea one of the girls played the piano & we all sang (some noise!) like a tap room. We have only one gentleman staying at the rooms with us & he entertained us next. Some talent! Tired of singing, we went upstairs & played consequences. Some more laughter. We decided to go for a walk at 9:30 PM to make us sleep better, so we all set off for the cliffs on the front. My! Spooners were everywhere, in every corner. We walked 2 1/2 miles on the cliffs, inspected Uncle Tom's Cabin [but didn't go in the famous pub], then turned back. Having walked 5 miles, we were ready for bed.

We were supposed to have been in by 10:30 PM on Sunday nights, but it was 10:50. When we arrived we had to pay a penny fine. As we were all famished (hungry) after the sea breeze, we ate a good supper. Then retired for bed after family prayers. Then we started arguing which bed to sleep in. Finally, all in bed. Doris & Sarah slept in another room. We tried to sleep but Moyra wouldn't let us. She kept the light on & sat on the bedroom floor in her night dress reading. She looked something like cupid. Ivy fell asleep, but Eva threw a pillow at her. Poor kid, nearly scared to death. But she kept the pillow so Eva had to sleep without.

Next morning Lily awoke at 4 AM & went around waking us all up. We then prepared for sea bathing. Some sights! Finally all ready in our bathing suits and caps. We set off at 4:30 AM for the sea. It was very cold at first but was a bit warmer as we went deeper in. We played all kinds of games—such fun! There were crowds watching the bathers. We stayed in the water about 1/2 hr. & then slipped our shoes and raincoats on & went home to dry ourselves. Some sights, all fighting for towels, clothes, etc.! All were dressed at last & went down for breakfast. More fun at the table & more cute tales were told.

After breakfast, we all decided to have some pictures taken together. Some terrible sight! That hard task done, we all took a 2d ride to North Shore. Some breeze blowing. Lovely weather. All sat on cliffs eating ice cream & listening to fellows telling fortunes. After sitting there about 1 hr., Sarah, Doris, Ivy & myself (Alice) walked home while the others rode. We arrived home in time for dinner consisting of remains of lamb, new potatoes, peas & sego pudding. One of the company played piano for us while we sang & then the gentleman gave a sketch turn [performance].

Tired of singing, Annie, Lily, Sarah, Ivy & I went upstairs. Doris, Peg (Eva) & Moyra went to see if the photos were ready & came back with them. They were good, just like "The Terrible Eight". We all stayed home in the afternoon in the bedroom, Doris making us scream with laughter. Then we had an early tea & got ready to go to the Tower, a fine place. First we went to the menagerie & watched the monkeys perform. Then we went into the ballroom to watch the kiddies.

Ivy & I went home about 9 o'clock as we were smothered with a cold. Ordered our supper & went to bed. As it was our turn to sleep in the other room, we never heard the other girls carry on, so we had a good night's sleep.

Next morning we went into the girls' bedroom, but all were asleep but Sarah. So we awoke them all & 4 of them went to bathe in the sea but Ivy & I were still smothered in a cold so we took care of their raincoats & shoes & as it was cold, they did not stay in very long. Then they went home & I watched them squabble for their clothes, etc. Some sight! All dressed, we went down for breakfast, but as we saw the postman across the street, we waited to see if there was any news from Home. I can tell you, plenty of mail for us! Then we had breakfast & went upstairs & had a good laugh as usual. Then went out shopping for bread, cards, etc. & came back & commenced writing cards home. Ivy & I then proceeded to get our pictures taken together, as we were dressed almost alike.

Had dinner—Yorkshire pudding, new potatoes, sausage & bilberry pie. After dinner we all went upstairs & lounged about on the beds eating chocolates. Don't they make your mouth water?

Then all at once someone decided to go wading in the sea in the sunshine. It was hot after the thunderstorm. Lily & I took care of the shoes, etc. Lily is reading with her umbrella up to keep the sun from frizzling her up & I am trying to write this diary but can't for watching people wading, making sand pies & castles. That's the worst of being a busybody. Some of the waders are back & we only have one towel with us & of course all want it at once. Annie dropped her stockings into the sea but put them on anyway.

Annie, Lily, Ivy & I all visit an oyster stall. Some slip-down! Lily's slithered down in no time. Ivy's jumped out of her mouth as soon as she put it in & mine refused to go down, so I chewed. Some taste!

We all returned home to have some tea & then go for a stroll. After walking a mile or so, we reached the South Shore (amusements). What fun! First we have a penny'rth of aerial flight, then walk around & then four of us decided to have a ride on the Velvet Coaster. Wish you could have seen us! Lily rolls in head first & I on the top of her. She struggles to get up but all in vain as I was holding her down & crowds were watching us. At last a fellow came to rescue her up. Annie & Ivy sat behind bent in two with laughing. Finally we all set off for the ride talked about—up hill & down dales. I thought we were on a rough sea. Some ride, though.

Tired of the South Shore we went out & walked on the Promenade. Saw some boys. Come across a wounded soldier being wheeled out by his pals so we dared Sarah to push him. So off she went & the boys left us to wheel him the length of the Prom & back in our turns. I guess we were practicing, eh? I can tell you he was quite a nice young man & he had quite a nice time with us girls, first one cracking jokes & then another. I guess he felt happy amongst us. We asked him if he would like to go back to his pals but he said he was quite alright with us.

We left him at about 9:30 PM as he had no lamp on his chair. Then we walked up & down the Prom, as we heard there was going to be a high tide at 10:29 PM & we thought we would like to see one. While we waited we picked up with some boys & had some fun with them & then clicked with 2 more & stayed until 10:29 but no high tide ever came. It was a false alarm. Crowds were waiting, but we were all taken in. Nevertheless, we had a good time.

About 10:45 PM we all returned home & ordered supper & returned upstairs. We had all undressed & just finished family prayers when the three girls from the opposite room knocked on our door. So we let them in & all sat on our beds in our nightgowns while Doris did nothing but make us laugh by telling all kinds of cute tales. Our sides fair ached with laughing! About 12:30 the three girls left, so we all jumped into bed & went to sleep.

Next morning we all overslept & a servant came to wake us & we all started searching for clothes. Such fun! We could find anyone's but our own. Sarah goes down to see if the postman has made his daily visit. Comes back with an armful of letters & cards. All read them & go down for breakfast. More fun while eating.

After all had lounged on the beds it was settled then to go for a sail. Whilst in the boat Sarah writes a letter & I write my diary. It shows how calm the sea was. After being on the water 1/2 hr. we came off & next we visit Punch & Judy show. Then return home eating ice cream. We wrote some more cards home & ordered dinner which was meat & potato pie & stewed pears.

After dinner, lounge on the beds. Then some of us got ready to bathe. Go down to sea & have pictures taken in the water. All come back. Put on shoes & raincoats. The usual scrap for towels. Returned home.

Had an early tea & we all go to Winter Gardens as it was called Bradford Night & we sat in the balcony & watched dancers & watched the children perform all dressed up in soldiers' uniforms representing the different Allies' countries, pretending to be in the trenches fighting. Then pretending nurses came to attend the wounded. It was sure a great performance. Next we watched Mr. Gladhill & daughter from Bradford introduce a new waltz. They clapped it back on twice. Then we left the ballroom & walked around the roof gardens. Very pretty. Next we visited a group of singers where all the latest songs were introduced & then we left for home.

Had supper. Retired upstairs & had family prayers & jumped into bed & then 2 girls knocked on our door & we let them in. As usual, more fun & performing in nightgowns. At 12:00 PM the girls left & we all fell asleep.

Next morning Annie & Lily who were sleeping in the other bedroom came in about 7 AM to wake us all up & some of us went shopping. Gobs of bread & 1/2 lb. of butter every day. I can tell you, I'll never be a mother again. Ha. Ha. After breakfast we all prepare to go for a stroll. The sun is shining & makes all things look glorious. Sarah & I went for an ice cream sandwich & then stood watching & talking dolly on the sands. Left the beach as the tide was fast coming in.

We all go for a ride around Fairyland. The scenes were sure lovely. Fairies dancing, dwarves pretending to chop wood & another scene representing washing day. We all go for a stroll on the North Shore. We watch the rough sea & some write cards & some read. We go home at 12 PM for dinner: Liver & onions, new potatoes, ice cream. As usual, laughter at the table.

After dinner, a boy played the piano. Then we go lounge on bed until 2 PM. Then some of the girls get ready to go bathing. Annie & Lily & I lay on sands taking care of clothes. After being in the sea for 1/2 hr. the girls come back on the sands to wipe their legs & all their costumes become sandy so they sit in a pool nearby to wash off. (Loud laughter.) Then the usual fight for towel, etc.

Finally all dressed. We then go shopping. All are fed up with married life (housebuying of food). Came back & played games in the garden. Then we prepared to go to the Palace. (Some place!) First we went through the wax workshop & then through the monkey house & then into the ballroom. There were just eight of us so we were able to make up a set of lancers [dance] & after going through it three times we felt tired & decided to go home & have supper & retired upstairs. Undressed & had family prayers & Eva & Moyra had not yet come up so we decided to play a trick on them. We put 2 hair brushes in their beds. Doris put one in the bottom of Eva's & I put one in the middle of Moyra's. Moyra slept all night & never felt it, but when Eva put her foot on it, we all laughed when she gave out a yell.

Peg (Eva) woke up with no bedclothes on her & Doris & I had a sheet around our necks. All get up. The usual fight about clothes, etc. Lily goes down for mail & comes back with her arms full of letters & cards. Lots of laughter & then down to breakfast.

That done, all go upstairs & start packing. Some job, first one saying "Whose is this? Whose is this?" It was like a ball game when someone had scored. One looking under the bed & then another to see if anything was left.

Then dinner was ready, after which all go out to buy presents & rock candy & pack. Then take off to station & send our luggage home & then come back & have tea. Fun as usual. Then we go looking for seaweed & then go wading & have a ripping time. The sun was shining glorious after a heavy shower.

After being in the water 1/2 hr. we dried our feet. Annie & Lily go to fish & chip shop whilst we get supper ready. Then after supper we got to bed at 9:30 PM to prepare for the tramp home the next day.

We woke up at 7:30 & have breakfast & wait for the postman with registered letters, etc. After reading mail, all get ready to set out on our homeward journey. Caught Lyntham car at 9:15 AM for 8d. Pass through St. Anne's & also pass through beautiful sand hills, Squire Gate where wounded soldiers are stationed. Reach Lytham 9:45 & then set out on a 10 mile walk, passing through Wharton & Freckleton in Ashton. At 12:50 PM caught tramcar to Preston, 2d. Arrived at 1:15 PM. Have dinner on buscar for Higher Walton (fare 4d). Arrived at 2:30 PM. Have a ride on a coal car motor lorry to Cherry Tree, 5 1/2 mi. Get off with faces like black men. Catch car to Blackburn, 2d. Pass through Mill Lane. Arrive at 3:30 PM. Board car to Acorington 4d. Arrive at 4:15 PM. Catch a tramcar to Rawstenstall (2d). Arrive at 5:05 PM. Then catch a tramcar to Bucup. Arrive at 5:30 PM. Then set out on a 5 1/2 mi. walk, eating our tea on the way. Pass through the Pennine Chain (the backbone of England). The scenery is beautiful. Reach Todmorton 7:30 PM. Catch a tram to Eastwood (2 1/2d). Then walk 1 3/4 mi. to Sandbed. On to Hebden Bridge & took a tram to Halifax. Arrive at 10:10 PM. Catch a tram to Queensbury, then to Bradford 6d. Arrive home at 11:30. Tired out. After supper, to bed & a well-earned rest.

~

[In Ivy's handwriting, on the final page:]

This was written by Alice Brooks. All the girls were members of the Church of Jesus Christ of Latter-day Saints. All were good girls. Moyra Homes—I'm not sure if she was a member & she was the only one we lost track of. Alice, Annie & Sarah have passed on [this is 1982]. Eva (Peg), Doris, Lily & Ivy are all in their eighties & keeping well. Those were happy days.

—Ivy

~

Uncle Noel clasps his fingers over his tweed waistcoat, leans back in his chair, and nods with scholarly superiority. I had quite forgotten, in the midst of a joyful storytelling, that we were conducting a scientific study.

"They were fun-loving people," my uncle declares. "Going to church was fun. It was the most fun they had all week. 'Fun' is what we're seeking a definition for. I don't suppose we're going to find it. Something akin to a medieval mystery, taken on faith. There are those who'd deny altogether."

"And the church made them feel special in a place without much room for special."

After a breath, a shift of the silly grin on my face, I can speak academia as well. "It gave them a place across the sea to turn their hopes to."

"Spirit, preaching, lessons, scripture, service—all of this meant little if it wasn't fun." Uncle Noel adjusts the glasses on his nose and concludes, "Pathetic."

So as assignment, I compare and contrast with the church girlhood I knew. No group of Mormon girls I knew would—would be allowed to—call themselves "terrible." My great-aunts and their friends organized this trip themselves; no adult supervision, no priesthood hovering by. No one bore testimony, no one preached. How unlike the Brighton Girls' Camp in the Wasatch Mountains of my girlhood. How glad I was when my mother said it was too expensive anyway, and I didn't have to go. One's willingness to pay for such things was not, I was glad to learn from my family, a measure of religiosity.

Same with one's tolerance for prepackaged fun. That word became key to me. If we heard over the pulpit that "You'll want to join in this fun activity that Brother and Sister Davis have planned for us—and we all know what a fun couple they are. We'll have fun games and fun food and—"

That many "funs" in one announcement sent up red flags. I knew I would stand alone, miserable in some dark corner the whole time wishing heartily for a book. Until I learned to bring one along. And then decided, I could read better at home. And no, I don't have a testimony that there was something wrong with me.

None of my relatives participated in that keystone of active Mormon life, the temple, while in England. The London Temple wasn't dedicated until 1958, when the theological shift away from Utah as Zion began. Zion had reached capacity. That can be seen as a sea change in my family's theology, too. But of course, since nearly all of them had immigrated by then, the big personal crises had already occurred.

My mother, all the aunties agreed, is much like their mother. As much like this binding force as I'll ever know. Only there is this difference. My mother was yanked from her life in England for her mother's faith at sixteen—just when stability is most important, she always says. And she should know. She mothered us six. And twenty-four foster children, and hundreds of Head Start and kindergarteners she bent to teach with her master's degree in mathematics, since she couldn't quite attain her grandmother's eight on her own.

Yanked away just when she was discovering her own Zion on a farm in Somerset during the first bright days after World War II. The smell of bruised tomato leaves hit her with the force of revelation. The yearning never lets her out of its grasp.

My mother visited all of the aunties in Salt Lake constantly. As charity? Or because she was homesick?

My mother, like her mother's mother, is a good prayer. At least, she prays as often and as hard. Something, however, seems wrong with the transmission at this close range. She prays constantly that I will fail at writing, so I'll stop telling lies for a living. That my sister will stop acting. She tells us she does so.

When my other sister—the good one—was in the hospital dying, leaving four children under the age of six, a crow came to the playground where my mother was watching the grandkids and praying, praying hard. In England, crows are a sign of death.

My mother left her prayers and threw stones at the bird. "No one is dying," she yelled, under the wide-eyed gaze of the children. "Go away. No one is dying."

The black bird did not go. He merely hopped from slide to jungle gym and back again.

The old pine tree near my father's office on the U of U campus blew over that same night.

"If one of your children dies before you," my mother heard the stake president's wife from the world of car rallies and road shows preach over the pulpit the next Sunday, "one of you has sinned." My mother, who never argues with anyone, had words with that woman afterwards.

When my grandmother died, my own mother confided to me, with tears in her eyes, "I am so happy. Now I can go to the church I want."

She wanted the Anglican of her English girlhood. "The music's better."

This shocked me. Not that the music was better. I knew that. I always knew my mother was self-sacrificing, but not to this degree.

That she would force herself, Sunday after Sunday, to attend a church she didn't care for, that she would ask in substitutes for the tithing lesson and the missionary lesson when she taught Primary, for her mother's sake. That she would force us, thinking we were pleasing her—

But of course, my mother's vacation at All Saints' was short lived. Soon one sister needed her attendance to keep the artifice of her perfect LDS life together. Then the other. My mother sacrifices her faith to this day.

However, my mother loves self-sacrifice. Mormonism isn't all that bad. My earth-mother mother believes in not using gas—and in Utah, no one has to drive to the ward house, just as she didn't have to drive to St. Mark's in England. She'd go to the mosque if she lived in Cairo—or in Muslim Bradford today.

Stake car rallies were "fun" (read "required religious") activities of my Mormon youth. At least Mom confirmed my suspicion that, contrary to press, this was an immoral activity, church sponsored, and didn't make me go to them. She allowed me thus to struggle with deep theological issues of good and evil, a discussion I never got at church.

My mother, like her grandmother, loves giving charity.

She likes the Mormon visiting teaching program to point her in the right direction. They always give her six or seven (way above quota) of the hardest cases, the ones no one else wants, that have to be visited every week or more. Mom likes an outlet for her bumper crops of peaches or zucchini. She likes to listen to three-hundred-pound women who can't get out of their chairs when no one else has given them the time of day for years. Mom doesn't have to talk.

She likes knowing what's on at the ward; she can weed in the back garden when some ward activity means gardening in front would require her to greet too many people as they go by in their dress heels.

Everyone in the ward knows they can drop off their fall leaves and their old newspapers on her doorstep. She puts them on the garden. She gets the sweepings from the floor of the local barber shop and puts them out, too. I remember one of the few girls from the ward who ever came to my house stopping in horror out the sight. "It looks," she said, "like a scene out of Auschwitz." She never visited again what was just normal life—and death—to us.

Mom hates weddings, and will never go to one in the ward cultural hall with the yellow roses strung pathetically through the basketball hoop. On the other hand, she loves funerals, and will make funeral potatoes (with her own potatoes) for complete strangers, just to be allowed to attend. I once watched her walk into another room at the funeral home, the room with the viewing no one was at, and whisper to the stranger in the coffin, "Well done. You've won the race."

She, like her ancestors, has not been to the temple, and was not allowed to attend my sister's wedding there. So much for "families are forever."

My mother is the most religious person I know. My cousins call her St. Betty. She's a hard act to follow. And I can't hope to sacrifice my religion for her.

"I'll never be as good as you," I sometimes mourn. "I can't garden like you can. I can't volunteer at the cancer institute and with the immigrants like you do."

She agrees. That's why I disappoint her. "But you can write about it," she concedes. "You learned storytelling from them, from my mother and her sisters. And they from their father, no doubt." She drops back into the dialect she lost the first day she had to stand in front of an American classroom and let her mouth go lazy. "'E could sing a song and tell a tale."

At least I got the "tell a tale" part.

That's why she prays as hard as her grandmother.

I do not answer her prayers. Neither does God. I have not stopped writing.

Hey, writing is easy, as someone famous—not an LDS general authority—once said. You just sit down at the typewriter and open a vein.

Car rallies and weddings with roses strung through the basketball hoop try and fail, in my case, to bind up the wounds.

And you thought people came to America, to Zion, to practice religious freedom.

Facts of Life and Death

BARBARA REMEMBERS DISTINCTLY where she was when she heard the news that day in early August 1914. Everyone had been on edge for several days: would it be war or peace? She was walking home from the factory. She remembers the lowering light, the open windows, the warm air, the tar soft between the cobbles. And then she heard the paper boy shouting—

It was war.

They promised it would end quickly. Month after month, year after year, however, the boy continued to shout: victories won, defeats sustained, the thousands and thousands dead and maimed for life in the trenches.

The home front endured hardships, too. Light was restricted and food scarce. The "ruthless enemy" tried "to starve us into surrender." Bread was rough and dark and rose to 9d. a loaf. Fat became hard to get, even drippin'. Barbara remembers standing in a line for four hours to get half a pound of margarine. Violet says, "If you saw a line, you stood in it, no bother to find out till t' end what you were waiting for."

Things got better when rationing began. Shopping became easier, although you still had little idea what you were going to get. And then one terrible day when Mary Jane was standing at the door with all the ration books for the family for a week, a strong wind came up and blew them out of her hand.

"I don't know how she managed," Violet remembers, "but people kept finding and bringing the books back for weeks afterwards."

Violet also remembers being sent to the store and losing the book herself in another such accident.

Sometimes there was only one egg allowed for the whole family in a week and sometimes that one was bad. If you went back for another, they wouldn't give it to you unless you brought the first one for them to sniff at. "An' then you'd to pay for it." They learned to keep eggs in the cellar in a solution that made them rubbery, but kept them all right for baking.

Being Mormons, they didn't drink tea and would always trade their tea rations with neighbors so they could get a little more butter or cheese or a few more eggs. People close to farms had an easier time of it that those in the cities. Hannah remembers buying a cake or two during World War II and her children wouldn't touch them. "They was like sawdust."

Many of Barbara's friends went to work in the munitions factory to earn more money. They would come home covered with dust— "drugs, all yellow." The Whitaker girls remained in the textile mills and had to deal with no worse than the shoddy khaki material that was constantly breaking, going to clothe column after column of boys marching to the Channel. Ivy, the English working class, minded her two machines, one weaving khaki for uniforms and the other weaving luxury fabrics to rajas' taste.

If a zeppelin were sighted, an alarm would sound and all lights had to go out. But every time a plane flew overhead, the children rushed out to see. Planes were something new then.

One day there was a terrific explosion at Lowmoor Iron Works, an ammunition factory. It was sometime in April, because Violet had just had her birthday. She'd received some Plasticene (modeling clay) and sat on the steps playing with it when the explosion shook the whole house. Many children were out playing in a park near this factory and might have been seriously injured as the fire raged if a quick-thinking coal man had not snatched them all up, tossed them in his cart, and driven away with them as fast as he could make his old nag trot.

The threat of more explosions always existed. "They was goin' t' blow all West Bowling up," Frances says, re-creating panic. So Ralph packed up his family and took them to Leeds where all ten of them slept on the floor of their uncle John's that night. In the morning, the threat had passed, and things settled back to war-normal. But, having to come from Leeds, the girls didn't get to work "while eight." That was the only time Frances missed the pennyhoilman and his half-past-six shutting of the factory gate in all her career.

At the end of the war, every child was given a medal for bravery at school. That evening the armistice was signed and, despite the nasty weather, Barbara took her little sister Violet down to the town square where there was singing and dancing in the street. Alas, Violet lost her medal in the crowds, so the day ended not so happily for her.

Ralph often wondered why the Lord had sent him only girls. When the war came, he didn't wonder any longer. All of his girls, if they'd been boys, would have had to serve in either the First or Second World War.

So many boys killed. Thousands and thousands of boys from Bradford. Even the millowner's son was killed. They were all the boys the girls' age or a little older. Just at the time they began to look for sweethearts and husbands, there were hardly any left. The list of their friends who never married at all is a long one indeed.

∾

Our Ivy knew she was going to die. For the last three days, blood had stained her bloomers. Quietly, alone, she had rinsed them out and hung them to dry each night, hidden behind the bed.

But all the water in the world would not heal the terrible state of her insides.

At last, trembling, shuddering with tears, she found Barbara alone in her room. "Tell Mother I'm dying," she told her older sister, "and that I love her."

Clinical Barbara none too gently set her younger sister straight about this fact of life that had slipped Mary Jane's mind.

By the time Frances came along, their mother had devised a new solution to the problem so no one would be caught unawares again. She gave her twelve-year-old a book called *On the Threshold of Sex* (for readers aged fourteen to twenty-one, by F. J. Gould.) "Go and read it" was all the introduction Mary Jane gave.

"I bet that was well thumbed," Uncle Noel interjects.

"It were all about chickens an' eggs and things, you know. An' I remember it said, 'Never go in a dark passage with a man.'"

All her reading left Frances hardly more enlightened than Ivy was when she thought the doctor brought baby Violet in a black bag. Babies, Frances thought, came from kissing. The first time a boy kissed her, she came home sobbing. She was now utterly disgraced, condemned like a distant cousin who got pregnant by one of the railroad men who boarded at their house. When it came time for the cousin to have the baby, her mother left her by herself up in Craig Siding and came down to Bradford for a visit. She wanted no part of the disgrace. The girl went out on the moors alone and had the baby there. She left it among berry bushes to die, but the authorities caught up with her and took her to court for murder. Grown-ups spoke of this in whispers and shut up whenever the children came near.

And no one at all mentioned what might have happened if Ralph hadn't married Mary Jane in their own good time.

Despite only a vague understanding, anything even distantly connected with this taboo topic was enough to bring about "awful" feelings of shame. My grandmother experienced them when, at eight years old, her mother's haphazard packing let a pair of Frances's own knickers tumble out of the cart the day they moved house to Moulson Street. The moving men laughed.

At night school, when they were sixteen or seventeen, over the hats they were trimming and their embroidery, the girls "used to talk about them things. Like them girls in *Miss Jean Brodie*." This clarified matters—a little.

Ivy remembers the first boy who asked her out. She was walking home from work one evening. She was so tired that she was walking the familiar route with her eyes closed, just peeking with one eye every once in a while to make sure she was still on track. All at once, she came to a spot in the sidewalk where a flagstone was missing, and no one had bothered to set a cordon around it. Ivy tripped into this hole and tumbled head over heels down a long embankment.

A young man she didn't know happened to see her fall and came running to help her up. "I must 'ave looked a sight!" she says, "me petticoat showin' and dirt all over." The young man was laughing and asked her to step out with him. Ivy was too shy and embarrassed to answer anything. She ran all the way home—and kept her eyes open after that.

Doris remembers that a boy might buy a girl four ounces of chocolate in a little bag nearly every time he came. "Much more sensible," she says, the flesh of her plump arms swaying gently, "than a whole box. It isn't good for us to eat too many, is it?"

A young man at the mill took a fancy to Ivy and asked her out. She was almost engaged to Gerald Craven at the time, which gave her the chance to say, "I'm sorry, but I already 'ave someone."

We learn that the disappointed young man gave a report of his failure to a friend. "Well, since she's turned thee down," his friend consoled him, "I won't bother to ask 'er."

This friend was my grandfather, who'd met and was attracted to Ivy years before he met my grandmother. They say Ivy and Frances looked very much alike, except that Ivy was blonde with blue eyes and Frances had the Welsh darkness.

"It were our Frances 'ad more boys 'an any o' 'em."

Everyone agrees on that. All of the girls had pictures of themselves taken when they were in their teens. Most seem prim and angelic, with their hair tied back in a demure ribbon. But there is my grandmother—with a comb in her hair like a Spanish dancer!

Any night she wasn't busy with night school or the orchestra, our Frances stepped out with someone. Courting was both her major interest and her life's greatest triumph. Of course, anybody's courting will do for entertainment, but as none of her granddaughters seem very willing to gratify her, she must continue to gloat over her own.

First "there were t' young mission'ry from Brighton." Her father didn't like him, although all the sisters thought her very lucky to have found a member of the church. They had only a few months to wait for that young man's mission to be over before things could get serious. But "Father always had great powers of discernment,"

Mona says, since Grandma is a little slow to provide further details. "Hardly a person ever impressed him as bad who didn't sooner or later turn out to be so."

Not long after, the missionary was discovered pilfering the tithing fund. "'E were shipped 'ome in disgrace an' our Frances were spared."

Another Mormon boy, Fletcher Talbot, took Frances out once or twice. ("'Is father played t' double bass an't were bigger an' 'im.") Then Fletcher came over to ask her mother (not her father) for her hand.

"Well, you'll have to ask her about it," Mary Jane said. All the while, "our Frances were listening it t' kitchen," trying to keep her shrieks of laughter from being heard—with her voice! "I 'ad no use for 'im, e'en though 'e were a Mormon."

Most of her suitors were, of necessity, nonmembers. "But I'd al'ays give 'em over if they didn't like t' church," she assures us.

There was Frank Webster—"'E thought a lot about me"—whose family owned a pub. One day Ralph went to tune the Webster's piano, and Frank told him, "I'd 'ave married your daughter, Mr. Whitaker, if she'd 'ave 'ad me." But she'd refused him, too. "'E's too much Wesleyan an' tha'rt too much Mormon." Her father agreed she'd made the right decision.

"Think o' me, married to a pub owner, wiping down t' counter to this day."

A friend fixed Frances and Hannah up with two soldiers on leave from the army.

"I don't think mine liked me," Hannah sighs. "I were too tame. We sat in t' park an' I never said a word." With most boys, she remembers, it was like that. As soon as they saw Frances—

"'E liked me all right, though," Frances giggles, and remembers how he wrote her instead of Hannah as soon as he got back to his regiment.

"But I soon set 'im straight," Frances says with a flirtatious toss of her grey curls. "I told 'im I wouldn't 'ave me sister's castoffs."

Hannah wasn't so proud. Robert Tomlin, a thin, quiet man at church soon gave up Frances for her. "Our Frances were too gay for 'im," she says. "'E liked 'em quiet, an' that were fine wi' me."

Then the orchestra got a new cello player. "I didn't like 'im at first," my grandmother recalls. "'Eyup, 'oo's this funny fellow?'"

She told him, in no uncertain terms, that she did not like his foot stomping time. If they were to play "t' cello together," he would have to stop. But she didn't tell him to stop smoking at that first garden party. That was the first cigarette he ever took. If she'd told him to stop, he would have. He always blamed her for the habit that lasted the rest of his life and, in the end, killed him.

("I were wearing a white 'at," Grandma remembers.)

My grandfather was going with his boss's daughter when he met my grandmother, "but 'e soon gave 'er up." Every night after a performance or a practice, he would see her home, carrying both cellos at once. "That kept 'is 'ands busy."

"What dost tha think I am?" One day, early in their courtship, my grandfather asked this of Grandma, who'd accused him of still dangling after his boss's daughter for the perks at work. "A bloomin' Mormon?"

"No, but you're talkin' to one," my grandmother replied with a saucy shake. "An' if tha don't like it, tha can' never speak to me again."

"Wi' some o' t' boys, that'd 'ave made 'em leave off," my grandmother says. "But wi' 'Arry, 'e come all t' more!"

Part of their hesitation was that Harry's mother never liked Frances—in good part because she was a Mormon. When they were married, she cried, "Look what you're doing, taking me best boy from me!"

"But 'oo made 'im 'er best boy?" my grandmother demands. "It were me. I made 'im 'er best boy. I'd tell 'im: ''Arry, 'tis tha mother's birthday. Tha'd best buy 'er a card. 'Arry, tha'd best go visit tha mother. Buy 'er summat nice fer Christmas."

Harry had a motorbike, and one day he took Frances for a long ride up into the dales. It rained all the time, but the English country lanes in the rain smelled sweeter than the ground ever smells here. Here, there is an alkali smell, Grandma wrinkles her nose, but there, everything is sweet and fragrant.

Halfway home, the cycle broke down, and Harry couldn't get it fixed. They had to spend the night. They sent a telegram home to explain the predicament and took two rooms in a local inn. They weren't married; the innkeeper winked and smiled. He knew. Or thought he knew.

"You may be sure I locked me door good and tight," Grandma assures us. Then again, she has to reiterate, "We never did anything wrong."

It seemed my grandparents were always "'aving a row." All the time I knew them. I loved my grandfather so dearly, I was sure Grandma was to blame. She was insensitive, never understood him. Why did he never go back to the boss's daughter? That might have led to advancement—

I begin to think now maybe my grandparents liked fighting. They had no better entertainment than getting on each other's nerves and carrying on about it with full-throttle drama.

Hannah recalls, "it were t' same when they was courtin'." She and Robert would double date with them, "Me an' 'im in one doorway, them in t' other." When they'd seen the girls home, Robert and Harry would run down the hill to catch the last tram to the other end of town at 10:00 p.m.

"I don't know what it was," Hannah says about my grandparents, "but them two'd al'ays 'ave a row. Nine time out o' ten, 'Arry'd say, 'Go on wi'out me, Robert. I'll walk tonight.' 'E wouldn't leave 'er in the middle of a row."

Once Frances and Harry had a tiff and weren't seeing each other. Frances promised to take Violet to see a show on the night she and Harry usually went out. Violet was so looking forward to it. She thought all her older sisters were marvelous and used to hang around, watching them get ready to go out. It used to shock her to go to friends' houses and hear them sass their older brothers and sisters. She would never dream of such a thing. In the end, however, "our Frances never took me to that show." She and Harry were back together again before night came.

Often when he'd left her at around midnight and walked all the way to the other side of Bradford, uphill and down, Harry would still be unable to sleep. He'd sit down and write her letters, great long letters of all the things he'd wanted to say but hadn't dared or hadn't thought of until his long walk home. He'd mail them in the morning in his hurry to work. The mails were such "in them days" that they'd get to her house the very same afternoon and be waiting for her when she got home. Grandma kept all those "love letters". She burned stacks and stacks of them when he died, but she still keeps a few of the most precious. "Maybe some day I'll let tha read them." But I can tell it won't be until after she dies. There are some things that should not be shared, even with a granddaughter.

Still, it was six years before they were finally married.

"An' tha'd to come along," Grandma shoots the barb at Uncle Noel in passing. My grandparents married when she was twenty-eight and nearly a spinster.

❧

Violet's wedding was probably the most glorious. It was held at St. Stephen's Church, a relatively new construction, built during the reign of Victoria. Its simple, dignified lines, the red-roofed bell tower to the left and smooth, white walls rose just east of Manchester Road. Their parents had been married there, as had Frances and Harry, Hannah and Robert.

Marriage in a Mormon temple was out of reach.

Violet made all the dresses herself—lilac ones for the bridesmaids and a pink one for my young mother who was the flower girl. My uncle Arthur was the page boy, carrying a white satin cushion for Violet to kneel on at the altar. Uncle Noel was not part of the party. He was "at an awkward age"—neither young enough to be cute nor old enough to be a responsible usher. He just sat at his mother side in the pew.

They had a wedding breakfast afterwards, avoiding any disaster like what happened with Frances. At her wedding breakfast, a ketchup bottle broke all over her dress. In the fuss that followed, Ralph kept asking, "What 'appened? What 'appened?" because he couldn't see, and no one could stop to tell him.

When Violet was married, her father put his arm about her and said, "There's the last one taken care of. An' I'm right proud of you all."

"'E'd reason to be," Hannah agrees.

PART THREE

WUTHERING HEIGHTS

He . . . put on her pillow, in the morning, a handful of golden cro-
cuses. . . . "These are the earliest flowers at the Heights! . . . They remind me of soft thaw winds, and warm sunshine, and nearly melted
snow. . . ."

"The snow is quite gone down here, darling . . . and I only see two
white spots on the whole range of moors; the sky is blue, and the
larks are singing, and the becks and brooks are all brim full. . . ."

. . . The full, mellow flow of the beck in the valley came soothing-
ly on the ear. It was a sweet substitute for the yet absent murmur of
the summer foliage, which drowned that music . . . when the trees
were in leaf.

—Emily Brontë, *Wuthering Heights*

THESE LINES OF THE OLD ROMANCE echoed in Doris's ear as
she stood on the porch of the inn, looking along the narrow, twisting, uphill-and-down lane of the little village before her. Although
she couldn't see, for a tumble of small cottages stood on the rise before her, she knew that lane led up and out into countryside so gothic
it put the classic words to shame. Haworth Moor was the heart of
Brontëland. Beneath that steeple to the left, Emily and her sisters
had grown up, dreamed their dreams, and set them on paper for
generations to come.

Doris had come to Haworth with her two best friends, the two
girls she'd converted, Annie Groom and Lily Briggs. Doris herself

had never read *Wuthering Heights*. She never had the patience to sit still and read anything on her own. But if reading were made a social affair, then she liked it well enough.

Annie was much more inclined to literature. She insisted that, as part of this holiday, some little time at least be devoted to the improvement of their minds. She had taken it upon herself to read a few chapters of *Wuthering Heights* aloud every night. These were the words she had read last night—and now Doris was very glad.

She would never forget her father reading *Jane Eyre* aloud from his big Braille book by firelight. The experience was compounded because of the good, blind hero. She remembered how the entire family circle had wept together at the lines:

> Reader, I married him.... When his firstborn was put into his arms, he could see that the boy had inherited his own eyes, as they once were—large, brilliant, and black. On that occasion, he again, with a full heart, acknowledged that God had tempered judgment with mercy.

This was farewell to England, to her family, Bradford, all. Doris was going to America. She had earned enough money, and she had already given notice at the mill. Her mother had given her a party, and her friends had shed their tears and given tokens of esteem: the traveling case that lay now under the bed upstairs in the inn, the bottle of scent that wafted up from her wrists and from behind her ears. She had meant to save both until she was actually on the ship, but Annie and Lily had lured her away for this last holiday in her native land. And then, this morning, for some reason she couldn't quite name, she had been tempted to crack the seal on the perfume bottle.

"This is certainly a beautiful country," Doris repeated Emily Brontë's words to herself. Surely nothing in wild, untamed America could ever inspire literature like that. It would be big, brazen, and terribly, terribly lonely.

No, she had set her mind to it. What other choice did she have? There was no future in burling and mending. She didn't have the education to pursue any other line of work, and what she really longed for was a home and a family.

If I stay in England, she reminded herself, I'll live and die an old maid. The war has taken them—almost all. Only one Mormon boy returned from the war alive. He took me out once and asked me to marry him that very night. I turned him down. I had to. How can he love me? He doesn't even know me. Well, now he's married my girlfriend Rose. He pulled the same trick on her, but she was so desperate she said yes!

Doris had decided she wouldn't marry a man who wasn't a member of the church, so she set out to convert her own. She'd tried it two or three times, but it seemed easier to convert girlfriends than boyfriends, and she had always failed. It was too hard to become close to a person and then have to break up like that. She knew she couldn't bear to go through that again.

No, she had to go to America, to Utah, where the odds would be more in her favor. She had to go now, and not waste any more time about it. She was past twenty-two. Every year would make her chances slimmer, even among an all-Mormon population. She must bid farewell to *Wuthering Heights* along with all the rest.

Annie and Lily came out of the inn, then. They had taken so much longer than usual to get ready that day, Doris thought impatiently. Even now, here they were, still fussing with their hats.

But, Doris told herself, I do seem in a hurry today. I was up before dawn and couldn't sleep. Breakfast was tasteless. I can't even remember what I had. Why should this be? I can't imagine. I'm not leaving for America for another three weeks yet. Today is just another pleasant, lazy, holiday, this Easter week that is warmer and drier than Easter had a right to be.

Her friends were already down the steps, making their way along the lane in the opposite direction, towards town and not towards the moor. They hadn't even seen her. But how could they miss—

"'Ere," Doris called after them. "Where are ye off to?"

"Well, we thought we'd stop at the stationer's and buy some post-cards," Annie replied.

Lily took up the cue. "Yes, and then we thought we'd take up a nice quiet seat on the bench near the Brontë house and write home."

"That should take us till dinner time at least. And then we thought we'd—"

"But we were going out on t' moor today," Doris protested.

"No, not I," Annie said. "Me feet are sore from our jaunt yesterday." She did seem spry enough on those cobblestones now, however.

"I'd enough of 'Aworth Moor yesterday," Lily agreed. "You've seen one moor, you've seen them all," Annie concluded with an uncharacteristic lack of romance.

"We 'ad it all planned," Doris protested. "'E's coming to get us, you know. 'E'll be 'ere any minute, in point of fact."

"'E?" Annie repeated. A merry twinkle danced in her eye as she exchanged a glance with Lily.

"Yes." Really. The pair of them. "You know very well. Albert."

"Albert? Albert who? I don't know an Albert. Do you, Lil?"

"No. No Albert."

"Albert Shutt. The gamekeeper's son."

"Oh. Maybe I do remember something about a gamekeeper's son." Annie scratched her head with exaggeration.

"Albert? Were 'is name really Albert?" Lily pushed on. "Not Allen?"

"I thought it were Rupert."

"Really, you two. You know as well as me 'ow we met 'im yesterday, an' 'e offered to take us on a ramble today to discover all the hidden places o' t' moor 'e knows and—"

"Aye, 'idden places o' t' wuthering 'eights and all." Annie came sauntering back to the inn steps.

Lily was in her wake. "Aye, well, an' we also know something tha doesna—or else tha won't admit it."

"Even though it's as plain as the nose on young Halbert's face."

"What's that?" Doris asked.

"That it's tha 'e's taken a fancy to. We're second fiddles, an' if 'tis all the same wi' thee, we'd just as soon leave you two alone today." Annie's tone was not in the least malicious, but cheery and obliging.

Doris saw their little joke now and joined it, laughing. "Very well. I'll admit it. 'E did seem to give me more than my share of the attention."

"Rather!" Lily exclaimed in her best swanky voice.

"But I didn't encourage 'im," Doris protested. "And I certainly didn't ask for it."

"Didna tha, now?" Lily asked.

Annie: "Surely you found 'im 'andsome."

"Well, yes," Doris admitted.

Lily: "And mannerly."

"Oh, aye."

Annie: "'Oh, aye.' And great fun to be with?"

"Aye, that as well. But you both know I'm not going out with any more non-Mormon boys. I'm not going to 'ave me 'eart broken one more time. I'm going to America."

"Aye, aye, aye. We know tha's going to America. So what does it matter? 'Ave one last fling. Tha know' tha won't get serious, so at t' end of t' week, tha can' break 'is 'eart instead."

"Really, Annie, that wouldn't be very nice."

"See?" Annie said to Lily. "I told thee. She's already soft on 'im."

"I'm not soft," Doris insisted. "I only think 'e's a nice young man what don't deserve such treatment."

"Well, I know you'll treat 'im right, Doris." Lily giggled and the two girls swung off down the lane.

Doris wanted to run after them, but just then, Albert appeared in the opposite direction, swinging a stick and looking even smarter than she remembered in a tweed cap and jacket and a sporting pair of knee-length britches. He was not a large man, but he had pleasant, fine features, ruddied by an outdoor life, and fair hair. Doris couldn't help but smile, although inventing excuses for her girlfriends was going to be difficult.

As it turned out, she needed no excuses. "'Ullo," Albert said. "Don't tell me you lasses drew lots to see who would come with me." And he laughed as if at a private joke.

Doris asked him what he meant, but he only smiled in the friendliest fashion and said, "It were nothing."

But she did find out later. This was after a day so perfect that, had she been given the gift of words, Doris felt she might have outdone Emily Brontë. She and Albert were sitting on a little hillock where heather and wild mountain thyme scented the air. His great knowledge of the moor had allowed him to show her a nest of young grouse, a den of foxes, and numerous soft, wild-eyed rabbits that seemed so appropriate at this Eastertime of new life. Now they sat, too tired to go on farther, but loathe to start their way back to civilization, even though shadows from the clumps of heather were as long as trees. A lark gave its final song of the day, and the last notes faded away like the ring of fine crystal.

Heather. Doris breathed in the fragrance one more time. In far America, if she ever had a daughter, she would name her Heather in memory of this day.

"'Tis 'ard to fathom," Albert said quietly, as if afraid to disturb the peace, "it weren't two year ago, all the world were at war."

"Aye," Doris agreed. "Tha served in t' army, didna tha?"

"From t' very beginning," Albert said. "There's not a man me age did not. Actually, I signed up for t' navy, but they needed the men, so they moved me to the army." And then, after a pause, "I were in t' Dardanelles."

A shiver ran up Doris's back as if a dark cloud had just sailed in front of the setting sun. The Dardanelles. "Churchill's folly," they called it, and the campaign had all but ruined that statesman's career. One hundred thousand young British lives had been lost—thrown away—in a few short but hellish months of a Turkish summer that nonetheless ended in a total defeat for the Allies.

"Tha'rt a lucky man." Doris didn't know how to put any more sympathy in her voice, but she wanted to.

"Very lucky," Albert replied. Then, "I'd three whole battalions, all killed, officers, soldiers, every man killed but me. They just kept moving me from battalion to battalion."

Doris gave an involuntary expression of horror.

"T' lads used to draw lots to see who would cross no man's land with me 'cause I al'ays came back alive.

"One of me jobs were to go 'round and pick up all t' dead limbs of men and 'orses, indiscriminately blown together. That's when I started to smoke. Not a clean 'abit, I'm afraid."

Doris was taken aback. He hadn't smoked once that she'd seen, but she knew it was against God's commandments.

"They told us it were a disinfectant. Maybe it were t' smoking, maybe just more luck, but I didn't get sick, wi' all o' that.

"Finally, in the heat of August, I were wounded. Got a bit o' shrapnel in me leg. You'll notice I limp."

Doris hadn't noticed.

"Tha will'. When t' weather is wet. It wouldn't be so bad except then I got dysentery. Not soldiering, mind, but while I were in t' field 'ospital. I got down to ninety pound—can' tha believe it? I'm not such a big fellow, I know, but still—they despaired of me life, so much so that when t' order came to pull out t' 'ospital and, while getting to t' boats, we came under heavy fire—well, me and a number of other 'helpless cases' were left behind as dead on t' beach."

"Goodness!" Doris exclaimed. "What 'appened then?"

"Well, a bomb went off—no further from me than tha ar' now. The sand and bits of metal rained down on me like 'ail and all but covered me. When t' air cleared and t' shooting ceased, I saw that t' bomb 'ad uncovered a case of evaporated milk, covered first, perhaps, by an earlier bomb and given up, like me, for lost. I crawled—I were too weak to walk—into t' 'ole the bomb 'ad made and 'id there, living on t' milk for three days. The milk were like a miracle. It cured me o' t' dysentery when all t' doctors' medicines 'ad failed. And, at t' end o' those three days, a fighting battalion also made their retreat from that same beach. They 'eard me calls for 'elp and were able to take me wi' them. After that, they sent me back to England, and I were released from t' service."

"Someone," Doris said with emotion, "were looking out for thee."

"Funny tha should' say that," Albert said. "I've felt the same thing so strongly meself. In fact, I'll tell thee summat else 'at 'appened to me. There were a time when t' Turks was dressing up in our dead officers' uniforms. They'd signal us up one by one through a narrow defile and 'round t' corner of this embankment. There they'd pick us off on t' other side as easily as if we was ducks in a carnival game. When it came me turn to go, summat—or someone, for I 'eard that voice as plain as day—told me, 'Don't go 'round that corner.' I took another step. Again: 'Don't go 'round that corner.' This time, I believed 'im. I turned on me 'eels and ran. I know someone were looking after me.

"A lot o' me friends—those what lived through it, or those I met in 'ospital—they've turned atheist. 'How can there be a God,' they ask, 'if 'E causes such things to 'appen?' 'Tis funny, that. 'Tis made me more religious than I've ever been in me life. There must be a life after this one. If this life is so cheap that millions can be thrown away like that, I've no choice but to believe there must be summat better to come."

Doris spoke a few words about her own conviction that there is a loving Father in heaven. She said that she, too, was certain that all his slaughtered chums were alive now, in heaven. "I believe they're even 'aving t' truth of Jesus Christ preached to them." But here she stopped. She didn't dare go on to say that she was a Mormon for fear of spoiling the splendid day.

"I've found it 'ard to explain my belief to people." Albert went on when she couldn't. "I don't go wi' me mother to church because t' Church of England don't satisfy me. ''Ow can' tha call thaself religious?' she asks me. 'Tha won't even come to church.' I can't seem to make 'er understand. Tha'r' t' first I've told that story to—about t' voice. Everyone else, I were afraid they'd laugh at me. Think t' war turned me 'ead or summat."

"I'm not laughing," Doris said.

"Nay. For that I thank thee. I thought—I 'oped tha might understand."

"Surely the very fact that tha ar' alive is some sort of proof. Proof, at least, that tha shouldna be laughed at."

"Well—" Then Albert stopped and began again. "I really do feel God were sparing me through it all, sparing me for some reason. 'Tis 'ard, now, back in old 'Aworth, to imagine what that summat could be. Perhaps—" He paused to let the sun slip behind the hills in silence. "Perhaps it were for just such a moment as this."

Albert, it turned out, though he visited his family in Haworth on holidays, had a job in Bradford as an accountant in the fruiter's market. He came to visit Doris every evening after they returned to the city and then spent all Saturday afternoon with her. He took her out to tea in a little shop, and Doris's heart beat wildly. For days the thought had been pounding in her brain: "I've got to tell him. I'm getting to like him too much, too much. Once he learns I'm a Mormon—I've got to tell him now and get it over with."

"I suppose tha'l've noticed—" Doris cleared her throat of huskiness and fiddled with the linen serviette in her lap. "I supposed tha'l've noticed by now that I never drink tea."

"As a matter of fact, I 'ave," Albert said, nodding towards the cup of tea and the glass of sarsaparilla on the table between them. "Why is that?"

"Well, t' religion I belong to 'as a Word of Wisdom." And Doris proceeded to explain the Mormon ban on tea, coffee, tobacco, and alcohol.

Albert felt for his little pouch of tobacco and cigarette papers in his coat packet, as if he would throw them away that instant for her. Doris knew she had to speak quickly before he made a fool of himself for a religion he couldn't possibly like.

"The religion I belong to"—she took another breath, her eyes down—"is the Mormons."

"Not the Utah Mormons?"

"Aye, 'tis." The tone of shock in his voice convinced her it was all over now. It no longer mattered what she said. Nothing could make it better, so she just kept going.

"And that's why I can't meet thee tomorrow. I've got to go to church." That's right, she told herself. You call it off first. It's better that way.

"Go to that church? Not wi'out me, tha doesna." Albert exclaimed. "I won't let thee go alone to those people 'oo steal young girls off to their temples and marry them by t' dozens to lecherous old men!"

The next day was Conference. The speaker was President George Albert Smith.

("I could tell," Doris says, "as soon as ever 'e opened his mouth that Albert were converted.")

He gave up his "disinfectant" smoking that very day and was baptized within the week in the River Aire. The elders confirmed him a member there on the riverbank.

And so, dear reader—as wrote that other Brontë who grew up in that desolate parson's house in Haworth—she married him.

Only not quite yet.

～

"Ello, 'ello!" Albert and Doris called. "Oh, and by the way, don't bother to waste that rice. We're not married."

"Not married?" The faces that crowded around the doorway dropped with disbelief. All the families and friends were gathered for the wedding breakfast, and now they told them, just fresh from town hall, that they weren't married?

"Albert was supposed to post his papers in 'Aworth—" Doris tried to explain—but burst into tears of frustration instead.

"Didna tha do' it, Albert?" his gamekeeper father asked severely.

"Of course I did it. For the twentieth time, I swear I posted them last Monday."

"It's got stuck in t' postbox," someone suggested. "You'll 'ave to quick, take t' train back up there and find them."

"No use going all that way," said another. "'Tis town 'all. Someone at town 'all's gone and thrown them away."

"Oh," cried Doris.

"Nothing quite that drastic," a third said in appeasement. "They've just misplaced them, that's all."

But none of these suggestions were any consolation. All anyone could do was to sit down to a glum "wedding breakfast." Albert continued to sleep on the Whitaker sitting room floor, and Doris up in the big double bed with two of her sisters from that Saturday until Tuesday when the papers finally appeared.

～

Even then, "I never should have married him," Doris admits.

"Why ever not?" we ask, astonished.

Many reasons. Although he survived the Dardanelles, Uncle Albert's health was never great after that, certainly not enough for the rigors of frontier America. I didn't know him; he died quite young so that Auntie Doris was a widow more than half of her life. She got her daughter named Heather, and five other children besides. Nobody has the words for it, but I get the feeling he suffered what we today would call post-traumatic stress disorder as well.

"'E 'adn't even a job," Auntie Doris says now instead.

Albert had lost his job at the fruiter's market when the merchants went on strike, and he was now out of work. Doris had managed to get her old job back at Ripley's—but she had given up her boat passage to stay home with her new love. They were living on her wage alone and trying to save up so they could both go to Zion at the same time.

One evening when they were out walking, they passed the mayor's house. "T' mayor's a good friend of me dad," Albert mentioned. "You know, 'e's always bringing in poachers and all."

"For goodness sakes, go ask 'im for a job," Doris exclaimed.

It was a lifetime job: accountant for the city of Bradford. He left it after only three weeks. They were already booked to sail. That was their honeymoon. The other men in the office thought he was a fool.

They took the mustering-out pay Albert had received upon leaving the army. They also took advantage of an emigration scheme the British government devised after the war to take the stress of all those returning veterans off her own cities. The couple made this combination of benefits take them as far as it could.

That is how newlywed Doris and Albert Shutt stepped off the train, not in Zion, but in Manitoba, "the wilds of Canada" in the early 1920s. Winter wheat gone golden and hillocks of hay stretched as far as the eye could see. They were on the right continent, but as part of the scheme, they would have to spend two years working off the rest of their passage in the British colony before moving on.

Albert's experience gamekeeping on the moors looked good on paper. They were hired on as "farmers"; that looked good on paper,

too, conjuring visions of healthy air and independence. Their assignment was a ranch a hundred miles north of Winnipeg, "in t' bush."

～

"We found out we weren't farmers," Doris, now forty years a widow,
says sadly.

"It were so far north that we saw t' northern lights there. I didn't
know what it was and called for Albert to come and see. I thought
t' whole world were on fire. It were like a rainbow gone mad—great
flashes of reds and blues. Oooh, it startled me no end!

"When we got there, I were so green I didn't even know what a—"
And now she searches the mind under her grey halo of hair; this
foreign word is among the first to go. "Co-rel" is what she finally
comes up with, closer to "coral," the fauna of a vast sea of a different
sort; in this context, she means "corral."

"As me first job, they sent me to hunt for eggs in the co-rel. I didn't
know what that were. Then once they left us on our own, telling us
we had to milk the two dairy cows that evening. Neither Albert nor
I had ever milked a cow before, and when it came time, we couldn't
find them. They were mixed in with a hundred beef cattle, and we
couldn't tell them apart. I finally found one because it had a patch of
curly 'air I'd noticed before and liked. But we never did find t' other.
And you hadn't to leave them, you know.

"We saw them—oh!—chop t' lambs' tails off and plug t' pigs' ears
and shear t' sheep an' all sorts of things. I'd to cook for t' threshers,
for t' shearers. Once they brought in a whole sheep that'd just 'ad its
throat cut and told me to cook it for dinner. Oh, dear, I worked 'ard.
I grew up, I tell you!

"We'd some terrible experiences there. When it were me twenty-third birthday, me first away from 'ome [29 October, through the
first crust of snow] Albert asked, 'What do' tha want for tha birthday?'

"I said, 'A box of chocolates.'

"The merchandizing store, which sold everything, were ten miles
away. So, after we'd finished all our chores, after six o'clock and
already twilight, we set off on that long walk without telling anyone
we were going.

"We'd got t' chocolates and was coming home. It were full dark by then, and it started to snow. And we 'eard some dogs barking, 'way off. And then, as we walked along—I were singing and 'appy as could be—Albert said, 'I believe them dogs is coyotes. They seem to be getting nearer.'

"By t' time we turned onto the road to the ranch, we could 'ear them barking quite loudly.

"When we reached t' light of t' ranch 'ouse, we was so surprised! Everyone were saddling up t' 'orses and getting ready to ride out to seek us. Oh, we were bawled out! 'You must never, never go on foot into the bush at night.'

"They were wolves that were closing in on us. And they said, 'Last year, a man 'ad to let go one of 'is 'orses to save 'imself from the wolves in the bush.'

"You see, we'd thought about English woods." Doris sighs. And perhaps she's thinking about that beautiful first day on Haworth Moor. "We 'adn't thought about t' wild woods of Canada."

After a wistful pause, Doris goes on. "In wintertime, it freezes sixty below, so they can't keep chickens. They kill them all and buy them fresh in the spring. So one day she brings all these dead chickens in. I don't know 'ow many they were—twenty-one, maybe. I'd to clean them all and put them in the deep freeze: just take them outside and put them in a shed, that were t' deep freeze.

"I'd never cleaned a chicken before. That were always our Barbara's job. And I were pregnant, very, very sick. I'd a bucket at one side for t' chickens' insides and one at t' other, for me own insides!"

Doris eventually became so sick that they had to leave the ranch and go back to Winnipeg, Albert finding other work. There, on the third of June, she gave birth to a little boy they named Francis (after my grandmother) Calvin.

"He were such a wonderfully well boy. Then, suddenly, in the depth of that next winter, in February, he took what they'd call intestinal flu today. Then they called it gastroenteritis, and he died."

Her father's first grandchild, finally, a boy. Born so far away and dead so soon.

"They don't bury t' dead there in wintertime. They put them in a room under t' chapel 'cause t' ground is froze so 'ard, you can't dig a grave. But they do dig a few, for t' rich people. This year, they'd one left over and that we bought when winter were over. We buried 'im in t' ground in May. T' next day we left to go further west. It were sad to leave him so soon, alone."

She was never able to return to Winnipeg.

Doris and Albert spent that next summer on another ranch—a huge ranch, two thousand and eighty acres—just over the U.S. border from Lethbridge, Alberta, Canada. Finally, they earned enough to come to Salt Lake.

"It were a real pioneering venture them days," Doris says. "We were like 'Those of the Last Wagon.'"

She is referring to the famous Conference eulogy President J. Reuben Clark delivered in 1947 to commemorate the centennial of the arrival of the first Saints in the Salt Lake Valley. I heard the words reread over the pulpit on a sweltering July Sunday morning when I was a girl; Auntie Doris and Uncle Albert heard them when they were first spoken.

"Those souls, in name unknown, unremembered, unhonored in the pages of history, but lovingly revered round the hearthstones of their children and their children's children," the prophet said.

"Back in the last wagon," the eulogy goes on,

> not always could they see the Brethren way out in front, and the blue heaven was often shut out from their sight by heavy, dense clouds . . . of dust. . . .
>
> Then the morning came when from out that last wagon floated the la-la of the newborn babe, and Mother love made a shrine. . . . But the train must move on. . . .
>
> And the Lord wanted little Bill with Him. So a few mornings later a weeping mother and a grief-stricken father and that last wagon swung into place in the line, leaving beside the road under some scrub brush, a little mound.

～

But some of the hardships were new. Doris and Albert were disappointed in many respects. Sons of those first immigrants, the missionaries who had devoted themselves to the members in England, now forgot all about them as they got wrapped up in their own, prosperous lives.

So Doris and Albert took it upon themselves to befriend other immigrants in the same lonely situation as themselves. Not only British immigrants won their compassion, but Germans and Scandinavians as well. Doris and Albert had them all over for Christmas and other dinners throughout the year. Like at home, they set table leaves between chairs for them all to sit on.

One particularly sad case was old Brother Matthew. His only family in the world, two sisters, had died of consumption caught in the workroom of a London shop where they hand-sewed pearls on evening dresses. Come to Zion, this good brother spent all his days in the temple and his nights all alone in a tiny rooming house.

Soon he, too, died of the same disease, and his bishop called up Doris and Albert in distress. They'd lost the man's body. All the mortuaries in town took charity cases in turn, but a round through the city revealed nothing. Finally, the police were called in, and poor Brother Matthew was found. In those days, Murray was a long way out of town, not just a continuation of State Street's fast food restaurants and pawn shops as it is today. No one had thought of looking clear out there, but that was the mortuary that had taken him after all.

Doris and Albert were surprised to be called in on the case. They didn't know the man very well. But the bishop had gotten the notion that they were his relatives. As his dying wish, Brother Matthew had asked that his father's old watch, the only thing of value he owned, be given to Brother Shutt "because he's been kind to me."

～

"What sad lives some people are called to lead," Doris sighs.

NURSE WHITAKER

OUR BARBARA, DORIS SAYS, was the prettiest of them all. She had, as a girl, "t' face of a saint." Yet "she 'ad no use for t' boys. I don't think she ever 'ad a date." It seems she just wanted to work, and becoming a dependent wife was not important to her.

"I learnt to plush weave, velvet weave, and the complicated box pattern," Barbara says. "And when I'd learnt it all, it grew monotonous. At first I considered emigrating, going to Zion to join Doris. But I should 'ave to work me passage on one of them emigration schemes, and after what 'ad 'appened to Doris and Albert, Father didn't trust them. But 'e knew I needed a change."

For the most part, the public, tired of war, was trying to forget trenches and gas with flappers and dancing and a carefree spirit. Yet every day in the streets of Bradford, Barbara saw human wreckage, reminders that the war had not been just a bad dream. The young men who should have been courting her, "taking care of her" as young women were promised, were in wheelchairs, empty sleeves pinned over missing arms, faces burned to horrid masks like melted wax.

She knew there were hundreds she didn't see, men kept out sight of the public. Men who seemed whole but were in truth more injured than the halt and maimed. Shell shocked into jittering heaps of flesh, they woke screaming like infants in the night. No woman could expect such a man to care for her.

And then, one day in November, Barbara stood shock-still to see a busload of young women come from St. Luke's to be dropped off along Manningham Road. An army of sorts, with their own uniforms: white aprons emblazoned with a red cross, or blue with the crisp, white trim and nun-like veils. Each carried before her a tray, her own miniature burden of a Flanders field.

In Flanders fields the poppies blow
Between the crosses, row on row

as the Canadian army doctor John McCrae had written in his famous verses before he, too, had been cut down in 1918.

"Buy a poppy, sir?" the nurses called their wares. "Remember those who gave so much. Remember the wounded soldiers this Armistice Day. Miss?"

Barbara paid sixpence for her own poppy and added another two, just for charity.

That night, she perched on the arm of her father's chair as if she were still a child and told him her plan. She reminded him how she had enjoyed both first aid and home nursing classes in night school and passed the highest exams in both of them. He reminded her how her mother had been a nursing student herself, long ago, when he'd first met her and fallen in love. When he gave approval to her plan, Barbara planted a happy kiss on his forehead.

Yet application after application came back, rejected. The reason was, a health-visitor friend of her father's advised, "They think factory workers are all slum."

So Barbara quit work and stayed home for a year, scrubbing, baking, and cleaning. Then she was able to put "Mother's Help" on the form and was accepted immediately at Fulham Hospital, Hammersmith, London.

Her parents spent the whole sum of fifteen pounds on her uniform.

∾

"I was thrilled about my venture," she says. "I used to dream at night what it was going to be like.

"A friend of mine at church came and said, 'Oooh, I'm so jealous of you.' Her father was a doctor and he wouldn't let her go nursing, although she wanted to. It was something very daring, to go off like that."

As it turned out, many years later when she'd immigrated, Barbara found herself working with this doctor's daughter. She'd immigrated and finally gained her dream of becoming a nurse, too.

Barbara's other friend Hettie Gelder was already in London, having taken a civil service job in the excise office. Hettie met her at King's Cross Station that April 15, 1920.

"We took the underground to Barons Court instead of Hammersmith, so we had quite a way to walk with my luggage, past distilleries, coach factories, poorer terraces. We met a bobby who did not know which way the hospital was, but showed us the direction he thought it ought to be. After walking a block, we saw what we thought was another policeman and asked again. It turned out to be the same policeman, and we all laughed. But he directed us right.

"Hettie left me at the door. The first person I met was the Church of England minister. He asked me if I was a member of his church. I was so scared they would send me home if they knew I was a Mormon. I said, 'No, I'm a Nonconformist.' That satisfied him, and he had no further interest in me."

Then, as she was walking through the ward carrying her luggage to her room, Matron stopped her and said, "Go back and try that walk again. You walk like a mill girl, not a nurse!" Barbara would have to overcome the remnants of rickets that still bowed her legs and learn to glide like Florence Nightingale.

At last, without being sent home for being either a Mormon or a mill girl, Barbara got installed, safe and sound. She was "shown over the cubicles where nurses on probation slept. They were eight-bedded rooms curtained off with a dresser and chair each. We put our suitcases under the bed.

"It was all very strange and new, and there was plenty of unpleasant jobs to do: scrubbing floors and latrines and very sick patients. But my heart was in my work. In them days, a nursing trainee had to devote her life to her work. She had to live in the hospital nurses' home. She had to have no other responsibilities: no children, no husband. If you did it well, it was a life of devotion. I noticed many girls came from Ireland where there was very little work for girls. They came just for a job, and if that were their only object, they were never a success as nurses.

"I was determined to succeed, even though I was at a disadvantage in education," having left school at twelve. "I studied hard and passed the preliminary exam. I was signed on for three years. The first year concentrated on physiology and anatomy, second on medicine, and third on surgery. I did very well—always in the first six of my class.

"The hospital had only just reopened after the war for training nurses, and they had very few trained staff. So we were given great responsibilities. We worked sixty hours a week and then put in time for lectures and study. We were often left in charge of wards of forty people or more on night duty. All the help we got was two wandering trained nurses who had to spend most of the night helping nurses of other wards who had a patient they couldn't manage alone. The trained nurses came around twice a night to check drugs or would come special if we had an emergency.

"There was plenty of real nursing to do, for we had no penicillin, no antibiotics or other modern drugs, and so many now-curable diseases were all terminal. We had a lot of battles with pneumonias. There were lots of TB incurables, pernicious anemias died, septicemias had little hope. All cancers died, heart cases. Bronchitis was a long, tedious complaint. I don't think nurses today can imagine what nursing was like them days.

"At one time, I remember I had forty-six babies, and seventeen of them were on bottles. And they were not healthy babies that grabbed at a bottle. They had no appetites and had to be coaxed to suck. I used to place them all on a table with a bottle each propped up a little. I spent my time agitating first one and then another until they

would suck. Lots of them had diarrhea and needed constant changing, or they got a sore bottom.

"I made mistakes sometimes, but with the Lord's help, there were no
serious consequences. I will never forget one or two of them and learned
great lessons. Once I was in charge of a mental observation ward. We
had to watch carefully so they wouldn't escape. One did scale the wall
and was off home in bedclothes. Thank goodness it was my night off!

"There was a woman with a delusion about Jesus Christ. She was
very noisy, keeping all the other troublesome patients awake, including the escapees. The old lady was on a quieting drug if necessary,
which she usually spat out all over me and the bedclothes. I had so
many troublesome patients, I was determined she would swallow
this medicine somehow and get some sleep for her.

"That was a night, I tell you! At the same time, the other nurse on
with me had had to run out after this escapee to the toilet else she'd
have been over t' wall that night. I'd heard of holding a child's nose
to make it swallow medicine, so I thought in desperation I'd try it
on this old lady.

"She were as determined as I. When I thought t' medicine were
gone, I discovered that she had gone, too. At least, she wasn't breathing. Poor soul, she must have been in such a weak condition. One
wonders how she could make such a noise. I did artificial respiration
and, oh, what a relief to see that breath come again!

"When she got her breath, she immediately cursed me and said
that I'd choked her, which was all but true. The Lord sure helped me
out that night!

"I once gave the wrong medicine, but fortunately it was only a
purgative and did no harm.

"Then, once, I was in great distress at an operating theatre. The
patient had been so nervous, she had retained the enema I had given
her until she was on the table. What I should have done was stop
the operation, which I thought I'd no right to do. But they didn't
give you much training, you know. You just had to use your own
judgment.

"I never thought I'd be able to say, 'You can't do that because she
hasn't had an enema yet.'

"I remember the doctor so well. His name was Swaine, and he wasn't very well liked. You can imagine what I went through! He threatened to report me to Matron, and I cannot imagine what that would have meant. The sister in charge of the operating theatre advised me to go beg him not to do that. That seemed to do the trick, and nothing happened but plenty of anxiety and tears.

"We had happy times, too. We had dances occasionally. Hettie and I visited the Pughs who lived in Barnes. They were well-off. No better than we are now, but we thought they were rich. They had a nice home and a car, and that's where I had me first car ride. It made me so sick, t' fumes and all.

"I passed my final exams, but not as well as I ought to do. I was aiming at the Civil Medal and the free midwifery training, but a Nurse Braman took it from me. Matron gave me a good testimonial and asked me to stay on the staff, but I didn't feel like that. I went home for a rest and then took jobs as a private nurse to save up enough money to take my midwifery exam. Private nursing wasn't much of a profession, but I gained lots of experience. I learned how unhappy people with lots of money can be."

The sickroom smelled of hot resin and boiled onion, the things Barbara used, bound in muslin, for her poultices when the cold settled into a desperate case of pneumonia. Under these, however, on that warm May morning, was already the sweet, creeping smell of death. For Mrs. Smith's infected lungs had strangled her. She had died just as her husband's temperature plunged from the 103 it had been in the late afternoon to subnormal, and his heart rate raced. He, too, had entered the crisis.

It was no use burdening his fevered mind with the sorry news of his wife's death. The next hour or so would decide if he were to join her—or live to face the terrible grief of life alone. And, since there was nothing more she could do for her, Barbara daren't leave his side. She slapped another hot muslin bag on the raggedly rising chest with its damp-twisted hair. This was her time in the trenches. Hers and his.

And then, near dawn, it was over. Mr. Smith would live. She may have lost the first engagement, having been called in too late, but she'd won the war. He slept. When she felt for his wrist, the pulse was stronger, steady and slow. He stirred at her touch, turned his clammy hand over and grasped hers in his.

Time at last to call for the local parson from St. Mary the Virgin's. To hear the birds in the blooming honeysuckle outside the cottage's little white door. To watch the rainbows made when the sun struck the beveled glass set in diamonds in the open windows. To sit with her knitting and watch the sleeping form, to admire the handsome brown hair with the curl in it, grey just starting to appear at the temples. The hair swept with dignity back from the high forehead. She hadn't had time to notice it before, nor the strong nose and chin. Mr. Smith was late forties, maybe early fifties. Old enough to have been spared the trenches, twenty years her senior. He and his wife had never had children, and now she never would. But he was not too old.

Time at last to pray thanksgiving to the Lord for having given her hands such skill. And maybe, to ask—one blessing.

She'd seen it too often. She didn't want to die alone.

This was Mirfield, near Huddersfield, but miles and miles, it seemed at last to Barbara, from hell. Local legend had it that all three Brontë sisters, Emily, Charlotte, and Anne, had attended boarding school here. Charlotte had been miserable enough to write those dreadful school scenes in the early part of *Jane Eyre* where rain poured and pneumonia killed. Yet she had come back to the same institution as mistress later.

For a moment, Barbara remembered how Doris had found her Albert on Haworth Moor.

Barbara scolded herself for foolishness. She didn't believe in fate. A woman worked her own destiny.

And yet Roe Head School, in its lowering Georgian manor house, was not the only bit of romance in this place. Brightly painted barges on the canal sailing through the locks past malt kilns and abandoned coal pits were not the sum of Mirfield's parts. They said Robin Hood himself had come to Kirkless Priory, of which only the fourteenth-century guest house remained, tucked behind the

Three Nuns pub for working men. Robin Hood had come here to be nursed, as she had come to nurse—

The outlaw of Sherwood's end in Mirfield was tragic, of course. The prioress, Elizabeth de Staynton, had treated him with that barbaric old sovereign methods, bloodletting. The remedy had naturally failed. Weak and dying, he shot his last arrow from one of that guest house's mullioned windows.

"Bury me where the arrow lands," he'd said.

The moss-covered gravestone bore the ancient epitaph:

> HERE UNDERNEATH DIS LAITL STEAN
> LAZ ROBIN EARL OF HUNTINTUN.

In a lingering practice from more primitive times, chips of the stone, the locals said, cured toothache.

No such claims were made for the neighborhood's newest stone, glaring white among the rest in St. Mary's yard:

> BELOVED WIFE
> OF CHARLES MARGERY SMITH
> NÉE BLACK
> 1890–1925

"I am so sorry for your loss." Barbara heard herself less sympathetic than she meant to be. The practical actions of crisis care came easily to her, not the words so much, nor the long, convalescent aftermath.

For his very first outing beyond the garden where he sat bundled in rugs on fine days, Mr. Smith had taken the short walk down Easthorpe Lane to St. Mary's. His wife had been lain to rest while he'd been too weak to attend.

On the return trip, he took Barbara's arm. Was it weakness? She hardly bore enough weight for it to be more than a gentlemanly gesture.

Later, in the garden, he asked after her family. It took a long time to recite everything about every sister, but he kept her going.

Barbara peeled new grapes for him, one by one. Peel was not good for the delicate, invalid stomach, although the fruit itself was known to be beneficial. Barbara could peel, even if she couldn't express her condolences with much grace. Even if she wished she didn't have to mention Nellie to make the tally complete.

And even though sometimes, especially this time, peeled grapes and the open, invalid lips connected in her mind not with the sickroom, but with the Roman debauch.

"You are so well recovered, Mr. Smith, thank the Lord. I shall be taking a new post at the end of the week."

Grape juice trickled over Mr. Smith's protesting lips.

Barbara reached him a serviette. He caught her hands and held them. Their eyes met, too.

"I am not—I am not a man who can live without a woman."

She hadn't known him before his illness, but Barbara had begun to suspect—to hope—it might be true. "Nonsense, Mr. Smith."

"Nurse Whitaker—Barbara, if I may. Your care has seen me restored to health. I see now I would like it for the rest of my life."

Barbara felt her own heart race. She would have diagnosed "crisis" had she been in charge of her own case. But she was beginning to think, just this once, she wasn't.

"I must think it over," she stammered.

"Of course you must."

The church. She'd only mentioned that in passing so far. He'd said he didn't mind what she was. But would he mind her devotion, day in and day out, if he couldn't share it? And her father. She must ask her father's opinion—

"I will see you on the train to London Friday afternoon," she promised instead. "I have the address of the sanitorium, and you have mine on Moulson Street. Let us write, and we shall see."

Only with that promise did he let go her hand, although even then the clasp lingered, stuck together with grape juice.

"I did think of marrying him," Barbara says briefly. "But it hadn't to be. 'E went to convalesce in London, met up with another nurse there and married her. I am glad, now, it happened so."

"Soon"—Auntie Barbara is in a hurry to go on to other things—
"Soon I had saved enough money to get my midwifery training at
Queen Charlotte's Hospital, one of the most famous hospitals in
midwifery. I enjoyed this training, but it took longer than they told
me it would. I had to borrow some money from Hannah.

"The district work I did while training inspired my intention to go
into district work." In the U.K., district nurses provide care within
the community and make house calls, allowing patients to remain
at home.

"I had some experience among the squalid parts of London," she
relates. "I remember one emergency delivery. There wasn't a thing
in the house. No baby clothes, so I took my petticoat off to wrap
the baby in. The only vessel to hold water was a chamber pot. Just a
bare mattress on the floor. These people! They'd wait until they were
just 'aving it before calling us because they knew we wouldn't deliver
them under those conditions, you see."

Another time, Barbara arrived to find the husband had the bed
stuck halfway down the staircase as he tried to make arrangements
for his wife. Barbara couldn't get up to see the woman who was in
heavy labor in a chair. Fortunately, the many times Barbara had
directed her father at moving pianos came in handy now. She finally
got the bed unstuck and back upstairs so she could come up herself
to deliver the baby.

Because they nursed many people for free, it was part of a
nurse's duty to collect contributions, too, and not just once a year.
In November, of course, Barbara carried her share of poppy-strewn
trays.

"I spent a month's holiday and then had an interview with the
Queen's District Nursing Association for training in district work.
They sent me to Harpurhey, Manchester, for six months' training.
There were eight nurses, all fully trained, and a matron, Miss Jones,
who was very strict. It wasn't a very happy place. It was very hard work,
and so much to do! And you couldn't do a good job! Nevertheless, I
enjoyed it and was pleased when the term was finished.

"When I had finished this training, I took a post in Witton Le
Wear in County Durham, a pretty little village that wanted a nurse

who could cycle. Well, we never had such a thing as a bicycle in Bradford. My good friend Ethel Forbes Clark had taught me to cycle when I had gone to stay with her on holiday in Sussex. We used to cycle down to the sea with her children sat on behind us. Still, I wasn't right sure I could do it, for it had been several years. I remember the first day: I was more worried how I was going to get on my bicycle than of any sickness. I didn't dare mount my bicycle in the village, knowing that many people would be appraising the new midwife. I took a walk with it till I got right out of sight and then made a successful mounting. Everything went well after that."

Barbara also learned to drive in the thirties, the only one of the girls ever to do that in England. Because she was a nurse, she got plenty of petrol, even during the Second World War. She is still the main taxier in Salt Lake whenever her sisters want to go anywhere.

"District nursing suited me very well," she continues. "My resourcefulness, humble life, and intuition were all used to best advantage. There were always lots of problems to be tackled. Think of this one: a female patient weighing two hundred pounds in a narrow, single bed in a very over-furnished room, desperately sick with pneumonia and nobody to help but a ten-year-old child. It were a little tiny room with furniture all round and knickknacks everywhere. There wouldn't be above that much space"—Auntie Barbara gestures to a small coffee table—"for you to walk beside the bed, and that's where I'd to nurse her all that week. A desperate week of poulticing, washing, and all other nursing needs. Pneumonia, and we'd no penicillin then, you know. It was a fight, I'll tell you. But we made it."

I catch a glimpse in her eyes at the end of this tale of that other pneumonia case in Mirfield, with the man she thought of marrying, but it quickly vanishes. Behind her glasses, Auntie Barbara is back to her old, busy self.

"I were well liked in these small villages, but had to battle with handy women—untrained doctors' helps—who did deliveries. In 1936, the health authorities finally paid these women off to stop them practicing. Surgical cleanliness is the key to success, and we didn't have access to a bath, but had to use a bowl. I had a very sad and trying case while I was at Witton Le Wear. It was not my own case, but that of the neighboring village midwife. We used to relieve each other so we could get some time off. Nurse Milner started this case, then went off duty and left her to me. When we had complications, we always turned the case over to the doctor, and we carried out his orders. This case had already been turned over to him, but doctors were sometimes neglectful. He left her too long in a very obvious obstructed labor. Poor girl! She had been a couple days in hard labor, and he sent us to another doctor who saw at once it needed hospital treatment. He wouldn't touch her. The little hospital wouldn't do anything, either, and sent us forty miles to a bigger hospital. By now the baby was dead, and the mother in dire distress. I was exhausted, too, and sick. They did a craniotomy, but the mother went septic and died of septicemia."

Auntie Hannah remembers Barbara telling her that as long as something could be done, she enjoyed nursing. It was only when the case was terminal that it upset her.

One family in Witton Le Wear had been too poor to pay Barbara, but they gave her a little Yorkshire terrier instead. "It was lousy. Had to delouse it. Then it was a beautiful little dog. Mickey, they called it. Doctor told me not to give it potatoes. 'Nothing but raw meat.'

"But I took it into the nursing home, and there was a woman there—she spoilt it. She said, 'Oh, poor thing. 'Tis 'ungry. Let's give it summat.'

"She would persist, and its tongue went gangrene. I had to take him to his doom."

In many parts of England for more than forty years, Barbara pursued her career, becoming sanitary inspector, public health visitor, midwifery training sister, tuberculosis visitor, school nurse, infant protection visitor, lecturer and trainer for nurses in the mobile unit during World War II, driver for supply wagon to set up an emergency hospital in an invasion area, supervisor of refugee children from London—

She delivered my younger uncle as well as his oldest daughter. ("That were another one. Showed up on me doorstep without a stitch of baby clothing, not a nappie, nawt.")

She helped my grandmother through the first anxious days with Noel.

In this round of work, the singing, teaching, and playing the piano and the many holidays abroad with which she filled in the cracks are described as "extravagances."

In a testimonial, one grateful employer wrote:

February 3, 1933

... Nurse Whitaker's work is invariably good and characterized by sound common sense. She is a most excellent midwife, careful and conscientious to a degree, and has a wonderful way with mothers and babies. She carries out her duties with a cheery hopefulness that is most encouraging to others whilst her capacity for work is unfathomable.

～

Uncle Joe makes her read that letter aloud while I am visiting. Then, taking her hand, he said, "Add my testimony to that, too. Her capacity for work is still unfathomable."

LETTERS HOME

WHEN SHE WAS JUST SEVENTEEN, our Ivy began to see a young man only a few months older than she. Even better, his family were members of the church, the only young man in Bradford with such qualifications, although his family did live quite a ways out of town, at Clayton. He was the only boy she ever went out with in England, and his name was Gerald Craven.

Ivy and Gerald used to arrange to meet in downtown Bradford. That way he wouldn't have to walk all the way up the hill to Moulson Street after taking the half an hour's tram ride in from Clayton. Then they'd have more time together, time for a show "or summat."

One night, Gerald waited and waited, and Ivy never came. When he walked up the hill to her house, he found she was fast asleep in bed, exhausted after ten hour's work.

Gerald played the trumpet in the church orchestra.

~

"That were lovely, playing in t' orchestra—'cept fer t' midges." Grandma mimes waving the insects away with her cello bow.

Then she tells how, right in the middle of the *Messiah* one Christmastime, the spittle came out of the bell of Gerald's trumpet and dribbled into her carefully curled hair. "I never forgave him that."

∼

In spite of these disasters, Ivy and Gerald continued to see more and more of each other and were soon engaged. Gerald was sent into the army, but fortunately the war ended before he saw action.

Soon after the war, Gerald's family, like Doris, became part of the mass immigration of Saints to Salt Lake. Gerald wrote Ivy every week, sometimes twice a week. She had saved enough money to pay for her own passage. She was only waiting for him to ask her to come and join him.

Then the letters stopped coming. After six long weeks, one came. With shaking hands, Ivy opened it, but she never read it. She gave it to someone else to read and went up to bed where she stayed for days.

Salt Lake City Zion USA
July 25, 1923

. . . Mother thought it best that I marry her. . . .
God bless you the rest of your life,

G. Craven

Frances's Harry Maud, when he heard the news, brought a small present of condolence to everyone in the house.

Later, when she had regained her strength, Ivy carried down the box of all Gerald's letters she'd been saving and laid them, one by one in solemn ceremony, into the fire, with her sisters in attendance.

("In America," the sisters say, "if a girl wants a man, she gets 'im." Cautionary to me, "You watch tha 'usband, lass.")

Ralph wondered how his quiet, gentle third daughter would survive the blow. What she did surprised them all.

September 12, 1923

My dear sister Doris,
I don't know how I had the courage to do it, but I've done it. I've

booked passage to sail to America next month. I should be in Salt Lake City by the end of October. Gerald couldn't wait for me, so I'll just show him I can do it on my own!

Hoping to see you soon,
Ivy

The Latter-Day Saints'
MILLENNIAL STAR
[Established 1840]
No. 41 Vol. LXXXV Thursday, October 11, 1923
Price: One Penny

Beneath the "Extract of a talk by President David O. McKay given at Rotterdam Conference January 14th, 1923," entitled "By Their Fruits Ye Shall Know Them," this notice:

FAREWELL SOCIALS

Tuesday the 18th ult., a farewell social was held at the home of Sister Mary J. Whitaker (Bradford branch, Leeds Conference) in honor of her daughter Ivy, who is leaving for Zion. A delightful program, which consisted of instrumental and vocal solos, and recitations and readings, was given under the direction of the Mutual Improvement Association. Sister Whitaker was the recipient of several beautiful gifts.

Ivy sailed on the *Queen Mary*. When she was over one hundred years of age, she went to the same ship moored in the Long Beach harbor and turned into a hotel. On the high-lacquered floor of the grand ballroom, her grandson, a professional dancer, took her tiny frame in his arms and gently glided her across the floor.

Stopping to catch her breath, she confessed, "I never got to see this when I were coming to America. It were for t' others."

The tiny cabin Ivy was assigned she had to share with a room-mate, a stranger. "And I don't know to this day whether it were a man or a woman."

"Good heavens, Grandma, what do you mean?"

"I mean, she stayed out all night like a man. I stuck to me cabin."

～

On terribly yellowed paper in ink gone brown, dictated to Mary Jane and sent to:

Miss Ivy Whitaker
c/o Mrs. Shutt
760 West Jackson
Salt Lake City, Utah USA

From R. R. W.
Moulson Street
Bowling Old Lane
Bfd. Yks.
Jan. 28th

Dear Ivy,

I will just write you a line or two in reply to your boxing day letter. I am glad you think about me when you are walking about the street, wondering how I should manage. I don't think I shall want to travel to Salt Lake City alone. If I ever do come it will not be to travel about as I do here, but to sit in the corner by the stove & play with the babies. I think you are right about the houses. . . I would like something. . . [with] an upstairs, where you can get a little privacy. If we take note of all the great men in Literature, art & science, they have done the greater part of their study in garrets, far above the noise & rabble of the streets. At any rate we are in the fashion with our detached villa at 4 Moulson Street. The motor cars are very cheeky here & people get knocked down almost every day here in Bradford. We have not much convenience at present on our Railways as there is a strike.

There is our Barbara here correcting my Grammar every other sentence. She finished her case on Sunday (25) & she is turning the wringing machine now. I am surprised about the piano business. I have always been made to understand from the elders that all the citizens in America had pianos. . . . I think the Children's party was a success but you will have heard all about it. I am sorry that your work is slack but it will brighten up in spring. Sorry you have broken your violin bow. Hope you will get a good one. Well, we have got a Labor Parliament in England. Ramsey Macdonald is the Prime Minister. We have two Bfd. members who are on the Cabinet, Mr. Jowell & Mr. Leech. I think every day is about the same with me. You will find me at home at the usual hours if you happen to pass this way. I am just going out with Barbara shopping so I think I will close now for the present.

With love & best wishes to you & Doris & Albert & [baby]
Barbara
From your loving Father

~

Salt Lake City, Utah
28 March 1925

Dear Dad, Momma and Sisters,

. . . Yesterday afternoon in the County Building on her 25th birthday, our Ivy became Mrs. Harry Mason. If you are surprised, so are we! But you know our Ivy was always very private about her life. They didn't even tell us until after. But a friend of ours married them, a Scots immigrant named Brother MacCloed. Ivy said he teased them and made it very pleasant.

Harry is a very nice, quiet man, and Ivy seems very happy. He's an Englishman, too, just newly immigrated. He served during the War in France in the cavalry. Ivy says he's always talking about his horse and how many scrapes the creature saw him through. Sometimes she wonders if he doesn't love that horse more than her and she's just a substitute now that the War's over. . . .

. . . You should see our little Ralph! He can pull himself up on anything, and Barbara is quite a little mother to him—just like our Barbara at home. . . .

. . . Dad, I must thank you for the 5 copies of Handel's Messiah. Next year our chorale director will not have to borrow my copy again because that best English edition is unavailable in America. I shall be able to give him his own. Won't we have a sing then!

Much love to all,
Doris

~

CABLEGRAM

Salt Lake City, Utah USA
6 Dec 1925

Baby boy to be called Frederick stop Ivy and baby fine stop
H Mason

~

Salt Lake City, Utah USA
19 December 1925

Dear Dad, Momma and Sisters,
. . . Hope this gets to you in time to wish you all the very best of Christmases and to send you our love. The baby seems to gain strength every day, although he was very small—only 5 lb. 4 oz— and five weeks too soon. Harry, when he saw how little he was, sighed and said, "Ivy, is that all we could do?" But the doctor said if he lives the first two months, he'll be a big man, he has such large shoulders. Everything looks very hopeful.

I'm feeling better, too. The months in bed helped me, I'm sure, after I nearly miscarried last August. I can almost hear my Dad saying, "Is she still alive?" It's been hard, but Harry has been so good to us. . . .

Best Christmas wishes to all,
Ivy

～

CABLEGRAM

Salt Lake City, Utah USA
8 Feb 1926

Harry Mason killed last night stop
Doris

～

Salt Lake City, Utah USA
10 Feb 1926

Dear Dad, Mother and Sisters,

. . . I knew our Ivy would be in no condition to write and tell you how this tragedy happened so I thought I'd better. The mere thought of it is almost too much for the poor girl to bear. And the baby just two months old. . . .

Harry, as you know, worked at the new mill in Magna turning the mountainside at Bingham Canyon into slag and copper. The train he took there and back every day began to slow coming into the Salt Lake station just as he could see the lights from their little house on 2nd South across the fields. We imagine he thought about his lovely wife rocking and singing their dear little boy to sleep. He could even see the nappies hung out—stiff as boards in the cold— and the soft mounds of snow in their yard.

Last Saturday night, it must have occurred to him: Why should I ride all the way to the station and then have to walk all the way back here again to be home with them? I'll just jump off the slowing train and run across the field. . . .

He must have slipped on the ice on the siding and fallen backwards as he jumped. They found him on the tracks, his head quite severed from his body by the wheels. It was a closed-casket funeral.

. . . We've heard from Gerald Craven. It seems he was so upset when he heard about Ivy being widowed that he had to come home from his own work and spent the day in bed. He still loves her, it seems. But he's married somebody else and there's nothing to be done about it. . . .

And we thought to escape the dangers of working in the mills here in Zion. . . . I'm sure I don't know how our Ivy'll live through it, the baby just two month old and all. . . .

How we miss you now,
Doris

～

Letter written in Braille on stiff brown paper. Ralph always began each letter with the alphabet so that deciphering was made easier. The dots are all but worn away by now so one does need eyes to read it.

A B C D E F G H I J K L M N O P Q R S T U V W X Y Z

I V Y D E A R E S T
B R I N G T H E B A B Y A N D C O M E H O M E
S O W E C A N C A R E F O R Y O U A T
M O U L S O N S T R E E T.

D A D
X X X X

～

4 Moulson Street Bfd. Yks.
Jan. 30, 1927

Dearest Ivy and little Freddie,

. . . Hannah has finally got her visa to go to America. You know, they won't take you unless you're perfect, and she's had some difficulty. No difficulty saving up the money. You know our Barbara was not told how long her midwifery training would last, and she hadn't saved enough to finish the course. Hannah lent her what she needed to finish the year, and Barbara has now returned it in a lump sum.

We're a little hesitant to let Hannah go to you. Three of our girls gone. Not only will we miss her sweet, quiet ways, but you know she is friendly with that nice Robert Tomlin in the branch. He is a fine young man, and I think he would marry her. "Perhaps he'll follow me," she says, but he's already been turned down by the consulate because of his bad eye. Still, she won't wait. "My only thought is for my poor Ivy all alone with that little baby," she says. . . .

Love,
Mother

~

Salt Lake City, Utah USA
September 29, 1927

Dear Mother and Dad,

Little Freddie seems to have recovered from that terrible fall he had out of the second-storey window at the Neighborhood House. I must say, it gave us some anxious hours. Ivy sat up all night at hospital with him until they assured her he would be all right. I don't know what would have happened if he'd been killed. She was nearly distract from her husband's death when I first got to Zion, now this. She seems to be doing better.

. . . Every morning at six o'clock we put little Freddie in the red wagon—or on the sled when there's snow—and pull him to the Neighborhood House. Then we both take the bus to town. Yes, I got Ivy on too. When I first went to Utah Woolen Mills, the boss, who'd been on a mission to England, said, "If you come from England and you say you can sew, I know you can sew." When I asked to bring my sister, and that I'd teach her myself and take out the mistakes she made on my own, he trusted me then, too. Now she's on piecework and making almost as much as I am. We live quite well for two poor immigrant girls and a fatherless orphan!

Although we've learned not to trust the Neighborhood House too much since the accident, we really have no choice but to leave little Freddie there. They take him for free because she's a widow.

Freddie really is the joy of our lives. He is such a happy child, always running around on his little bowed legs and laughing and prattling. I think he's been Ivy's salvation during these dark months. It is simply impossible to be sad for long with him around. He's a joy for me, too. He runs around the house singing, "My Nauntie! My Nauntie!"—"My Auntie!"...

... Have they told you the news yet? Doris's little George took his first steps while we were visiting them last Sunday. The other three children are doing just fine.

. . . Still, to hear Ivy playing "The Hours I've Spent with You, Dearest" on her violin. Sometimes it nearly breaks my heart....

Love to all,
Hannah

～

A B C D E F G H I J K L M N O P Q R S T U V W X Y Z

D R I V Y

W E A R E A L L A L I V E & W E L L...

I H A V E P U T A F E W C O N T R A C T I O N S I N T H I S L E T T E R. I H O P E Y O U W I L L B E A B L E T O M A K E I T O U T. W E H A D U N C L E E D G A R & A U N T B E R T H A H E R E F O R H O U R S O N T H U R S D A Y. T H E Y A R E A L R I G H T. J U S T T H E S A M E A S U S U A L. W E L L I W I L L C L O S E N O W.

W I T H L O V E & W I S H E S F R O M Y O U R L O V I N G D A D,

R R W H I T A K E R X X X X

∽

Salt Lake City, Utah USA
April 3, 1929

Dear Frances,

I've bought the most lovely lace here for my wedding dress. I can't wait to show it to you. With your veil (if you're still willing to let me borrow it), I'll be very pretty indeed! Robert deserves it. He's waited so long.

I should be home on the 20th. Tell Dad it isn't necessary, but if he wants to come all the way to Liverpool to meet me, he knows there's nothing I'd like better than my first sight of dear old England to be him standing with his cane and waving his hat at the sound of the steamer's horn.

. . . So glad to hear your precious Noel is taking his food better. It was a worry.

. . . By the way, do you remember that quiet young man we told you about that Doris invited to her Halloween Party? You remember, the one she had dress up as a preacher, and such a tall and lanky one he made, too! Harry Brooks is his name. Well, he and Ivy have been seeing more and more of each other. I think she likes him, although she'd never say, and he couldn't be nicer. He has a couple of sisters here. They don't want him to marry her because she's a widow and three years older than he is. But I've overheard him call her Buttercup. (Don't tell Ivy I heard. She'd be so humiliated.) And Freddie likes him, too. I don't think busybody sisters can stay in the way of this for long. Dear Ivy. It's about time she had some joy in her life. And that he should be named Harry, too. Very convenient, to avoid embarrassing mistakes.

Looking forward to seeing you all soon. So hard to believe it's been over two years.

My best love,
Hannah

∼

Bfd. Yks.
10 June 1929

Dear Ivy,

Robert and I have been married a month now, and we're very
happy. How happy we are you can tell by how long it's taken me to
finally write you. But you know, when I walked off the boat and saw
our dad waiting for me, I went straight to him, hugging and kissing
and crying for joy. Dad was the one who had to tell me, "Robert's
here, Hannah. Go to Robert now."

I have to tell you something very funny that happened at Riddles'
when I went there to see if I could get my old sewing job back. I
walked in, and the whole room (you know, there must be two hundred work there) all began talking at once. The boss came out of his
office to see what the matter was, they were making so much noise.
It was because they were so surprised to see me. Someone had gone
to Salt Lake City with the Mormons and escaped!

Anyway, I have my old job back and that will help us save up for
our own place. Right now Frances is kind enough to let us live with
her. You know our Frances, always money bags. . . .

. . . When Dad and I drove up to the church in the taxi, there
were some men there, and they laughed, "Look, there goes another
one!" We must have been the third or fourth wedding that day. You
know me, I was very shy, and I shrank back. "What have you got to
be ashamed of?" Dad says. "You've got nothing to be ashamed of,
Hannah," he said. "You're doing what's right."

Dear Ivy, I certainly pray that you might know the same happiness someday soon. Still, I often long for the days when we were
together in Salt Lake, just we two and little Freddie. I always say,
anyone who can't get along with our Ivy, it's their fault. . . .

Love,
Your sister, Hannah

~

Auntie Ivy's handwriting at the top of her father's stiff, brown Braille paper notes: "Sept. 1940."

A B C D E F G H I J K L M N O P Q R S T U V W X Y Z

D R HARRY & IVY & FRED & NUMBER FOUR

WE RECEIVED YOUR CABLE SATURDAY
MORNING ELEVEN O'CLOCK FOR WHICH WE
THANK YOU. WELCOME TO NEW LITTLE
BYRON.
I TOOK IT TO HANNAH & VIOLET THE
SAME DAY.
EVERYBODY IS DELIGHTED & THANKFUL ALL
IS WELL....

BEST LOVE TO YOU ALL & BEST WISHES FROM
YOUR LOVING PARENTS

RRW & MJ WHITAKER

~

And finally, Ralph's last letter:

A B C D E F G H I J K L M N O P Q R S T U V W X Y Z

SUNDAY
OCT 26TH

DR IVY & ALL

I WAS INTERESTED IN YOUR LETTER
PARTICULARLY ABOUT
BYRON BEING SO CLEVER.
I SHOULD LIKE TO PLAY YOUR NEW
PIANO FOR FUN.
V'S BABY IS LOVELY: FOURTEEN

POUNDS AT SEVEN WEEKS AND SHE
SO LITTLE. HIS NAME IS
MALCOLM STUART.
HE IS A GOOD BABY....
I WILL TRY AND WRITE OFTENER,
SHORT LETTERS JUST TO LET
YOU KNOW WE ARE ALLRIGHT. I
WISH YOU AND YOURS EVERY JOY
AND BLESSING IN THIS LIFE
AND IN THE LIFE TO COME.
FROM YOUR LOVING DADDY

RRW   XXXX

MONA AND THE DEVIL

M. WHITAKER
FIRST YEAR BIOLOGY TAXONOMY FINAL EXAM
INSTRUCTOR: MISS HAWTHORNE
24 FEBRUARY 1926

Mona's black Welsh eyes ran quickly over the pages filled with her neat, tight penmanship.

DOMESTIC DOG—Kingdom: Animalia; Phylum: Chordata; Class: Mammalia; Order: Carnivora; Family: Canidae; Genus: Canis; Species: Familiaris.

EUROPEAN WOLF—Animalia Chordata Mammalia Carnivora Canidae Canis Lupus.

EUROPEAN RED FOX—Animalia Chordata Mammalia Carnivora Canidae Vulpes Fulva.

DOMESTIC CAT—Animalia Chordata Mammalia Carnivora Felidae Felis Catus.

She'd made a perfect paper. She'd known she would.

She loved taxonomy. Her years of Latin made the technical terms self-evident. But it was more than ease. "How Wondrous and Great, Thy Works, God of Praise" was a favorite hymn. Even poor Nellie, whining wordlessly, tunelessly at their mother's side, was imbued, through that hymn, with a sense of the majesty of God's creation. But only she, Mona, of all the sisters could chant that creation through both the plant and animal kingdoms, fifty phyla, and all the classes of living creatures on earth.

That man Linneaus, she decided, must have been inspired—moved upon by the spirit of Christ—to come up with such a system. Human beings could now classify God's creation and thereby come closer to him through understanding. "The glory of God," as the revelation said, "is intelligence."

Mona had loved learning the singsong of creation. She enjoyed matching the names to the stuffed exhibits in the natural history gallery of the Liverpool Museum. She enjoyed classifying algae, molds, and nematoda under the microscope. She enjoyed collecting members of the Insecta class to form a gradated display on cardboard with pins stuck through their bodies as neatly as our Frances could pin a gore in a skirt. Even some fossil specimens Mona had labored over had given her no trouble. She just ignored the label, which suggested the impossible years before Christ someone thought the creatures must have lived.

She had enjoyed this work so much that at times she regretted her choice to specialize in geography and history. The sciences needed more teachers, she was told, and pay was better. The same source assured her that, with her diligence and intelligence, she could do equally well in either field.

Only a favorite English teacher in grammar school (where she'd been head girl her last year) telling her, "Mona, you stick to arts!" had won her devotion away from the headmistress, who was a "Cambridge maths person."

Now Mona had graduated and been accepted to Edge Hill Training College in Liverpool. Here, Miss Hawthorne, the biology lecturer, was a woman one could admire. Mona never felt she could confide in this woman, as she had done in many teachers—her best friends had always been teachers. But Miss Hawthorne exuded brilliance. So much so, in fact, that some were put off and thought she was proud.

Mona, however, knew better. She showed something of the same pride herself when she shut out her sisters' foolishness to study, when she had not minded that she was not asked to go dancing or skating with the others. It was not that she thus avoided the embarrassment of her lame foot. She was always submerged in reading a book at the moment—more often than not about her hero, Oliver Cromwell—compared to which dancing would have been both a frivolity and an annoying interruption.

Yes, Mona thought she understood the tall, strong person behind the horn-rimmed glasses and severe hair knot. Perhaps more than the study of biology itself did she love going to that dark, echoing hall every day, getting a seat near the front, and meeting those intense grey eyes with intensity of her own. And if she did not go up to Miss Hawthorne at once and declare herself ready to change her specialization (in English schools, no small step), it was only because she wanted to prove herself absolutely worthy of that brilliant woman's returned respect.

A perfect taxonomy exam must surely have given that proof. And yet, that "Excellent" scribbled by her name in a rather florid hand gave Mona no pleasure at all now. It seemed, instead, a most dreadful betrayal.

That morning, after returning the graded exams, Miss Hawthorne had unfurled, like a banner of war, one large chart upon the classroom board. At first, Mona had missed its martial character. She had smiled with excitement at the colors: a rainbow of tints faded into one another on the branches of a great, blooming tree.

Then she had read the lettering. Mona was the secretary of a genealogical society that had recently been formed there in the Liverpool branch of the church. She knew a family tree when she saw one.

Up shot Mona's hand. "Miss Hawthorne, surely you are not going to expect us to learn—" She paused, for the very word was blasphemy. "Darwinism?"

"Miss Whitaker is very astute today." Irony bit the older woman's voice. "Yet we should no more call this natural law after the name of the man who merely discovered it than we should call the law of gravity Newtonism. Evolution is the term that has come to be generally used for the laws by which living things change. These laws were first brought before the world some fifty years ago by our own countryman, Charles Darwin. Yes? Miss Whitaker?"

"Call it what you will, Miss, isn't it still the—the delusion that man is descended from an ape?"

"That is a gross oversimplification. As we shall see, and as leads directly from our just-completed study of taxonomy, evolution—"

Mona shocked the whole class then by daring to interrupt the teacher in the middle of a sentence. Pulling herself up to her full height, with a vision of the ancient prophet Abinadi before wicked King Noah in her mind, Mona declared, "Miss Hawthorne, don't forget the word of God: 'In the beginning, God created the heavens and the earth. . . . Male and female created he them.'"

"The Bible," Miss Hawthorne said, "may satisfy some as to the why of our existence. But science is the best-qualified tool to answer the how. Better, surely, than the legends, however pious, of a people who lived so very long ago, when human knowledge of the world around us was still very primitive. Please sit down, Miss Whitaker, and let us proceed with the lesson."

Time and again as Miss Hawthorne lectured, Mona raised her hand and stood, even when the girls next to her tugged on her skirt and begged her to keep her seat. Miss Hawthorne began to ignore her. Miss Hawthorne, whom Mona so wanted to impress.

Mona had remained determined, until the end of the hour, with the help of the Holy Spirit, to bravely defend the Right.

And yet, now in the quiet of her room, the Right did not seem as eloquent as it had been with an audience. Like a lion cub raised in captivity which, upon reaching full size, suddenly turns on the hand that feeds it—so with her knowledge. Learning had been so tame and friendly before, purring gently inside her brain. Slowly, subtly, Miss Hawthorne had built up her arguments with no warning as to where they were leading. Now, in spite of herself, Mona found them almost irrefutable.

And the light in Miss Hawthorne's eyes, when she looked at her student in the front row, had extinguished.

Some of the girls had sought to explain, to quieten Mona, that perhaps God had created the earth—but by means of evolution.

Then what should become of the "in six days, the Lord made heaven and earth" and "the seventh day is the Sabbath . . . in it thou shalt not do any work"? Was that one commandment, too, merely a myth of primitive people? What of the other nine, then? If this were the case, why did she, Mona, a scholarship-winning college student in the 1920s, bother to follow these ancient superstitions? Why did she rush to finish her studies on Saturday night so Sunday could be restful? Why did she even get dressed in her best clothes once a week and walk to church on her crippled leg?

The Latin growled ferociously; the neatly ordered mind of God had grown claws. They tore at her to reject layer after layer of the scientific argument until there was nothing left to believe in that direction, either. Even so basic a thing as the word "genus," which she had used with so much ease and freedom, now reared its ugly head. It reminded her that the original meaning had been, not a biological class, but the tribal or clan system by which the ancient Latins determined with whom they would fight or against, who their kinsmen were—in other words, their direct genealogies. Mona felt herself persuaded, pursued, by this beast gone wild, to the very edge of a deep and dark abyss, no matter which direction she turned to flee.

Lead kindly light amid th' encircling gloom,
Lead thou me on.
The night is dark and I am far from home,
Lead thou me on!

Suddenly it seemed to Mona that she heard those words, sweet and clear, in her mother's voice. Suddenly her soul, like the room, was filled with light. She was able to crumple the exam and toss it away as if ridding herself of physical pain. Better to fail out of school altogether, give up the scholarship, than to ever deny the Truth.

Later, her roommate Agnes rescued the exam from the trash, straightening it out. "I can't believe you threw it out," Agnes said. "A perfect paper? I'd send it home to my parents if I could ever get such marks."

Mona was still in no mood to see biology papers, but she forgave Agnes her misplaced rescue because of what she said immediately afterwards.

"Mona, you've heard me talk of our Christian Society, haven't you? Well, we've been having slack attendance lately, and the girls asked if I would see if you'd come and be our speaker next Friday evening. To liven things up a bit."

"Me? I've told you I'm not interested in your—"

"You're not interested, but we are. We want to hear you speak on 'why I am a Mormon' or 'what Mormons believe,' something like that. A real live Mormon! I mean, what could be more exciting than that?"

Agnes was the daughter of a Methodist minister. A frail girl with thin lips, mousey hair and eyes, still excitement could bring such color to her face that none would call her plain. Mona looked at that face, propped up on her elbows, glowing across the expanse of bed between them.

Mona could not say no. Besides, as she later described, a voice came to her saying, "You have received the privilege of a college education, which all of your sisters were denied because they had to go work in the mills. You will do great things for me because of your learning." God had a purpose for her after all.

Friday came, and Mona walked through the wet drizzle that came off the wintry Irish Sea. The cold always made her limp worse, and she felt much more self-conscious about it than a great missionary— St. Paul, say—should have felt. Still, she persisted in trying to collect her thoughts over the bubble of Agnes's excited voice at her side. Fortunately, they had given themselves time, and she still had half an hour to spare for meditation when they reached the warmth and light of the lecture building.

The Christian Society usually met in a small room around a single long table. "We're ten—fifteen at most," Agnes had described the audience to Mona. The usual room was lit but empty when they reached it. This was not because they were so early, however. Hastily scribbled across the chalkboard was the announcement: "Christian Society to meet in main lecture hall tonight due to large turnout."

Agnes glowed and clapped her hands. "Come on, Mona," she said. "To the main lecture hall! You're coming off just grand!"

A dozen or more girls were standing before the lecture hall door, talking excitedly. They immediately silenced when they saw Mona coming, however, and parted like the Red Sea for Moses before her. Their bodies came together again after she passed, and they watched her through the door. Their voices closed in after her, too, but in whispers now.

A similar silence fell upon the rows of girls seated inside. Three rows were full already, and more people were coming in every moment. Mona saw at once that they weren't just girls from the college. Many had brought their young men—young men!—their families and friends. She saw the white collar of a Church of England minister and the somber black robes of some professors who had come to the college from Liverpool University.

Agnes gave Mona no time to hesitate, but dragged her at once—like a prize fish to show off—to meet the officers of the society and one or two other people of importance. Each one took Mona's hand, but only briefly, as if they were afraid of contagion. Mona longed for more human contact and warmth. Her own hands were drained of blood and numb.

Agnes showed her a seat behind the table that spread behind the podium in front of the room. A pitcher of water and glasses stood at Mona's elbow. She didn't think she could trust her hands not to shake if she poured herself some. This was the time she ought to spend collecting her thoughts, but she couldn't find a single one. More and more people kept pouring into the hall, the tide increasing as the time drew closer. From one side of the room or the other, there was always a finger pointing at her. Following every point, heads bent together in excited whispers.

The true gospel of Jesus Christ, Mona tried to remind herself, gave their lay clergy—every member, from earliest childhood—great practice in public speaking. In such a small branch as Bradford, it was even more so. Mona herself had raised her voice to preach on street corners with the missionaries. She had stood in front of congregations to bear her testimony so many times that some of her sisters would plead with her, "Not this month, our Mona, please." She had even taught the baby's class for a year in Sunday School, and what more demanding audience could there be than the three-to-five-year-olds?

Then a figure in a grey coat walked into the hall, and Mona recognized Miss Hawthorne. With her strode the head of school, Miss

Beecham. Mona's courage fled to the same hiding places as all her carefully plotted thoughts.

I must pray, she thought, and did so with facial expressions she hoped would let the audience know that she talked with God. Looking heavenward, however, she saw the ribs of the vaulted ceiling like the ribs of the carcass of some animal she had dissected for biology. She had thought the animal dead and in her power, but it seemed now to have swallowed her alive. Eerie pools of light played on the ceiling, making its plaster seem insubstantial. Rather than leading her mind beyond that roofing as a similar phenomenon in the branch meeting house had always done, it tricked her eyes like a wavy mirror. She felt unsure of even her most solid beliefs.

She looked to the floor, closing her eyes at the point where they should have taken in the masses of people between the ceiling and it. The floor was liver colored with a pattern of dirty, sick green in the tile. In the corners of the room, shadows turned the floor into the mouth of a bottomless pit. No place to look with safety presented itself.

The success of the evening turned the lively Agnes more talkative than ever. Throughout the half-hour wait, she kept jumping up and running to greet new arrivals, then returning to the speaker's platform, poking Mona, and giving reports: "There's so-and-so. And look, there's so-and-so, as well. Just grand, Mona, just grand."

Now Agnes was at the podium. The audience rustled to silence. She will address them a long time, Mona thought. I still have time to think and pray. But the first thing she heard as this thought unfuddled her brain was Agnes saying: "But you didn't come to hear me so I will turn the time over—"

Mona got to her feet. You could hear a pin drop. The clumsiness of her lame leg crossing the platform echoed throughout the great hall like a log dropped on a bandbox.

Mona gripped the edge of the platform. It offered precious little support. She shoved her glasses up on her nose. Then she opened her mouth to begin. "My dear brothers and sisters—"

"Can't hear you," someone shouted. "Speak up," said another. These voices came from only halfway back. People in the rear stood and cupped their ears. She would have to yell. She wished she had her sister Frances's voice. She filled her lungs with air, as much as the constriction in her throat would allow. Her voice boomed. She wanted to hide from it, but there was no hiding now.

"Neither do men light a candle, and put it under a bushel, but on a candlestick; and it giveth light unto all that are in the house. Let your light so shine before men." These comforting words of scripture suddenly came to her, and she found breath again to continue on after another beginning, covering the slip of the first. "My brothers and sisters—I call you brothers and sisters because I believe, Mormons believe—"

What she said after that, though it came with increasing ease in memorized phrases, might have reached the back of the hall, but it failed to reach the speaker's own brain. Automation took over. The spirit of God! she exulted, and the words of the Doctrine and Covenants came to her: "It shall be given thee in the very moment what thou shalt speak . . . and they shall hear it, or I will send unto them a cursing instead of a blessing."

"I know that the things I have spoken here tonight are true," Mona heard herself say in closing. She had so little recollection that perhaps she couldn't make that statement at all.

She closed in the name of the Savior, then turned to take her seat. But Agnes caught her arm and herded her back to the podium. She must now field questions.

Hands shot up like bristles on a hedgehog. A lot of edginess, Mona noticed, filled the voices that addressed her. Some were out-and-out hostile. A red-faced minister had opened his Bible and was flipping from quote to quote with the ease of a man who has the book memorized. When Mona found herself unable to answer rationally, or even with calmness, she felt inspired to raise her shrill voice and exclaim, over and over, "I know what I say is true." Sometimes this brought nervous chuckles, but she, at least, felt no one could assail her after that.

At last it was time to close. Agnes stepped to the podium to say so, but two or three questions were shouted up even after she'd made that announcement.

"Thank you all for attending," Agnes said. "This evening has certainly been an interesting one and given us all food for thought. Thank you and good night."

The audience spilled from its seats now, many leaving the room in hot discussion with their neighbors. Mona saw some stop and talk to Miss Hawthorne and Miss Beecham at the door. The women coughed and shuffled their feet a lot. But many more came rushing down to surround Mona and Agnes, who held her roommate firmly by the arm so she could not escape. A full fifteen minutes passed before they could even step off the platform. It seemed to Mona, however, at the end of the tally, that more girls had come up to her asking to be taken to attend a church meeting than there had been people wanting to attack.

Although the attacks were brutal.

At least, faith told her their numbers were close to equal.

Mona found the cold, dark out-of-doors not bitter but welcome to cool the flush of her cheeks and to hide the hot tears of gratitude that ran down them.

By Sunday, all those who had promised to come to church with her had dwindled down to three. Even Agnes bowed out, giving her dour minister father as an excuse. But Mona had never exulted more. Even a less-than-inspiring speaker could not disappoint her elevated spirits. When the girls took a polite but cool leave afterwards, only one took the Book of Mormon Mona had gone to great expense to purchase for each one.

Mona was still very happy. God had sent her to Liverpool for a purpose.

∾

"All rise!"

Monday morning, a great rumble filled the college chapel as several hundred young women got to their feet for the headmistress's entrance. Miss Beecham, short and stout with the features of a bull-dog, strode to the podium (her stride was another woman's waddle) and cleared her throat to announce the morning prayer. Mona's heart faltered as she both saw and felt those tiny but fierce eyes fix her—and only her—with a steady glare for nearly a full minute before they closed to address the Almighty. An extra emphasis hit the three-in-one and insubstantiality of God—the most un-Mormon doctrines—that morning.

Immediately after convocation, somebody came to tell Mona that the headmistress wanted to see her in her study. Now Mona used her limp as an excuse to walk slower than she'd ever done before down the long, poorly lit passage. The door to the study was open, waiting for her, and holding it was Miss Hawthorne.

"Miss Beecham will see you now," the biologist said.

Mona looked back and saw those brilliant grey eyes, magnified by the glasses, as heavy upon her as two stones. She looked back again when she was further inside. The weight did not let up.

"Sit down, Miss Whitaker," the headmistress said.

The headmistress squatted behind her massive desk, her jowls heavier and more bulldoggish now with gruffness.

Mona had had a friend here. It was through the auspices of Miss Beecham, who was a friend of her favorite teacher back at the grammar school in Bradford, that she had earned this scholarship and been able to come to college at all. But Miss Beecham, it seemed, had forgotten.

"I'll come right to the point." The headmistress turned the light on her desk under its green shade off her papers and let it shine into Mona's eyes. "Either you give up this mad religion of yours"—she said "religion" as if the word must be insulted to find itself in such a place—"or you must leave this school."

Mona had expected anything but this. For a moment or two, she blinked dumbfounded into the light. Then, as some defense seemed called for, she rattled off a chain of platitudes she had heard the missionaries use in similar tight spots.

None of these had any effect on the stern face before her.

Finally, Mona thought to say, "Miss Beecham, Edge Hill Training College is a nondenominational school, the first in Britain. The other college for women in Liverpool is run by the nuns. I chose to come here for that very reason, and you cannot exclude me because of my faith."

That was not precisely true. She had been glad to be accepted anywhere, and religion, at first, had had nothing to do with it.

Nonetheless, she knew she had the headmistress there. It was true. She could not be dismissed because of religious persuasion, and she knew it. Inspiration, Mona thought gratefully, had been able to call the bulldog's bluff. The woman retreated into a subtler process of bargaining.

"I may forbid you, however, from ever using any room on this campus to preach your nonsense again."

Yes, Mona supposed the head of a school did have the right to do that.

"And I must ask that you do not take any more of your fellow scholars to any of your meetings again. Young ladies are entrusted to me by their parents. I cannot allow anything that might jeopardize that trust of youth's morals."

Mona was not at all certain that any of the girls would be willing to go with her again. Their closed-mouth farewell yesterday indicated that perhaps they were not as impressed as missionaries' testimonies always said they ought to have been. Mona felt very lonely and frightened, very small and very clumsy in the face of that massive desk, like bulwarks, and the John Bull behind it.

"Very well." That much Mona could concede. "But," and she pulled herself up in her chair and made her eyes flame against the desk lamp like, she hoped, the eyes of Shadrach must have done in the fiery furnace. "If you are standing between these girls and the Truth, someday, Miss Beecham, you'll have to answer to a Higher Judge for it."

Mona was pleased by the silence that fell then. The foolish things of the world have confounded the wise, she congratulated herself.

When Miss Beecham spoke again, however, it was with the restricted vocal cords of someone who has only just refrained from beating a petulant, saucy child.

"Miss Whitaker," the head of school snarled, "I have taken the liberty of writing a letter to your mother, asking her to come and consult with me on this matter. Your mother knows you consort with these Mormon madmen?"

My mother is herself a "Mormon madwoman," was Mona's first reaction. Fortunately, she managed to keep those words inside. "My mother," she said instead, "is a very devout Mormon, too. She has been president of our women's organization now for ten years. It is at her knee that I first learned right from wrong."

"I see," Miss Beecham replied. "Nevertheless, I've sent for her. She should be here tomorrow afternoon, and I expect you to be here, too, to try to defend your behavior to me in her presence."

"Yes, Miss Beecham," Mona said, and was then dismissed.

Tomorrow. There was no time now for Mona herself to send a letter of explanation home. Her mother must come, leave Nellie untended, leave all her many other responsibilities. Her mother never enjoyed leaving the house unless it was for church work. Now she must come all the way to Liverpool.

Mona's mind would not leave her in peace as she dragged herself to her next class—biology. Here was I, given the opportunity to go to school when none of the others was allowed. I should be the least bother to Mother, being the most blessed. Yet here I am being the biggest bother of all. Ever since I was born. The polio, all those days of warm baths and olive oil. All the years telling the others: "Hush, Mona must study." When will I ever grow up and be a blessing to her instead of a care?

That evening after classes, Mona left school and took the quick, five-minute walk up Edge Lane to number 295. Durham House was the church headquarters for all Europe. It also served as the home of the mission president and his wife as well as the local meeting house. There she found Sister Talmage, the wife of the apostle and president, who was considered something of a mother to all the Saints from Dublin to Prague.

Sister Talmage was a thin woman, for all that she was the mother of eight, the youngest of which was already married. She had deep, dark, motherly eyes well set above prominent cheekbones. Her black, lustrous hair was only just streaking with grey. Her mouth seemed intelligent but, contradictorily, honest. She could, in certain lights, seem the very epitome of an old school marm. To ears used to taking the dropping of aitches as a sign of provincial upbringing, she gave the impression of being foreign—French, perhaps, because of her dark features, or Swiss: proper and well bred, although not on the King's English. Mona understood that "foreign," that "alpine": Sister Talmage had spent her girlhood in the tiny village of Alpine, Utah.

First, Sister Talmage offered Mona use of the mission telephone to call her mother. The call, however, would have to go to the pub on the corner since 4 Moulson Street had no phone. Mona didn't want to draw her mother into that atmosphere, the shame of it so public. So she refused. Instead, to this motherly woman from so far away, over cups of hot cocoa, Mona poured out her tears and her story. Sister Talmage's sympathy was like the cocoa, warm, dark, and sweet.

"Now, don't you worry anymore," Sister Talmage said at the end of the interview. "We'll take care of Miss Beecham."

The president's wife promised she would be present at the confrontation, too. Better than that, she would pick Mona's mother up at the train station. For, as she drank the cocoa and it made her more and more homesick, Mona's fear for her mother grew. Had it been her father called to this confrontation, Mona would not have feared. Although he was blind, his daily practice with public transportation would get him to Liverpool with ease.

Mona was not so sure of her mother. To her knowledge, her mother had never left the boundaries of Bradford unaccompanied since her marriage. And her mother had that implacable air that expected sainthood not only of herself, but of anyone allowed to associate with her or hers. If she failed to find it, she could not turn it with humor as Mona's father did.

Mona had thought to improve upon her mother's converted sainthood in herself through education. Now she was stumbling in that very search for learning. Her mother's disappointment would be harder to bear than Miss Beecham's wrath. But now that Sister Talmage had stepped into the fray on her behalf—Sister Talmage who was saintly not only by conversion and profession, but by birth, breeding, education, marriage, and endowment as well—things seemed much, much better.

~

"Mrs. Whitaker, I regret to inform you that your daughter is a religious maniac."

Miss Beecham began with that indictment. She proceeded to cite the student's behavior in biology class and at the Christian Society. In the headmistress's mouth, these and other deeds did at best sound as if Mona had been willfully disruptive, disrespectful, and insulting to her instructors. That was at best.

Mona had once, in grammar school, received an "unsatisfactory" in behavior. Miss Beecham had that record; such behavior was not completely foreign to this student's nature.

Mona remembered the mark. "The work is boring," she had explained to her father. She always finished before any of the other students, and she had to do something to keep awake in class.

"Now, Olive Mona," her father had said in a deep, stern voice, and she had known he was not jesting this time. "Even if you were a child who couldn't do the lessons, you could always behave yourself."

Since that scolding, Mona had always tried to behave, and it became less and less difficult as the lessons grew more and more challenging. These disruptions Miss Beecham alluded to sounded like the same thing all over again.

No, it was worse. They were cited in her mother's presence.

And Miss Beecham seemed to think this was not mere childish naughtiness. Mona was, by implication, hopelessly insane. Surely no school in Britain could take her on staff at the completion of her studies.

Now Miss Beecham cited, in her gruff, intellectual tone, all recent scholarship on the subject of manias in general and religious manias in particular. "Freud, Kraepelin, Kretschmer, Jung—" She rattled off these names as if such German gentlemen were her most frequent houseguests. "Characterized by middle height, rounded figure, a short, broad face—" That described Mona to a tee. "Hereditary taint, delusions often occur, changeable and ridiculous in character, grandiose in type, false ideas of persecution, heightened aggressiveness, feelings of failure, hopelessness, and sinfulness, the drive toward self-destruction can be overwhelmingly strong—"

Mona looked over to her mother and Sister Talmage. Would neither of them speak in her defense? She wasn't these things, or not all of them. Surely not.

When she'd first seen her mother's familiar figure trudging down the hall beside Sister Talmage, all Mona could think was how comfortable it would be to bury her face in that ample bosom. She would hear that sweet voice murmur a little prayer, and then, even as it had been during the worst of the polio, she would know that all was well.

Now, Mona saw with different eyes, eyes altered by Miss Beecham's presence—and by education. Her mother had dressed for the occasion, but the strenuous journey had slipped even her best back into squalor. Her brown hat was twenty years old. Her hair, between washings, was greyer and rattier than usual. It was flyaway, as if she'd ridden all the way to Liverpool on the cowcatcher. Her grey-brown suit, practical, without dignity, gaped in several places. A few seams needed mending, and Mary Jane Whitaker had not had time to do it. Mona cringed as she even saw the silver glint of pins and white underthings beneath.

Her mother poofed in the hard chair like a very soft cushion, but it was not comfort that made her look that way. Her mother was even quieter than usual; Mona could tell her mother was nervous and out of her element. She did not even raise a protest at the words "hereditary taint," though Mona knew she must have heard them. Her mother must have thought, when she did hear, of Nellie left at home.

Mona had to do the protecting now, and she didn't feel up to it.

Sister Talmage was neater and trimmer than her mother. A dark blue, tailored suit with white lace lapels slanting in at the waist emphasized this impression. The American woman sat stiff as a board. The headmistress might have directed the wife of the mission president to sit on a chair where some child had left his tin soldiers. "One knows what Americans are like, encouraging bad discipline, lacking manners," hung in Miss Beecham's air, and Sister Talmage knew it.

Sister Talmage was still bent on giving the impression that she was at ease. She seemed not to notice, or at least not to protest, at the suggestion that "all recent scientific data concerning mania" fit Mona to a tee.

No hope was forthcoming from that chair, either.

"Mrs. Whitaker, the best thing I can recommend to help your daughter—and you must realize that we do want to help her—is for her to visit a psychiatrist."

"A psychiatrist!" Mona heard herself explode with indignation. But she found her voice lonely and unsupported. All three women in the room looked at her as if this outburst merely substantiated the evidence.

Mona bowed her head quietly and let the blows continue in silence. "I have a friend, a Doctor Seymour Adler, very trusted in his profession, studied in Vienna, appointment on Friday—"

Mona followed her mother and Sister Talmage out of the school building. The two grown women talked quietly together about things that had nothing to do with Mona's predicament.

"But what am I supposed to do?" she interrupted loudly. "I could leave school right now, Mother, and go home with you."

"No, dear. I think you should stay. You worked very hard to get here, and you shouldn't give up now." Tension in her mother's voice indicated that Mona's interruption of grown-up talk had been bad manners—yet another example of instability.

"But I can't go on like this. You see what I'm up against."

"I'm sure, with the Lord's help, that you can, Mona, dear," Sister Talmage said.

"But a psychiatrist? I can't go to a—"

"I think you should go," Sister Talmage said.

"But I thought the church taught that such men were of the devil. Such men teach you to say bad things against your parents and to put an off-color"—she didn't dare say the word "sexual" in front of these women—"slant to everything."

"Yes, the church suggests that you not put too much faith in the wisdom of men. But my husband has a favorite saying," Sister Talmage said. "'Within the Gospel of Jesus Christ is room and place for every truth thus far learned by man, or yet to be made known.' Even psychiatrists may have useful knowledge it would not be good for anyone to ignore who believes 'the glory of God is intelligence.' I do think you should go, my dear young sister. A time or two, at least, and see if you can't learn something to help you from this doctor—something to help the king-dom as well."

Mona turned in exasperation from the apostle's wife to her mother. "Mother—"

"I agree with Sister Talmage." The betrayal struck Mona dumb.

"Give this science a chance, at least."

"But what about the money?" Mona cried. "Mother, that's ten pounds a visit."

"We'll manage, love. You know, they said my violet-ray treat-ments for lupus were expensive. Others tried to tell me they would never work. But I tried them and prayed and had faith in God. And they did work. There's no price too high for your health."

But I'm not sick! Mona wanted to scream.

But she said nothing. Everything she'd said so far had only made the women look at her with more helpless concern and pity. She couldn't stand pity. She wanted pride in their eyes.

And now they turned from her to each other, talking as only two longtime members of the Relief Society can, both of whom have eight children. They spoke of things Mona had never known—would never know—because God, for some mad reason, had allowed her to catch polio long before she'd even reached the age of accountability. Because of this whim, she would never marry, never fulfill the mea-sure of a woman's creation, never be "a mother in Zion." The low tone in her elders' voices was enough to tell her that, denied these things, there was really nothing worthwhile left in the world for her to do.

Mona went to the doctor's on Friday. He was a tall, thin man with a well-tended Vandyke that made him look like a goat. Mona felt very uncomfortable, lying prone on a couch, alone with a man. Especially a German. She'd heard about war atrocities.

The doctor talked a lot, hardly gave her a pause. He repeated many of the things Miss Beecham had said. He had the headmistress's very intonation—he must have taught her how to say them. Or perhaps she had taught him, and through his thick glasses, he was unable even to make a diagnosis on his own. He did say some other things besides, things interspersed with a questioning "Hmm?" to which Mona always replied in the affirmative, even if she thought what he said made no sense at all.

After the hour's session (which seemed like three days), the first thing Mona told herself was "Well, if I'm crazy, that man's even crazier! I won't go again."

She said it aloud, because she wanted to make certain her self still existed. Fortunately, she waited to say it until she was outside the office, down the steps, and on the sidewalk. Unfortunately, a passerby heard her. The passerby looked at her, looked at the plaque beside the door she'd just stepped out of, then hurried on.

Mona remembered Nellie's ravings. She closed her lips very tightly and set off in the other direction.

As her feet brought her closer and closer to the college, however, they grew heavier and heavier, slower and slower. At last she couldn't lift her lame right leg off the pavement at all. She dragged it for a few steps, then the good left leg gave up as well. She had to sit down where she was, on a bench in the botanic gardens on Edge Lane. To one side was the laburnum arch walk, lacking its bright yellow flowers at this early time of the year, flowers whose snapdragon shape put it in the Legume family—

No. She could not believe that a tree and tiny pea plants were related, that God had not created each separately. Laburnum was poisonous, after all—

She had to shut down her thoughts completely.

When at last Mona came to herself, it was to see the mothers and nannies packing up their knitting and prams to take the children home for their tea. She thought of her sisters, Doris and Ivy, who were fulfilling the role God made for them as mothers and wives. Frances, Hannah, and even young Violet had plenty of beaux. And they were doing useful work in the dressmaker's shop until the greater calling came to them. Even Barbara, nursing babies and healing the sick, was answering the measure of her creation better than this selfish, confusing pursuit of sterile book learning. Who did that leave? Only Nellie. Only Mona and Nellie, still dependent, still, because of weaknesses in the mind, a care and a disappointment to their parents in their old age.

"You thought you were so smart with your Latin and your history dates." A very black voice entered her mind. "What good is history? It is dead. It can never be like God, bringing forth new life. You. Yes, you, with your nose in a book. You are so proud. You could shut the silly jabber of your sisters out to study while you were home. And all the time, you didn't realize that you were the silly one. They were concerned with life, 'about my Father's business,' what is truly good and beautiful upon this earth.

"Remember? Do you remember how little Violet would have nightmares when you stayed up late to study. She would sleepwalk and call out, 'Momma, Momma! A pencil! I need a pencil for our poor Mona who 'as to work so 'ard.' Did you appreciate her? No. You only snapped at her for messing up your papers. She cared for you. They all cared that you make something of yourself, but you have made nothing. You cared only for stale books, books written by men and women whose last care on earth was for the building up of the kingdom. What eternal good is that? It isn't even earthly good. 'The foolish things of this earth confound the wise.' And you, after all these years and sacrifices on the part of those who love you. What earthly good are you? You might as well be—"

Out of the corner of her eyes, Mona saw a flight of something across the sky. A butterfly, she thought at first, and turned to its beauty and light like a famished soul to bread.

But it was not a butterfly. It was too early for butterflies. Even the illiterate would know that. It was only a dry, yellow leaf, wafted along by the wind. The moment she recognized it for what it was, it dropped dead to the ground.

In Liverpool, everything from the paper-littered streets to the lowering sky seemed to live up to its name—to be the color and smell of a pool of cod-liver oil. No, even had that leaf been alive, it would have been no lovely, bright butterfly of the heathery moors, but a dingy old moth. *Amphydasis (Biston) betularia.*

Mona'd caught many of that species for biology. They'd laughed at her at home, where a cry of "Moth! Moth!" set the whole household adither, chasing and clapping hands at the shadow fluttered against the lamp flue. Little concern for preserving the thorax intact. Mona, with her gamby leg, was usually more of a hindrance that a help in this chase. Again, she was no use at important things like trying to keep moth holes out of the woolens.

And only that day, the name of the moth, that common moth every layman in the Northern industrial towns knew as the plain peppered moth, had come up in class again. Fearing things worse than a psychiatrist another outburst might bring down upon her head, Mona had kept quiet for once, and found herself really listening.

Amphydasis betularia had been cited as clear proof of the theory of evolution. Animals did change to suit their environment. Survival of the fittest did exist. Two hundred years ago, that moth had had peppered white wings.

"If its common name were not evidence enough of that"—Miss Hawthorne had shot a glance in Mona's direction—"I refer you to naturalists who gathered specimens and drew beautiful hand-colored etchings in their early attempts at scientific classification. We cannot deny it. The moth used its color to blend in against white stones, white birch bark, white picket fences along country lanes. It thereby hid from its enemies: hungry birds, hedgehogs.

"Then came the Industrial Revolution. Stacks belching out smoke blackened the sky. A fine layer of ash shifted over the countryside. Now, on dingy grey tree trunks and sooty stone walls, a white moth would stand out (to use the phrase Kipling did in his *Just So Stories*) 'like a bar of soap in a coal scuttle.' The birds could pick them off with the ease with which you pick up apples in the market, already harvested and polished. Then, in stepped evolution to save the day.

"Some *betulariae* always tended to darker coloring. Now these had the survival edge—all others were eaten. More of the darker young survived. Within just two hundred years, the entire species has changed from white to black. You can see it."

Mona herself had only ever observed dark moths during all her life in the dark industrial towns. It was true.

Then what did that mean? The Bible was wrong. It had taken more than six days for the world to be created—a good deal more than six days. How could God let something so wrong get passed as his word among people so desperately searching for purpose? Perhaps because he—if indeed he did exist (the horrible thought came to her for the first time in her life)—he didn't care.

"Man." Miss Hawthorne had allowed herself to slip into a rather nonbiological posture at one point, but it was no less impassioned a declaration. "Man must make his own meaning."

The thick, black emptiness Mona found engulfing her now was almost comforting in the oblivious end it promised. So. How was this end to be accomplished? At first she just sat, thinking oblivion would come of its own accord if she just sat cold and dark and miserable long enough. It did not. "Man must make his own meaning."

She would have to take things—her own life—into her hands.

How did one do violence to oneself? Mona had never considered the problem before. Even the novels she had read so voraciously, full of violent passions and broken hearts, had all been so carefully Victorian as to remain remarkably barren of necessary details. "Incapable of her own distress" was all she could remember from Shakespeare.

Though it aptly described the feelings, it only covered the actual biology with poetry.

"We cannot complain of life. It keeps no one against his will." Seneca had said that. "Tranquility can be purchased at the cost of a pinprick. . . . Wherever you look, there is an end to troubles. Do you see that precipice? It is a descent to liberty. Do you see that river, that cistern, that sea? Freedom is in their depths. . . . But I am running on too long. How can a man end his life if he cannot end a letter?"

At last. Useful information from the letters of Seneca.

Mona got to her feet at once. There was her little penknife, ink-splattered, sitting on her desk back in her room. Agnes would find her afterwards, when the deed was done. That would be a shock for the poor minister's daughter.

Very well, it need not be that way. As Seneca said, there were exits at every turn: the Mersey River, a four-story building—she would find what she needed quickly, and she would know what it was when she found it. One thing was certain, she would never find it there in the safety of the botanic gardens, not even in the laburnum. A bobby stood over there, cheerfully whistling and swinging his club.

Ah, there was something. Something Seneca had not known in his day, but something very useful—a street full of automobiles. These had the added attraction that they could make it look like an accident. "Crippled Girl Killed by Lorry." Such headlines were common. That would be kinder to her family and friends.

As fast as her lame leg would carry her, Mona stepped off the curb and into the midst of the traffic.

Horns blaring, tires screeching, a sharp pain in her arm. But the next thing Mona knew, she was safe on the sidewalk again, face-to-face with the cheery-faced bobby.

"'Ere now, miss. You should watch where you're goin'. Like to get 'urt, you are, if you go running amongst cars like that. Good job I saw you, eh?"

Mona did not think it was a "good job" at all, but she said nothing. She only looked down at the ground and rubbed her arm where the policeman's hand had been none too gentle.

"I been watchin' you," the bobby continued. "You don't look so well. Why don't you let me see you 'ome? Tell me where you live."

I can't even kill myself properly, Mona thought, feeling a more dismal failure than ever now. She was humiliated and embarrassed to the point that only death could cure her of it, but the bruise on her arm made her conscious of the pain that must be involved. On top of everything else, she knew now that she was a coward. She would need some time to "screw her courage to the sticking point" before she could attempt it again. She smiled weakly at the bobby and nodded her head toward the school.

The bobby asked her a few questions. Mona only replied with monosyllables, so the young man took up the burden of conversation on his own. He spoke of his wife, to whom he'd been married only a couple of months, and of how happy he was in their life together.

This testimony to wedded bliss, even without the blessings of the gospel, did more than anything to bring all the dark hopelessness seeping back into Mona's soul. If the bobby had not politely taken the curbside, she was certain she would have walked into the street again. This time, she would have had better success.

A walk from the botanic gardens to Edge Hill Training College required passing the high grey stone wall of Durham House, the church headquarters. Mona was too desperate to lay claim to inspiration. She did it more to escape the bobby who held her so tenaciously to life. She suddenly indicated that her way led through this gate now. "Thank you, sir. I have no more need of accompaniment."

The bobby politely took his leave with a touch of his club to his hat. But he stood watching her so she could not avoid the long walk down the gravel path.

The leafless limbs of sycamore and oak in the yard of Durham House drew the awful blackness over her head once more as the afternoon faded. One of these trees will be gracious, she hoped, and fall on me. Or one of these limbs will serve me for a gallows if only I can find a rope.

In all of this blackness, the little lamp glowing in one of the house's great bay windows seemed no more than a pinhole. Very easy to lose sight of. Mona wandered off the path into the demon-fingered wood. Although she'd never left that path in the hundred times she'd walked it, the damp grass and mouldy leaves away from it seemed more familiar to her soul.

Somehow, Mona found herself on the doorstep. She must have knocked, though she didn't remember it.

The maid answered. She was not the usual stalwart Sister Perkins, but a new girl Mona had never seen before. The girl had bright red hair and a face thick with freckles. She greeted the visitor with an Irish brogue that seemed as steeped in the supernatural as the woods had been.

Mona must have blurted something about wanting to see Sister Talmage, for the girl said, "Just a minute. I'll see if she'll see you."

Then the great paneled door heaved shut.

For one moment, as the warmth and light of the hall had fallen on her, Mona had felt like a drowning person granted one more gasp of air before the seas closed over her. She'd felt almost human once more.

Now she plunged into darkness again, as thick as ever. "They don't want me here, either," she realized. Slowly she turned, stepped off the porch, across the drive, and into the dark arms of the woods.

"Mona! Mona, child. Good heavens! Come inside at once." Mona heard the foreign tones bred in Alpine, Utah. She felt arms about her. A moment later, darkness lifted enough to allow her to know that she was lying on damp grass, chilled to the bone. The white face and dark eyes of Sister Talmage bent over her.

Mona made an animal sound of recognition. "Please, please, forgive me," the apostle's wife prattled as she helped a numb-legged Mona inside. "This is Kate's first day. I'm afraid we haven't taught her what's expected of a maid yet. I shall have to tell her that she's to show visitors into the parlor, not leave them frozen on the doorstep."

The light of the kitchen was blinding. Mona had been here before, but it still seemed very distant and surreal to her, like a room in a dollhouse viewed through one tiny window. Sister Talmage, dogged by a sulking Kate, bustled around to remove Mona's damp wrap and hat, then, on investigation, her wet shoes and stockings as well. Besides a running commentary on these actions, the older woman described, in the cheeriest tones, bizarrely distant to Mona's mind, the frightful time she'd had all day with a leaky water pipe. "My husband has too much to do to bother calling a plumber. The man wouldn't come when I asked, so here we sit bailing buckets like a ship a-sea."

Despite impending disaster to woodwork and carpets, a pot of cocoa was made, presented to Mona, and then the maid was dismissed.

"Now," Sister Talmage said, taking the familiar green-painted chair across the oil-clothed table from her. "Suppose you tell me what the trouble is."

Mona opened her mouth but nothing came out. Something black weighted her tongue. She felt more coherent now—another sip or two of cocoa helped—but that coherency only made any explanation seem more implausible. Tears might say it best, she thought. Even coaxed, however, no tears came. All Mona finally managed was a shrug and a desperate toss of her head.

Sister Talmage worked tongue and teeth thoughtfully over her lips. Then she pushed back the green-painted chair and got to her feet. "You stay here, Mona, and finish your cocoa. I'll go see if my husband won't see you."

"No!" Mona managed to blurt out something at last.

"Now, I know I said he was too busy to see about the pipes. At least he thinks he is too busy. But he just might be persuaded to take time out for this."

She was gone. Mona closed her eyes and felt her heart sink to the pit of her stomach.

Not five minutes later—before she'd even finished off the mug— Mona found herself ushered into the study of the apostle of the Lord.

"This is the young lady you told me about, Maia?" the man said, getting to his feet.

"Yes, James."

"How do you do, Sister?"

"Sister Mona Whitaker," his wife supplied for him.

"Sister Whitaker. How do you do? Won't you come in?"

That thick, strong hand had encircled hers many, many times before. Every Sunday, she made a point of going up to the president after the service, just to be able to flatter herself for the whole next week that she had shaken the hand of someone who knew Christ personally. She had, she'd thought, come to know President Talmage so well, bragged about it to her sisters back at home. Now she saw that she was so insignificant that, after all those handshakes, he didn't even know her name.

"Please, take a seat, Sister Whitaker. Make yourself at home. I'll be right with you, in just a moment." The apostle shut the door behind him, and Mona found herself alone—dangerously alone—again.

The study was dark. A single lamp burned, a desk lamp with its shade turned against her. It illuminated some papers on which were written illegible characters. They must have been a sort of short-hand. The width of these papers was all the flat space there was on the desk. The rest lay deep under unstable piles of books. She discovered a Book of Mormon, but only after a search. It was nowhere near the top of a stack.

Now Mona saw that soft, comfortable leather, cracked with loving use—many hundreds of book spines—lined the room from floor to ceiling. James E. Talmage, she remembered, was a full-fledged professor, a respected geologist and chemist, as well as a leader in the church. She saw at once that he had several presentation copies of his own works: *Jesus the Christ*, *The Great Apostasy*, and *The Articles of Faith*. But there was also a pair she suspected very few Mormons had ever read: *The First Book of Nature* and *The Great Salt Lake, Past and Present*.

Then Mona looked closer at the other books by other authors. Every one of mankind's studies seemed represented: literature, philosophy, physics, astronomy, chemistry, biology, religion—not only his own, but many different persuasions. Mona even saw, tucked away here and there, the words "Psychiatry" and "Evolution" on some of the spines. One could be a scholar and a Mormon. But maybe not a Mormon woman.

Mona's gaze returned to the desk and lit on something she had passed over the first time because of all the clutter. It was an irregular chunk of white rock about as big as a cone of sugar. Sandstone, Mona identified it at once. Looking closer, she found that she was right. The specimen had been carefully labeled as such with the date of discovery and the place—a little town near Dover—written beneath it.

Coming close enough to read the label also brought her close enough to notice something else about the specimen: it was a tumble of (she identified them at once) gastropods and ostrea bivalves.

Mona stretched out a hand and touched the stone. Her fingers could not distinguish the once-animals from their medium. She knew perfectly well the geologists' explanation for how such phenomena came to be—an explanation that went against all religion. But as she touched the curious unity of living and dead, faith and fact, that permeated this room and centered in this rock, she suddenly felt something of that wholeness of the irreconcilable seep into her soul.

And then the tears came to her eyes, washing away the darkness like good strong soap.

President—Professor—Talmage returned, and Mona thought she could tell he had been praying. An apostle praying on her behalf! And now, though she had seen him so many times before, she saw for the first time that, beneath two great creases in his brow—the product of years of thought—this man wore a pair of round, black-rimmed spectacles just like her own.

That evening, President James E. Talmage laid his hands upon Mona's head and gave her a blessing:

"Sister Whitaker. Thou wert one of the most valiant spirits in the pre-existence. Obey the laws of health, for they are the laws of God. Thou shalt have equilibrium. The Lord loves thee very much, and thou hast always loved him. This blessing will be recorded in the highest heaven, and that is where the Lord wishes thee to be when thy time on this earth is through."

Mona was glad heaven was taking notes. Only bits and pieces of the blessing stayed with her, however. At the time, besides weeping freely, Mona felt more attached to the chunk of sandstone on the desk—and through it to heaven—than to any words of men.

But the devil was not banished. Not yet.

It was dark when Mona left Durham House to race back to school. It was dark in the morning when she woke to the haunting sound of bare limbs scratching against her windowpane in the bluster of another storm. The sound reminded her of the trees and the awful darkness trying to close around church headquarters, trying to crush the church out of its toehold on European soil. This impression loomed much, much clearer than the blessing and the stone. Those seemed to have been only a dream.

All that Saturday was very uneasy. Mona kept looking around her, as if expecting claws and fangs to jump out at her from behind every door. What sort of beast could lurk here in the heart of civilized Liverpool? Something that would prove once and for all that the relief she had found the night before was only air. That seemed a very real, horrible possibility.

Somehow she managed to hang on until Sunday morning and another trip to Durham House.

> Thanks for the Sabbath School,
> Hail to the day,
> When evil and error are
> Fleeing away.

Mona sang this song on her way to church, more from a desire to show bravery. The bravery to screw her courage "to the sticking point"? Not from a sense that all around her was blooming, warming, fresh from Saturday's storm. She made a little deal with God. He would show her she had not dreamed, that she was not losing her mind, by having this be the opening song that morning.

God did not keep his part of the bargain. They sang "In a World Where Sorrow Ever Will Be Known" instead.

Mona noticed at once that the new maid—"a fresh convert from Ireland," as the chorister announced from the pulpit—Kate had been elected pianist for the day. The girl was no better than the usual run-of-the-mill pianists. Mona had her father for comparison. But Kate plunked out the tune with a lively sort of vehemence for the sentiments the hymn contained. Kate wore a forest-green dress (that went frightfully with her red hair and complexion), and her hair was done up in a sharp little braid bun on either side, like a pair of animal's ears. Mona did not find it an edifying sight.

In the middle of the hymn, four men entered late. The first was President Talmage. He took his accustomed seat behind the podium with two of the others. One was heavy, his jowls covered with bushy black hair. The other thin, long-limbed one with sandy hair, had spindly hands clutching his scriptures. Those seemed to be monkey hands on the trunk of a tree. They were a pair of new missionaries just fresh from Zion. Along with the pug-nosed, double-chinned chorister, this made up the grouping on the stand that day.

The fourth man to enter made Mona's heart skip. He wore a greying Vandyke, shaped and pointed just like her psychiatrist's had been. In fact, at first glance, he did seem to be the very Dr. Adler.

He's come to laugh at us with his superior knowledge, she panicked. Next time I go to him (forgetting she'd already decided she wouldn't go again), he will throw all of this in my face to prove that I'm out of my mind.

A closer look revealed that this man was not the doctor. He was heavier than the psychiatrist, shorter, and balding on top. Still, when he took a seat among the congregation with his back to her, Mona could not reassure herself it was not the same man. Only an investigator brought by the missionaries, he nonetheless exuded the same air of dangerous, skeptical, tempting knowledge.

Mona's heart raced through the opening payer and the president's first remarks. She found herself growing hotter and hotter, and the meeting room—what had once been sitting and dining room in this old, fashionable home—growing more and more cramped and dingy.

When the sacrament was passed, Mona choked on a terribly dry piece of Sister Talmage's bread. Before it could help her catch her breath, Mona spilled all the water down her blouse. The emblems of Christ, too, rejected her.

Now the monkey-like missionary got up to speak. He began by reminding the congregation that when the British mission was first opened nearly one hundred years before, Satan had trembled in his cloven boots and tried everything he knew to try to stop the work. The first pair of missionaries, all alone in a strange land that first night, had seen the wall of their little room open up. All the dreadful imps and beasts of hell came pouring out at them, gnashing their teeth and shrieking the most dreadful curses.

At this point, President Talmage, who must have caught a cold, took out a great white handkerchief to catch a pair of trumpeting sneezes. Kate the maid exclaimed loudly, "God bless!" The speaker and almost everyone else tried to carry on as if nothing had happened.

But something had happened to President Talmage, at least how he was perceived in Mona's fevered mind. His fleshy jowls and neck grew heavier and greyer. His eyes behind their round, black-rimmed glasses grew piggier. His hair, which needed a trim anyway, grew long and shaggy, and the great white handkerchief turned into neither more nor less than a "really truly" elephant's trunk.

"*Elephas maximus,*" Mona murmured as if responding to questions on a taxonomy exam.

Mona had long ago forgotten the elephant in Halifax zoo that, everyone told her, had, with a sneeze, caused her polio. But those two sneezes from the stand brought back the fever and terror of that time in a single moment. And it was not just the president who seemed transformed.

The speaker had become a monkey, his squeaky Utahn chattering and scolding at the audience.

"*Cercopithecidae simia*," Mona responded, feeling the pressure to excel mount.

His companion was a lumbering black bear. "*Ursus americanus.*"

The double-chinned chorister?

"*Sus scrofa*," a grunting pig.

The visiting gentleman, the investigator—now the very image of the psychiatrist—bleated and wagged his beard like a goat.

"*Capra hircus.*"

Kate the maid's red hair and its two pointed knots turned her into a quick little fox.

"*Vulpes fulva.*"

And Sister Talmage, even kind Sister Talmage, who from time to time shot a concerned glance in Mona's direction, seemed a dignified domestic cat.

"*Felis lybica domestica.*"

Then came the final, most difficult question. "Miss Whitaker, who are you?"

The perfect exam paper stopped. Mona couldn't answer. It seemed that "*Homo sapiens*" might satisfy the examiner, but it didn't satisfy her. That would mean that she was indeed just a link in an arbitrary tree of chance descent. She struggled, squirmed in her chair, trying very hard to remember. She wanted the end of a pencil to chew on. Little Violet, sleepwalking. "Our Mona needs a pencil."

Minutes passed. How long would they give her to come up with the right answer? No answer at all was probably better than the wrong one when a girl's self was the subject of inquiry. Mona thought until perspiration bloomed on her forehead and the fever seemed about to make her burst like a kettle on the fire. She looked at the chattering monkey, at the elephant still wagging his trunk. They offered no clues.

The fox opened the instrument to pound out the closing hymn. The pig got up to lead. That black bear gave the closing prayer. Even as she responded "Amen," Mona bolted from her seat to escape that zoo, that final, awful question still ringing in her ears: "Miss Whitaker, who are you?"

But the missionaries got to the door before she did. The monkey reached out and grabbed her hand. At first she couldn't feel it. It was neither animal nor human, and her mind could not conceive of the gap between them. Then, all at once, those tree-grasping fingers grew warm and human, and Mona saw that he was only a pimply faced nineteen-year-old American, away from home for the first time.

As was she.

"How are you, Sister Whitaker?" the young man said in his western drawl. "I'm Elder—" The name meant no more than had he said, "I'm *Homo sapiens*," and she didn't remember it. But she did remember what he said then. "I've heard what your trouble is. We'll all pray for you."

Mona's heart stopped dead as if it had suddenly raced full speed into a wall. That wall seemed made of sandstone chunks, all like the one she had seen and felt two nights ago. Behind this young missionary, she saw President Talmage smiling, pushing his round, black-rimmed glasses just like hers back up onto his nose. He'd betrayed her confidence. He'd told. Everyone knew—everyone was laughing—

And suddenly, the wonderful unity and peace and, in the apostle's word, "equilibrium" came back to her, bringing her to the verge of tears.

"Thank you," she managed to murmur. "Thank you very much."

Kate, who found her duties as a pianist now at an end, came up to the group of young people then.

"Mona," she said. "What do you say you and I go for a little walk together? It's such a nice day, and we could be friends, two girls both alone in a big, strange city."

They went out into the sunlight. Mona noticed for the first time that it was spring and that there were daffodils blooming in Durham House garden.

Kate spoke about her mistakes as a maid as they walked.

She had such a lilting, carefree tone that Mona was soon laughing with her. When she saw that the girl intended to lead her through the botanic gardens, Mona hesitated. But the girl's laughter scared all the shadows away. Mona stepped forward, not completely fearless, but brave.

"I'm the only one in my family converted," the girl was saying. "They're all staunch Catholics, don't you know. My father wouldn't speak to me after I was baptized. I've to fend for myself. I've come only as far as Liverpool. But 'tis on the seaside, just waiting for the boat, 'tisn't it? I'll be in Zion soon, I know it.

"But before I get too far from home, I'd best get what genealogy I can done, so I'll have plenty of ancestors to carry with me when I finally get to the house of the Lord. Sister Talmage says you know a lot about genealogy, Mona."

"Well, some—" Mona hesitated. Was it only missing link apes she knew?

"'Tis a fair sight more than I do. Will you help me then?"

"Maybe."

"See this?" The girl pulled a scrap of paper out of her pocket. "I copied it from the parish records on the sly, just before I left."

"It's in Latin." Mona didn't bother to remark how badly spelled the whole was.

"Yes, and I can't read a word. Good little Catholic girl, and I can't read a word of Latin. Say my 'Aves,' and 'tis the lot of it. All our parish records are in Latin over in Ireland."

"So are our English ones, before a certain date," Mona mused.

"Still, I think it does have to do with my ancestors, this notice here. Hennesy's our name. My mother's a Sullivan. Do you read Latin, Mona? Is this something important?"

"Yes, I read Latin," Mona said.

"Ah, fine. Tell me, then, what does it say? The trouble I went to, to get this, and 'tis all I've got to go on. What does it say?"

Mona stopped in her tracks. It wasn't the paper, which seemed simple enough. Up ahead, she saw the tall, grey figure of Miss Hawthorne. Armed with a magnifying glass and a notebook, the teacher was engaged in decidedly non-Sabbath behavior. She was foraging among the botanic gardens' specimens, the myrtle and ferns, making copious notes.

"What is it?" Kate whispered. "Do you know that woman? She must be someone famous."

"It is nothing."

Mona turned their path in the other direction without allowing the biologist to see them. And she felt only the briefest twinge of sorrow as she began to translate.

"Christened 13 Jan 1856—"

∿

I send Uncle Noel Auntie Mona's tape.

The next Christmas, he gives me a book on Jungian psychiatry. "Auntie Mona put the name of Satan on her experience," he holds forth.

"Hallucinations, nervous breakdowns, religious mania."

He tells me the names to put on it instead. So now it's tame. Like years with the therapist have helped him to tame—what haunts him.

"Thank you," I tell him. I don't tell him Satan works well, too. Because some things just can't be domesticated.

EMULATE HER VIRTUES

~

I see the Deep's untrampled floor
With green and purple seaweeds strown;
I see the waves upon the shore,
Like light dissolved in star-showers, thrown:
I sit upon the sands alone,—
The lightning of the noontide ocean
Is flashing round me, and a tone
Arises from its measured motion,
How sweet! did any heart now share in my emotion

MONA NODDED OVER HER STUDY OF SHELLEY, and when she came to herself again, the pages had flipped to the book's inside cover where it lay next to the morning mail.

At first her waking mind was confused. She wasn't having a recurrence of those awful visitations from the devil, was she? Were the two foreign postage stamps pressed against her sleeping face a portent?

Then she remembered that, among the mail she'd brought up that morning there had been the anomaly of a letter from Germany for her roommate Agnes. This mixed with the reality before her eyes: the nameplate pasted in the front of the poetry collection indicated how the book had come into her possession.

Mona had won this book as a prize for scholarship while still at grammar school in Bradford. Other years, she'd won other books with similar nameplates in them. A German had immigrated to Bradford, made his fortune there in woolens, and set up an endowment to reward young ladies for good work at school. His name was Mr. G. Ernst Peters, the bookplate reminded her in a heavy Gothic script; Mona herself had never met the man. His "dearly beloved wife," in whose memory the endowment was made, was a woman of Bradford origin. She had loved him while he was still only a poor immigrant. Her name was Mary S. Peters. The young recipient of the prize was admonished, amidst scrolls and flourishes, to "Go forth and emulate her virtues."

Mona smiled to herself with just a hint of the dejection she'd been discovering in Shelley's poem (and through it, in her own heart). The nameplate gave no indication as to what Mrs. Peters's particular virtues might have been.

And how am I to emulate them, Mona thought, when I never knew the woman? Unless—and she laughed out loud at the absurdity of this thought—unless it be to likewise marry a German.

～

Her "bout with Satan," as Mona always describes it, turned her passionate about another sort of family tree, genealogy. She was already secretary of the local Mormon Society for searching out ancestors. This was the way the hand of God led her out of the abyss into which she had fallen. Suddenly her knowledge of Latin, French, and history had a useful purpose in the kingdom. And, she says, it was for this very reason that Satan had thrown all his forces at her, to try to steal her soul for himself. He knew she would be instrumental in doing much work for the salvation of the dead.

When she'd first shown this interest at home, her father had discouraged her. "Aw, leave t' dead alone."

But whenever she came back from visiting some of the old relatives to collect their memories, he'd be the first one to greet her at the door. "What did' tha find? What did' tha find?" When she'd tell him, he was always pleased and enthusiastic.

～

Footsteps down the hall, a rummaging at the door.

Agnes burst into their room, excited about something, as she always was. She tore off her hat and coat and sang a merry "Hullo, Mona. Still swottin' away?"

Mona decided she might as well add to the jollity and replied, "You've got some mail. I put it on the dresser."

"From Germany!" The girl tore into the envelope.

"Who's it from?" Mona asked.

"Fraulein Siegelinde Bauer, Wiesbaden." Agnes stumbled over the foreign words and didn't umlaut the "a."

"Who's he?"

"I think it's a she," Agnes replied. "At least, she says she likes sewing, and I don't think a man would reply to that."

"But who is she?"

"My new penfriend. At last! How exciting! I'll write back right away."

"How did you get this penfriend?" Mona asked. Curiosity had brought her to her feet now, and she dearly hoped Agnes would share such an interesting letter with her so she wouldn't have to read it over her shoulder.

"The Christian Society. We thought it would be nice. You know, promote international understanding so there won't be another war, that sort of thing."

"Have you—have you any names left?" Mona asked. The idea was so thrilling to her that she could hardly keep that excitement from her speech and making her sound like a beggar. She hated to sound like a beggar over anything, for the church should make a person self-sufficient.

"Sorry, Mona. They were all given out weeks ago. In fact, we had to turn some away, it raised so much interest among our members. Nothing like it since your Mormon night."

Mona didn't like to be reminded of that night.

But the mousey-haired girl wasn't paying her any attention. She had thrown herself into her letter writing with a passion she never showed for classwork. "Dear Fraulein Siegelinde Bauer" was all Mona managed to read without appearing rude.

She returned to her Shelley but couldn't concentrate. They didn't have any names left for me, she thought. Well, I'll just get my own penfriend, then.

By the time Agnes had finished what must have been a rather flighty letter, Mona had a plan. The moment her roommate went down the hall with a towel to wash her mousey hair, Mona got out her own letter-writing materials. She addressed the envelope to the church mission headquarters in Basel, Switzerland.

"What do you want this for?" The little old man looked up from the rugs covering his knees with bright, sharp eyes that belied his feeble condition. He was John Robinson, Mona's father's mother's brother.

Oh, dear, Mona thought. If I tell him I'm a Mormon, he'll throw me out of this house with as little ceremony as an old man can muster. I won't learn anything more.

She decided then, a lie, or at least a half-truth, was called for.

"I'm making a family history," she began.

"Oh, no," the old man stopped her. "It's something else you want it for."

Now Mona knew that nothing short of the truth would do.

But he's told me all I want, she thought, looking down at the notebook full of names, dates, places and, here and there, a nice little anecdotal tidbit she'd spent the past two and a half hours scribbling down as fast as she could write. Let him throw me out. I've got it all, and he can't take it away.

So she began to tell him all about the church and the work done for the dead in the temples.

The old man listened very intently. When she was finished, he said, "I believe every word you've told me. Every word. Will you do something for me?"

Mona nodded.

"I love my wife." He nodded in the direction of another rug-wrapped figure that had fallen asleep during the discussion. Mrs. Robinson was very deaf and, after a few fruitless "ehs?" at the beginning of the visit, she must have decided this was the politest thing to do.

Had this been Barbara visiting, she would have cleaned up their kitchen for them and never got down the information. Mona had her priorities straight.

Mona found it difficult to imagine the flame of romance one invalid could have for another after fifty years. She could tell, however, by the fresh, young crack in the old man's voice that he was in earnest.

"I love my wife," he reiterated. "But we're both too old and sick to come down to your meeting house for church every week. Will you do this for me? Will you do that sacred work for my wife and me, after we've gone? Will you have us baptized and sealed to one another for all eternity? Will you do that work for us in your temples?"

A bony hand, cold for all the covers, like a cadaver's, reached out for hers and pressed it.

Mona nodded very hard. Yes, indeed, she would.

"Don't forget" were his last words to her.

And she didn't.

~

In the pigeonhole was another envelope inscribed in a foreign hand with German stamps on it. But this time, it was not from "Fraulein Siegelinde Bauer," who seemed to have lost interest in Agnes after the first letter. This was addressed to "Miss Olive Mona Whitaker." Mona dashed up the stairs with it almost as fast as if she had never had polio.

"Dear Miss Whitaker," it began, then continued in textbook English:

"Please may I introduce myself. My name is Mr. Fredrich Sohn. I am twenty-six years old, and I live with my mother, my uncle, and his family in Frankfurt am Main, Germany. You may find it on the map. It is a large, industrial city.

"My father was killed in the war, on the Yugoslavian frontier. Let me assure you, if you are of delicate sensibilities—"

He must have read some English literature, Mona decided, probably Jane Austen. Or maybe, for practice, cheaper Victorian romances.

"Let me assure you that my father was a good man. He did not fight at all but delivered supplies. One day while out delivering, a wall fell on him, and he died.

"Now you must know what is the most important thing about me: it is my religion. I am a member of the Church of Jesus Christ of Latter-day Saints. I am what they say in slang, a 'Mormon.' Indeed, it was through the church that I got your name and address."

Mona did not know at the time, but somehow the mission headquarters had not understood that she, too, was a very devout Latter-day Saint. "Here," they'd told him when they gave him her letter. "Maybe you can convert this person."

Fred Sohn was certain he could do just that. He had defied mission authority to make that trip to Basel. They had wanted him to go to Luzern, but he had felt a stronger impression to ignore those orders. Until he'd received that letter, he had no idea why.

Fred Sohn lived his life on very strong impressions, inspiration from the Lord.

Mona now found herself faced with the most impassioned testimony she had ever read. The mundane facts of the story were that Fred's mother had been converted by missionaries before the war, while he was still a child. When his father had died, his uncle had taken them in, but refused to let young Fred join his mother at church, insisting that he be raised to be a Lutheran minister or nothing at all. Fred declined to be swayed and, at the time of his letter writing, was just completing a three-year full-time mission for the church (the Mormon Church) in Switzerland.

Much of this time had been spent translating *The Star* into *Die Stern* and Germanizing the works of President James E. Talmage, from which he quoted profusely. As soon as he had earned enough money, he told her, he intended to emigrate to Zion and send for his mother soon afterwards.

"And so," he closed the letter in apology, perhaps, for having come on so strong on the side of his ulterior motive for writing. "I am glad to correspond with an English person so I may improve my ability in your language."

Had Mona been a nonmember, the vibrancy of this curious man's faith might well have frightened her off. Instead, she answered him at once, setting him straight: she was a Mormon, too and, incidentally, one of the most fervent and knowledgeable in all England. She answered quote for quote of Talmage.

~

Ralph Robinson Whitaker, being blind, had learned to listen when he was a boy. And all the grown-up talk he'd overheard, he remembered. It was a great help to Mona when she came to filling in the gaps in her genealogy.

Mona listened, too, and now, in turn in Salt Lake, requires an audience for tales of all our ancestors. The other sisters warn me if ever I call her up for a single name or date that I'd better have an hour or two to kill in a very one-sided—hers—conversation. And I must go armed with twice the number of blank tapes I need for any other session.

The tapes I record of her have the most curious background noises— echoing voices and the click of dress shoes on highly polished tile, the periodic ringing of bells, a recorded message about Mormon genealogical work for the dead played over and over again. I meet her in the main hall of the Church Office Building in front of the old Genealogical Library. Tours keep going through, playing the little dioramas and explanatory accounts. General authorities and their aides "lengthen their strides" in a rush for the elevators.

This, I am assured—not by Mona, who remains blissfully unconcerned, but by others—is much better than going to her house. In spite of her lame leg and cane, it is better that we meet downtown. I should look for her old red sweater draped over a chair at the microfilm machine under the clock in the far back corner of the British Isles section of the library.

Her house, I am told, is filthy, especially now that all the children are gone. Housecleaning always took a backseat to reading, research, and study for Mona. Barbara, Mona says, used to spank her for her negligence at home and then yell in desperation when she grew too old to spank. To no avail. The first time my grandmother was in that house upon their arrival in Zion was the last, thirty-five years ago.

Mona had the biggest house, so my grandmother, grandfather, and their children were invited to stay there when they first arrived in the U.S. After a cross-country trip by train, all Grandpa longed for was a bath.

Mona had the biggest house, but she also had seven children of her own—and a single bathroom. And the bathtub, my grandmother is always glad to declare, "were full of genealogy." Dust on the books and papers betrayed the fact that they'd been there for years. "They're there yet, I wager." My family moved in with kindly Ivy instead.

Ivy had the beds all made up. "I knew you wouldn't stay there," she said in her quiet way.

Ivy remembers one terrible trip she took on the train across the U.S. with Mona. Mona was eight months pregnant. Ivy, who was still weak from a combined miscarriage and appendicitis—her father writing anxiously from England, "Is Ivy still alive?"—had to carry all the luggage. Ivy had packed lightly. Mona had not. Not that she needed a lot of clothes. In Mona's mind, one maternity smock was quite sufficient to see her across the country, thank you. Mona nevertheless had a trunk—full of books.

A porter finally took pity on Ivy and came to help. "Lordy massy!" he exclaimed. "What you got in that thing, miss? I can't carry it, I tell you." He went to get reinforcements

Now Mona delivers her tales in what can only be described as a tone of decided conspiracy. It's as if she and I were plotting together the damnation of all lesser, more ignorant souls who will not take the time to listen. She assures me as she leads me through the maze of parish records, naval dispatches, and mossy, deserted graveyards, that I am descended from nothing but "a very nice person," "a very bright little boy," "a very progressive family," "a very kind little person," "of very good conduct," they all "loved learning, you know." She, of course, is descended from such superlatives as well.

There is the man who lost the brand-new house he'd just built with all his life's savings. A lawsuit determined he'd built twelve inches over the boundary. It made him so angry, he went and knocked every inside wall down—"Welsh temper, you know."

There is kindly Anne Holbrook—"you look like her, you know." (Mona herself never saw the woman alive.) A niece of Anne's—an old woman in Mona's day—related how she once scalded her arm, and her mother was rough with the bandages. So she said, "I'm going down to Aunt Anne's. She's gentler than you." Anne spent all of one day nursing some children sick with the measles and went to bed very tired. She woke in the night, telling her husband she'd had a dream. In the dream, she saw her own little tombstone with her name and the date on it, and a little dog barking at it.

"Go back to sleep," he said. "It's just a dream."

In the morning, they found her dead, and Mona herself went to the cemetery and found that very little tombstone.

There is the salty old tar who spent more money on tobacco than on soap.

There is the woman who went to bed sick with grief when her husband died and never got up again for ten years.

Another lived as a widow on a shilling-a-week pension, which the city of Bradford kept trying to get out of paying her. She was buried in a pauper's grave.

There is the dashing John Johns who swept our ancestor's fiancée off her feet just as they were about to be married. Our ancestor had to content himself with the older, plainer sister while the John Johns ran off to Chile to make their fortunes in the copper mines.

"There," Mona says triumphantly. "You can give that some color in your book."

And maybe I will someday.

~

On his way to America, Fred Sohn stopped off to visit Mona. When he left, they were engaged to be married.

"You'll do all right," her father told her. "'E's a bit of religious maniac. You'll suit just fine." He patted his daughter on the cheek and, had his eye been capable of it, he would have winked.

Frau Sohn sent a red knitted shawl to her son's intended. Ralph put it to his nose. It smelled of mothballs. "Hmm," he said. "Tha'lt do all right wi' 'im. But tha'lt have a time with 'is mother."

Mona taught school for two years in England after graduation. But then she began to receive letters from Fred in America that made her father say, "I think tha'd better go. I think 'e means business."

It was the middle of the Depression, and the church authorities asked all immigrants to stay in the East rather than coming immediately out to the hard-pressed West. Fred made himself useful by meeting boats of German Saints, easing them through customs, and then helping them get established in the bewildering world of New York City.

After all this experience with immigration, he was certain getting Mona in would be a snap.

When he went down to meet her boat, however, he waited and waited. He saw all the Germans and Swedes off the gangplank—no Mona. He even made a search through the luggage. To no avail.

Then Fred heard his name called over the public address system. He had to go up the gangplank and onto the boat himself.

On board, he found Mona in tears at a table surrounded by customs officials.

"Do you know this man?" they asked her gruffly.

"Yes, yes!" she cried, her face lighting with relief.

But they would not let her out of her chair to run and greet him.

"Do you know this woman?" they asked him.

"Yes," he replied.

"Are you certain?"

"Of course. She is my fiancée."

"Fiancée, huh?" The officials grunted and exchanged knowing glances among themselves. "Then you would have no objections," they continued, "if we called up the ship's captain and had him marry you this moment."

"But that can't be," Fred and Mona exclaimed together.

"I see." The officials nodded.

Fred and Mona took turns trying to explain. "It's our religion, you see."

"We want to be married for time and all eternity."

"In one of our holy temples."

"We don't believe in spur-of-the-moment marriages such as the world practices."

Mona began to cry again.

"Very good one." The officials were impressed. Never had anyone come up with such a tale before. "I'm sorry. We still don't buy it."

"What do you mean, you 'don't buy it'?"

The indignity made Fred's accent even more pronounced, which brought mocking snickers from the officials.

"Maybe you have never interviewed a couple of Mormons before," Fred retorted, "but we testify that what we say is true!"

"Mormons, huh?" The officials laughed aloud. "Better and better. At least calling it 'polygamy' comes closer to the truth."

Fred poised to launch into a tirade. Mormons no longer practiced polygamy.

One of the lesser officials could keep the full range of his thoughts hidden no more. "Polygamy. What she really is—is a little whore."

It seems that Mona, in the blank for "Purpose" on her immigration form, had written "marriage." She should have written "religious reasons," "to join family," anything but "marriage." Customs knew only too well that "marriage" is what certain pimps told their exotic, imported merchandise to fill in. The officials could not be convinced that as soon as they released this couple, Fred would not start peddling his "fiancée" in Times Square, lame leg and all.

Their hesitation to marry "shotgun" under the captain only increased suspicion.

Finally, after hours, they were released, but only on the condition they be married within the week. They were, by the local Mormon bishop instead of in the temple, and without the dress and ceremony they'd both always longed for.

～

Then Mona began to look for work. It wasn't easy in 1931. At first she hired on as a governess and nanny, but "those New York kids 'bout drove me daft."

Then some Swiss sisters who had known Fred on his mission got Mona on with them at a garment factory in New Jersey "sewing corsets and brassieres." This was Mona's first experience—and in the promised land—with the sort of life her sisters had been leading since they were twelve.

At lot of Italian girls worked in the factory. Mona could not understand their chatter, which kept pace with their sewing: "They could sew like the wind." They made over twenty dollars a week on piecework, while Mona only ever worked up to fourteen. As with swimming, perhaps, the polio affected her coordination. And fully half of that fourteen dollars had to go to her fare: "one bus to the ferry, the ferry over, and another bus up to the factory."

At home, things were no less disappointing. Frau Sohn, Fred's mother, who lived with them, was not a very strong woman. She was always sick with something. And when she was sick, she expected the housekeeping still to be kept to the strictest German standards.

Soon, to add to the difficulties, Mona was pregnant.

After the birth, she continued to work, leaving the baby girl every day in the care of the grandmother, with whose principles she found herself more and more at odds. Almost immediately, a second pregnancy followed.

Then, the strain reached a peak. And crumbled into tragedy.

When the second child, also a girl, was thirteen days old, she died. "Laid on her stomach" by the grandmother, "she couldn't get her head up off the mattress. Her little nose was pressed against the bedding, and she suffocated."

Mona remembers that the day before she found the baby dead, the child smiled at her, "the most beautiful smile I ever saw on a baby girl." At less than two weeks, she thought, "that is very strange." Later she thought, "it was meant to be, that that baby gave me a gift before she went."

Grief exhausted Mona. She took their remaining daughter to upstate New York, to a convalescent home, for recuperation.

"What they didn't tell me there was that my roommate's child had pneumonia."

When they got back to the city, little Margaret, with the beautiful red-brown hair, who'd never been sick a day in her life before, kept coming down with one thing after another. At just under two, she died of pneumonia.

Now Mona threw herself into work, sewing corsets and brassieres, one job during the day and one at night, until she had saved enough money to sail back to England. When she left, she was pregnant again, but this time there was the comfort of home and our Barbara to deliver it. She gave birth to a boy. He was very healthy. Very healthy, indeed.

Mona accuses my grandmother, who had only very picky eaters. "Our Frances just loved to see this boy eat and fed him more than he should have had." He was named Ralph, of course (everyone has a Ralph, down to the third and fourth generation), but everyone since has always called this boy "Mona's Fatty"—to distinguish him from the rest.

∾

"Mother!" one of my sisters exclaims when she first hears that name. "That's mean. Why would you call him that?"

"Well," my mother replies, completely without malice. "Wait 'til you see him. If you just saw him walking down the street, you may not know he was Mona's, but you'd know he was somebody's Fatty."

∾

When her son was eleven months old (and she could still get him over for five dollars' fare), Mona could make excuses no longer. She had to go back to America and rejoin her husband. By then, Hitler was in power in Germany. Mona knew she had to return before war broke. She did get out just in time—with a trunkload of genealogy. Two weeks later, Germany invaded Poland.

The first thing Mona did when she got to New York was to go to their bishop. The bishop called Fred in and told him in no uncertain terms he should send his mother on to Salt Lake. "She can be kept happy doing temple work, and you can give Mona a home of her own."

Frau Sohn didn't want to go, Fred didn't want her to go, but Mona invoked the virtue of obedience. Frau Sohn went to Zion alone. Although he always blamed Mona for "throwing his mother out," things did seem to go better after that. Mona, whom their father had feared would never marry, ended up "'aving more'n any of 'em," nine children in all, counting the first two little girls who died.

∽

One day not too long ago, I was studying on the bus for an anthropology course—a book on the Bene Israel of Bombay. A funny little old man with the sharp esses, round vowels, and no "ths" of a German noticed what I was reading. He engaged me in a long conversation about the lost tribes and related subjects.

Oh-oh, I said to myself with an anthropologist's cool regard. Here's a religious maniac if I ever saw one.

It wasn't until I saw where he got off that I recognized him as my great-uncle Fred (neither he nor Mona ever learned to drive). I watched him limp down the road with his cane as if he were catching polio from his wife in old age. He wore a ratty old suit he looked after himself if anybody did, heading for that dirty old house with the books in the bathtub.

Then I was very glad Auntie Mona had done as Mr. G. Ernst Peters had admonished and had "emulated her virtues."

THE END

GRANDMA IS PICKING A BOWL full of "tomahtoes" from her vines against the thickly painted grey of her "garage" (pronounced with the emphasis on the first syllable). "I do love a tomahto" of all vegetables. "I eat it like an happle."

She's telling us about a man who died and left her father two houses in his will because "'e could sing a song and tell a tale. That were a Mr. 'All, 'oo were right well-off, 'oo used to like to go out wi' me father to t' pubs."

Once when the man came to their house, little Frances asked him, "Where do' tha get all tha money from?"

"'Oh,' says 'e, 'I just go out in t' garden in t' morning an' take some money off t' tree.'" Her dented aluminum basin settles with its distinctive thunk on her back steps. The metal is so thin, it gives like mesh when she does so.

"If ever me dad were tight, 'e'd lend 'im some money. An' when Mr. 'All died, me father owed 'im some money. 'E 'ad a housekeeper, 'ad this Mr. 'All. 'Is wife 'ad died, an' t' 'ousekeeper were a right bossy thing. An' me father were a fool. 'E went straight back to 'er and paid 'er this money. An' Mr. 'All would never 'ave wanted 'im to give it 'er. She'd keep it for 'erself."

"And he left him two houses when he died?"

"Hmm. But there were three o' 'em. There were six 'ouses. An' 'e left these six 'ouses to three people. Two to me dad and two—two to somebody else. But—there were a connection." (She means a stipu-

369

lation.) "They'd to pay funderal expenses." (There's always a "d" in "funeral" when my grandmother says it.)

"Now, that were ridi'lous."(Grandma's "ridiculous," frequently used, is always missing a syllable.) "Me father 'adn't enough money to pay any funderal expenses. Mr. 'All would never 'ave expected 'im to do that. But somebody got—that—that flaw"—she means "clause"—"in for these three people to pay funderal expenses. An' 'e 'ad to come from Morecambe to Bradford to be buried, which would cost a lot o' money them days."

"So your father never got the houses?"

"Well, 'e did get t' 'ouses because our Violet used to go collect rents from them. But 'e'd to borry money to pay fer t' funderal."

"But then the rents helped out."

"Aye, but they wasn't very much, really. They was poor back-to-back 'ouses."

"Five bob a week?" Uncle Noel asks.

"Probably six. Mr. 'All would never 'ave wanted me father to do that. 'E loved me father, you see."

"My pathetic grandfather, a slum lord." Uncle Noel shoves the glasses up on his nose in amazement when Grandma has gone to answer the doorbell to take a customer in her sewing room for a fitting.

Barbara was nursing in Wisbech in the South of England, and Hannah, in the first five years of her marriage before her children were born, had come to visit her older sister.

They were sitting eating their "tea" ("hot cocoa," she is careful to remind me; when I was a child, I never thought "tea" was anything else) when they heard steps on the walk and the rap of a cane on the window.

Barbara, Hannah says, jumped up as if she'd been shot. "Oooh, that's me dad!" she said.

And so it was. He'd made it all the way down from Bradford on his own, walking, riding trains and trams, getting lifts in carts and wagons, in a single day. They put him up with some friends of Barbara, and "Oooh, 'e did enjoy playing their pump organ!"

Ralph went on a tour with Barbara to Ireland where he climbed all over the Giants' Causeway, a great step-like rock formation creating a steep cliff at the seaside. "I'd to put 'is cane on t' stone, and 'e'd put 'is foot on it. And I'd put it on t' next one, and 'e'd put 'is foot on it." They also went several times to the seaside closer to home. "'E'd go in swimming. 'E liked swimming, if you'd guide 'im."

~

"Leave 'im be. Let 'im cry it out," Ralph told Violet and Mary Jane. The women were trying everything to get Frances's little Arthur to be quiet. My little uncle had been left at 4 Moulson Street while Frances went to a "funderal" and could do nothing but hang onto the doorknob and sob. After an hour or so, "'e'd come troopin' to Daddy an' put 'is 'ead on 'is knee."

Although he thought nothing of travelling himself, to Ireland, to Wisbech, the seaside, or all the way to Liverpool to greet a daughter coming home, Great-Grandfather Whitaker hated good-byes. He would never go to the station to see one of his daughters off, but would go to the field near their house where Ivy had collected her little mounds of ground glass. He would stand on the hill and listen.

Then, when he heard the train rumble by, blowing its whistle, he would pull out a great white handkerchief and wave until the sound (and that was long after the sight) disappeared in the distance. He waves to the air, a passerby might have thought. But the family always knew better.

~

And now time goes quickly, all too terribly fast. It's as if marriage were the high point of an arc on a roller coaster. Now, after chugging slowly, so slowly to this peak, the girls' lives go hurtling down at speeds that take the breath away.

Mona remembers how her father walked clear across town when he learned a friend of hers had got the first crystal radio set. Soon enough, he got his own, and would sit at the table, wires stuck in his ears, trying for the best sound. Hannah thought the sight so funny, she never could keep from giggling and had to leave the room. On the crystal set, he could hear the broadcast of the Mormon Tabernacle Choir on a Sunday morning. And it was on the crystal set that he first heard the voice of Adolf Hitler. Always a discerner of character, Ralph told his family, "That man has the worst voice I've ever 'eard. 'E'll cause a lot of trouble in t' world."

~

In the midst of that World War he was not to live to see to the end, forty years and six months after his wife, Ralph Robinson Whitaker was baptized a member of the Church of Jesus Christ of Latter-day Saints on the fourteenth of June, 1941. Barbara, Frances and her three children, Hannah and her two children, and Violet with her three were all there to watch. The rest sent telegrams of congratulations from Zion.

As he sat waiting in the thin white shirt and bare feet, Ralph whispered to Hannah, who sat next to him to lead him to the font when the time came, "Eee, me feet's cold!"

Hannah quickly took off her fur hat (she'd made it herself from somebody's castaway coat—"A fur hat? In June?" "This were England." "Oh. Right.") and stuck it on his feet.

"Oooh, that's nice," he said. "What's that?" She didn't tell him because it was time to go.

Afterwards, in the next room, he was confirmed a member, given the gift of the Holy Ghost, and had the priesthood conferred upon him. For some reason they gave him the Melchizedek, or higher, priesthood first. Hannah looked up, startled, for usual practice is to give the lower, or Aaronic, priesthood first, wait a year or so, and then advance him. No one seemed to notice. Violet kept her head bowed, and Hannah couldn't see Barbara's face. "Frances were crying—she al'ays were emotional"—too hard to hear.

("They didn't even know they'd done it until afterwards," Hannah says. And then, with typical Mormon philosophy towards "mistakes" in religious matters: "I suppose it 'ad to be. The Lord knew 'e didn't 'ave long to live and would never really 'ave strength to attend to all 'is duties afterwards.")

So finally, after all these years, priesthood entered the home.

Ralph's baptism was, indeed, his retirement. He never played the pubs again nor ever smoked his pipe or even drank tea.

("'It were too weak wi' rationing, anyway,' 'e'd say.")

Perhaps it was a sort of withdrawal, as Hannah suggests, that made him fail so immediately afterwards.

Hannah does remember the last piano he tuned. It was one he himself had rebuilt and given her and Robert so their daughter Rita could learn to play, with lessons from Auntie Barbara. Ralph came in and sat down on the bench as he always did. Barbara helped him remove the top, and he tuned it. When they came to America later, Hannah dearly wanted to bring the instrument with them, but that was impossible.

She sold it to the owner of a pub where her father always used to play. The man was so delighted it had once belonged to the life and soul of his establishment, Ralph Whitaker. He made the movers stop as soon as they got it to the sidewalk and played "Excelsior" on it right there.

After that, Great-Grandfather was mostly bedridden.

One day, Hannah stopped over to see her parents after having bought Robert a wallet for his birthday. Her father took the wallet in his hands to "see" it.

"'Ere. Give 'im that," her father said, handing it back. Hannah looked and saw he'd put ten shillings—his whole pension—in the wallet. "That's the sort of man 'e were."

And then, very near the end, Hannah remembers how she walked into his room. He knew it was she by her step, and he struggled to get to his feet and walk over to her. He threw his arms about her. "Oh, 'Annah, lass, I love thee," he said. "I love thee. Don't worry about me. Me time's almost gone, but tha'st still tha life to live yet. An' when tha time comes, I'll come for thee. I'll come for thee, if they'll let me."

("I can 'ardly wait," Auntie Hannah adds for the tape.)

And Violet remembers the last thing he said to her before he finally closed his milky eye to open two perfect eyes on eternity. It was from Proverbs. "He that watches over thee will never sleep."

("'E weren't on that little 'ill to wave his 'andkerchief when I set off for Liverpool to come to America," Barbara says, "for it was not too far from there that I laid him and Mother side by side to rest.")

Ralph Robinson Whitaker was buried on December 1, 1944, in Bradford, Yorkshire, England. Six days later, the girls in Salt Lake took his name to the temple and had the work of eternity done for him.

Sorrow, and the miserable winter weather on the day of the funeral quite overcame Mary Jane. She caught pneumonia, was in a coma for two weeks, and the doctor said she wouldn't live. Then one morning, she woke with a start. To Barbara, who'd never left her side, she said, "Your father's been here."

("And our Barbara says she felt 'is presence.")

"He's been here, and I asked him to take me with him. But he said, 'Doris is on her way from America. It would be a tragedy if our Doris came and found neither one of us alive. You must stay for our Doris.'"

When she'd heard about her father's failing health, Doris determined to leave her husband and five children in America to come and see him. It was the middle of the war, however, and the only way she could get across the Atlantic was to sign up as a chaperone for a boatload of English children who had been sent to America for safety and were now returning to their families for Christmas. They had to convoy with warships. Many of the children were sad and bewildered to have been dragged first from one family and then from another. Still, they were all very well behaved—"Not like these cheeky American children."

They set out under sealed orders at night, but the next morning they found themselves back in New York again. U-boats had been sighted, and the entire convoy had returned to port for safety.

Doris called her family from New York. They were all at dinner at a neighbor's, but the operator somehow managed to find them. That was how she learned about her father's death, for the telegram had reached them during the night.

"Shall I come 'ome again?" Doris asked.

"No," Albert replied. "There's still your mother. You must go and comfort 'er."

The boat left again that evening, this time going by a southern route so they had balmy weather all the way. All the children and chaperones arrived in England safely.

When Doris walked into the bedroom at 4 Moulson Street, all her sisters were standing around their recovering mother. Mary Jane held out a frail hand to her returning daughter and said, "Isn't she lovely? But isn't she lovely?" It had been twenty-five years.

Doris mostly remembers with sadness how things were not the same as when she had left. Besides the sorrowful times, they themselves had changed. Years of separation and different experiences communicated only by letter had created a gulf. Before, because she was the eldest, Doris had had a very close camaraderie with her mother. Mary Jane, who was never one to gossip over the back fence with neighbors, had shared with her daughter instead. But now Barbara had usurped that position with her long years of nursing, care, and attention undivided by other family. It hurt Doris deeply, and the full year and a half she spent in England before her mother died did not seem to remedy the situation much.

("If it's like that in 'eaven," Doris confides quietly, almost off the tape, "I don't want to go.")

Those daughters who stayed in England, however, remember how their mother always helped with their children: my mother slept in her grandmother's bottom dresser drawer when she was only one month old and her older brother had the measles she had to be protected from. Mary Jane gave Hannah a large box of talcum powder when her eldest was born. She keeps the last little bit to this day in her bathroom on Salt Lake's Avenues, and sniffs at it from time to time to remember.

∾

"She's al'ays at church," Ralph used to tease his wife. "She'll die at church."

And his prophecy, given even before he received the priesthood, all but came true.

Barbara, who had a car and plenty of petrol even in those times of rationing because she was a nurse, remembers the last week of her mother's life. Mary Jane asked her to drive her to visit all the married daughters and their children.

Then, on Sunday, a beautiful, warm day in June, they were ready for church with half an hour to spare, so Barbara drove her mother to the park where they looked at the flowers. Barbara gave the Sunday School lesson and noticed that her mother seemed "very alert." They ate lunch between meetings, and Mary Jane went around the chapel admiring the new paint job just completed in all the nooks and crannies of that dear old building.

("In two days, that new paint job would be hidden in flowers for her own funeral—white roses. We al'ays have white roses. For York, you know.")

Then, as they were making their way to their places in the choir for sacrament meeting, Mary Jane suddenly said, "I do feel queer. Let me sit down." Then, "Oh, I've a pain!" reaching to her head with her hand.

She slumped to the floor.

Several brethren helped to carry her to the vestry where they laid her on a table, but she was already unconscious. Although she lived for a day or so longer in hospital, her last living memory was of the little chapel in Woodland Street where the choir had already begun to practice their number for that day:

When I leave this frail existence,
When I lay this mortal by,
Father, Mother, may I greet you
In your royal courts on high?
Then at length when I've completed
All you sent me forth to do,

With your mutual approbation,
May I come and dwell with you?

~

Because of the heavy post-war traffic, Doris had to write a letter to the prime minister himself explaining her situation before she was at last given priority to sail back to America and her waiting children. Frances went to Liverpool to see her off, and as she waved good-bye, a voice came to her which said, "If you want to see your sister again, you'll have to go to Zion."

Every sister has her own reason why "Our Frances suddenly took it into 'er 'ead to come," which started the second exodus that finally included them all.

~

"When Mother had died," Barbara says, "I came out and told our Nellie, who was waiting in the car, that Mother had gone to be with Father."

"I wish she'd taken me wi' 'er," Nellie said.

"You see how sensible she was?" Barbara exclaims. "But I couldn't keep 'er at 'ome all day while I worked, so I decided the only thing was to put 'er in a 'ome. All 'er life, she'd 'ad 't 'ome' 'eld over 'er like a whip for good behavior."

"She didn't!" exclaims one sister.

"I never 'eard me mother say anything like that," says another.

"She never would 'ave put 'er in a 'ome," a third insists.

But Hannah substantiates Barbara's story. "I went wi' our Barbara the day she took 'er to t' 'ome. I think it were the worst day of me life. I were nearly 'eart-broken, the way Nellie trembled and were so scared."

"I always heard they killed her in the home," Uncle Noel prompts, with a hard look at his mother, who told him the tale.

"No," Barbara says firmly. "She quite liked it after she got used to it. She stayed there ten years, so they didn't kill 'er."

"I think they was glad to 'ave 'er," Hannah says. "She could mind t' babies and 'elp in t' laundry. She earned 'er keep, didn't she, Barbara?"

"And I went every week to see 'er," Barbara agrees, "and take 'er out very often, as often as I could."

"I spent the whole day wi' 'er afore I came to America," Violet pipes up. "We sat out in the field where me dad al'ays stood and watched the children playing cricket. I think she were content."

"Well, tell us how Nellie died," my uncle says.

"She took sick, and they let me know she were sick." Barbara reclaims the table. "I went one day, and they were trying to give 'er oxygen. But it were such a backwards place, they never knew t' cylinder were empty. And they were putting t' mask on 'er and making 'er worse, you see. She were fighting it, swearing an' all."

"They were strangling her," Uncle Noel declares triumphantly.

"So I told 'em." I'll bet Auntie Barbara did. "And next morning, when I went in, she said, 'I like that,' pointing to the cylinder.

"I says, 'Dos' tha?'

"She says, 'Aye.'

"The night nurse 'ad got a new cylinder. You see 'ow sensible she were, right to the end."

"Sensible, indeed, to know when you're being strangled," comments Uncle Noel in an undertone.

"That afternoon, she were breathing badly and in bed, of course."

"It was pneumonia?"

"Yes, I think she 'ad pneumonia, and that poisoned 'er, you see. She 'adn't slept. They told me she 'adn't slept all night, couldn't take 'er soother. I gave 'er a little doll—she couldn't 'old anything, she were so weak—but I gave her this doll."

The image is clear to us all—the great fat woman, her pasty face sagging with age, her wild grey hair—holding what had been her favorite doll all her life.

"She were 'olding this doll, and she went to sleep wi' the doll. 'Thank goodness, she's gone to sleep,' I thought, 'for a while.'

"I sat about an hour I should think. An' 'er breathing started to get shallower and shallower. 'She's going to die.'

"So I went to the nurse. I said, 'I don't want to make a fuss. I know I should be leaving soon, but I'm going to stay wi' 'er. Our Nellie's dying.' And I went back, and she did. She took about ten minutes, probably, to go. She never woke up. She just went to sleep. Just lovely. I were so 'appy because I knew there were nothing for 'er to live for."

∿

After Nellie died, there was only one problem left for Barbara, and that was what to do with her own Auntie Ethel.

Auntie Ethel was her father's cousin, a woman over seventy who'd never married and who'd come to live in Moulson Street at retirement. Auntie Ethel was "a genteel soul." She'd been in service as a lady's maid all her life and learned high-class manners. She would always insist on serving tea—real tea—whether anyone else stopped to take it with her or not. Uncle Noel liked her and remembers little phrases she had such as "Oh, was that your favorite?" when she'd stepped by accident on your foot. Or "Always face the enemy" accompanied even in the retelling by a shift of one's chair in a stalwart stance of defiance against "the enemy"—the draft coming in at a door or a window.

Barbara applied to the government for a little house for Auntie Ethel to live in "and they gave it to her right away because she'd been 'twelve year in lodgings'—living with me. And she was thrilled because that was her first home of her own in her life, and she was over seventy. I had some friends look in on her, and she had friends, so she just enjoyed the last few years of her life in that new home, you see."

Barbara had to do this because the city of Bradford bought 4 Moulson Street—all Moulson Street, in fact—in a forced sale to build high-rise subsidized council houses.

"And then I were free," Barbara says. "Me parents 'ad died, me sister 'ad died, all me friends 'ad died. I were free. I could come to America."

∿

So she came. When I learned my new Auntie ("Auntie" being reserved only for great aunts, only for my grandmother's sisters; every other female relative is a mere "aunt") was a nurse, I took my doll to her for diagnosis.

I'd carefully looked up all the symptoms of polio. I wanted my doll to have the drama of polio, like Auntie Mona.

Crutches at least. Maybe an iron lung.

"Give 'er some milk o' magnesia," Auntie Barbara said, refusing to get into the game. "She'll be better in t' morning."

It took me a while after that to appreciate this new auntie—who could peel a grape for the sick when it really warranted it.

They are sitting now, all seven together again, in a circle of lawn chairs in a large, well-tended yard on Tenth Avenue overlooking the Salt Lake Valley. It is my grandmother's birthday again, her sixty-third, and, as she falls "in t' middle," the others range in age on either side of her.

Interspaced between them are children, grandchildren, great-grandchildren. Here and there sits a son-in-law or grandson-in-law, always a little bewildered at the bubbling scene punctuated by wild explosions of shrill laughter he wasn't born to.

(It was the same with the Whitaker girls' own husbands all their lives. At least most of them had the advantage that one didn't have to translate for them. "Please pass the jelly" doesn't mean "Reach for the homemade strawberry jam," but "Pass the wobbly thing made with gelatin, fruit, and whipped cream."

If someone offers you a "biscuit" after dinner, don't refuse, saying you already ate three of Auntie Ivy's homemade rolls and having eaten "nasty," you're ready for dessert. If you do, you'll miss out on your chance at a delicate English butter cookie, stale though it may be from somebody's last visit to the homeland.

And never, never ask for a "napkin" to wipe your face and hands. You'll put everyone into fits of laughter. "Nappies" are what babies wear, and they're usually wet and smelly. You mean a "serviette," of course.)

Every gift giver gets a fortune written on a strip of paper. My grandmother, wearing a gypsy turban, has cut them out of an old calendar. Auntie Barbara's says, "You'll marry early."

I think this is a rather nasty joke, like when my three-times-divorced second cousin got a fortune at Grandma's party that said she would be happily married. Being American, the cousin did not take it with such good grace.

When my mother tells me her mother does not give those fortunes out by chance, that Grandma actually thinks out the recipients in advance, I feel the joke is even meaner.

Auntie Barbara, at sixty-five and ready for retirement (in the hospital's books, of course, never in her own mind) is still an old maid. And then she gets the fortune, "You'll be married early."

"Early in t' morning, p'r'aps," Barbara says in good humor, setting everyone in stitches of laughter.

My mouth stands open with shock, as when my sister first heard about "Mona's Fatty."

But I see now that maybe they all knew then what was only to be an incredible surprise to me a few months later.

Auntie Barbara was married in a proper temple ceremony (the only one to get that blessing right off the bat) to Joseph S. Nelson, the missionary who'd come to Bradford during World War I. Of one of Salt Lake's most illustrious families, the grandson of prophets and presidents, a wealthy, retired lawyer with a house on the East Side, he was the best catch any of them got at all. A widower, Joe Nelson had found the best possible mate to see him through his last, fading years: an "unfathomable" worker.

("'E married 'er 'cause she were a virgin," my grandmother—a little jealous?—tells us with a warning finger. "Men always like virgins best.")

"Uncle Joe," as I learned to call the man with the shiny bald head, had, by his previous marriage and in good Mormon style, numerous children, and now "She 'as more grandchildren an' great-grandchildren 'an any o' us!" the others exclaim in amazement at this major thing by which they measure success.

And then, as if sixty-three were only yesterday, Grandma is eighty-two and throwing yet another party. By now all of the Whitaker sisters have outlived their husbands, on their own again. Except that they are in brilliant cotton or polyester prints instead of somber woolen dresses and pinafores, and except that their bodies are bloating, sagging with age and the bearing of many, many children, it is the same as it once was in 4 Moulson Street.

Doris has her newspapers and "t' television graphics" to take her "'ome." She always was one to follow royalty, even if it's only a president.

Barbara has her house and garden and kettles of soup to the sick in the ward.

Ivy has her garden—many peas now all in a row, although they're harder to weed than the single one in a flagstone crack. And they die so quickly in Utah's summer heat. She has her weekly luncheon for the girls, too, where she does all the cooking.

Frances still takes in sewing. "I'd a'most do it fer nothing, just to 'ave t' company."

And Hannah has her house to make into a home. "I'd rather be domesticated than educated." (She is domesticated, too, like a fluffy, white Persian cat.)

Mona is educated, and has her house full to the bathtub with genealogy.

And Violet is the only one ever to follow in their mother's steps and attain the honor of Relief Society president ("For two years only, thank goodness"). She does all the ward's flower arranging ("'old 'em up 'igh") and has taken up oil painting, now that she can no longer dance.

No one under sixty gets the luxury of a chair with a back at this party. Some of the kiddies have had "buffets" made for them of low, over-turned garden buckets, and I am trying to keep comfortable on a backless wooden bench, the grey-blue paint peeling since Grandpa's not here to repaint.

It shouldn't be all that difficult, should it? It's the same bench that I used to sit on outside my grandfather's garage-turned-weaving-room, where I would spend hours talking to him as he worked at the machine he refused to leave in England, though my mother had to leave her violin, and Uncle Noel got left entirely (in the Air Force at the end of World War II). I remember trying to mimic Grandpa, making a rat's nest on the iron foot of a bed when I got home. That loom is now in a museum. It is on this same bench that my only brother (a Ralph, too, of course—everyone has a Ralph) got stung by wasps because he wouldn't relinquish his Hostess cupcake to them.

Still, I'm not as young as I once was when I wove up the foot of the iron bed, either. Pregnant with my first, it's not so easy on this bench anymore. And yet, the waves of four or five conversations going on all at once wash over me and recede in the familiar rhythms of broad Yorkshire.

As they do, I come to feel much more comfortable. So comfortable, indeed, that I forget the role I'm supposed to play as observer here and have to consciously call my mind back to the task at hand.

Slip in another tape.

All conversations briefly fade to one as Auntie Hannah tells the story of how she was promised in a blessing when she left England for America that she would live "as many years there as you 'ave 'ere." "I were forty then an' I'm eighty now," she says. "I can go anytime."

Everyone laughs heartily at these and assures her she has years yet.

Now she begins to tell again the story of how her father, barely able to walk, came to her, threw his arms around her and said, "'Annah, I love thee. An' when tha time comes—"

"I used to think the same thing," Barbara says, for the tale only needs half telling for the others to pick up on it. "I used to think it'd be me dad'd come for me, too. But now I think it'll be Joe." And she blushes—Auntie Barbara blushes, as romantic as a sixteen-year-old. It's come to her at last.

Everyone assures her they'll both be there, "An' Mother an' our Nellie."

I imagine Uncle Noel shuddering.

"They'll all be there."

But suddenly I am an observer again. I sit back and think, How interesting! Here she is, Auntie Barbara, who never had time for boys and nonsense after World War I. Now she's idealistic as can be. Uncle Noel even remembers a time when she whispered doubts to him about the truthfulness of a religion that could preach that spinsterhood was a sure condemnation to the lower realms of ministering angels. No doubts now.

Ivy, too, although she still hasn't managed to read the Book of Mormon, seems more believing than all the irrational tragedy of her life allowed her to be for many, many years.

They say it came over her on her recent trip to the Holy Land, but what that comfort is, she doesn't put into words.

Perhaps it is beyond words.

Doris, on the other hand, is now much more sober than the wild-eyed, flirty girl her mother always called back into the house to pin up her neckline decently. Already her husband and two sons are gone before her—she's been a widow longer than she was married, for all her six children. She wonders, "Will they be there, indeed? Or will we have changed so much that none of the companionship is there at all?"

Others try to quell her fears. Still she insists, "Life is more sorrow than joy. I've learned that now, and I never imagined that before. I remember only too well how it was when I went back to see my mother.

"She said, 'Oh, look, girls. Isn't she lovely?' But I remember. It wasn't the same. Something had faded. I don't know if I want to go to heaven if it's going to be like that. If we just look at one another and say, ''Ow lovely!' then 'ave nothing to say to one another."

Auntie Doris confides in me, too, although she won't tell the others, that she, that girl who so fervently denied tea that she won herself a husband on Wuthering Heights now drinks a comforting cup whenever she doesn't feel well.

"And that's nearly every day now!"

So I sit and look over the full century since my great-grandfather was first blinded. I see gaps in the circle: those who have fallen away, those divorced, those with illegitimate children, those fallen into bad company, drugs, alcohol, those ostracized by the Saints already established when they came—all the ills any modern American family is heir to. Here in Zion, we are not so special, such a "peculiar people," as they once thought in Yorkshire. Life is neither so happy nor secure as they knew it to be, with a blind father and the fate of millwork hanging over their heads.

What Zion and the future were for them, Bradford and their past have become for me. Such a perspective makes one more pessimistic. It gets harder and harder to be excited about what is billed as "fun" in the ward these days, and all the various preachments about "mutual improvement" and "eternal progression." The days when the Myth was lived and breathed have already come and gone. They cannot be captured again.

This child I am carrying, whatever can I give it to pass hope on to it? I draw a blank and escape only in another doze as a rousing chorus of "Ilkla Moor Bat 'At" begins. Often sung to round out an evening, it requires footnotes, in spite of frequent repetition.

Where 'as' tha bin sin' I saw thee,
On Ilkla Moor bat 'at?
Where 'as' tha bin sin' I saw thee?
Where 'as' tha bin sin' I saw thee?
[*Chorus*]
On Ilkla Moor bat 'at,
On Ilkla Moor bat 'at.
On Ilkla Moor bat 'at.

Tha's' bin acourtin' Mary Jane.
On Ilkla Moor bat 'at?
Tha's' bin acourtin' Mary Jane.
Tha's' bin acourtin' Mary Jane.
[*Chorus*]
On Ilkla Moor bat 'at,
On Ilkla Moor bat 'at.
On Ilkla Moor bat 'at.

Tha's' boun' t' get thee death o' cawld.
[*Repeated Verse and Chorus*]

Then we shall 'ave t' bury thee.
[*Repeated Verse and Chorus*]

Then t' worms'll cum an' eat thee up.
[*Repeated Verse and Chorus*]

Then t' ducks'll cum an' eat up worms.
[*Repeated Verse and Chorus*]

Then we shall cum an' eat up t' ducks.
[*Repeated Verse and Chorus*]

Then we shall all've e'ten thee.
[*Repeated Verse and Chorus*]

No more patriotic song will ever be sung than this "national hymn of Yorkshire" by women whose "true religion" is suspiciously like having been born in the East Riding.

I'm saving this place on the little grey-blue bench in case my uncle decides to make one of his grand entrances and surprise his mother on her birthday. He probably won't come. But he might, like fresh air from the world beyond this easy, gentle doze on a July afternoon.

~

"Is she still alive?" Ralph whispers quietly. "Is our Ivy still alive?"

Mary Jane smiles and points down.

Ivy is making Mrs. Tracy's favorite recipe for meatballs and complaining because one of the nieces who comes to check up on her has set the flour canister where she, shrunk to less than four and a half feet tall, can no longer reach it. Meatballs need flour, don't these fool girls know that? "Those fool girls" are all over sixty themselves.

Ivy still lives alone in the little four-room bungalow in Rose Park where she's lived for fifty years. Neighbors on both sides now speak Spanish, and the nice black man on the corner comes to shovel her walk whenever it snows. Her grandson came and redid her front porch with a railing and new shrubs on the hottest day of the year.

Ivy has shaken hands with three different Utah governors at the annual party they give for citizens over a hundred years old. Ivy, whom they never thought would live during her first three months, never through her dropsy, through the death of her husband and raising her son alone, through miscarriages and the appendicitis— Ivy is one hundred and six years old and six months. She has lived through every minute of the twentieth century—and then some. All her sisters are dead now, both husbands, one of her two sons.

(My grandmother died with the measuring tape around her neck—"In the yoke," Uncle Noel likes to say. "Work conquers all," he wrote in her obituary.)

"Sometimes I think they don't want me up there," she says sadly. "They've forgotten to invite me. Every once in a while, me dad looks down, 'Is she still alive?' An' 'ere I am."

She still hasn't read the Book of Mormon, still can't get past Laban getting his head chopped off, one man dying so a whole people won't "perish in unbelief."

"Maybe when I've done that—"

The wonderful, earthly smells of cooking meat and onions fills the tiny kitchen out of which she fed the dwindling circle of her sisters every Thursday for thirty years, where she fed children, grandchildren, great-grandchildren crowded into the equally tiny living room Thanksgiving and just last Christmas.

At least there'll be something for her niece when she comes. That girl never eats enough. And her niece will pick up sacred text and try to read on from Laban—although Ivy is often secretly grateful she's too deaf to hear much of that anymore, and can let her mind wander all the while.

Her mind wanders back, then there is a strange light—

And I stand with my mother and sister on the bright slope in Salt Lake City cemetery in the mid-October air that has a nip in it. The last of the Whitaker lasses is laid to rest here, so far from home, and yet so close. Flanking the spot are a pair of yew trees. The ivy twining up them is not English ivy. It has turned a brilliant red with the season.

"Is she?" Ralph asks—then he, too, joins his wife's smile, breaking into the song he always had for that one sickly daughter:

But yet to cheer the mournful scene
The ivy liveth on.

Mom, my sister, and I can hear laughter blowing through the solemn yews. "There's a party in heaven tonight," we agree.